MRS. THATCHER'S REVOLUTION

MRS. THATCHER'S REVOLUTION

The Ending of the Socialist Era

PETER JENKINS

HARVARD UNIVERSITY PRESS
Cambridge, Massachusetts

Excerpt from ''Annus Mirabilis'' from HIGH WINDOWS by Philip Larkin.
Copyright © 1974 by Philip Larkin. Reprinted by permission of
Farrar, Straus and Giroux, Inc.

Library of Congress Cataloging-in-Publication Data

Jenkins, Peter.
  Mrs. Thatcher's revolution : the ending of the socialist era /
  Peter Jenkins.
      p.   cm.
  Bibliography: p.
  Includes indexes.
  ISBN 0-674-58832-0 (alk. paper) (cloth)
  ISBN 0-674-58833-9 (paper)
  1. Thatcher, Margaret.   2. Great Britain—Politics and
  government—1979-   3. Socialism—Great Britain—History—20th
  century.   4. Conservatism—Great Britain—History—20th century.
  I. Title.
DA591.T47J46 1988   88-7231
941.085'8'0924—dc19   CIP

*To Polly, Amy,
Milly, Flora and
Nathaniel*

Contents

Illustrations

The author and publishers would like to thank the following for
permission to reproduce photographs: Agence France Presse (no.
22); Associated Press (nos 28 and 30); Camera Press (nos 7, 10, 11,
18, 20 and 26); The *Independent* (no. 9, nos 19 (Brian Harris) and 31
(Jeremy Nicholl)); Popperfoto (nos 8, 14, 15, 16, 17, 24, 25, 27, 29, 32
and 33); The Press Association (nos 6, 12 and 21); and Syndication
International (nos 1, 2, 3, 4, 5, 13 and 23).

Introduction to
the American Edition

Seldom has the leader of another nation been as widely acclaimed in the United States as Margaret Thatcher. Not that she is without honour in her own country – far from it – but although respected, and twice re-elected, she has not been the best loved of British prime ministers. Her popularity among her own people does not compare with Ronald Reagan's popularity with Americans, even after the failures and disgraces of his second term. No one since Winston Churchill between the wars has aroused such strong passions as Thatcher. Adored by some sections of the population, she is detested by others, who spit with hatred the very name 'Thatcher'. These strong feelings cut somewhat across conventional party lines: through patriotic and populist appeals she has won the support, even the adulation, of many working people, while on the aristocratic wing of her own party, within what used to be the Establishment, she is widely regarded with misgiving or snobbish disdain. As for the liberal intelligentsia, they loathe her.

Americans took to Mrs Thatcher before the British did. Shortly after she replaced Edward Heath as leader of the Conservative Party in 1975, she visited the United States, stopping in New York, Chicago – for her the Mecca of monetarism – and Washington. On that trip she made her debut as a star of the early morning network shows, and in Washington she captivated the National Press Club. Partly this was because of her novelty value as a woman, the first ever to aspire to be Britain's Prime Minister, although she brusquely rejected all feminist blandishments. Also her anti-socialism was music to the ears of most Americans, although it got her into trouble at home, where a Labour government was in power. The custom was to refrain from partisan politics when overseas. Eric Sevareid told CBS viewers that Harold Wilson, then Prime Minister, was 'the passing figure and she the arriving one'. He proved to be correct, but that was not how she was generally seen in Britain at the time. The columnist George Will was closer to the mark when, after her election in 1979, he compared the bewilderment and shock of many of the British to the reaction of Americans to Barry Goldwater's capture of the Republican nomination at San Francisco in 1964.[1]

In the period between May 1979, when she became Prime Minister, and January 1981, when Ronald Reagan was inaugurated, the tide in the United States was flowing towards the Conservative right. Britain was of special interest to American commentators as a laboratory for a monetarist experiment. Thatcherism was seen as a rehearsal for Reaganism. But already in 1981 some of the New Right commentators, who earlier had held her up as an example, were presenting her as a cautionary tale. According to George Gilder, for example, she had 'failed to combine her reduction in basic monetary growth rates with a reduction in government taxing and spending'.[2]

The truth was that she had never been a supply-sider, and it is this more than anything else that sets Thatcherism apart from Reaganomics. She remained an old-fashioned fiscal conservative. A tax-cutter, yes, for cutting taxes was a way to sharpen the incentives to enterprise, but she never came to believe, with the supply-siders around Ronald Reagan, that tax cuts themselves would increase revenue to cover borrowing. Reaganomics was a magic formula by which inflation would be conquered, taxes cut, and the defence budget massively increased all at the same time. For her, monetarism was closer to good housekeeping, or storekeeping; for governments it meant not printing more money, in exactly the same way that a housewife should spend no more money than is coming in. 'We don't have to choose between inflation and unemployment – they go hand in hand', declared Reagan in 1981. In her seminal budget of that year Margaret Thatcher chose fiscal rectitude, and throughout her first term rising unemployment was one of the hallmarks of Thatcherism.

There are other differences too between the style we call Thatcherism and the politics of Ronald Reagan. The Moral Majority, that unappetising brew of ultra-patriotism and social puritanism, fermented by religious fundamentalism, does not exist in Britain. Margaret Thatcher seldom mentions God and has no political need to do so. She supported the legalisation of abortion in 1967 and has not bowed since to the anti-abortion lobby. Ronald Reagan may have kept the Moral Majority at bay, but it was a part of his constituency nonetheless. The first non-governmental group to receive an audience in the Reagan White House in 1981 was the March for Life.[3]

All the same, there are striking similarities between Thatcherism and Reaganism, and between Ronald Reagan and Margaret Thatcher. Both are of humble origin, almost mandatory for an American president but rare in the case of the leader of the British Conservative Party. Both were born above a small-town store, although her father owned his store. As politicians, both played the outsider role, he not belonging to the Eastern Establishment which mostly dominated Washington and she not belonging to the charmed upper crust which dominated the Conservative Party. Each came to office possessed of a vision, he of a golden age restored and she of an American Dream come true in Britain. Each, by the same token, believed it their mission to arrest and reverse a process of national decline. The Reaganites spoke of a 'Reagan Revolution', or, as their opponents saw it – a counter-revolution, an attempt to repeal the New Deal.[4] She was no less explicit in her ambition to roll back the tide of socialism and put an end to what she called 'consensus politics', which, she claimed, had governed Britain since the election of a Labour government in 1945. She shared with Reagan a belief in the efficacy of market economics, scarcely remarkable in an American politician and certainly not in a Republican, but somewhat more novel in a British leader, even a Conservative. For in Britain the neo-Keynesian consensus has been far more pervasive. Both leaders were pledged to cut government expenditure, but not on defence. She vied with him as a gut anti-Communist and earned herself in Moscow the soubriquet 'Iron Lady' – in which she reveled – before Reagan inveighed against the 'evil empire'. Both were novices in foreign affairs, and both were gut nationalists. They were also populists, mixing patriotism and pocket-book economics to appeal to blue-collar workers. Both won election by making major inroads into the traditional coalitions of their opponents.

A theme of this book is that the Thatcher Revolution was as much the product of her times as the shaper of them. I describe how and why the collapse of the old political order brought her to power and enabled her to practice her brand of right-wing 'conviction politics'. In this she also resembles Ronald Reagan, the twice-rejected conservative (1968 and 1976) and belated heir to the Goldwater coup of 1964. For at first Reagan, like Thatcher, was seen as something of an aberration, brought to power through the default of opponents. Neither his sweeping victory in 1980 nor hers the previous year was immediately seen as a 'watershed', or critical elections like those of 1932 in the United States and 1945 in Britain, events which resulted in profound and lasting changes in the political landscape. The subsequent course of British politics seems to confirm that in Britain 1979 was such a watershed year. Whether the same is true of 1980 in the United States remains to be seen. The most general opinion seems to be that there has been dealignment rather than realignment, and this could turn out to be true in Britain also, although after three elections the defection to the Conservatives of a substantial part of the working-class vote looks to be hardening into a habit.

In Britain the decline of the Labour Party as an electoral force invites comparison with the plight of the Democratic Party. They are, of course, very different political creatures inhabiting quite different cultures. Nevertheless, almost everywhere – West Germany is another striking case – parties of the left appear to be increasingly unable to reconcile the wishes of the special interests to which they are prey and those of their own activists with the preferences of the electorate at large. This causes them to alienate even many of their own traditional supporters.

In the case of both the Democrats and Labour, this drawing apart of party and people was exacerbated by changes in rules and procedures. In the American case the McGovern reforms of 1972 had the effect of enfranchising party activists at the expense of the party bosses and their proverbial smoke-filled rooms. In Britain the so-called democratisation of the Labour Party took the form of removing power from the parliamentarians and conferring it upon the party in the country. Members of Parliament were made liable to mandatory re-selection by party activists in their constituencies. The leader (who is, in effect, the candidate for Prime Minister), instead of being elected exclusively by MPs, henceforth was to be chosen in an Electoral College in which the trade unions held 40 per cent of the votes, constituency activists 30 per cent, and MPs only 30 per cent.

As the party became more responsive to its activists, for example adopting policies such as unilateral nuclear disarmament, it made itself more repulsive to the electorate. The consequence was comparable to that of the excesses of anti-war politics in the McGovern period. In the United States the proliferation of primaries, and the rules concerning delegates to the Democratic Party convention, has meant that the credentials of a candidate for nomination are likely to be in inverse proportion to his qualifications for winning a presidential election and for governing thereafter. In Britain the Labour Party is similarily tugged between the vested interests of the trade unions and the middle-class radicalism of party activists; the preferences of these groups not only conflict but are unattractive to the electorate in equal degree.

The Mondale campaign of 1984 has been described as 'interest-group liberalism in its worst possible incarnation – serving the lobbies without rousing the voters'.[5] The words would do as well for the Labour Party. At Britain's 1979 election, law and order and educational standards had become more salient issues. In much the same way as Richard Scammon and Ben Wattenberg's 'social issue',[6] these concerns helped to drive former Labour voters into the arms of Mrs Thatcher. When sections of the Labour Party later took up sexual politics, championing gay and lesbian rights, traditional working-class supporters became still more alienated. The shrill anti-racism of the left in Britain has had the same effect in driving away blue-collar workers as black caucus policies have had in disaffecting white Democrats, especially in the South.

As the Democrats have suffered disproportionately from the decline of partisanship and the weakening of party, so has the Labour Party. Some of the reasons are similar. Media influence has contributed to more volatile, issue-oriented voting behaviour. However, candidates play a less important role in British campaigns, where party is still the crucial factor. Single issues also play a relatively small role. We have no PACs, and campaign finances and political broadcasting are strictly limited. Demographic and socio-economic factors have played a larger part in the erosion of party allegiances in Britain than seems to be the case in the United States.[7] In Britain there has been a marked decline in size of the working class and, more controversially, of class voting in a country where politics has been predominantly class-based. The disintegration of the old Roosevelt coalition is an important aspect of the decline of the Democrats as a presidential party. As William Schneider put it, contrasting the vote for Adlai Stevenson in 1956 and for Walter Mondale in 1984: 'Both got about the same share of the popular vote . . . But the nature of their support was very different. Mondale did significantly better than Stevenson among black voters, college graduates, women and professionals. On the other hand, Stevenson's support was much stronger among whites, Southerners, blue-collar workers, union members and Catholics.'[8] Mrs Thatcher's new majority – or, to be accurate, her new plurality – in 1979 was founded on an unprecedented level of support among blue-collar workers and trade union members.

The Labour Party and the Democrats today are both victims of political geography. Britain is increasingly polarised between north and south, city and suburb, town and country, with the weight of the population increasingly concentrated in the south and moving away from the cities. The result is that Labour piles up useless votes in its mostly northern class strongholds while the Conservatives hold sway across the bulk of the country. The arithmetic of the Electoral College is similarily hostile to the Democrats, especially as a result of the continuing defection of the white South.[9]

It is often said in Britain that we are moving towards a more presidential style of government. That may be true with regard to the imperiousness of the Prime Minister (not only Mrs Thatcher) and the use of modern media techniques for promoting party leaders. Moreover, there is more superficially American razzmatazz at election times than there used to be. But the purpose of a General Election in Britain is to elect a House of Commons; whoever leads the largest party becomes Prime Minister. As partisanship declines, voters may identify more with the party leader than with the party, but come election day, the voter has no choice but to make a party choice. There is no way to split a ticket, no way to elect one party to a majority in the legislature and the leader of another to head the government. The American voter can choose a president from one party while, ostensibly, maintaining his traditional allegiance to the other.

For all that, I am tempted by the theory that in spite of differences in political systems and traditions, voters in advanced democratic societies behave rather similarly. Inside the British voter there is a ticket-splitter trying to get out. The nearest equivalent phenomenon in Britain is the growth of electoral support for third-party politics. In 1951 the two major parties in Britain monopolised 96.8 per cent of the votes cast, by 1983 this monopoly was down to 72 per cent, and in 1987 it recovered only to 75 per cent.

Mrs Thatcher and Thatcherism, and the decline of Labour and the tendencies towards a realignment of party politics are two themes of my book; a third is Britain's decline. That too may have a topical resonance for American readers. Mrs Thatcher came to power pledged to arrest and reverse the long downward trend of the British economy relative to others, and by 1987 she could lay claim to having succeeded at least in arresting the trend, although how permanently is a question I discuss. For decline is a matter not simply of relative economic performance but also of the longer-term determinants of future performance. The literature on the British case, now voluminous, has increasingly discovered the roots of Britain's malperformance in cultural factors or structural deficiencies which have their origin in Victorian times. One of the chief culprits has been the neglect of education, especially technical education, from the mid-nineteenth century onwards.

In the present case of the United States, the resilience and adaptability of its vast continental economy has been so prodigious that it is difficult to take altogether seriously the latest cries of gloom and doom. However, Paul Kennedy in an influential book has shown how even the mightiest empires can fall when their economic resources prove inadequate to the military demands upon them.[10] Meanwhile, that most prolific of prophets, Felix Rohatyn, warns that the United States already has lost its independence, has become 'a first-rate military power and a second-rate economic power'.[11] Strategic overextension was an important cause of Britain's long decline, as it was of Rome's downfall. There is also, perhaps, some analogy between the industrial and technological challenge which Britain, then the predominant industrialised nation, faced towards the end of the nineteenth century from the United States and the nascent economies of Germany and France and the challenge which the United States faces today from Japan and the economies of the Pacific Basin. Moreover, some of the symptoms of the 'British sickness' are today part of the American condition: low investment, technological lag, educational neglect, and possibly some waning of the spirit of enterprise, all adding up to uncompetitiveness. But in Britain's case, remember, an economy utterly dependent upon international trade and with a small, though ravenous, domestic market was required to adapt over a short period to a major transformation in the global economy. In the process Britain disposed of an empire and saw her overseas assets wiped out by war. The task facing the United States in adjusting to a relative decline in power and wealth strikes me as in no way so severe.

The organisation of this book may require a word of explanation to readers not wholly familiar with the course of post-war history in Britain. My story ostensibly begins in 1979 with the advent of Margaret Thatcher as the first Prime Minister in the post-war period determined not merely to postpone the march of collectivism but to drive it into permanent retreat. However, in order to explore the roots of what I present as the end of the *ancien régime* in 1979, it is necessary to look back as far as 1945, when the first majority Labour government came to power and laid the foundations for the new age of Keynesian economic management and welfare. Indeed, when I come to the politics of decline (in Chapter 2) it is necessary, as I have already mentioned, to track back as far as the Industrial Revolution in the nineteenth century. In this way I have treated the narrative thread of my account of the Thatcher years rather in the manner of a clothesline on which to hang laundry as it comes to hand. For example, the moment of her election in 1979 seemed the appropriate point to discuss electoral trends over the previous decade and more (Chapter 5). And the moment of schism in the Labour Party in 1981, with the breakaway of the Social Democrats (Chapter 4), seemed the place to chart the capture of the Labour Party by its activists, which had begun as early as 1973, and (in Chapter 5) the rise of third-party politics during the 1970s. These chapters may help to clear up perplexities remaining from the earlier ones. Gradually, I hope, everything will fall into place.

There is scarcely a mention of foreign policy, of Anglo-American relations, or of Margaret Thatcher's 'personal relationship' with Ronald Reagan (or her remarkable empathy with Mikhail Gorbachev) until (in Chapter 12) I reach the point in 1986 at which the nuclear issue came to a head in British politics. Then it blew apart the alliance between the Liberals and the SDP and severely damaged any chance Labour might have had of winning the 1987 General Election, while Neil Kinnock adhered to his position of unilateral nuclear disarmament.

Some American readers may be puzzled at the omission of Ireland, apart from a passing mention. That is not because Ireland is unimportant or uninteresting, but because it is peripheral to the story of Mrs Thatcher's Revolution. It is part of the tragedy of the Irish Question to be of no relevance to anything happening anywhere else in the world save, possibly, the techniques of counter-terrorism. It throws no light on any of the themes of this book.

Since the publication of this book in Britain, nothing has happened to cause me to revise my assessments of the Thatcher era. If the world is sucked into recession as a result of the market crash of October 1987, the British economy will be sucked down with it. That would be bad luck and, depending on its severity and duration, a recession could affect the outcome of a General Election in 1991 or 1992. Nevertheless, since September 1986 the fundamentals of the British economy have, if anything, grown stronger. This supports my tentative view that Britain's decline has been temporarily arrested, although I doubt permanently reversed.

The further disintegration of the political centre has reinforced my conclusion that if anyone is the realigner of British party politics it is Mrs Thatcher. There are now two centre parties in the field, a merged party of Liberals and Social Democrats calling itself the Social and Liberal Democrat Party and a rump of the SDP loyal to Dr David Owen. Under the iron law of the British winner-take-all electoral system, this can only damage the prospects for a third party and further postpone any remaining possibility of a realignment on the centre-left. So far, the beneficiary has not been Labour, as the only credible alternative to Mrs Thatcher, but Mrs Thatcher herself.

Meanwhile, she has pressed ahead with the third phase of her revolution, meeting – as in her second term of office – a good deal of opposition from within her own party. The crisis in the National Health Service, which was an issue in the 1987 campaign, came quickly to the fore once more. As a result she was obliged to add the NHS, the last remaining pillar of the Post-War Settlement, to her agenda for radical reform, although how radical remains to be seen. The National Health Service remains a popular institution in Britain, supported by all classes. Behind her rhetoric Mrs Thatcher is a shrewd and, often, a cautious politician.

At the beginning of 1988 she became the longest-serving Prime Minister of this century. She shows not the slightest intention of retiring. She speaks as if she will run again for a fourth term of office in 1991 or 1992. No successor to her is in sight. In peering into the future, however, we should take heed of some wise words of George Orwell: 'Power-worship blurs political judgement because it leads, unavoidably, to the belief that present trends will continue. Whoever is winning at the moment will always seem to be invincible. If the Japanese have conquered South Asia, they will keep South Asia for ever; if the Germans have captured Tobruk, they will infallibly capture Cairo; if the Russians are in Berlin it is not long before they will be in London, and so on'.[12]

London
February 1988

Notes

1. Quoted in Allan J. Mayer, *Madam Prime Minister*, 1979, p.197.
2. Quoted in Peter Riddell, *The Thatcher Government*, 1983, p.14.
3. Lou Cannon, *Reagan*, 1982, p.316.
4. Ibid., p.321.
5. Robert Kuttner, *The Life of the Party*, 1987, p.25.

6. Richard M. Scammon and Ben J. Wattenberg, *The Real Majority*, 1970, p.21.

7. Martin P. Wattenberg, *The Decline of American Political Parties, 1952–1984*, 1986, pp.141–6.

8. Quoted ibid., pp.141–2.

9. Kuttner, op. cit., p.112; Martin P. Wattenberg, op. cit., pp.147–9.

10. Paul Kennedy, *The Rise and Fall of the Great Powers: Economic Change and Military Conflict from 1500 to 2000*, 1987.

11. *New York Review of Books*, February 18, 1988.

12. Quoted in C. A. R. Crosland, *The Conservative Enemy*, 1962, p.134.

Chronology

1945

July
: General Election. Labour 393, Conservative 213, Liberal 12, Others 22. Labour majority 146

  Prime Minister: Clement Attlee
  Foreign Secretary: Ernest Bevin
  Chancellor of the Exchequer: Hugh Dalton

October
: Dalton's first Budget: income tax reduced, profits tax introduced

1946

April
: Dalton's second Budget: purchase tax reduced, income tax allowances increased

1947

January
: Fiercest winter in living memory, with acute fuel shortages

  Coal industry nationalized

April
: Dalton's third Budget: profits tax, purchase tax, Stamp Duty, and tobacco duties all raised

August
: Sterling made convertible into US dollars causing a run on the pound. Convertibility suspended

November
: Dalton's 'Austerity' Budget: profits tax, purchase tax, and alcohol duties raised

  Dalton resigns as Chancellor after leaking contents of the Budget to a newspaper, Stafford Cripps succeeds him

1948

January
: Railways nationalized

March
: Marshall Plan aid begins

April
: Electricity supply industry nationalized

  Cripps's first Budget: capital levy, tobacco and alcohol duties raised, betting tax introduced

July	National Health Service inaugurated by Aneurin Bevan

1949

April	NATO treaty signed
	Cripps's second Budget: income tax relief reduced, alcohol duties cut, betting tax raised
September	Sterling devalued from $4.03 to $2.80
November	New agreement reached with Trades Union Congress (TUC) on wages freeze

1950

February	General Election. Labour 315, Conservative 298, Liberal 9, Others 3. Labour majority 5
April	Cripps's third Budget: income tax reduced, fuel and purchase tax increased
September	TUC votes against incomes policy
October	Cripps resigns as Chancellor, Hugh Gaitskell succeeds him

1951

February	Steel industry nationalized
March	Herbert Morrison appointed Foreign Secretary
April	Gaitskell's first Budget: income tax increased, purchase tax and petrol duties raised
	Aneurin Bevan resigns over the introduction of health service charges
October	General Election. Conservative 321, Labour 295, Liberal 6, Others 3. Conservative majority 17
	Prime Minister: Winston Churchill Foreign Secretary: Anthony Eden Chancellor of the Exchequer: R. A. Butler

1952

March	Butler's 'set-the-people-free' Budget: tax thresholds lowered, fuel subsidies cut
May	London bus strike
July	France, Germany, Italy, Netherlands, Belgium, and Luxembourg establish the European Steel and Coal Community. Britain plays no part

1953

April	Butler's second Budget: Excess Profits Levy abolished, income tax and purchase tax cut
May	Steel industry denationalized

October	Labour Party conference in Morecambe. The Bevanite left make important gains on the National Executive Committee

1954

April	Butler's third Budget: new 'investment allowance' scheme introduced
October	Rationing finally abolished
	Government reshuffle. Harold Macmillan becomes Minister of Defence
November	Nasser becomes President of Egypt

1955

April	Winston Churchill retires as Prime Minister, Anthony Eden succeeds him. Harold Macmillan becomes Foreign Secretary, Lord Home Commonwealth Secretary
	Butler's fourth Budget: income tax cut, personal allowances raised
May	Warsaw Pact signed
	General Election. Conservative 344, Labour 277, Liberal 6, Others 3. Conservative majority 58
October	Butler's fifth Budget: purchase and profits taxes raised, housing subsidies cut
December	Cabinet reshuffle. Selwyn Lloyd becomes Foreign Secretary, Harold Macmillan Chancellor of the Exchequer, R. A. Butler leader of the House of Commons
	Hugh Gaitskell succeeds Clement Attlee as leader of the Labour Party

1956

April	Macmillan's first Budget: income tax relief, profits tax increased, tobacco taxes raised, Premium Bonds established
	First protest march to the atomic weapons research establishment at Aldermaston
July	Nasser nationalizes the Suez Canal
November	Anglo-French invasion of Suez causes domestic and international furor
	Soviet forces enter Hungary
December	Anglo-French forces leave Suez under American pressure

1957

January	Anthony Eden resigns as Prime Minister, Harold Macmillan succeeds him. Peter Thorneycroft becomes Chancellor of the Exchequer, R. A. Butler Home Secretary

March	Treaty of Rome signed establishing European Economic Community (EEC). Britain plays no part
April	Thorneycroft's first Budget: purchase tax reduced, company tax concessions increased

1958

January	Thorneycroft resigns as Chancellor, Derek Heathcoat-Amory succeeds him
February	Campaign for Nuclear Disarmament founded by Bertrand Russell and Canon Collins
April	Heathcoat-Amory's first Budget: company tax concessions, purchase tax reduced

1959

April	Heathcoat-Amory's second Budget: income tax cut
July	Transport and General Workers Union supports unilateral nuclear disarmament
	Bad Godesburg conference of West Germany's Social Democrats rejects Marxism and accepts the role of markets
October	General Election. Conservative 365, Labour 258, Liberal 6, Others 1. Conservative majority 98
	Hugh Gaitskell unsuccessfully attempts repeal of Clause 4 of Labour Party constitution committing Party to wholesale public ownership
November	European Free Trade Area agreement signed as British response to EEC

1960

March	Sharpeville massacre in South Africa
April	Blue Streak missile cancelled, casting doubt on Britain's future as a nuclear power
July	Heathcoat-Amory resigns as Chancellor, Selwyn Lloyd succeeds him. Lord Home appointed Foreign Secretary, Edward Heath Lord Privy Seal
October	Labour Party conference adopts a policy of unilateral nuclear disarmament. Gaitskell vows to 'fight, fight and fight again'
November	Polaris submarine bases in Scotland announced
	John F. Kennedy elected American President

1961

May	South Africa withdraws from the Commonwealth
July	Emergency Budget: pay pause and Government spending cuts

August TUC and employers join new National Economic Development Council established for the purpose of accelerating economic growth through indicative planning

1962
March Liberals score sensational by-election victory at Orpington

July In the 'night of the long knives' Macmillan replaces seven members of his Cabinet. Reginald Maudling becomes Chancellor, Peter Thorneycroft Minister of Defence

Policy of economic expansion and income restraint launched

October Labour Party conference votes against British membership in the Common Market

December Macmillan and Kennedy meet at Nassau and reach historic agreement to provide Britain with US Polaris missiles

1963
January Hugh Gaitskell dies

General de Gaulle vetoes Britain's attempt to join the EEC

February Harold Wilson becomes leader of the Labour Party, defeating George Brown

June John Profumo resigns as War Minister in scandal involving call girls

October Harold Macmillan resigns as Prime Minister. Fierce contest for the premiership ensues, from which Lord Home emerges, renouncing his peerage to become Prime Minister as Sir Alec Douglas-Home. R. A. Butler, denied the succession, becomes Foreign Secretary, Edward Heath Minister for Trade, Selwyn Lloyd leader of the House of Commons, Henry Brooke Home Secretary

November John F. Kennedy assassinated

1964
April Maudling's Budget: tobacco and alcohol taxes increased

Home postpones General Election until autumn

October General Election. Labour 317, Conservative 304, Liberal 9. Labour majority of 4

Prime Minister: Harold Wilson
Chancellor of the Exchequer: James Callaghan
Foreign Secretary: Patrick Gordon-Walker
Home Secretary: Frank Soskice

November Callaghan's first Budget: prescription charges abolished, pensions increased

1965

February   Prices and Incomes Board established

April   Callaghan's second Budget: corporation tax introduced

November   Unilateral Declaration of Independence for Rhodesia by
            Ian Smith

1966

March   Wilson calls General Election and wins handsome working
            majority. Labour 363, Conservative 253, Liberal 12, Others
            2. Labour majority 96

May   Callaghan's third Budget: selective employment tax in-
            troduced

July   Seamen's strike deals a blow to the economy and to ster-
            ling

1967

March   Steel industry renationalized

July   New economic crisis forces emergency measures. Cal-
            laghan resigns as Chancellor, Roy Jenkins succeeds him

November   Sterling devalued

1968

March   George Brown resigns as Foreign Secretary, Michael
            Stewart succeeds him

May   Student riots in Paris set off wave of unrest in France

August   Soviet Union invades Czechoslovakia

1969

January   Government publishes White Paper 'In Place of Strife' pro-
            posing legal constraints on collective bargaining

April   Franchise extended to eighteen-year-olds

July   Wilson finally defeated in Cabinet over 'In Place of Strife'.
            Attempt to reform unions abandoned

August   British troops sent to Northern Ireland

1970

January   Selsdon Park Conference of Heath's Shadow Cabinet

May   Equal Pay Act passed

June   General Election. Conservatives score surprise victory.
            Conservative 330, Labour 287, Liberal 6, Others 7. Conser-
            vative majority 30

            Prime Minister: Edward Heath
            Chancellor of the Exchequer: Iain Macleod

Foreign Secretary: Alec Douglas-Home
Home Secretary: Reginald Maudling
Education Secretary: Margaret Thatcher, the only woman
Cabinet member

Britain reapplies for membership in the EEC

July Iain Macleod dies, replaced as Chancellor by Anthony Barber

1971

February Decimal currency introduced

First British soldier killed in Belfast

June EEC negotiations completed

October House of Commons votes for entry to the EEC, 356–244; Labour splits, 68 Labour MPs following Roy Jenkins into pro-Europe lobby

1972

January 'Bloody Sunday', 13 killed in Ulster

February Government capitulates to striking miners

April Roy Jenkins resigns as deputy leader of the Labour Party protesting the plan to submit EEC membership to a referendum

July Maudling resigns as Home Secretary, replaced by Robert Carr

October New Liberal revival marked by victory in the Rochdale by-election

November Cabinet declares three-month wages and prices standstill

December Liberals win Sutton and Cheam by-election

1973

January Britain accedes to membership in the EEC

July Liberals win Isle of Ely and Ripon by-elections

October Labour Party conference accepts radical socialist programme

November Miners begin overtime ban

Yom Kippur war. The price of crude oil doubled by OPEC, heralding energy crisis

December Three-day week imposed on industry in response to miners' action and to save energy

Cuts in public expenditure announced

1974

February   Miners vote to strike

Edward Heath calls General Election asking 'Who rules Britain?' Labour 301, Conservative 297, Liberal 14, Others 23. No overall majority

March   Heath resigns as Prime Minister after negotiations with Liberals break down, Harold Wilson succeeds him. Denis Healey becomes Chancellor of the Exchequer, Roy Jenkins Home Secretary, James Callaghan Foreign Secretary

Miners' demands met in full

October   Harold Wilson calls a new General Election seeking a Parliamentary majority. Labour 319, Conservative 277, Liberal 13, Others 26. Labour majority 3

1975

February   Edward Heath deposed as leader of the Conservative Party, Margaret Thatcher the surprise successor

June   Referendum on continued membership in the EEC, 67% vote Yes

July   Government and TUC announce £6 voluntary pay policy

Unemployment passes 1 million

1976

March   Harold Wilson resigns suddenly

April   James Callaghan becomes Prime Minister, Anthony Crosland Foreign Secretary

Denis Healey announces tax cuts conditional on 4% pay policy

May   Jeremy Thorpe resigns as Liberal Party leader

July   David Steel elected Liberal Party leader

September   Roy Jenkins resigns as Home Secretary to become president of the EEC commission, Merlyn Rees succeeds him

Sterling crisis obliges Denis Healey to call in the International Monetary Fund (IMF)

December   Cabinet agrees to package of expenditure cuts in order to obtain further IMF credit

1977

February   Anthony Crosland dies, David Owen becomes Foreign Secretary at age 38, the youngest since William Pitt

March   Liberals enter into parliamentary pact with Labour to keep the Government in power

| July | Denis Healey outlines Phase III of the incomes policy |

1978

January	Special Liberal Assembly endorses Lib-Lab Pact conditionally
May	Notice given that the Lib-Lab Pact will end in November
June	5% decreed as limit for Phase IV of pay policy
September	Callaghan cancels expected election
October	Labour Party conference rejects 5% pay policy
December	House of Commons votes down sanctions against companies breaching the 5% pay policy

1979

January	Seven-nation summit in Guadaloupe discusses deployment of Cruise and Pershing missiles in Europe
	'Day of Action' in the public sector, followed by six weeks of strikes, the so-called 'Winter of Discontent'
March	Referendum rejects devolution in Wales. In Scotland it fails to result in 40% positive vote necessary. Leads to new parliamentary crisis
	Government defeated on confidence vote, 311–310
	Election called for May 3rd
May	General Election. Conservative 339, Labour 269, Liberal 11, Others 16. Conservative majority 43
	Prime Minister: Margaret Thatcher Chancellor of the Exchequer: Sir Geoffrey Howe Foreign Secretary: Lord Carrington Home Secretary: William Whitelaw
	Edward Heath rejects post of Ambassador to US
July	House of Commons decisively rejects death penalty
August	Soviet Union invades Afghanistan
November	Mrs Thatcher calls for £1000 million cut in Britain's EEC contributions
December	NATO agrees to deploy Cruise and Pershing missiles in Europe

1980

October	Unemployment passes 2 million
November	Ronald Reagan elected American President
	James Callaghan resigns as leader of the Labour Party. Michael Foot defeats Denis Healey on the third ballot to become, surprisingly, the new leader

1981

March	Budget: road, alcohol, tobacco, and petrol taxes raised
	The Social Democratic Party (SDP) launched by four former Labour Cabinet Ministers
April	Riots in Brixton, South London. 191 arrests
May	Local elections. Ken Livingstone defeats the leader of the newly elected majority Labour group on the Greater London Council to become Labour leader of the GLC
July	Riots in the Toxteth area of Liverpool. The police use CS gas for the first time
	Roy Jenkins standing as a 'Social Democrat with Liberal support' cuts the Labour majority from 10,274 to 1,759 in the Warrington by-election
September	First major purge of Mrs Thatcher's Cabinet. Three of her sternest critics replaced
	Liberal Party conference in Llandudno approves alliance with the SDP
October	Liberal wins the Croydon North-West by-election from the Conservatives
November	Shirley Williams becomes the first SDP candidate elected to Parliament in the Crosby by-election
December	Arthur Scargill elected president of the National Union of Mineworkers (NUM)

1982

March	Budget: road, tobacco, and petrol taxes raised
	Roy Jenkins becomes second elected SDP MP in the Glasgow Hillhead by-election
April	Argentine forces capture Port Stanley, capital of the Falkland Islands
	First Saturday sitting of the House of Commons since Suez
	Foreign Secretary Lord Carrington and Lord Privy Seal Humphrey Atkins resign. Francis Pym becomes Foreign Secretary. Naval task force sails for the Falklands
May	Argentine ship the *General Belgrano* sunk. Argentine navy withdraws from the Falklands conflict
June	Port Stanley recaptured by British task force
July	Roy Jenkins elected first leader of the SDP, defeating David Owen 26,000 to 20,000
	Rail strike defeated

1983

January	John Nott replaced by Michael Heseltine as Defence Secretary, Tom King becomes Environment Secretary
February	Liberal Simon Hughes wins the Bermondsey by-election from Labour after a bitter campaign and the largest-ever by-election swing
March	Budget: alcohol, tobacco, and petrol taxes raised
	President Reagan launches his strategic defence initiative with his 'Star Wars' speech
May	Mrs Thatcher calls a General Election
June	General Election. Labour receives 28% of the vote, lowest since 1918. SDP/Liberal Alliance is close behind at 26%. Conservative share of the vote goes down but their majority goes up. Conservative 397, Labour 209, Liberal/Alliance 17, SDP/Alliance 6, Others 21
	Cabinet reshuffle. Francis Pym replaced by Geoffrey Howe as Foreign Secretary, Nigel Lawson becomes Chancellor, Leon Brittan becomes Home Secretary, replacing William Whitelaw who receives a hereditary peerage
September	Unemployment falls for the first time since 1979
October	Neil Kinnock elected Labour leader. Roy Hattersley, defeated for the leadership, is elected deputy leader
	Cecil Parkinson resigns as Secretary of State for Trade and Industry in scandal over affair with his secretary
November	First Cruise missiles arrive at Greenham Common air base, Berkshire
December	30,000 women demonstrate at Greenham Common

1984

January	Staff at General Communications (intelligence) Headquarters in Cheltenham are deprived of the right to union membership
March	NUM begins strike action in protest at the projected closure of 'uneconomic' pits with the loss of 20,000 jobs
April	Lawson's first Budget: tax reforms
	Minor Cabinet reshuffle. James Prior replaced as Northern Ireland Secretary
June	SDP gains Portsmouth South from the Conservatives in a by-election
July	Violent clashes at Orgreave coking plant in Yorkshire

November	Bill abolishing the Greater London Council and six metropolitan local authorities passed in the House of Commons
	Ronald Reagan reelected American President
December	Soviet heir apparent Mikhail Gorbachev visits London

1985

February	Gorbachev becomes General Secretary of the Soviet Union
March	Miners' delegate conference votes 98–91 to return to work. Strike ends in defeat after a year of action
May	County Council elections, big swings to the SDP/Liberal Alliance
July	Liberals win Brecon and Radnor by-election by 559 votes from Labour, forcing the Conservatives into third place
September	Cabinet reshuffle. Patrick Jenkin replaced by Kenneth Baker as Environment Secretary and John Selwyn Gummer replaced by Norman Tebbit as Conservative Party Chairman. Leon Brittan replaces Tebbit as Secretary of State for Trade and Industry. Douglas Hurd becomes Home Secretary, Tom King Northern Ireland Secretary. Lord Young and Kenneth Clarke, both in the Cabinet, replace King at Employment
	Riots in the Handsworth area of Birmingham. Two Asians are killed
October	Riots in Tottenham, north London. A policeman is murdered by rioters
	Nottinghamshire miners vote to form a breakaway Union of Democratic Mineworkers
November	Geneva summit between Ronald Reagan and Mikhail Gorbachev
December	Westland helicopters controversy erupts

1986

January	Heseltine resigns as Defence Secretary over Westland crisis, George Younger succeeds him
	Printworkers dispute at News International headquarters in Wapping, east London, begins
March	Lawson's third Budget: income tax cut by 1%, cigarette and petrol duties raised
April	Labour gains Fulham from the Conservatives in by-election
	The Shops Bill to introduce Sunday trading defeated despite a three-line Government whip
	America bombs Libya using UK bases

May	Conservatives lose one safe seat to Liberals in the Ryedale by-election and hold a second by only 100 votes in West Derbyshire
	Sir Keith Joseph resigns as Education Secretary, replaced by Kenneth Baker. John Moore enters the Cabinet as Transport Secretary
September	Liberal Party conference rejects SDP/Liberal Alliance defence policy
October	Conservative Party conference puts forward radical plans for a third term of office
	Labour Party conference advertises Labour's new look, symbolised by red rose
	Reagan and Gorbachev meet at Reykjavik. Summit breaks down but makes progress on INF treaty
November	Lawson announces £5 billion increase in public spending
December	British Gas privatised

1987

February	SDP easily wins the Greenwich by-election from Labour who have held the seat since 1945
April	The Prime Minister visits Moscow, spending 5 hours with Gorbachev
	Neil Kinnock visits Washington, spending 20 minutes with Ronald Reagan
May	Local elections show Labour weakness after Greenwich defeat
	General Election announced
June	General Election. Conservative 375, Labour 220, Liberal/Alliance 17, SDP/Alliance 5, Others 28. Conservative majority 102

Abbreviations

ABM	Anti-Ballistic Missile	DTI	Department of Trade and Industry
ACATT	Association of Cinematograph, Television and Allied Technicians	EEC	European Economic Community
ALC	Association of Liberal Councillors	EEPTU	Electrical Engineering and Plumbers Trades Union
ASLEF	Associated Society of Locomotive Engineers and Firemen	GCHQ	Government Communications Headquarters
ASTMS	Association of Scientific, Technical and Managerial Staffs	GDP	Gross Domestic Product
		GLC	Greater London Council
AUEW	Amalgamated Union of Engineering Workers	GMBATU	General, Municipal, Boilermakers and Allied Trades Unions
CAP	Common Agricultural Policy	ILEA	Inner London Education Authority
CND	Campaign for Nuclear Disarmament	IMF	International Monetary Fund
CBI	Confederation of British Industry	INF	Intermediate-Range Nuclear Forces
CLPD	Campaign for Labour Party Democracy	IRA	Irish Republican Army
		MOD	Ministry of Defence
COHSE	Confederation of Health Service Employees	MORI	Market and Opinion Research International
CPS	Centre for Policy Studies	MSC	Manpower Services Commission
DHSS	Department of Health and Social Security	NAAFI	Navy, Army and Air-Force Institute

NATO	North Atlantic Treaty Organisation	PSL	Private Sector Liquidity
NEB	National Enterprise Board	PUS	Permanent Under-Secretary
NEC	National Executive Committee (Labour Party)	SALT	Strategic Arms Limitation Treaty
NHS	National Health Service	SDI	Strategic Defence Initiative
NUPE	National Union of Public Employees	SDP	Social Democratic Party
NUR	National Union of Railwaymen	SERPS	State Earnings-Related Pension Scheme
OECD	Organisation for Economic Co-operation and Development	SPD	Sozialdemokratische Partei Deutschlands
OPEC	Organisation of Petroleum-Exporting Countries	START	Strategic Arms Reduction Talks
		TGWU	Transport and General Workers' Union
ORC	Opinion Research Centre	TUC	Trades Union Congress
PAYE	Pay As You Earn	TVEI	Technical and Vocational Education Initiative
PLP	Parliamentary Labour Party	VAT	Value-Added Tax
PPE	Philosophy, Politics and Economics	WEA	Workers' Education Association
PSBR	Public Sector Borrowing Requirement	YTS	Youth Training Scheme

Author's Note

Where possible I have tried to make attributions or give references either in the text or in the notes, but a good deal of the material for this book is drawn from the elaborate notebooks in which I record conversations and thoughts and make notes from television, the radio, newspapers and other reading. Some of this information has to remain unattributed in any case within the conventions of political journalism.

1
THE OLD ORDER CRUMBLES

I

Post-war Discontents

'I am not a consensus politician . . .' Margaret Thatcher said, in what was to become her most remembered statement, 'I'm a *conviction* politician.' The self-designation stuck: 'conviction politics' became the brand mark of her style, as well known as Harold Wilson's belief that 'ten days is a long time in politics' or Harold Macmillan's nonchalant shrugging off of a Cabinet crisis as a 'little local difficulty'. In these ways do politicians type-cast themselves.

But what did she mean when she said that she was not a consensus politician? For it is there we must begin, with the foundations of the post-war order which were to crumble and fall with the rise of Margaret Thatcher. The consensus she imagined herself to be smashing was founded more in myth than in reality. Because myth is as powerful in politics as reality, however, I shall refer to the 'consensus' as if it had literally existed. The word implies that throughout the post-war period the parties had had more in common than the differences between them and that government, and especially the management of the economy, had proceeded according to a broad agreement. They did no such thing. Indeed Britain suffered unduly compared with some other, more successful, countries from sharp and usually ideologically-inspired changes in direction – enactments and repeals, nationalisations and denationalisations. It is true that in 1945 all three parties – Conservative, Labour and Liberal – went to the country committed to principles of economic reconstruction and social reform which they had jointly endorsed within the war-time Coalition. 'A massive new middle ground had arisen in politics.'[1] Some of the spirit of the war-time consensus – although even the extent of that can be exaggerated – had lasted into the immediate post-war years but not for long: the austerities of 1947 – food rations cut, no petrol for private motoring, no currency for foreign holidays – soon put paid to it and in 1950 and 1951 the middle class voters in the towns and suburbs of the south who had crossed class lines in the euphoria of 1945 returned, chastened, to the Tory fold.

After 1951 the Conservatives set about dismantling the panoply of war-time and post-war controls which Labour had relied upon to plan production and arrange fair shares in conditions of austerity. The Welfare State was not attacked but there was no agreement about how it was to be financed, and whether to introduce charging and means-testing or not became a running battle between the parties. For reasons of prudence, Churchill – no union lover – pursued a conciliatory policy towards organised labour which endured, more or less, until the great London bus strike of 1957. By 1964 the privileged position of the trade unions, with their immunities from the law,[2] had become a party issue and by the late 1960s the 'union question' had come to dominate party politics.

'There never *was* a consensus . . . The parties never came together in their policies. Even the idea of "Butskellism" was sloppy and inaccurate,' said Edward Heath in 1971.[3] The notion of 'Butskellism' owed more to the easy elision of the names Butler and Gaitskell than to the similarities of their economic policies. To be sure, both R. A. Butler and Hugh Gaitskell made some use of Keynesian techniques of demand management but so would have any Chancellor of the Exchequer, or the Finance Minister of any other country, attempting at that time to maintain full employment with reasonably stable prices. They differed quite sharply, as Philip Williams has shown, on monetary policy, the convertibility of sterling, state controls and the distribution of wealth.[4]

Certainly, nothing resembling the civility of 'Butskellism' extended to the shop floor of British industry, where the battle lines remained sullenly drawn between 'them' and 'us'. On foreign policy a broad consensus in support of the Atlantic Alliance operated between the front benches – until Eden shattered it at Suez – but did not reach down into the Labour Party which was consistently split between Bevinists and Bevanites. In the 1960s the parties divided, and split within themselves, over British membership of the European Common Market. In short, the post-war consensus had never been much of a consensus. It became a convenient scapegoat for the economic failures and social dislocations of the 1970s which, as we shall see, it suited the Thatcherites to blame on a Keynesian collusion between the parties. What did break down towards the end of the 1970s was not so much a consensus as the Post-war Settlement which had grown out of the brief war-time suspension of party politics.

Like the 1688 Act of Settlement which finally resolved the constitutional issues of the Civil War, the Attlee government's social legislation, much of it inspired by the forethought of the Coalition, was designed to call at least a truce in the class war which had disfigured the politics of the 1920s and 1930s. Full employment and the maintenance of the Welfare State became the accepted goals of both parties, if for no other reason than that to depart from them would be to court electoral defeat. They set not only the framework but the agenda for post-war politics, for neither full employment nor the Welfare State could be maintained without an expanding economy. How to achieve faster and sustainable growth was the unsolved but ever-pressing question of post-war economic policy. Growth was inhibited by a balance of payments constraint which became increasingly severe from around the end of the 1950s, and by the tendency of the economy to 'overheat' and generate price inflation which exacerbated the balance of payments difficulties. Harold Macmillan, always the performer, described the task of managing the post-war economy as requiring the skills of 'a new Cinquevalli', a juggler capable of keeping four balls in the air simultaneously – full employment, an expanding economy, stable prices and a strong pound.[5]

Of these full employment was the first imperative because of memories of the mass unemployment of the 1930s; in countries where inflation had been the greater scourge, Germany for example, the folk memory worked in the other direction. In Britain the pattern of post-war economic government became bouts of inflation brought to an end by balance of payments crises. This was the depressing but seemingly inescapable 'stop-go syndrome' which defeated each and every government until the 'long boom' came to its end in 1973 and stop-go gave way to 'stagflation' – all stop and no go.

For Labour governments, growth was an even greater imperative than for Conservative governments living down their reputation of the 1930s. Growth was not only necessary for maintaining full employment, the cornerstone of the Post-war Settlement, but was indispensable if resources and wealth were to be redistributed in accordance with socialist priorities. This was the essence of Anthony Crosland's 'revisionist' insight: it was unnecessary, as well as undesirable, to engage in wholesale nationalisation; the mixed economy under Keynesian management had no need to approach socialism by means of a command economy; social justice and equality – the central values of the 'revisionists' – could be achieved by the re-allocation of resources and wealth, in other words by public spending. But all this was possible only if resources overall expanded at a sufficient pace. For redistributive justice would be acceptable enough if everyone was growing richer in absolute terms; the contrary strategy of soak-the-rich-to-feed-the-poor offered no way forward, for to redistribute wealth and income meant soaking not just the rich but also the mass of the better-off working class. That was a recipe both for inflation and electoral defeat.

Crosland later confessed that he had been too sanguine about growth. To all intents and purposes he had regarded the problem of production as solved, leaving all good socialists to get on with what more concerned them, and fell within their competence, the creation of a more just and equal society. It was a happy vision and one which by giving the State a lesser and more indirect role in the achievement of socialism seemed to remove the tension between equality and liberty.

In this he embodied the hopes of a generation. Not only in his thought, which was immensely influential, but also in the example of his lifestyle he combined social commitment and private freedom. With his seminal work published in 1956 he liberated socialists not only from the encumbrances of the Marxist tradition but also from the earnest worthiness of Sidney and Beatrice Webb, who had spent their honeymoon collecting information about trade unions in Dublin with no time to visit a theatre or a gallery. A famous passage towards the end of *The Future of Socialism* was headed, 'Liberty and Gaiety in Private Life; the Need for a Reaction against the Fabian Tradition', and it ended with the words: 'Total abstinence and a good filing-system are not now the right sign-posts to the socialist Utopia; or at least, if they are, some of us will fall by the wayside.'[6]

A figure of dazzling glamour and charm, Crosland had shaken off a stern religious upbringing by the Plymouth Brethren to become in the early part of his life a playboy intellectual, although the two roles were pursued in relentless parallel, the one not permitted to interfere with the other. The war had punctured his Oxford career and when he returned to complete his degree he stayed on for three years as a don, teaching economics. One of his pupils was Tony Benn. While still an undergraduate Crosland had been talent spotted by Hugh Dalton, then Chancellor of the Exchequer. Dalton, a roistering Old Etonian with a penchant for bright and beautiful young men (of whom Rupert Brook had been one) helped Crosland win a seat in Parliament as member for South Gloucestershire. That this in 1950 was a Labour seat (although no longer by 1955) is a measure of the times straddled by his career. At first he hated Parliament. It bored him and offended his fastidious intelligence. Perhaps this was as well for, when not drinking or womanising, Crosland settled down in his armchair and, with expensive fountain pen, wrote his great work. He was thirty-eight when it was published. At twenty-two he had declared in a letter: 'I am revising Marxism and will emerge as the modern Bernstein.'[7]

So he did. The book made him at once the *bête noire* of the Bevanites and fundamentalists but gave inspiration to a whole generation of socialist reformers. It provided new foundations for an ethical socialism centred on the pursuit of equality. It became the bible of so-called 'revisionist socialism' and, although never formally accepted by the Labour Party as its doctrine, in practice it coloured the approach of the Wilson and Callaghan governments.

The Future of Socialism provided an ideological basis for Hugh Gaitskell, who in the year before its publication had triumphed over Aneurin Bevan to succeed Attlee as Labour leader, and his supporters. Dalton had introduced Crosland to Gaitskell's circle – the 'Hampstead set' it was called by the Left – and it was Gaitskell who helped Crosland back into the Commons in 1959. Although the chief theorist of 'revisionism', he had not been in favour of Gaitskell's ill-fated attempt to revise the Labour Party's constitution to remove the commitment to wholesale nationalisation contained in Clause Four. Like many intellectuals he tended to make a cult of pragmatism. He liked to cite Max Weber's distinction between the 'ethic of ultimate ends and the ethic of responsibility', insisting that, 'he who follows the former has no interest in political power'. Rewriting the tablets, he thought, would prove more trouble than it was worth. He was right.

After Gaitskell's untimely death in 1963 he had gradually ceased to be a Gaitskellite. He did not change his views about socialism but he was not a man for faction. There was also a rivalry touching upon jealousy between himself and Roy Jenkins, who had been Gaitskell's other favourite protégé. Jenkins's view was that Gaitskell had preferred his company but Crosland's brain. The Jenkinsites became increasingly identified with the cause of 'Britain in Europe'. Crosland chose to regard this as a symptom of socialist atrophy. He remained in favour of Britain joining the European Common Market but insisted that this was not an overriding question. Those who believed it to be so did so because of their increasing inability to believe in the central values of socialism.

For these reasons he declined to join the pro-European Right, mostly former Gaitskellites, in the government lobbies in the historic division on 28 October 1971 which took Britain into Europe and prefigured the schism in the Labour Party ten years later. Crosland took to insisting that he was a democratic socialist, not a social democrat, claiming that the definition of the latter appeared to be somebody who was preparing to leave the Labour Party.

As time went on he donned a protective hide of populism, relegating a growing number of issues to a place so low on the list of the concerns of his Grimsby constituents as to be not worth the attention of serious people. 'Serious' was a favourite Crosland word, his anathema against all that was 'trivial' or 'fashionable' but also, increasingly, against what was uncongenial to his position. As a gilded youth he had become accustomed to being excused (or even loved) for bad behaviour and would sometimes use this to bolster the integrity of his convictions. For example in restaurants he was liable to complain loudly about the noise of 'frightful upper class voices'. He refused even when Foreign Secretary to wear evening dress (he would stoop to a dinner jacket) although on occasions (chiefly in his constituency) he affected to wear a flat cap. In *The Future of Socialism* he had advocated 'uninhibited mingling between the classes' – a phrase he had picked up from Dalton.[8] He remained to the end a fiercely egalitarian spirit.

But by the time of his sad and sudden death in 1977 his world, as we shall see, was collapsing around him. When the IMF foreclosed on Britain it foreclosed on Croslandism. The 1970s had confronted him with the implications of his theory in conditions of slow growth. As resources were withdrawn from personal consumption in order to finance the public expenditure needs of a Welfare State, the problem of inflation was exacerbated. That, combined with low productivity, 'sometimes makes the British economy seem unmanageable', he wrote; but he did not alter the primacy he attached to growth. 'We may take it as a certainty that rapid growth is an essential condition of any significant re-allocation of resources.'[9] In 1970 that was a pessimistic observation; after 1973, when the world was plunged into recession, it became tantamount to an admission that further redistribution had become impossible, or at least without the dire consequences which flowed from Crosland's own theory.

Not only that but, as he recognised, the problem had long since become not how to achieve a further re-allocation of resources but how to pay for what had already been created. With slow growth the financing of the Welfare State became increasingly problematical.

From the early 1960s Britain was trapped in a vicious circle as the rising costs of welfare resulted in higher taxation, resulting in accelerating wage inflation, resulting in higher welfare costs and more taxes, and so on. The cost of welfare increased partly for demographic reasons as proportionately more old and young became a charge on proportionately fewer wage earners and taxpayers but also because of a vast expansion in the numbers employed in the welfare bureaucracies. Moreover, many benefits were linked to inflation either directly or indirectly and in some years raced ahead of real earnings. In 1965 government expenditure, central and local, accounted for 37 per cent of Gross Domestic Product (GDP); by 1970 it had risen to 41 per cent, by 1975 to 50 per cent. In 1965 taxes financed four-fifths of the expenditure, by 1975 only three-quarters. The Welfare State was financed increasingly by borrowing.

The fast-rising cost of public spending, together with inflation, brought more and more wage-earners into the net of PAYE. In the 1950s the average wage-earner paid no income tax; in 1960 his tax and insurance contributions took some 8 per cent of his earnings; by 1970 they took nearly 20 per cent. In 1972 a married man with two children and with average industrial earnings paid 19 per cent of his gross earnings in taxes, direct and indirect; by 1976 he was paying 26 per cent.

This in itself represented a change scarcely less profound than that brought about by the Welfare State which had ensured universal access to medical care and social security. The working classes were not used to paying income tax. Now the great mass had for the first time become taxpayers. In the lowest income bracket the rate they paid was the highest in the world, according to Denis Healey in his 1976 Budget speech. The Welfare State had made us into a nation of taxpayers.

For Conservative governments too, growth was the means of keeping the people happy, of winning elections and of not putting too great a strain on the Post-war Settlement. Macmillan had never been able to forget the unemployment he had seen in Stockton in the 1930s and other Conservatives, with less developed or patrician social consciences, kept it in mind that memories of the 1930s had lost them the General Election of 1945, or so it was widely supposed. During the 1950s Britain boomed, although in fits and starts. Between 1952 and 1960 real earnings (that is, what money would buy after tax and National Insurance deductions) increased at an annual average of 2·8 per cent. When Gaitskell tried to make growth an election issue in 1959 Macmillan, although himself always at heart an expansionist, could brush the thought aside as a new-fangled craze to be compared with the twist, at that time the fashionable rage of the dance floors. But by 1961 he was himself dancing to another tune. The balance of payments constriction was now tightening, due to an overvalued pound and to Britain's over-extended post-imperial role. 'Stop' abruptly followed 'go', this time accompanied by a 'pay pause' – the first essay in pay restraint since the Cripps freeze in the austerity conditions of 1947. The 1960s had arrived.

The Post-war Settlement had placed another item on the political agenda – the collective bargaining system or what was to become the 'union question'. It dominated the politics of the 1960s and 1970s. Full employment had transformed the bargaining power of the unions. Slowly it became apparent that free collective bargaining, certainly on Britain's fragmented, competitive model, was not easily compatible with the maintenance of full employment with reasonably stable prices. From this realisation flowed two consequences, both of them profound. In order to defend full employment, promote economic expansion and avoid policies of crude wage restraint, trade unions were drawn into sharing responsibility for the management of the economy. To their members this appeared as a collusion with government and employers for the purpose of reducing real wages. The authority of national leadership was undermined, the power of shop stewards enhanced, and the fires of militancy fuelled. By the same process the government came to be held responsible for what people were paid, not only for the general level of wages but for the disparities between the pay of a nurse and a miner, a general and a policeman. Government soon found itself carrying a can of worms marked 'social justice'. The consequences were scarcely less disastrous than assuming responsibility for the English weather.

However, within the terms of the Post-war Settlement there was no alternative. There was no other way of keeping Harold Macmillan's four balls simultaneously in the air. When Harold Wilson came to power in 1964, on a growth ticket, he found himself obliged to query the traditional division of Labour whereby the political wing of the Movement concerned itself with governing the country while the industrial wing got on with its own business of collective bargaining. The then general secretary of the Trades Union Congress, George Woodcock, also saw that things could not go on as they were; if the unions themselves failed to come to grips with the 'wages problem', government would step in to do it for them, either by legislation or by abandoning full employment. Incomes policy was the chosen instrument for resolving these contradictions and for filling the lacuna left by Keynes in his theory of employment. If workers would restrain their demands for money wages, freeing themselves from the 'money illusion', prices would rise more slowly; this would permit sustained and faster growth, in consequence of which *real* wages would rise faster than would have been possible under conditions of free-for-all. That was the theory. It could never be put to proper test for the reason that the patience of the union members ran out before the completion of each experiment. Nevertheless, in order to obtain the co-operation of the unions, or, at least, as the TUC put it on one occasion, their 'reluctant acquiescence', governments were obliged, first, to intervene directly to obtain a commensurate restraint in prices, and, second, to endeavour to operate the policy fairly between one group and another and with some regard to economic efficiency. A Prices and Incomes Board was set up to study cases with regard to these criteria. The task which its chairman, Aubrey Jones, undertook with invincible confidence might have daunted Solomon with a computer. The Board pronounced on the marketing of soap powder, the productivity of baking and of brewing, the working practices of busmen employed by the Corporation of Dundee, the fees of solicitors and architects, the need for overtime in banks, and, altogether, 170 similarly arcane matters.

The Prices and Incomes Board was the archetypal institution of the Wilsonian era; it represented the apogee of the expert and of the belief in the powers of problem-solving social science. Aubrey Jones saw it as an opportunity to give institutional expression to Keynesian theory, no less. 'The Board's task was to prevent the opportunity for full employment opened up by Keynes from being defeated,' he wrote later.[10] But defeated it eventually was.

Incomes policy had begun as an instrument for achieving Labour's ambitious plans for faster economic growth. In no time it became part of the desperate deflationary defences of an over-valued pound and an over-extended frontier which, Wilson had claimed ludicrously, extended to the Himalayas. The use and misuse of incomes policy contributed to rising industrial unrest. In the two years 1963–4 some four million working days were lost through strikes. In the two years 1968–9 the total was 11·5 million. Wilson's answer to this problem was to try to reform the unions themselves. If incomes policy could not control the proceeds of collective bargaining the government would reform the processes of collective bargaining. The legislation proposed in the White Paper, 'In Place of Strife', resulted in the 'Battle of Downing Street'.[11] Wilson lost. The next year, in 1970, he lost the General Election.

In this way the attempts to sustain the Post-war Settlement had produced a crisis within the Labour Movement, its most severe since 1931 and the Ramsay MacDonald secession. The crisis was to continue through the 1970s and into the 1980s. Free collective bargaining, as practised or malpractised by British trade unions – 'free collective chaos', James Callaghan was to call it in 1978 – was simply incompatible with the preservation of full employment and the financing of the Welfare State, except at rates of inflation which would become intolerable. At the same time, the umbilical links between the Labour Party and the trade unions prevented a Labour government from effectively resolving this contradiction within the social democratic approach.

The Post-war Settlement now came under real strain. In the six years of Wilson government unemployment increased from 376,000 to 555,000. At about 2·5 per cent of the registered workforce this was scarcely a departure from 'full employment' but the upward trend was already a sign of what was to come. Then, about 1967, inflation really began to take off. This was not solely due to the contradictions now inherent in upholding the Post-war Settlement. The USA, at war in Vietnam, was running a huge balance of payments deficit, thereby swelling the world's money supply and exporting her own inflation to others. Pseudo-revolutionary events in France in 1968[12] triggered industrial and student unrest in other countries, including Britain. By the end of the decade inflation was running at an annual rate of over 8 per cent, compared with around 3 per cent at the beginning of it. Crosland, looking back on the 1964–70 Labour government, believed that no government could govern with 8 per cent annual inflation but by 1971 the annual rate was an alarming 13 per cent.

From 1964 the annual rise in living standards, an accustomed and expected feature of the post-war period, slowed almost to a standstill. Between 1964 and 1968 it averaged no more than 0·5 per cent a year. Then, in 1966 and 1967, real living standards on average actually declined for the first time ever in modern memory, apart from a few months during the Korean war when wages had temporarily failed to keep up with rising prices. Over the whole six years of Labour government real disposable income had increased on average by scarcely more than 1 per cent a year compared with 2·8 per cent in the 1950s. Increased taxation had bitten into real incomes. Indeed, taxes under Wilson had risen at twice the rate of average earnings. Yet little if any redistribution had been achieved in the direction of the working class. For the bulk of the population the Welfare State was probably largely self-financing: that is, people by and large paid for what they got.[13] By 1970 some five million people were living below a Labour Government's own declared poverty line. In that year *The Economist* commented: 'the failure to advance, or even maintain, the differential between the low-paid and pensioners on the one hand and the average wage earners on the other is a real increase in inequality which becomes more apparent as wages spiral.'

In 1970 it was the Tories' turn again. Edward Heath began by trying to govern the hard way. He came in pledging 'to change the course of history of this nation, nothing less.' He did not see it as his task to uphold 'consensus' which, as we have seen, he regarded as a fiction. The economy was to be set free again, as in 1951, but in contrast to then, the trade unions were to be put in their place within a framework of law similar to that envisaged in Labour's 'In Place of Strife'. Incomes policy, meanwhile, was discarded and pay claims were contested on a one by one basis; planning, brought into disrepute by the Labour government, was virtually discontinued; 'lame duck' industries were to be left to the mercies of market forces. By these means inflation was at first brought down, until in February 1972 the sheer industrial strength of the miners prevailed over the government. The coalfields dispute brought a new character on to the stage, one who was to epitomise 1970s man. At the gates of the Saltley coke depot in Birmingham the police retreated in the face of a superior force of flying pickets from Yorkshire, estimated to be some ten thousand men. The young Yorkshire militant, Arthur Scargill, clambered on to the roof of a public lavatory and proclaimed: 'This is the greatest victory of the working class in my lifetime.' The miners' pay claim was settled at 27 per cent. 'A little blood-letting may do no harm,' Lord Carrington was advised. 'What do you mean?' he demanded indignantly. 'This is true blue Tory blood and it's been spilled all over the carpet.'

Other workers followed on the militant coat-tails of the miners. The workers of the Upper Clyde Shipbuilders were occupying their bankrupt yard. The local Chief Constable advised the government that he could no longer be responsible for public order. Meanwhile unemployment was rising towards the million mark. In January 1972 it had reached 928,000. A million was the round number at which it was widely believed unemployment would threaten social and political stability. The events on the Clyde gave support to this view. Heath was too much the political child of the 1930s to regard that prospect with equanimity. He performed a U-turn far more spectacular than Macmillan's in 1962. In February the Upper Clyde Shipbuilders were rescued with new subsidies. The Budget that spring was strongly reflationary; monetary policy was relaxed. In August a powerfully interventionist Industry Bill was enacted. Meanwhile, Heath sued for a new compact with the trade unions. When his series of talks at Chequers failed he went ahead, and on 6 November 1972, a fateful date, legislated statutory controls on pay and prices. The times were not favourable to incomes policies. World commodity prices were exploding. The Yom Kippur war[14] in October 1973 resulted in a quadrupling of the world price of oil. By the beginning of 1974 inflation was running at 13 per cent. The incomes policy could not possibly take the strain. Inflation was by now in the blood. This time the miners advanced in the wake of the Gulf Sheiks. In December 1973 industry had to be put on to a three day week. In February Heath went to the country asking, 'Who rules Britain?' He lost. The miners ruled Britain.

Heath had tried first to escape from the Post-war Settlement, then to prop it up. The crisis had deepened since Wilson's days, even before OPEC took a hand. 'We have to find a more sensible way of settling our differences,' he had said at the end of the first miners' strike in 1972. But his bid for an incomes policy was made more difficult by his Industrial Relations Act of 1971. At first the unions refused to talk at all, especially when in June 1972 five dockers' pickets were committed to Pentonville Prison in contempt of the Act. The law had to be bent in a hurry to get them out before they became martyrs. The law was now an ass. However, the Industrial Relations Act remained on the Statute Book and Heath was not prepared to lose face by repealing it. This gave the TUC its excuse to break off the Chequers talks.

The point had been reached at which it was probably politically impossible for the unions to enter into any kind of effective agreement on pay with a Conservative government. The legal status of the trade unions had become too contentious an issue. Following the débâcle of 'In Place of Strife' the unions had moved towards a still closer relationship with the Labour Party. The object was to prevent anything like the Battle of Downing Street from occurring again; the effect was to increase the power of the unions within the Labour Movement. Rather than come to terms with Heath the TUC leaders preferred to await the return of a Labour government.

When the Tories had returned to power in 1951 the TUC had declared its readiness to work with the elected government of the day whatever its political complexion and Churchill had seized the outstretched hand with a kid glove. Now, in 1973, the unions were entirely hand in glove with the Labour Party, part of the government when it was in power and an extension of the Opposition when it was not. In this way the politics of the 1970s became polarised around the union question.

Moreover, the fall of the Heath government dealt a blow to the authority of government itself. When Wilson had been prevented from legislating against the unions, that had been a crisis of the Labour Movement. When the unions moved into confrontation with an elected government it was altogether a more serious matter. And when Heath had had to resort to the ultimate deterrent by a dissolution of Parliament and his bluff was called, he had disarmed not only himself but his successors. The country had taken a massive step towards the condition known in the 1970s as 'ungovernability'. Parliament was no longer sovereign. The courts could be flouted. Violence had become a feature of the industrial scene. Power could be exercised only if shared with non-elected bodies such as the TUC. Or so it seemed in the aftermath of the Heath débâcle. 'No Government in Britain can hope to succeed today without the good will of the unions,' wrote Norman St John Stevas in 1976.[15]

Trade unionism was one of the chief growth industries of the 1970s. This was largely due to the burgeoning of the public service bureaucracies. Between 1961 and 1975 central government employment had increased by 27 per cent and local government employment by 70 per cent. For example, the National Union of Public Employees (NUPE), which was to play a leading role in the Winter of Discontent of 1978–9, grew from a membership of 265,000 in 1968 to 712,000 in 1978. This trade union expansion was also an unforeseen consequence of the incomes policies of the 1960s and 1970s. In order to ensure that their noses too were in the corporatist trough, the middle classes unionised themselves. Even the top civil servants, who included the people running the incomes policies, affiliated themselves to the TUC in brotherhood with the Transport and General Workers' Union. Clive Jenkins organised Midland Bank managers. In 1973 there took place the first ever major strike in the National Health Service. Doctors now learnt to engage in what they pleased to call 'industrial action'. Recorded in my notebooks is a BBC-TV news bulletin which began: 'Tonight militant consultants . . .' Thus were the professions proletarianised. We were all militants now.

Who governs? Heath had asked. Many now thought the answer was the leaders of the TUC, whom they saw on their television screens, coming in and out of Downing Street. With Wilson's return to office in the wreckage of Heath's confrontation with the miners the Social Contract came into force. This Rousseauistic euphemism was the brainchild of Jack Jones, militant shop steward turned left-wing statesman. After the Labour Party split of 1931 Ernest Bevin had acted to enlarge the influence of the unions within the Party to prevent such a débâcle from happening again; after the débâcle of 'In Place of Strife', Jones, Bevin's successor at Transport House, had done likewise. He had established a Liaison Committee consisting of representatives of the General Council and the 'Shadow' Cabinet and National Executive Committee of the Party. It was there that the Social Contract was hatched.

The notion was that if a Labour government pursued economic and social policies acceptable to the unions a positive response would be forthcoming. 'A government which is prepared to tackle the problem of prices in the shops, rents and housing costs and put up pensions will certainly get the co-operation of the trade union movement and there will be moderation,' Jones had promised as Labour moved back into power. In the first year of the Social Contract inflation soared to 27 per cent. The miners had been bought off for 22 per cent. By the June of 1975 earnings had increased by an average of 26·6 per cent, weekly wage rates by a staggering 33 per cent. In exchange for their restored legal immunities and for the food subsidies, price and rent controls contained in Denis Healey's first Budget, and the 'howls of anguish' he had promised to extract from the rich, the unions had delivered nothing. The Social Contract, said the *Daily Mirror*, was 'a shameful flop'. Joel Barnett, the Chief Secretary to the Treasury, wrote later: 'To my mind the only give and take in the contract was that the government gave and the unions took.'[16]

Who governed? A Gallup Poll found that 52 per cent thought Jack Jones the most powerful man in the country, only 34 per cent the Prime Minister. The truth of the moment was that no one had power. With inflation soaring frighteningly out of control, the Cabinet committees concerned with economic matters 'merely watched passively the slide towards hyper-inflation during the spring and early summer of 1975,' according to another inside witness.[17] People began to imagine they could hear not the tumbrils but the wheelbarrows of Weimar rolling in the streets. In fact it had been mass unemployment, and not the earlier hyper-inflation, which paved the path for Adolf Hitler and brought down the Weimar Republic. Nevertheless, amid now fast-rising unemployment, Weimar with its hooligan violence, aimless sexual freedom, its superstitions and cults, and intellectual proletarianisation, offered tempting analogies to pessimists.

By the summer of 1975 something had to be done. The government now had a majority at Westminster, though a slender one. The referendum on Britain's continuing membership of the Common Market was safely out of the way. A run on the pound in July helped to concentrate the minds of the unions. Jack Jones was converted to the need to restrain wages below the level at which prices were rising. The pay restraint was to be voluntary; everyone was to get a flat £6 a week up to £8,500 a year, and above that nothing. For two years the policy worked not badly. By the summer of 1977 average earnings were increasing at an average of 14 per cent while price inflation was down to 13 per cent.

By that time, however, the real living standards of the average family had fallen in two successive years, by about £7 a week in total. In December 1973 the real weekly take-home pay of a family (a married couple with two children) averaged £70.20, in 1977 £63.10. Deteriorations on this scale were quite unprecedented. Annual increases of two or three per cent a year in real incomes had come to be regarded as a standard feature of post-war capitalism. The French philosopher and commentator, Raymond Aron, had dubbed this the 'revolution of rising expectations'. In 1973 55 per cent of people looked forward to higher living standards in the following year; by 1977 this figure was only 23 per cent. The counter-revolution was in progress.

Not only were average wages failing to keep up with inflation but the first two phases of the policy, combined with a new militancy among the unions of the unskilled, had put a fierce squeeze on differentials. The gap was narrowing between skilled and unskilled, manual and non-manual, male and female, older and younger workers. Income tax was up from 30 to 35 pence in the pound. No wonder the pay policy was beginning to break down. Meanwhile, something else had happened. When Labour returned to power in 1974, full employment was not as full as it had been, but with unemployment figures standing at just over half a million (less than 2·5 per cent of the work force) it could not be claimed seriously – although some did – that the goal of full employment had been abandoned. Some fifteen months later unemployment topped the million mark for the first time since 1940. Now the cornerstone itself of the Post-war Settlement was crumbling.

Not only in Britain was this happening. The recession was world-wide, and the deepest by far since the 1930s. At first governments had struggled to keep growth going but one by one they gave in. Deflation was back in business. Keynes was proclaimed dead: monetarism became the new orthodoxy. The Labour government held out until the last. As Joel Barnett recorded: 'The Chancellor . . . made the fundamental decision to react to the oil crisis in a different way from the Germans and the Japanese, and indeed from many other developed countries. Instead of cutting expenditure to take account of the massive oil price increase of 1973 . . . [he] decided to maintain our expenditure and borrow to meet the deficit.'[18] By 1976 public expenditure and borrowing were both out of control. In July there was a run on the pound, stemmed for a while by expenditure cuts and another tranche of borrowing from the International Monetary Fund. In the autumn a crisis broke out again. Healey was on his way to Heathrow Airport listening in his car to the news of the fall of the pound. Instead of heading for Manila, where the IMF was meeting, he diverted to Blackpool, where the Labour Party conference was meeting. There, to boos and catcalls, he stood amidst the debris of his policy and announced his application to the Fund for what would this time have to be a conditional loan. All other credit was exhausted. A conditional loan meant that the conduct of the British economy would be placed under surveillance. That was something which happened to Third World countries.

For Labour, 1976 was the year of the U-turn. In his Budget that spring Denis Healey, as we shall see later, had taken the decisive step towards monetarism. At the Labour Party conference that autumn Callaghan spoke words which effectively buried Keynes. 'You cannot spend your way out of a recession,' he asserted. But now, in November, while the bailiffs from the IMF waited in a London hotel, the Cabinet faced the bankruptcy of Croslandite socialism. Everything that he had predicted would be the consequence of nil growth and rampant inflation now came about. The Welfare State could no longer be sustained on its existing scale, social spending had to be curtailed.

The alternative approach insisted upon by the Treasury under pressure from the IMF made no sense to Crosland; to deflate when 1·25 million were unemployed stuck in his Keynesian throat; deflation would mean falling tax revenues, unemployment would increase the cost of benefits; the fiscal crisis of the Welfare State would deepen. But the government was no longer its own master. 'Even if the Government survives, does it make such a difference if Labour measures can't be implemented?' he wondered.[19] For Croslandite socialism had little or nothing to say about the creation of resources; it was concerned with their distribution. Now it stood empty-handed, offering sympathy and the dole. It was worse than that, for public spending was not an end in itself but one of the means to a broader social equality in which the cards of opportunity would be re-dealt.

The goal of revisionist socialism was equality. Nothing had happened to invalidate its goals, only the means were no longer available; and as Crosland, in his love of liberty, had always insisted, revisionism was a doctrine as much about means as about ends.

The Cabinet agreed to cut public borrowing from a planned £10·5 billions to £8·7 billions. The proportion of national wealth consumed by public spending (which in 1975 had reached 50 per cent) was reduced to 44 per cent by 1977. The world did not end. In fact the immediate crisis passed remarkably swiftly. The balance of payments was restored to surplus. Unemployment was rising but so were real living standards once more. By 1978 inflation was at last down in single figures again. But then, as Burckhardt said of the French Revolution, 'did the curtain rise on that great farce of hope.'

In the first weeks of 1979 a wave of industrial militancy spread across the land. In the months which preceded it economic logic prevailed over political prudence; greed and envy burst from beneath the skin, as is their way; and folly, vanity and cowardice played their familiar roles. These were the immediate causes of the events of the Winter of Discontent as it soon became known. Nothing that happened was quite inevitable, yet the roots of what happened can be seen stretching deep into the post-war period. They were a manifestation of what we shall call the politics of decline (see Chapter 2). The Winter of Discontent put the finishing touches to the destruction of the Post-war Settlement. It made a fitting obituary to the Old Order.

In the summer of 1978 the pay policy had been due to enter its fourth stage. One problem with pay policies is that they are more useful as temporary instruments of crisis management than they are as tools of regular government. It is relatively easy to impose a period of crude restraint in moments of grave emergency. The British are good at that sort of thing, going back to war-time rationing and the Blitz. But as the policy has to be relaxed and refined, made necessarily more flexible, resentments and envies mount. One consequence of pay policy is to draw attention to what others are being paid. Pay is news. As the official negotiators go slow, the initiative passes to the unofficial negotiators. The moguls of the TUC, observed coming and going on television, are seen to be in collusion with government and employers; even the authority of the shop floor leadership can become undermined, giving rise to the *unofficial* unofficial strike. Two years is about the limit of effective wage restraint; then comes the problem of 're-entry', how to return to normal collective bargaining without inflationary burn-out. Almost by definition re-entry has to be attempted when circumstances are improving, partly as the result of temporary wage restraint. As real living standards rise again, so do expectations. Invariably it is when things are looking up that heads appear above the barricades. All these factors were at work in 1978 and, in addition, there was a smell of North Sea oil in the air. Having already largely broken down in the public sector, the pay policy was now threatening to break down in the private sector. The spending cuts forced upon the Cabinet in 1976 had excited the militancy of the burgeoning public service unions. Callaghan's fears were amply justified when he warned: 'I say to those who are calling for a return this year to free collective bargaining that in my view that would be a return, this year, to free collective chaos.'

The writing was on the wall in the largest letters when, at the last conference of his union before his retirement, Jack Jones was repudiated by his members, who insisted on a return to 'unfettered collective bargaining'. Nevertheless, from the government's point of view there was no avoiding a fourth stage of the pay policy. Not only was it necessary for keeping up the fight against inflation but also the authority of the government depended upon it. Labour no longer had a majority in the House of Commons and was depending on Liberal support. Its credibility was heavily invested in its claim to a special relationship with the unions. Incomes policy was its alternative to confrontation of the kind which had developed under Edward Heath and which would surely be the result of the policies proposed by Margaret Thatcher. If the unions could not agree to a further phase of voluntary restraint they must be seen to acquiesce in the government's more responsible view of the matter. By implication the government was now saying that the country could not be governed effectively without some permanent substitute for free collective bargaining, some alternative to free collective chaos. Its policy was rejected by the annual Trades Union Congress and repudiated by the Labour Party conference. The government could act in what it took to be the national interest and appeal to the electorate as a whole only by defying the Labour Movement: it could appease the party and the unions only by alienating the country. The contradictions were closing in.

It is the unfortunate logic of incomes policies that they become more restrictive in money terms as they become more relaxed in real terms. Logic in this case required the 'norm' to be pitched below the Treasury's forecast of the rate at which earnings were actually likely to rise, which was estimated at 10–11 per cent. Nevertheless, when the Cabinet endorsed – which it did with some foreboding reluctance – the Treasury's figure of 5 per cent it did so in the expectation that this would serve more as a campaign point in an autumn election than as a realistic target for the coming pay round.[20]

However, on Thursday, 7 September, Callaghan flabbergasted his Cabinet by announcing that he had that morning informed the Queen that there would be no election that year. We may guess that the Queen was scarcely less astonished, for an October election had been regarded as a racing certainty. Transport House had started to press the buttons. Plans for election night television coverage were already under discussion with the broadcasting organisations. When Callaghan sang, 'There was I, waiting at the church', to the annual Trades Union Congress in Brighton earlier that week few took the hint, least of all the luminaries of Trade Unions for a Labour Victory, who on the way down had discussed battle plans at the Callaghan farm in Sussex. But behind the scenes there had been some frantic lobbying by a 'cold feet' group at the centre of which was Michael Foot, who thereby performed one of his many disservices to the Labour Movement. While no one can say whether Callaghan would have won in the autumn of 1978 – my own opinion was that he would not have – at least he would have been in with a chance. The discretion vested in a Prime Minister to obtain a dissolution of Parliament at a moment of his own choosing gives him an immense advantage over his opponents but it places an awesome responsibility upon him to get the timing right. Callaghan's problem as he pored over the entrails of the opinion polls was that he could not be certain of winning, and if he went for an election and lost he alone would be blamed; there was the risk that come the spring he would be certain of losing but, on the other hand, you never could tell . . . So he funked it. He put off the evil day and, when it came, it was indeed he who was blamed.

To set off into a final winter without secure means of parliamentary support and without proper defences against inflation was foolhardy in the extreme. As William Rodgers puts it, 'having embarked upon a courageous but fraught pay policy, the wise course was to submit to the electorate rather than to invite the unions to tear it apart.'[21] That is what they proceeded at once to do. With Jack Jones gone the Transport and General Workers' Union was out to smash the incomes policy. The 5 per cent target which the government had declared served not as a restraint but as a red flag to the inflationary bull. In December one Cabinet Minister was lamenting, 'Five per cent originally meant seven or eight, now it means nine or ten.' To the TGWU it meant 22 per cent. That was what it was claiming for the road haulage drivers who, having duly turned down a 13 per cent offer, came out on strike in January 1979. That was the beginning, in full earnest, of the Winter of Discontent.

Industrial disorder spread as by contagion. It was far from being a simple display of class grievance or trade union solidarity. In the 1970s the banner of tax revolt had been carried from California and Massachusetts into the social democratic fastnesses of Scandinavia. It was an aspect of 'overload' and 'ungovernability', one of the responses to the rising curve of government expenditure in conditions of economic recession. In Britain some 2½ million more people were paying tax in 1979 than in 1974 and the same number had passed from the lowest into the higher tax bands. 'Go anywhere in the country,' Thatcher told Callaghan in the no-confidence debate which finally brought him down, 'and the demand will be for two things – less tax and more law and order.' Healey's 'howls of anguish' were coming not from the rich but from the mortgage-paying, car-driving, foreign-holiday-taking affluent working classes.

Not only did the Winter of Discontent have the character of a tax revolt but also that of a peasant revolt. On the coat-tails of the proverbially acquisitive Ford workers, the tanker drivers and the general haulage drivers, came the low-paid in their hordes, the swollen armies of local government and health service employees. A recent estimate had put the number of male workers, manual and non-manual, earning £50 or less a week at some 600,000. Their pay compared with an average industrial earning of £78.40. There were now well over 2 million local authority employees in England and Wales of whom the bottom 10 per cent earned £40 a week. Dustmen were better off than this, averaging £56. In the National Health Service the bottom decile earned £48 a week. The government's own definition of a poverty line was £55 a week for a married man with two children. There were a million working men in Britain earning less. We were paying ourselves more than we could afford, said the bankers and the economic journalists. Our decline had reached the point at which we could not afford to pay ourselves enough to hold a decent society together.

The winter was cold. Snow lay on the ground. Callaghan was in Guadeloupe for an economic 'summit' meeting. He was photographed sitting under a palm tree. At the airport on his return he was asked about the crisis and is reputed to have asked (although there is no record of it) 'Crisis? What crisis?' This attempt at Macmillan-style nonchalance went down badly. Members of his Cabinet were under no illusions about the predicament now facing the government. Its authority was on the line. The question, 'Who governs?' had been asked again. It had brought Heath down. It would bring Callaghan down unless he acted. If the unions would not allow him the authority to govern the country he must appeal to the country for the authority to govern the unions. That was the position. Everyone knew it. 'Either Jim must stand up and read the Riot Act or he must go to the bloody country,' said one of his oldest and most loyal friends. He did neither. He appealed in vain to the TUC but the TUC had little or no authority over affiliated unions. At Congress House, the TUC general-secretary, Len Murray, was near to despair: this was not trade unionism, this was 'syndicalism'. It was taking over from trade unionism as he knew it. Just as the TUC had no control over the unions the unions had lost control of their members. In the trade union boom of the 1970s NUPE had recruited members faster than it could train organisers. Local militants were a law unto themselves, many of them self-appointed. A local officer of the TGWU in South Wales said, 'Talk about bloody-mindedness, this is bloody-mindlessness!' The unions, quite simply, were out of control.

A Callaghan aide at Number 10 complained, 'We're trying to hold the line with no weapons at our disposal.' There were weapons but the government was not prepared to use them. The crisis it faced in the January and February of 1979 was nothing like as serious as the one with which Heath had had to deal in 1974: then the power supplies of the nation were in jeopardy and workers had had to be put on a three-day week; but in January 1979 there were relatively few lay-offs (about 250,000 by the end of the month) and essential supplies were moving. There was some panic buying in the shops but little cause for it. There was no need to risk intensifying the conflict by declaring a State of Emergency as Heath had done in 1974. Even Rodgers, who as Transport Minister was the most 'hawkish' member of the Cabinet, agreed with that. But he wanted to use troops to take out what he called 'soft targets', for example to move a consignment of pharmaceutical drugs bottled up in the docks at Hull. Instead, the Home Secretary, Merlyn Rees, requested the permission of the TGWU leaders for the supplies to be moved. Even they were taken aback by this display of Ministerial subservience. The government stood petrified in the face of the trade union power it had done so much to promote – power now turned to anarchy. The Cabinet solemnly considered whether the troops could dig graves. But the use of troops in any contingency was anathema to Rees. Damage limitation was the government's only policy – in other words, appeasement. After 1975 anything which smacked of confrontation was not to be thought of. 'By God I'll confront them,' said Thatcher on the

Jimmy Young show. Her demeanour was in sharp contrast to the Prime Minister's. Would he call the unions to order? 'No,' said a Cabinet colleague, slightly misquoting Byron:

> A little still he strove and much repented,
> And whispering, 'I will ne'er consent', consented.

In the circumstances he faced it was not in his character to do otherwise.

No man alive better personified the old Labour Movement now dying than James Callaghan. He had grown up with it and of it. The son of a seaman and a domestic servant he owed everything to it, including his education. While each of Labour's three post-war leaders had been Oxford men he had had no university education at all, a fact he seldom forgot. Few who dealt with him as Chancellor of the Exchequer, Home Secretary, Foreign Secretary and, finally, as Prime Minister held his intellectual powers in the low esteem in which he held them himself. That made him a chippy sort of character. Born in 1912, his political apprenticeship was served against the background of mass unemployment and degrading poverty; he was the last of the 1930s generation to reach the top. It is one of the paradoxes of post-war politics that the men presiding over an era of expansive optimism were men haunted from their earlier lives by a sense of pessimism. He was of a foreboding bent of mind and it was appropriate, perhaps, that he should have come to the top as the 'long boom' ended, in time to preside over the passing of the *ancien régime*.

He had entered Parliament in 1945 wearing his Naval Lieutenant's uniform. The navyman in him accompanied him through his long career and he exercised his high offices with a jaunty authoritarianism. He was the first professional trade union official to become Prime Minister and almost certainly the last. He was the last of Bevin's breed. However, he had held no high office in the union movement and such were its snobberies that as a former organiser for the Inland Revenue Staff Federation, a collector of tax collectors, he was regarded by the vanguard of the working class in much the same way as the Service Corps or the NAAFI would be regarded by a crack regiment of the line. In the 1950s he made his career on the right of the Labour Party, which in those days was where the union leaders stood and where the power lay. He supported Hugh Gaitskell politically but was never a member intellectually or socially of the Gaitskell set. On Gaitskell's death in 1963 he played third man in the election in which Harold Wilson beat George Brown. His intervention helped to put Wilson in. At that time Callaghan had no base either in the party, the Movement or the country. It was later that he built the remainder of his career around an alliance with the trade union movement. 'Rebuilt' is a better word for what he had to do, for his career as Chancellor of the Exchequer ended in the ruin of devaluation. In 1967 there would have been few takers for Callaghan as Prime Minister. 'Policeman Jim' became Home Secretary – he had been a parliamentary adviser to the Police Federation. He gave more time and thought to his farm in Sussex. The controversies around the White Paper 'In Place of Strife' gave him his chance to establish, for the first time in his career, a real political base. By then, perhaps, the tanks of his ambition had been refuelled with sour grapes – Harold Wilson and Barbara Castle thought so. Be that as it may, both opportunism and tribal instinct placed him on the unions' side. Moreover, his political judgment told him that Wilson and Labour would not win another election by biting the hand which fed the ballot boxes. He knew his Labour Movement. He was a traditionalist – the 'Keeper of the Cloth Cap'.

When he became Prime Minister seven years later he was sixty-four. His position was weak in every respect. He had scarcely a majority in Parliament. He had been elected to the leadership of his party only narrowly, by 141 votes to Michael Foot's 133 and Denis Healey's 38. He had no mandate from the people, having not fought or won an election. The National Executive Committee and the party conference were no longer under the control of the parliamentary leadership. With the incorporation of Michael Foot within the Cabinet, Callaghan now faced in Tony Benn a much more formidable enemy on the left. He inherited a worsening economic crisis. Within a year he was governing by permission not only of the IMF but of the Liberal Party with whom he had been obliged to form a parliamentary pact. For all that, James Callaghan now found his métier. He was a good Prime Minister.

Vastly experienced by now, of solid conservative temperament, ungiven to ideological predilection, possessed of sound populist instinct, his talents were appropriate to a world rapidly falling apart, as it seemed to him it was. Wilson, by the end of his career, had become a master at avoiding unpleasant problems, most of which were familiarly insoluble. Callaghan preferred to take them on bluntly. He restored Cabinet government in some degree, even in the conduct of economic policy; he used his Cabinet as it should be used, a tool of government by consent. The great IMF trauma occurred within months of Wilson's hasty departure, like a day of reckoning come. Callaghan skilfully played both wings of his Cabinet, Keynesian and socialist, against the middle, himself; he managed at the same time to avoid calamity and face the inevitable. He steered his government through a change of policy more drastic than the U-turns of the Macmillan and Heath governments and did so without a resignation.

Mellowed by power, ambition now all spent, more confident in himself, or perhaps by now resigned to the limits of what might be achieved, he took to addressing the nation as if leaning – somewhat sternly – over a farmyard gate. He was the Stanley Baldwin of his day. Much of what he said was at variance with the policies of his party but in tune with the aspirations of the people. His populist instincts told him which way the wind was blowing. When he told the 1976 party conference that it was no longer feasible for a government to spend its way out of recession it was not that he had been converted to monetarism, which he would have regarded as too new-fangled for an old fuddy-duddy such as himself; it was Polonius speaking, not Milton Friedman. He had always had a keen ear for the concerns and prejudices of ordinary people. As Home Secretary he had understood well that concern for law and order was not the monopoly of Tory ladies in their hats. When he called for a 'Great Debate' about the quality and the content of teaching in schools he was voicing a widespread and growing dissatisfaction among working families. He told the ideologues on the NEC, 'If you want to retain power you have got to listen to what people – our people – say and what they want. If you talk to people in the factories and in the clubs, they all want to pay less tax. They are more interested in that than the Government giving money away in other directions.' Callaghan was one of the first to grasp the populist roots of Thatcherism.

He spoke his mind, 'Honest Jim', and restored to politics some of the dignity lost in the last Wilson years. The public liked his old-fashioned style. To his pleasure, and probably to his surprise, he found himself well liked, even fondly regarded – a bit of a national character. He was the popular Prime Minister of an unsuccessful government.

Like Baldwin, and Cincinnatus before him, 'Farmer Jim' enjoyed speaking of his return to the plough. No one took him very seriously, for he also enjoyed being Prime Minister. That was until the events of January and February of 1979. Now he meant what he was saying. The heart went out of him as the world he knew was stood upon its head. He was utterly perplexed by the things that were happening, paralysed and powerless. Everything he had stood for, and everything he was, was now in peril. 'Policeman Jim' was appalled by the lawlessness which now took place in the name of the Labour Movement. He was shocked, and deeply hurt – for his skin was always thin – at what he took to be the ingratitude of the trade union leaders. He, above all men, had championed them and now they were busy losing him the election. Yet psychologically he was incapable of acting, petrified by all of his past. How could he, a Labour Prime Minister, take on the unions? The Labour Party *was* the unions. As the Labour Movement tore itself apart that winter it was James Callaghan who was torn limb from limb.

In the Winter of Discontent television did for class war what it had done for war in Vietnam. The nation was brought nowhere near to its knees; people were not even seriously inconvenienced. It was nothing like as bad as it had been in 1974 when the lights went out. Outrageous acts there were, but many fewer than legend would have it. Not many emergencies were turned from the hospitals, schoolchildren came to no great harm, and only in parts of Lancashire were the dead unburied. It was the spectacle that was presented to the public which made the Winter of Discontent such an unmitigated disaster for Labour. For many years the unions had been unpopular in the land. High proportions of respondents to opinion polls agreed with the pollsters that the unions were 'too powerful'. With the signing of the Social Contract they had been admitted to an even more privileged and powerful role, or so it seemed. Their leaders strode through the corridors of power as if they owned them. Now, the spectacle, as seen on television, was not so much of power – as embodied in the coal miners – but of anarchy and pettiness. The country seemed to be in the hands of self-appointed Gauleiters, pickets and strike committees, who officiously decreed who and what should pass. Their permission was required for medical supplies to move or for ambulances to take the sick to hospital. 'If it means lives lost, that is how it must be,' said one of them. They decided whether or not heating fuels would enter hospitals or whether schools would open their doors to shivering children. The country seemed to be caught in the grip of a militant trade union psychology, with everything politicised and proletarianised. The National Union of Teachers felt obliged to instruct its members not to cross NUPE picket lines. Mr Geoff Davies, head of Parson's Down junior and infants' school at Thatcham, Berks, asked the parents of children who normally had school dinners to arrange for them to go home for dinner. He told them in a letter, 'We cannot allow you to provide packed meals instead, as this could be regarded as a form of strike breaking. Children who normally bring a packed lunch will not be affected.'

Hundreds of thousands of commuters, nursing their accumulated rage at ASLEF and the NUR, now saw acted out before their eyes on television everything that trade unionism had come to mean for them. The same must have been true of many motor workers sick of being press-ganged out on strike by militant stewards, of doctors (themselves far from blameless), nurses and patients who knew the sort of things that had been going on in hospitals, of council tenants with dripping walls awaiting the attention of Direct Labour departments, of ratepayers fed up with overflowing dustbins. Seen on television it may have all looked more dramatic and awful than it was, but to claim that the Winter of Discontent was created by the media is to ignore and demean the daily experience of millions of Britons at that time. What they heard and saw rang true. It is the people who best know what is going on among the people.

The Winter of Discontent was the moment when the Old Order crumbled. From the latter part of the 1960s and throughout the 1970s, the last and best hope of preserving the Post-war Settlement had seemed to lie with the trade unions. Barbara Castle and Harold Wilson had inaugurated the attempt to bring the unions within the law and make the practice of collective bargaining compatible with the achievement of prosperity. For a decade this project obsessed and eventually destroyed successive governments. As the 1970s advanced the co-operation of the trade union movement became increasingly indispensable if the Keynesian circle was to be squared in order to make possible full employment, economic growth and universal welfare, all at stable prices. Too much was asked of the unions in this; in return they asked too much of government. Neither side could deliver. For each side the negative aspects of their too ambitious bargain came to outweigh the positive: the unions practised wage restraint according to their lights but full employment was abandoned none the less and social spending cut; the government conferred all manner of privileges upon the unions, enhancing their negative power, but wage inflation continued none the less and there was no bonus in productivity. If there was something aspiring to be called a 'consensus', in the sense of a general disposition to uphold the Post-war Settlement by co-operation across the class divide between government, employers and trade unions, it was the events of the winter of 1979, not Margaret Thatcher, which put an end to it.

Could it have succeeded? In principle, yes it could, for something of the kind had succeeded in Sweden, the most socialist of the West

European democracies, and in Germany, one of the least socialist. But Britain was not a Sweden, or a Germany: the great Social Democratic project of the 1960s and the 1970s was attempted against, as we shall see in a moment, a backdrop of accelerating decline; moreover, it was superimposed upon a society in many ways malformed for modern purposes, whose traditions and folk memories were at war with the enterprise in hand. The pretension of the unions to become a partner in government was, to be fair to them, never wholehearted. Some of their leaders saw it as the only way of reconciling full employment and free collective bargaining but others did not, and correctly predicted that this enterprise would end in tears or something worse. The unions did not so much aspire to corporate status; they found it thrust upon them. It was an unhealthy and corrupting role. The Winter of Discontent was a comment not only on a failed government but on a union leadership which had compromised its independence. Moreover, if what the Labour Movement represented was an alternative and morally superior culture to the one which offered its embrace, then that too became a casualty. For after what had taken place in the hospitals and schools it would not be possible for some while to regard the collectivist thrust of the Labour Movement as synonymous with the forward march of humanity. The *ancien régime* and the old Labour Movement brought each other down.

2

The Politics of Decline

The Winter of Discontent was at the same time a manifestation of the politics of decline. For economic failure had gradually taken its toll on the social cohesion and stability which had made Britain for so long one of the political wonders of the world. The word 'decline' crept into the political vocabulary some time towards the end of the 1970s, although the condition it described had long been present. Slower growth than in other countries results in relative decline, and that had been the British condition not only throughout the long post-war boom but also throughout the twentieth century. More insidious are the consequences of persistently slow growth: the weakening of the industrial base and the deterioration of the human resources available to it. By this means slow growth engenders slower growth, and relative decline can lead in the end to absolute decline. This occurs when output falls or becomes insufficient to maintain the living standards of the people. Except for cyclical recessions it had never happened in the modern world. Could Britain be the first country to go from developed to under-developed?

The Establishment was slow to recognise the condition, and slower still to admit it. The political fiasco of Suez in 1956 had been a big jolt, not to the British people, who were quick to forgive and forget and to re-elect the Tories, under Harold Macmillan, in 1959, but to the governing class. The Empire had always been predominantly a ruling class affair, a point which eluded the many foreign observers who attributed Britain's post-war difficulties to the shock of losing it. The Suez incident, however, did administer a severe shock to the confidence of the governing class, bringing home some of the reality of Britain's post-imperial position. Yet Britain's leaders, misled by the Commonwealth and the much celebrated 'special relationship' with the United States, continued – well into the 1960s – to suppose that

Britain remained a Great Power. In the year following Suez the signing of the Treaty of Rome by France, Germany, Italy and the Benelux countries was viewed complacently in Britain and almost with indifference.

When the war ended in 1945 nobody predicted decline. To be sure, the country had been greatly enfeebled by the war – half of her overseas earnings had been wiped out, her export trade halved, and formidable debts accumulated – but the defeated and occupied powers of the continent had suffered far worse devastations. In the euphoria of victory there were few doubts that Britain would recover and hold her position politically as a member of the Big Three and industrially as the world's third greatest power. Policy was based on those assumptions. According to Kenneth Morgan, the historian of the Attlee government, later historians of decline have antedated their diagnosis. 'The post-war problems of the British economy should always be related to the belief, as widespread in Washington and Moscow as in London, that Britain between 1945 and 1951 was still a great power, and the leader of a struggling, exhausted continent in trying to generate a new and more stable international political and economic order.'[1]

Indeed, given the long years of relative decline which had preceded the war, the recovery after 1945 was remarkable. In the 1950s the decline in exports was halted and, for a time, reversed, and the balance of payments for the most part balanced. By Britain's own past sluggish standards the growth of the economy in the 1950s was good but nowhere near as good as that of others. Taking advantage of their access to American technology and of the favourable Keynesian economic environment of the post-war years the war-damaged economies of Europe recovered in remarkable fashion. While Britain grew at an average of 2·5 per cent per annum through the 1950s, growth in the rest of the industrialised world averaged 4 per cent. Germany was growing at more than twice the British rate. In the 1960s Britain, again by her own standards, did better still. Her economy grew at an average rate of 3·75 per cent but, again, the rest of the industrialised world averaged 5·5 per cent. Over the whole period of the 'long boom' (between 1950 and 1973) Japan averaged 9·7 per cent annual growth, Germany 6·0 per cent, France 5·1 per cent and Britain only 3·0 per cent. 'There is no record of any other power falling behind at such startling speed.'[2]

In terms of wealth per head of the population Britain grew between 1950 and 1973 at half the rate of Germany and France. In 1950 she had ranked among the very wealthiest nations of Europe, a little behind

Switzerland and Sweden, who had escaped the war, but comfortably ahead of Germany, France and all the others. By 1960 Germany was at the point of overtaking, by 1970 France had also moved ahead. In 1978, on the eve of the Winter of Discontent, the following countries were all more than 50 per cent better off than Britain in terms of per capita wealth: Germany, the Netherlands, Norway, Denmark, Belgium, and Sweden. By then France was exactly half as well off again and Japan very nearly so.

In 1950 Britain's 25·4 per cent share of world export trade in manufactured goods was artificially high as a result of the war. But already by 1953 it had fallen to 20 per cent as other economies recovered. Between 1951–5 her share of world markets averaged above 20 per cent while in the four years 1973–7 it had fallen to an average of 9 per cent. Over the same period Germany increased her share from 13 to 21 per cent, Japan from 4 to 14 per cent, while France held hers at above 9 per cent.

By all these measures of actual performance Britain experienced a steep relative decline during the twenty-three years of the 'long boom'. When it ended in 1973 the pace of relative decline accelerated. In the 1960s a growth rate of 3·75 per cent had compared with an OECD average of 4 per cent. In the 1970s Britain's 2 per cent compared with an average of 3·5 per cent. The growth in manufacturing industry was down to 0·1 per cent per annum, from an average annual 3·3 per cent during the previous decade. That compared with Germany's 3·6 per cent (6·6 per cent, 1960–70) and France's 2·1 per cent (5·4).

The measures of underlying economic performance tell a still more dismal tale. During the years of the 'long boom' productivity had grown at an annual average of 5·6 per cent in Germany, France and Italy while in Britain the growth rate had been only 3·1 per cent. After 1973 the growth of productivity in the three major west European economies slowed to 3·4 per cent but in Britain to 2·7 per cent. In manufacturing the deterioration in relative productivity growth was still worse. After 1973 Germany continued to improve by 2·5 per cent a year, France by 3·8 per cent but Britain by only 0·2 per cent. By 1980 output per head in manufacturing was only two-thirds that of Italy, half that of France and less than half that of Germany.

Economists quarrel about whether lack of investment is a symptom or a cause of Britain's decline. It is not disputed that we reinvest less of our wealth than others do. In the 1960s Britain devoted 17·8 per cent of her GDP to investment compared with an average of 20·8 per cent among industrialised nations belonging to the OECD. In the

1970s the proportion had grown to 18·7 per cent but the OECD average by more, to 22·2 per cent. Japan invests more than 30 per cent of her national product. A better measure of Britain's decline, perhaps, is the lag in *new* manufacturing investment. Between 1953 and 1960 we invested in new plant at half the rate of Germany. In the 1970s the British rate of capital investment per worker was half that of Germany and Japan and considerably lower than everybody else's.[3]

Britain lost not only her share of world markets but, increasingly after 1973, her share of her own domestic market. Others did not want our goods but neither did our own people. In 1963 we exported manufactured goods of twice the value of those we imported. By 1973 the surplus had almost gone. This was not due only, or in the 1970s even chiefly, to uncompetitiveness as measured by price but rather to uncompetitiveness in design, delivery, after-sales service or marketing. The British became increasingly habituated to the purchase of foreign goods in preference to their own. As this deterioration progressed, the providential oil from the North Sea began to flow in quantities sufficient to mask the deficit. Nevertheless, by 1983 Britain, once the proverbial workshop of the world, had become for the first time since the Industrial Revolution a net importer of manufactured goods.

A modern society cannot easily embrace the idea of decline. The idea of progress is too deeply embedded in the twentieth-century consciousness. In the post-war period Western Europe underwent a remarkable renaissance, literally a rebirth from the ashes of its civilisation. If progress could survive the experiences of the twentieth century then progress was indestructible. This belief was reinforced by the secular faith of the age. God was dead but hope of a heavenly kingdom had been replaced by hopes of an earthly one. Belief in the supreme power of science encouraged belief in the efficacy of social science too. Socialism became the religion of the age but a broader church grew up around faith in economic management and social engineering. It was complete with a clergy of experts of which the economist was the highest priest. John Maynard Keynes provided an Anglican version of the new religion and in the mixed economies and Welfare States of the West a generation grew up which took the advance of prosperity for granted. For these reasons the notion of decline was alien to the contemporary mind.

The Ancients of Greece and Rome had not made this assumption. They always took it for granted that States must rise and fall. For them it was written in nature that oceans flowed and ebbed, the sun rose and set, and wheels turned in their full circle. Man's own mortality provided a compelling model for the life and death of States and medical metaphors abound of which the 'English disease' is the latest in a long line. States are 'injured by time', said Aristotle, which is a view not very different from our contemporary theories of 'mature' and 'sclerotic' economies. Machiavelli, who lived through an age of decline, believed that 'since nature has not allowed worldly things to remain still, when they arrive at their final perfection, they have no further to climb and so they have to descend.' The belief that decline was more natural than stability had its psychological base in man's fallibility: he could be relied upon to sow the seeds of destruction within the city he had built. For the men of the Renaissance, as for many of the Romans, decline was thus a moral and, therefore, a political question. Luxury was commonly the corrupting agent. 'With greatness, riches increase, and with riches, vices increase, luxury, arrogance, lust . . . kingdoms which have been brought to the top by frugality have been ruined by opulence,' said the Venetian historian Giovanni Botero. 'It rarely happens that external forces ruin a state which has not first been corrupted by psychological or social ones.'[4]

Decline in those days almost invariably ended in the loss of liberty as the result of military defeat. Machiavelli, who lived to see the Italian Republics overrun by the outside powers of France, Germany and Spain, identified another aspect of political fallibility, what today we would call the boredom factor: 'Ancient writers were of the opinion,' he noted, 'that men are wont to get annoyed with adversity and fed up with prosperity, both of which passions give rise to the same effect.' His study of politics led him to the conclusion that it was virtually 'impossible to constitute a republic that shall last for ever.' Experience showed that cities 'had never increased in dominion or riches except while they had been at liberty.' But how was liberty to be preserved? Adaptability was Machiavelli's answer. The capacity to change was the key to a republic's survival. Modern economists give an answer very similar to Machiavelli's and make adaptability the key to economic survival. 'All empires seem eventually to develop an intractable resistance to the change needed for the required growth of production.'[5]

Following the example of seventeenth-century Spain the moral account of decline gave way to explanations of a more economic or social kind. In the earlier part of the seventeenth century the decline of imperial Spain was generally perceived in terms of the decline of Rome, but by the eighteenth century it was ancient Rome which was being seen in terms of modern Spain. Spanish critics of the time, the *arbitristas*, focused on inflation, over-taxation, the absence of a work ethic and many other factors which today are part of the diagnosis of the 'English disease'. Spanish gold was seen by some as a curse in blessing's disguise, in the same way and for, essentially, the same reasons that some have seen North Sea oil as an agent of de-industrialisation. But once more it was failure to adapt, above all, which was the downfall of imperial Spain. 'It was one of the tragedies of Castile's history that it found itself, by the end of the reign of Philip II, in a position where it seemed that readjustment to the new economic realities could be achieved only at the price of sacrificing its most cherished ideals.'[6]

Gibbon, writing in the shadow of imperial Spain's decline and fall, a haunting event for a European of his time, treated many aspects of decline but in the end preferred the moral to the economic explanation. His version of Rome's demise was similar to the Romans' own: decadence, luxury, effeminacy, despotism and military weakness were no match for barbarian frugality, discipline, manliness, freedom and military strength. In their turn those of the Victorians who saw the challenge which faced them at the very moment of their pre-eminence saw it in remarkably Gibbonian terms. Haldane for example: 'The name of the little territory which encloses Weimar and Jena stirs the imagination of thousands of our youth of both sexes, even as the name of Jerusalem moved the hearts of men in the centuries behind us.'[7] For barbarians read Prussians. The virtues which Gibbon so admired, and what Adam Smith, influenced by him, had seen as 'the irresistible superiority which the militia of a barbarous has over a civilised nation' were now applied not only to the military arts, although they were not lacking, but to the development and organisation of production in the service of the State. Meanwhile, it was Britain which was succumbing to the Roman disease.

An intimation of Britain's decline as a manufacturing power was given to the Victorians with the Paris International Exhibition of 1867. There the advances of German engineering (we would now say technology) were on display. One observer, Dr Lyon Playfair, reported: 'I am sorry to say that, with very few exceptions, a singular accordance of opinion prevailed that our country had shown little inventiveness and made little progress in the peaceful arts of industry since 1862.' Playfair, who was a campaigner for industrial education on the continental model, noted that all the major European countries possessed 'good systems of industrial education for the masters and managers of factories and workshops, and that England possesses none.'[8] The following year, 1868, a Royal Commission – they were legion – was established, and it reported in terms which echo in the words of James Callaghan and Sir Keith Joseph in the 1970s and 1980s: 'our industrial classes have not even that basis of sound general education on which alone technical education can rest.'[9]

Here then are two recurrent and interwoven themes of British decline and, most likely, two of its chief causes – technological laggardliness and inappropriate education – manifesting themselves at the very apogee of Britain's industrial power. Why did Britain begin to fall behind at about this time? 'This sudden transformation of the leading and most dynamic industrial economy into the most sluggish and conservative in the short space of thirty or forty years (1860–90/1900) is', in the words of Eric Hobsbawm, 'the crucial question of British economic history.'[10] There are many theories and all bear upon the crucial question of our own times which is why, during the 'long boom' of the post-war years, did Britain fall so disastrously behind?

Hobsbawm puts his question in a way which implies that virtues which were present in the first Industrial Revolution, say between 1740–1850, were absent during the second, from say 1870. But this is now disputed. We are told that the first Industrial Revolution was no miracle of enterprise or innovation but rather a slow plodding affair. Britain's rate of economic growth rate was slow then, later and now. Investment rates were low and too narrowly based on cotton, coal, iron and steel; incomes grew only slowly and the workers who left the land for industry were mere factory fodder and remained the most ignorant industrial peasantry in Europe. Britain emerged from the Industrial Revolution less than fully transformed; the earliness of industrialisation had meant that it had taken place within an obsolete institutional structure and was superimposed upon a still aristocratic society.[11]

In any case, the capacities required for success in the second Industrial Revolution were not those which had been required in the first. The day of the craftsman engineers was over. Their heyday had been in the early phase of the Industrial Revolution, in the eighteenth century when James Watt's steam engine and the early textile machinery and machine tools were designed and made. By mid-Victorian times the mechanical engineer, the romantic hero of the early industrial revolution, had become the victim of social snobbery. In 1847 the engineers split into professionals, who were the civil engineers, and mechanicals. The chief reason was the rise to prominence of George Stephenson, who could scarcely read and was not a 'gentleman'. More than a century of industrial decline is encapsulated in this professional exclusion of the engineer which typifies the 'gentlemen' and 'players' syndrome, of which Harold Wilson was to make much in his modernising campaign of 1964. Stephenson warned at the time: 'Unless the talent of England is concentrated, it is not unlikely that some of the continental talented men might take part of the business of this country.'[12] In 1977 a Department of Industry study reported: 'in manufacturing industry generally the status of mechanical engineering is low in itself, and production engineers are regarded as the Cinderella of the profession.'

In the second Industrial Revolution, out of which came the electrical and chemical industries and the motor car, it was the application of science to industry which was at a premium. In that Britain was already a laggard. Continuity may be the clue to the history of British decline. Certainly there is a continuity of lament. Many of the letters written to *The Times* in the late Victorian or Edwardian era could have been reprinted in the 1960s and 1970s, or indeed today. Educational failure, particularly in the matter of producing an adequately trained labour force, and the failure to apply technology to production were then, as again now, seen as the chief national weaknesses. For example, it was not until 1902 that Britain at last arrived at a national system of secondary education and even then local authorities were only empowered, not required, to provide post-elementary education in addition to that provided by the churches. The statutory school leaving age remained at 12, although local authorities could, if they wished, raise it to 14. Until 1876 not even elementary education had been compulsory. The Foster Act of 1870 created school boards to fill the gaps, if they thought fit, in the voluntary system. Until then elementary education had been regarded as a matter of charity rather than of national duty or purpose.

Prussia, in contrast, took education to be a duty of the State from birth to adulthood. Elementary school, secondary school and university were integrated into a national system. By late Victorian times the *Gymnasia* (grammar schools) had been complemented by the *Realschulen* (technical schools) which were given an equal status. Classics and science were provided on an equivalent basis and held in equal esteem. In Britain no start was made on technical education until 1889. Another Paris Exhibition had brought another shock of discovery and another Royal Commission had been instituted. At that time the Polytechnic at Zürich had 600 students, half of whom were foreign but none British. The Commission was told by the Professor of Civil Engineering at University College, London, 'I believe the reason is that among the English the class of boys does not exist who could take these examinations.'[13] By the turn of the century technical education was still only rudimentary. According to Halévy by Edwardian times it was widely agreed that the failure of the State to provide adequate technical education was the chief cause of the 'decline, or at least stagnation of British industrialism'.[14] Yet a government White Paper of 1956 approached the subject with all the thrill of discovery. 'From the USA, Russia and Western Europe comes the challenge to look to our system of technical education to see whether it bears comparison with what is being done abroad.' It concluded, 'we are in danger of being left behind.' Playfair had warned of that as early as 1853. At the time about which Halévy was writing, Germany was producing some 3,000 graduate engineers per year, while in Britain in 1913 only 350 graduated in all branches of science, technology and mathematics. Another sixty years on it was the same story. At the end of the 1970s there were 15,000 professional engineers graduating in Britain each year compared with, for example, 30,000 in France and 70,000 in Japan.

This paucity of technologists must have played a part in Britain's technological falling-behind in the late Victorian and Edwardian years. However, there was more to it than that. A sympathetic German observer, Wilhelm Dibelius, writing in 1922, blames not so much the educational system as 'the national aversion of the English people to systematic thinking.' Or, he might have added, to any form of systematic instruction. Samuel Smiles was pandering to the popular prejudice of his times when he wrote in *Self Help* (which, published in 1859, sold 55,000 copies) that, 'Anybody who devotes himself to making money, body and soul, can scarcely fail to make himself rich. Very little brains will do.' In 1974, at an examiners' meeting at the University of Birmingham, one of the examiners said of a poor student, 'Give him a third and let him be a businessman!'

Very little brains would do also for the gentlemen. When Harold Wilson hung the 'grouse moor image' round the neck of his Conservative opponent, Sir Alec Douglas-Home, in 1963, he was reviving the complaint first heard in 1909, in Arthur Shadwell's *Industrial Efficiency*, that the entrepreneur, the salt of the Industrial Revolution, had succumbed to the aristocratic embrace and the lure of English country life. Wilson, as we have already mentioned, invoked the image of the annual Gentlemen *v.* Players cricket match at Lords as a way of contrasting the professionalism of the technologist against the amateurishness of much of British management. Did he realise, I wonder, that it was in exactly those terms that Halévy had pronounced his epitaph on Victorian Britain?

It was no longer possible to pass over the fact that a young Englishman on leaving school was intellectually two years behind a German of the same age with the consoling reflection that he made up in character what he lacked in information and that, if more ignorant, he was better equipped for practical life. How was it that in London itself the business houses of the City employed a host of Germans whose presence was unwelcome but whose industry compelled admiration? If English bankers and merchants preferred them to their fellow countrymen, it was because they found them less devoted to sport, more industrious, more methodical, and better educated. Victorian England was beginning to lose confidence in herself. A nation of amateurs was being forced to recognise that they could not compete with a nation of professionals.[15]

The 'cult of the gentleman', the 'cult of the practical man': the English vices do not change.

Wilson in his modernising zeal of the early 1960s, frequently gave examples of 'brain drain' and of British failure to apply to industry the technology even of its own devising. Like the Tibetans who could find no better use for clockwork than the prayer wheel, or the Chinese for whom the invention of gunpowder led to nothing more than a firework industry, so the British had failed to exploit – in Wilson's favourite example – even the hovercraft. The very same complaints were being made at the turn of the century. For example, in 1896 a vogue book was published with the title *Made in Germany*. The *Daily Express* launched an 'England Wake Up!' campaign, the *Daily Mail* ran a series on the 'American Invaders'. *The Times* printed articles on the 'Crisis of British Industry'. There were complaints about the design and adaptability of British goods, of catalogues available only in English, of prices quoted only in sterling, and about the English weights and measures system which was a forbidding mystery to all metric-minded foreigners. The first inquiry into the shortcomings of the Foreign Office as an agency for commercial support was in 1886. Similar inquiries were held in the 1960s and 1970s. In a French magazine in 1903 this story was told:

There was a period, not more than thirty or thirty-five years ago, when England led the way in applied chemistry. A new era was opened up by the researches into the products of coal tar carried out by the celebrated chemist, Hofmann, when he was teaching in London. His pupil, Mr Perkins (now Fellow of the Royal Society) discovered the first aniline dye. Why has the benefit of this new branch of applied science been reaped by Germany? Simply because Professor Hofmann, meeting with no encouragement, returned to Germany and took with him his band of assistants. The coal tar industry . . . left with Hofmann.[16]

When war broke out in 1914 Britain was wholly dependent on Germany for aniline dyes. By then, says Correlli Barnett, we were 'well on the way to becoming a technological colony of the United States and Germany.'

Between 1870 and 1913 British industry doubled its output. World output grew fourfold. Some historians have sought to blame the entrepreneur himself for the failure of Britain to keep up with the Second Industrial Revolution. The 'cult of the practical man' had succumbed to the 'cult of the gentleman'; the grandsons of the men who from their backyards had made Britain the workshop of the world were now public schoolboys, proficient in team spirit and, perhaps, in Latin but lacking in the spirit of enterprise which had made England what it was; nowadays they spent their time in gentlemanly pursuits, leaving the mill to their foremen; in this way the battle for industrial survival was lost on the croquet lawns of Edwardian England. The theory of 'entrepreneurial failure' re-appears, as we have already seen, as a lament of our own times, in which the shortcomings of management are explained in class or cultural terms. Hobsbawm points out that most of the Edwardians were not gentlemen but, in any case, they did what is expected of entrepreneurs: they maximised advantage and profit. They are not to blame if the easiest way of doing this was to find new outlets for old staples in the captive markets of the Empire, leaving the tougher competition to the Germans and Americans. Even if we exonerate the late Victorian and Edwardian entrepreneur for taking the easier path but still argue that Britain lacked what today we call an 'enter-prise culture', we are merely saying that this lack of drive and foresight was not new – then or in our own times.

What did happen in the period between 1870 and 1914 was that the whole system of the State re-formed itself around the dominance which Britain had achieved. This was done at the very moment at which that dominance was coming to an end. A new chapter of modernity was opening in which Britain would fall behind, eventually losing her Empire and her markets. It was in this period that we 'retreated from industry into trade',[17] and began to live off our past and what had been accumulated.

Great Britain had emerged from the Industrial Revolution, as we have seen, a less than modern State. The middle classes had been strong enough to obtain on a piecemeal basis the reforms they wished to see: there had been no centralising revolution of the kind which had taken place in most of the States now emerging as industrial competitors. The year 1870 brought a great surge of Disraelian reform. The civil service, opened now to competitive entrance by examination, was reformed into a bureaucracy appropriate for the government of an Empire and its mother country. The trade union legislation of 1869 and 1871 was the beginning of the process, culminating in 1906 and 1912, by which class war was institutionalised within the framework of the Liberal State with disastrous results for industrial relations and industrial growth. Similarly, the educational system, centred by then on the public schools, was designed to produce the cadres of the governing class appropriate to the richest country in the history of the world and the hub of an empire on which the sun never – and would never – set.

The State apparatus created after the Second Reform Act of 1867 was not intended to perform the functions required of government in the nascent industrial nations of the continent. What need was there to imitate others? Britain's liberal institutions were widely admired and envied, seen as the secret of her success as the world's wealthiest and most powerful nation. Liberal institutions, and the liberal mind, were inimical to the growth of State power. Centralising forces, and the bureaucratic tradition, were weak. There was thus a failure of the State, at the very moment of modernisation. Britain remained, in Norman Stone's phrase, the 'last of the *ancien régimes*'.[18]

Correlli Barnett contrasts the late-Victorian State with countries such as Prussia which 'still believed, like Elizabeth and Cromwell, that a nation was a single strategic and commercial enterprise and that the national interest as a whole came before private profit.' He blames *laissez-faire* for a legacy of 'decaying industrial power, a brutalised and ignorant urban race, a ruined agriculture.'[19] In this he echoes the 'Prussians' of the times, the social imperialists. He is Gibbon-like in his contempt for the Evangelicals as the 'wets' of their day and, later, still more contemptuous of the Bloomsbury set who, it must be said, were the antithesis of a Prussian-style élite.

Pragmatism was the English vice. Lecky exemplified it. He saw politics as a process of 'perpetual compromise'.[20] The belief persisted down the years. So much was peculiar about the British system, its historical development so untypical, that there were always reasons for grafting the present on to the past. Even the disastrous 1870

Elementary Education Act Lecky hailed as a splendid example of the
art. In fact by leaving unresolved the question of who is responsible
for the schools and what they teach – the State, local authorities or
the churches – it bedevilled English education for a century.

Some time around 1970 Britain's downward progress gathered pace.
Britain's growth rate fell from 70 per cent of the OECD average in the
years 1967–73 to only 45 per cent of a reduced average in 1973–8. The
factors contributing to the vicious circle of slow growth were by now
chronic. Slow growth resulted in low investment, low investment
contributed to slow growth; inflation was rising but so also was
unemployment, the result – Iain Macleod coined the word for
it – 'stagflation'. Attempts to expand were constrained by recurrent
balance of payments difficulties; rising public expenditure meant
rising taxation and heavier borrowing; union militancy stoked up
inflation, inflation stoked up union militancy. At about that time,
however, a step-change seems to have taken place: Britain began to
lose market share with alarming rapidity. In 1964 her share in world
trade in manufactures had been still 14·2 per cent, by 1969 it was 11·2
per cent, by 1974 it had slumped to 8·5 per cent – a decrease of nearly
50 per cent since 1960. Stop-go had been seen as a cyclical phenomenon: now the evidence pointed towards a secular (i.e. long
continuing) decline. Britain made her living by exporting manufactured goods while importing her food and raw materials. World trade
in the former had grown more rapidly than trade in the latter and,
although the import of manufactures had been doubling every five
years or so, the scale of Britain's surplus remained a cushion against
the trend. That is until around 1970 when the absolute gap between
imports and exports began to close rapidly. Between 1961 and 1971
manufactured imports increased their share of the British domestic
market from 8 per cent to 13 per cent. By 1976 their share had soared
to 21 per cent. At the opening of the decade the value of exports
exceeded imports by £6,000 million, in 1977 by only £1,000 million.
'The external constraint began to grab us by the throat.'[21]
    Writing in 1976 two Oxford economists, Bacon and Eltis, asserted
that Britain's economic performance had become 'incredibly worse'
over the past decade:

In 1965 . . . the examination question, 'Can economies have
simultaneously, zero growth, rapid inflation, substantial unemployment and a balance of payments deficit?' was set in Oxford.
Undergraduates answered that this combination of failures was

only possible in an underdeveloped country. It has now been achieved in Britain.[22]

Manufacture was in relative decline in all the industrialised economies as their service sectors expanded and they moved towards what the American sociologist Daniel Bell had dubbed the 'post-industrial society'. The world-wide trade recession brought about by the quadrupling of the oil price after 1973 also slowed the pace of manufacture in all countries. Only in Britain, however, did manufacture go into *absolute* decline.

'De-industrialisation', as this phenomenon came to be called, and a precipitous fall in Britain's share of world trade, now came to present an alarming prospect. Wynne Godley and his Cambridge colleagues repeatedly warned that this deteriorating trade imbalance was no longer susceptible to periodic devaluations; it would become increasingly difficult to maintain full employment without balance of payments crises and the prospect would be of 'chronic recession'. Bacon and Eltis, by a different route, arrived at a similar conclusion. As the result of de-industrialisation, they said:

> . . . the plant is just not there to meet the country's requirements for goods. Hence articles which are normally produced in Britain have to be imported and the goods are just not available to exploit export opportunities . . . In consequence attempts by governments to move towards full employment produce vast balance of payments deficits, which make continued expansion impossible.[23]

What the 'New Cambridge' economists and Bacon and Eltis had diagnosed was the condition we now call by its name: *decline*. Still into the 1970s, the Establishment flinched from the word. It had too ominous a Gibbonian ring about it, too strong moral undertones. 'De-industrialisation', which sounded bad enough, could be presented as a natural structural shift, something which was happening to everybody; 'relative decline' was only a fancy way of talking about slow growth, a perennial complaint; and the Cambridge diagnosis was an excitable way of describing the balance of payments constraint which was an equally familiar symptom of the British disease. The word 'decline', on the other hand, suggested a cumulative process, a general and systematic falling behind, qualitative as well as quantitative. Britain's malperformance could be quantified easily enough in terms of growth rates, share of world trade, and so on, but less easily when it came to the factors which might determine future competitiveness. Persistent slow growth has cumulative consequences: for investment, for productivity, for the trade balance, and for social cohesion and political stability. At the point at which slow growth, or relative decline, results in an incapacity to sustain production and living standards, decline becomes absolute. By definition, absolute decline has to be a temporary phenomenon, otherwise output would dwindle to nothing in a black hole economy. What had happened to Spain in the seventeenth century was that relative decline, in the form of persistent failure to adapt to a changing world, brought about a phase of absolute decline, lasting from about the 1620s to the 1680s, a calamitous experience which ensured a long future of further relative decline.[24]

If the word 'decline' was uncongenial to the governing class, the thought of it had not escaped its mind. Macmillan's turn towards Europe in 1961 was born not out of belated enthusiasm for the European Economic Community which had been launched without Britain in 1957, but rather out of a growing lack of confidence in Britain's own future. In 1959, in his famous lecture on the 'Two Cultures', C. P. Snow anticipated the mood which was to pervade the ruling élite over the decade which followed:

> I can't help thinking of the Venetian Republic in their last half-century. Like us, they had once been fabulously lucky. They had become rich, as we did, by accident. They had acquired immense political skill, just as we have. A good many of them were tough-minded, realistic, patriotic men. They knew, just as clearly as we know, that the current of history had begun to flow against them. Many of them gave their minds to working out ways to keep going. It would have meant breaking the pattern into which they had crystallised. They were fond of the pattern, just as we are fond of ours. They never found the will to break it.[25]

In 1961 Iain Macleod, then Leader of the House of Commons, told the author of *The Anatomy of Britain*, Anthony Sampson, that if Britain did not join the European Economic Community: 'No question – we'll just be like Portugal.'

The economic failures of the 1960s forced a belated recognition of Britain's strategic over-extension. The withdrawal from east of Suez, decided upon in 1968, was – for the ruling élite if not for the mass of the public – an event scarcely less traumatic than the Suez incident of 1956. Loss of Empire tends to be regarded as something which happened at a stroke with the ending of the war and the independence of India, leaving Britain thereafter struggling, in Dean Acheson's always quoted phrase, to 'find a role'. In fact, the dissolution of the Empire was a slow, drawn-out business which to this day, in the form of the Falkland Islands, has been a drain on resources, a distraction from the real predicament facing the country and the source of much nostalgia and delusion. Strategic over-extension contributed to Britain's economic difficulties, as it had with Rome and Imperial Spain, and Britain's economic difficulties made it increasingly impossible for her to keep up her position in the world; but more important, perhaps, than the mutual causality at work here was the concurrent, and reinforcing, demoralisation of the governing class. For the people of Britain the 1960s were years of material advance, cultural excitement and individual liberation, but for their rulers it was a decade in which it slowly became more evident that Britain was experiencing a decline beyond their ability to arrest.

Although by the early 1970s those concerned with the management of the economy were only too aware of the intractable and chronic aspects of the British disease, it was still not politic to speak the language of decline. For example, in 1973 – the year in which Britain did at last join the Common Market – Edward Heath publicly reprimanded Lord Rothschild, the head of his own 'Think Tank', for predicting that on existing trends Britain's Gross Domestic Product would by 1985 be half of Germany's and France's and about on a par with Italy's. Rothschild had warned:

> Unless we take a very strong pull at ourselves and give up the idea that we are one of the wealthiest, most influential, and important countries in the world – in other words that Queen Victoria is still reigning – we are likely to find ourselves in increasingly serious trouble.

A year later the Wilson Cabinet had met at Chequers to review the economic situation. Denis Healey, then Chancellor, had said jokingly, 'If we do join the Third World it will be as a member of OPEC.' Crosland had said that they did not know how such a relative decline had taken place: 'All we can do is to press every button we've got. We do not know which, if any of them, will have the desired result.'[26]

Foreigners, perhaps, were better able to see the seriousness of the British condition or, at least, to speak more frankly and openly about it. In 1974 the Paris-based Hudson Institute made explicit the analogy with seventeenth-century Spain, quoting in a report on Britain the words of the British Ambassador to Madrid in 1640:

> Concerning the state of this kingdom, I could never have imagined to have seen it as it is now, for their people begin to fail, and those that remain, by a continuance of bad successes, and by their heavy burdens, are quite out of heart.[27]

On his return in 1979 from a tour of duty in Paris as British Ambassador to France, Sir Nicholas Henderson reported in his valedictory despatch: 'In France we have come nowadays to be identified with malaise as closely as in the old days we were associated with success.'[28] When, in a conversation with the Federal German Chancellor, Helmut Schmidt, I referred to Britain generically as among the developed nations, he pulled me up and said, 'Britain is no longer a developed nation.'

By the mid-1970s just about every mix of remedy had been tried, apparently to no avail. Many of the specific diagnoses offered did not stand up to comparative test: other countries were taxed more heavily than Britain, had more strikes, spent more on their Welfare States, and so on, and yet were capable of faster and more sustained economic growth. It seemed increasingly probable that the explanation lay somewhere in history, in class animosities or cultural attitudes towards industrial production, or in the shape of British institutions. Scholarly studies of the period 1870–1914 took on contemporary relevance and encouraged this view that there was something ineluctable about Britain's long slow decline. The sheer length of it invited cultural explanation; many of the weaknesses – investment deficiency, for example – seemed to persist through differing economic circumstances, while in other countries similar economic factors seemed to produce different results. 'An effective economic strategy for Britain will probably have to begin in the cultural sphere,' wrote Ralf Dahrendorf, the German director of the London School of Economics.

Correlli Barnett's *The Collapse of British Power*, which I have several times referred to, was published in 1975 and sought to demonstrate that, 'The English disease is not the novelty of the past 10 or even 20 years . . . but a phenomenon dating back more than a century.' The Hudson Institute saw Britain in the 1970s as 'very largely the creation of the mid-Victorian period'. The Marxist historians Perry Anderson and Tom Nairn noted how the aristocratic *ancien régime* had absorbed the new bourgeoisie to produce an élite in which capitalist values vied with the aristocratic in a State half modern, half feudal. This failure to produce a full-blooded capitalist class was perhaps a cause of the weaknesses of the industrial spirit so frequently lamented. The American scholar, Martin Wiener, gathering together this long literature of lament into what became an influential vogue book, attributed both Britain's political success and economic failure to 'the containment of the cultural revolution of industrialism' from towards the end of the nineteenth century. The late Victorians had laid the foundation for social stability but at the price of a lack of industrial innovation.[29]

The American economist Mancur Olson constructed a theory of 'the rise and decline of nations' around the paradox that war and political instability may be favourable to innovation and peace and social tranquillity conducive to stagnation. The reason for this is that stability strengthens in time the hands of interest groups, or 'distributional coalitions', and produces in societies 'an institutional sclerosis' which slows their adaptation to changing technology or circumstance. This, he suggests, 'helps to explain why Great Britain, the major nation with the longest immunity from dictatorship, invasion and revolution, had had in this century a lower rate of growth than other large, developed democracies.'[30]

In the first edition of his best-selling and influential *Anatomy of Britain* Anthony Sampson quoted a passage from J. H. Elliott's study of the decline and fall of imperial Spain. The words were clearly intended to have contemporary relevance:

> Heirs to a society which had over-invested in empire and surrounded by the increasingly shabby remnants of a dwindling inheritance, they could not bring themselves at the moment of crisis to surrender their memories and alter the antique patterns of their lives. At a time when the face of Europe was altering more rapidly than ever before, the country that had once been its leading power proved to be lacking the essential ingredient for survival – the willingness to change.[31]

Machiavelli's explanation of decline as failure to adapt became the common diagnosis of the British disease.

Cultural explanations were adduced also for Britain's class-divided industrial relations. Ronald Dore, the student of comparative technology, writing in 1973, concluded: 'It will be a long time before Britain loses the marks of the pioneer, the scars and stiffness that come from the searing experience of having made the first, most long-drawn-out industrial revolution.'[32] This, he argued, had led to the classes drawing apart and retreating into their separate cultures. Richard Caves of the Brookings Institution, Washington, reported that: 'Britain's economic malaise stems largely from its productivity problem whose origins lie deep in the social system.' Because of this, he added, 'one needs an optimistic disposition to suppose that a democratic political system can eliminate that problem.'[33] Chancellor Schmidt's advice to me at about this time was: 'You must get rid of that damned class system of yours.'

Our own people were slow to grasp the notion of decline. That was and had always been a part of the problem. How is one to speak of decline when output is growing and living standards improving? The seeds of decline are easily mistaken for the fruits of prosperity. Between 1870 and 1914 the industrial falling-behind was concealed behind the wealth and splendour of the imperial heyday. Between the wars the structural weakness in the economy was masked by the world-wide recession. During the long post-war boom which continued until 1973 Britain's relative decline was an undercurrent to a rising tide of prosperity. After 1973 the ending of full employment and the onslaught of inflation across the whole of the industrialised world obscured the extent to which Britain's cumulative decline had made her more vulnerable to, and less able to adapt to, the world-wide recession. Finally, North Sea oil, like a providential windfall, gave Britain a new lease of life beyond her means, and a new excuse not to adapt to a changing world, just as had done the accumulated assets of the Victorian climacteric.

However, as the underlying crisis in the economy grew deeper, and as the country was brought to the verge of ungovernability, the nature of the British disease became more clearly understood, more explicitly recognised – at least within informed opinion and among the governing élites. The 1979 General Election was fought openly on the issue of decline. The new Chancellor of the Exchequer, Sir Geoffrey Howe, said in his first Budget address:

> In the last few years, the hard facts of our relative decline have become increasingly plain, and the threat of absolute decline has gradually become very real.

The Bank of England agreed. It warned in 1979:

> The consequences of failure to arrest the country's industrial decline are likely to become more pressing and more obvious as

time goes on. Now condemned to very slow growth, we might even have to accept, if present trends continue, decline in real living standards.

In 1970 decline was still the unmentionable. Now it was official.

3

Consensus or Conviction Politics?

Margaret Thatcher and Tony Benn were the twins of their time. Between them in the 1970s they set out to smash what they alleged to be a collusive conspiracy between the political parties, the so-called consensus politics of the two previous decades. For Thatcher consensus meant the appeasement of socialism and the ineluctable advance of collectivism. For Benn it meant the collaboration of Labour governments with capitalism and the betrayal of the working class. In order the better to assault the consensus both of them exaggerated it. In retrospect, Benn minimised the achievements of both the Wilson and the Callaghan governments and Thatcher the differences which existed between the parties, especially in the first years of the Heath administration, in whose Cabinet she served. They both thrived upon the air of conspiracy which was implicit in their critique of consensual politics. 'Thatcherism' and 'Bennism' were founded in a theory of betrayal, the stab-in-the-back which is a common feature of the mythology of revolutions or revanchiste movements.

For Benn the betrayals were by Labour Prime Ministers who, once in office, soon became the tools of the City of London, the international bankers, the IMF, NATO and the Brussels bureaucrats of the EEC. Their treachery consisted in disregarding or defying the democratic decisions of the party conference. Hence the cry, 'all power to the conference', which was at the heart of the extra-parliamentary politics of the 1970s and 1980s of which Tony Benn became the champion.

For Thatcher the stab-in-the-back was Heath's U-turn on 6 November 1972, the day on which the Cabinet, of which she was a member, introduced statutory powers to control pay, prices and profits. That, together with the profligate reflation which had become the economic policy of the government, was, for her, to collaborate once again with the Social Democratic or Keynesian consensus which had ruled in Britain since the war with increasingly disastrous results.

Betrayal theories require that there be something to betray, an ark of the covenant, a tradition of some kind: grace to fall from, a Golden Age to recall. Where these do not exist they must be invented. In the case of 'Thatcherism', Edward Heath's specific act of treason was incorporated into a more general rewriting of history in which successive Conservative governments in the post-war period had departed from the true principles of Conservativism and collaborated in the advance of collectivism. Whoever was in office, Social Democracy had been in power. A certain confusion entered here, for Thatcher herself also spoke admiringly of Winston Churchill's post-war administration and, especially, of R. A. Butler's 1952 'set-the-people-free' Budget.[1] It can be argued that it was Heath who had thrown the first stone at the Post-war Settlement in 1970 with his Selsdon Park programme,[2] allowing inefficient firms to close, driving up unemployment, and legislating against the unions. In that case, the U-turn of 1972 was not a betrayal of any true Tory tradition, merely the abandonment by Heath of his own programme. Nevertheless, post-war Conservativism was alleged to have fallen from grace, to have departed from the true ark, and it was the Victorian age – although that of *laissez-faire* liberalism rather than Tory paternalism, the age of Gladstone rather than of Disraeli – which came to play the role of Golden Age in the nostalgia of Thatcherism.

For Benn the Labour government of 1945 served a similar purpose. He too was liable to be confused, putting the Attlee government forward sometimes as a reassuring model of moderate socialist reform and at others as an encouraging example of how true socialism could win popular support. He told an interviewer in 1981:

> the amazing thing was the extent to which we were able to mobilise young and old, left and right, men and women, Scots, English and Welsh, the trade union members and the Labour Party . . . Unfortunately that spirit escaped and evaporated during the period of successive Labour governments after 1951.[3]

Thatcher and Benn, each of them, came to preach a politics of new departure, a break from the recent past and a rejection of the notions which had governed it. They formed unholy alliance to dance on the grave of John Maynard Keynes, Thatcher because Keynesianism was an engine of socialism, Benn because it was the crumbling prop of capitalism. She, the shopkeeper's daughter, hated socialism with the same passion that he, the peer's son, had learnt to hate capitalism and his own class.

Both of them had experienced conversions. She, it seems at some point on the road between the February and October elections of 1974, turned from her past ways as an unprotesting member of Edward Heath's Cabinet and saw the true light by then emanating from Keith Joseph. Sir Keith was later to declare dramatically, 'It was only in April 1974 that I was converted to Conservativism. I had thought that I was a Conservative but now I see that I was not one at all.' Benn's conversion had occurred shortly after laying down the seals of office in 1970. He had been radicalised in office, he was later to say, but his moment of revelation came during the 1971 sit-in by the workers at the Upper Clyde Shipbuilders, a yard which he had endeavoured to save while at the Department of Technology. The occupation of the yard was conducted in a style reminiscent of the events in France in 1968; the cry was for workers' control. It was there, on the 'red' Clyde, that the Honourable Anthony Wedgwood Benn consummated his love affair with the working class. Looking back, he expressed his gratitude to:

> The shipyard workers who organised the work-in at Upper Clyde Shipbuilders, the brave men and women who fought so hard to set up Meriden and Kirkby Manufacturing and Engineering as co-operatives, and the brilliant and humane shop stewards at Lucas Aerospace combined with hundreds of others to give me an education in the real meaning of practical socialism which no books or teachers could have matched.[4]

In all countries at about this time a new radicalism was emerging on both right and left in response to the breakdown of the old Social Democratic order. Influenced as Benn and Thatcher were by the events and spirit of those times, they were revealed to have certain beliefs in common. One was their attitude towards the State. For Thatcher the power of the State had usurped the responsibility of the individual to the point at which not only economic enterprise but moral choice had atrophied. For Benn bureaucracy had become one of the enemies of socialism and he saw in participatory democracy the means of rebuilding society from the bottom up. Their common animus against government at the centre gave both of their politics a strong tinge of 'populism'.

The word populism is much misused to mean demagogic – although both of them could be that – or merely popular. The word properly should mean a direct appeal to the people, often above the heads of existing political institutions, Parliament or party. In its American forms, populism can be of the Right or of the Left and has often involved novel coalitions – blacks and poor whites against plantation owners, farmers and workers against the banks and rail-road companies. Benn and Thatcher could both be said to be 'populists' in their fashion. Benn, for example, appealed directly to the shop stewards' organisations over the heads of the trade union Establishment and took up the cause of workers' control. He made common cause with the excluded elements and groups of society – blacks, students, women, sexual minorities – in the hope of con-structing a new and broad progressive alliance. He inveighed in true populist manner against what he saw as an effete, corrupt and defeatist ruling class:

> The Vichy spirit in the top echelons of the establishment is quite astonishing. If you listen to those who inhabit the golden triangle of the City of London, Fleet Street and Whitehall, there is a lot of defeatism. Compare that with the mood at Lucas Aerospace, at Meriden, at Kirkby, at the shop stewards' committees up and down the country. They may be angry, worried, disappointed but they are not defeated. Compare them with the gloomy men who go to City luncheons and dinners in their boiled shirts for ever calling upon everybody else to face the harsh realities of technical change.[5]

Thatcher, a true outsider unlike the patrician Benn, shared his contempt for the Establishment, especially for civil servants and, more especially still, for Brussels bureaucrats and the Foreign Office. Her populism took the form of a direct appeal to the working class. She appealed to its acquisitive and patriotic instincts. 'Today,' she said in 1976, 'it is the Conservatives and not the Socialists who represent the true interests and hopes and aspirations of the working people.' In this she was echoing the radical Toryism of Lord Ran-dolph Churchill and Joseph Chamberlain except that theirs was a paternalist appeal and there was nothing paternal, or maternal, about the Thatcher-style. Rather she presented herself to the working class as the champion of the taxpayer against the Treasury, the worker against his trade union, the council tenant against the landlord and the citizen against the State. Shortly before she became leader the High Tory grandees feared she would be too petty bourgeois to command a majority in the land. In a speech at Amersham, January 30, 1975, Ian Gilmour warned against 'retreat behind the privet

hedge into a world of narrow class interests and selfish concerns.'
They could not have been more wrong about her.

One other thing she and Benn had in common was zeal. Together
they raised the temperature of British politics, arousing new passions
and inspiring new idealism. They were the twin agents of the polarisation which came to characterise the party politics of the 1970s and
1980s. She called her approach 'conviction politics' which was a way
of declaring that she was not bound by the consensual wisdom but
would be guided by her own passionately held beliefs. Benn admired
her for this and determined to put forward his own socialist beliefs
with similar conviction. It seemed not to occur to him that her
convictions were striking popular chords which his were not. Nevertheless, Benn – eyes gleaming – filled halls with huge audiences as he
travelled the land preaching his gospel of left-wing socialism.

Fundamentalism would seem to flourish in the rubble of collapsed
belief. Thatcherite and Bennite enthusiasm coincided with the revival
elsewhere of Christian and Islamic fundamentalism. Everywhere
people were groping for new certainties in an uncertain world. The
consensus which Benn and Thatcher so despised had been founded in
rationality: the age of Social Democracy had been the age also of the
social scientist as the age of Keynes had been the age of the economist. The Keynesian notion of 'managing the economy' suggested that
government was a technocratic business, comparable to the science of
management. But now, in the 1970s, as things went badly and as
economies declined to be managed and the governed to be governed,
the priesthood of the expert fell into disrepute and the magic men
were deserted by their skills. There now took place a retreat from
rationality. Monetarism was a mystical creed at the heart of which lay
the search for some Holy Grail of authority which would serve as
surrogate for God or gold. Marxism, reviving at the same time,
answered a similar need for a project which, unlike Keynesianism or
Social Democracy, was capable of transforming the human condition. It was amid this intellectual and spiritual ferment, born of a
dawning social pessimism, that Margaret Thatcher and Tony Benn
arose as peddlers of new and simple faiths. Between them they
changed the political vocabulary of the times. She placed herself at
the head of an intellectual offensive against 'a generation and more of
collectivist theory' which she blamed largely on Keynesianism, in
Nigel Lawson's words, 'that great engine of creeping socialism.' For
Benn, Keynesianism was the creed of declining capitalism, devoid of
remedy for ailing manufacturing industry. They were the first political leaders to face squarely the issue of decline.

Their alternative in each case to Keynesian macro-economic management was to approach the problem from the supply side: they looked to micro-economic inputs to increase the efficiency of products, whether through the intervention of planners or the freer play of market forces. By Thatcher's diagnosis the remedy was to let the market work its cure within a framework of monetarist discipline with supply-side measures chiefly directed at the rigidities of the labour market. For Benn, at the core of the decline was manufacture – it was he who coined the word 'de-industrialisation' – and the cause of it was a deficiency of investment. The patent failure of its economic strategy – if strategy is not to glorify it – had set in motion a reappraisal after the defeat of the Labour government in 1970. Benn at that time was shopping for new thoughts and inspirations, susceptible to the Pauline light. At an early stage of his conversion, as we have mentioned, he had been attracted by the idea of participation – one of the three P's studied in the Class of '68, the others being permissiveness and protest. Indeed, in a pamphlet published in 1970 and sub-titled 'A Socialist Reconnaissance', which was the result of consultations in the library with various gurus of the age, he had already reached the hard conclusion about participation, namely:

Workers are not going to be fobbed off with a few shares – whether voting or non-voting. They cannot be satisfied by having a statutory worker on the board or by a carbon copy of the German system of co-determination. The campaign is very gradually crystallising into a demand for *real workers' control*. However revolutionary the phrase may sound, however many Trotskyite bogeys it may conjure up, that is what is being demanded and that is what we had better start thinking about.[6] (My italics.)

The device of the 'planning agreement' became the quintessential instrument of Bennite socialism. The one hundred largest companies would be obliged to enter into planning agreements with the government, for which purpose a Ministry of Planning was envisaged. They would be obliged at the same time, and as a condition of the State investment they might receive, to involve their workers, through their unions, in the planning process. By this means the government would obtain the firm-by-firm information necessary to draw up a plan, information hard to obtain at the centre; at the same time it would have the benefit of the knowledge, wisdom and ingenuity of the workers; and by so involving the workers it would break down the factory class system and obviate any need for wage restraint or 'incomes policies'.

The Bennite package was innovative in a number of ways. It addressed the problem of over-centralised Statism; it appealed to fashionable desires for participation, accountability and an end to secrecy; it could be presented to the Right as a substitute for nationalisation and to the Left as a major step towards it; it got round some of the unions' hostility to any form of industrial democracy which smacked of shared-managerial responsibility; and it appeared to be addressing the problem of de-industrialisation. In the decade between 1973 and 1983, the concept of the planning agreement exercised a powerful fascination upon the left-wing mind. It became the point of reference for economic debate within the Labour Movement. It was the radical alternative to Thatcherism and, together with Thatcherism, one of the radical alternatives to the bankrupt Croslandite version of Social Democracy and to the Callaghan-style corporatism practised after 1975.

Whether it offered a real answer to the decline of British manufacture is another question. Economists would dispute that under-investment was a central problem. Resources might be inefficiently applied but that was another matter. The Bank of England pointed out in the mid-1970s that the real rate of return on investment, excluding stock relief, was zero. Why should anyone invest if there was no profit to be had? The Marxists, to the left of the Bennites, agreed. Moreover, Bennite socialism was based on a sentimental vision of the working class. Benn had been much excited by his dealings with the Lucas shop stewards. They were a talented, ingenious lot who might well have managed better than their managers; but most workers had no desire to be managers, and their unions most certainly did not want them getting their collective bargaining lines crossed. It might be one matter to plan the expansion of, say, the electronics industry but how likely were coalminers or steel workers to plan the contraction of their own hopelessly uneconomic industries? Benn spoke of the 'self-discipline of full democratic control'. Participation plus planning was his socialist remedy for decline, rather in the way that Lenin had supposed, or so he said, that the 'Soviets plus electrification' was all there was to socialism.

Somewhat later a third element was added to what became known as the Alternative Economic Strategy of the Bennites – protectionism. The Cambridge School of economists, by whom Benn was much guided, had argued that no amount of Keynesian reflation on its own could save British industry because the propensity to import had grown so great that a balance of payments crisis was the swift and certain outcome. De-industrialisation tightened this constriction and was a vicious spiral. Import control – 'planned trade' was the prefered euphemism – was the only way out. Benn gave protectionism a patriotic twist. He was not interested in import controls in themselves, he insisted, only in saving British industry and British jobs. Like Thatcher he was a nationalist, or had become one. In 1970 he was explaining to his electors in Bristol why Britain must join the European Economic Community (in 1963 he had been against it) but in Opposition again he soon sensed which way the wind was blowing. It was he who manipulated the 'Shadow' Cabinet into the promise of a referendum on Britain's continuing membership of the Community and in so doing wrong-footed the Revisionist Right of his party for the next decade. Increasingly he spoke the language of left-wing nationalism. The British ruling class had 'defected to Brussels', he said. The Common Market, NATO and the IMF were reducing Britain to the status of a colony. They were the agents of de-industrialisation and would make Britain into a 'Salazar-like society'; we would become the 'Kirkby of Western Europe'. (He had forgotten that, back in the 1960s, Barbara Castle, opening a housing estate in that benighted overspill from Liverpool, had said: 'This is your chance to build a New Jerusalem.')[7] 'If you say to nation states there is nothing you can do,' Benn said, 'you will end up with withdrawal of consent from elected governments.' By joining the Common Market, he solemnly warned the Cabinet, we had 'lit the long fuse to revolution'. Did he himself believe it? Who knows? But, like Enoch Powell, he plainly believed himself to be speaking great truths which were concealed from the people. 'You once called me an Old Testament prophet' (he said to Wilson) 'and that is just what I am. There are just certain ideas that I think ought to be spelt out and I spell them out.'[8]

By 1975 Benn was in the wilderness, where prophets belong. He remained a member of the Cabinet but had been sacked from the Department of Industry, where his industrial strategy had been progressively watered down by Wilson and the Cabinet, and exiled to the Department of Energy on Millbank. There, using his powerful position within the party apparatus as chairman of the home policy sub-committee of the National Executive, he concerned himself chiefly with preparing a socialist programme for a future Labour government. The events of 1975, traumatic for Benn and important for the future, compounded the myth of betrayal. As the Left saw it, the Bennite programme adopted at the party conference of 1973 had been the blueprint for socialism. Benn had told delegates, 'We are saying at this conference that the crisis that we inherit when we come to power will be the occasion for fundamental change and not the excuse for postponing it.' At that time history had seemed for once to be going the Left's own way. The quadrupling of the price of oil in 1973 produced a crisis of capitalism, at least of a sort; working class action by the miners had brought the Heath government down, although some would say Heath had brought himself down; miraculously Wilson, or so it seemed to him, was suddenly back in Number 10. But this time, the Left believed, Labour was equipped with a socialist programme, a programme which Wilson then proceeded to emasculate. Labour in 1974, Benn later insisted, had been armed with 'policies that had been fully worked out to open up a really new vision of industrial life that would have transformed the situation in a decade.'

The year 1975 saw Margaret Thatcher's accession and Tony Benn's banishment. Shortly before his dismissal he said at a luncheon:

> If I got knocked down by a bus as I left the Café Royal after this lunch, I don't believe anything would be changed one way or the other . . . There is a wind of change blowing gale force through British industry . . . I am no more than the weather cock showing which way it is blowing.

He certainly believed at that time that history was on his side. He had worked out that great radical change occurred in approximately forty-year cycles and that after 1945, which he chose to regard as an authentically socialist moment, 1984 would be the year, his year. He had an air of destiny about him in the 1970s but we had seen the same glint in the eye of Enoch Powell and that had taken him from high office to the farthest fringe of British politics. All the same, if I had had to have chosen one of them in that year, Thatcher or Benn, rival exponents of the politics of decline and the twins of their age, I think I would have given the future to Tony Benn.

While the New Left was busy taking over the Labour Party the New Right had been busy capturing the Conservative Party. The leftward shift in the Labour Party had been in part a response to the rightward shift by the Heath government. 'Stand on your own two feet' was the slogan of Heath Mark I. Then came the U-turn which produced a pay and prices freeze and the débâcle of the miners' strike in February 1974. Between the two General Elections in that year Sir Keith

Joseph had begun to develop a radical critique of Edward Heath's style of Conservativism. The moment the October election was lost Heath's leadership was at issue. It is the custom of his party to show no mercy to losers and Heath was now a three-time loser. Moreover, in February 1974 he had lost on an issue of class confrontation, a most serious setback for a party which saw itself as the natural governing party. Since the enfranchisement of the working class the Conservative Party had been remarkably successful in keeping Labour out of office, and socialism out of power even when Labour was in office. Now Heath had played into the enemy's hands. The débâcle, or so it could easily be alleged, never need have happened had it not been for the notorious 1972 U-turn which had brought in the statutory incomes policy, which led to the fatal show down with the miners two years later. It could equally be argued that the attempts to put into action the Selsdon Park programme during the first two years of the Heath administration had brought about a class confrontation which the 1972 U-turn was intended to avoid. In any case, Heath was unloved by his party.

A tetchy, uncomfortable figure, he was the first leader of the Conservatives in modern times who was outside the traditional mould. A grammar school boy, the son of a jobbing builder, and an organ scholar at Balliol, his background was similar to Margaret Thatcher's. Snobbishly nicknamed 'the grocer' because of his supposedly shopkeeper's bent of mind he was, in truth, a man of vision who had seen clearly at an early stage of his career that the future of post-imperial Britain lay with the nascent European unification movement. Brought up on the south Kent coast he had as a young man looked across the narrow English Channel to the Continent, and bridging that gap became his life's mission as a politician. He had been foiled by General de Gaulle in 1963 when he had been Macmillan's negotiator in Brussels, and the overriding goal of the administration he formed in 1970 was Britain's belated accession to the European Community.

By then Europe had become also Heath's remedy for Britain's decline. He saw the Common Market as a cold douche which would brisken British industry into competitiveness. Like Wilson before him, Heath was a moderniser. But whereas Wilson was a politician of infinite pliability, for whom party management was the first prerequisite of governing at all, Heath was full of impatience. For him ten days was a very long time in politics. Wilson had made a famous speech about the 'white heat of technology' but it was Heath who in his spirit and character was the technocrat. He adopted a brisk managerial response to government, expecting things to happen when buttons were pushed. Caught in a London traffic jam, he telephoned the chairman of the Greater London Council, who was visiting Tokyo at the time, and shouted at him about it. The style was 'abrasive', a word he first used himself, a characteristically Heathite word. But he rubbed too many people up the wrong way. For a man who had served his apprenticeship in the Whip's Office he was remarkably deficient in conducting normal human relations, although he inspired the loyalty and affection of his personal entourage. Much of his manner may have been due to gaucheness, shyness perhaps, for he was a kindly man and could be funny when relaxed although even when he laughed, the shoulders heaving, the appearance was of a man imitating laughter.

Heath was the last of the 1930s generation to lead his party. He had been moved and shocked as a young man by the unemployment and poverty which had so disfigured Britain in the years between the wars. When in 1971 unemployment spurted towards the – at that time unthinkable – million mark, he lost his nerve. He had no stomach for the class confrontations which his industrial policies were provoking. Being a man of no fixed ideology, he turned in his tracks. The policy of refusing all succour to 'lame duck' industries gave way to massive interventionism; stringent monetary and fiscal policies gave way to a new burst for growth; the policy of resisting inflationary pay claims one by one gave way to an ambitious and elaborate incomes policy which, when agreement with the TUC proved impossible, he imposed by statutory edict. A believer in the power of reason, Heath expected reason to prevail. He found it difficult to grasp that people, and at times society as a whole, could be thoroughly unreasonable. It was all very irritating. When he went to the country in 1974 asking, 'Who rules Britain?' he asked a silly question and received a silly answer. His political adviser at the time, Douglas Hurd, has testified that his real reason for going to the country was that the energy crisis threatened Britain with catastrophe and that his government required a new mandate to preside over a severe but inevitable decline in real living standards, something which had not occurred since the war. 'People would have to understand, because only with that understanding could their government do what was needed.'[9] So once more, seeing things clearly himself, he appealed to reason. He told the truth. He lost. Heath was the first victim of the politics of decline.

When he lost again the following October he would have to go. Sir Keith Joseph was the obvious challenger from the Right but he had embarrassed the Conservatives with a speech in Birmingham on 19 October in which he had suggested clumsily that the breeding habits of the poor threatened what he called 'our human stock'. Not only had he embarrassed his party but himself. A pathologically sensitive and nervous man, given to agonising intellectual and moral self-doubt, he was deeply upset by the reaction from press and public to what he had said. He peered into the kitchen and decided that it was too hot in there for him.

Sir Keith Joseph had played the Baptist's role in Mrs Thatcher's coming. The analogy is apt because in conversations at that time he (like Benn) had compared himself with a prophet come down from the mountains. Indeed, there was an Old Testament ring to his cries of woe from the wilderness as he urged repentance from the wicked ways of socialism and beat his breast in immolation for his own part in the betrayal of the ark of the Conservative covenant. Characteristically he was able to identify the exact moment of his conversion and date it, as we have seen, to April 1974. When there was a similar Damascan moment for Margaret Thatcher we do not know. According to one of her biographers it may have been at the election press conference on 1 October 1974 when she publicly disassociated herself from Heath's notion of a government of national unity which had been hinted at, though vaguely, in the Conservative manifesto. *Her* policies, on housing, she asserted with what was to become characteristic spirit, were not negotiable. She was a Conservative, not a coalitionist.[10]

After Heath's defeat in February 1974 she had joined with Sir Keith Joseph in setting up the Centre for Policy Studies, with its remit to 'secure fuller understanding of the methods available to improve the standard of living, the quality of life and the freedom of choice of the British people, with particular attention to social market policies.' This move had been regarded with extreme suspicion by Heath and the CPS was to serve as a Thatcherite 'Think Tank'.

That summer Sir Keith had become more openly critical of the direction which the Conservative Party had taken under Heath's leadership. His criticisms of the policies pursued by the government of which he had been a member, and on which Heath now proposed to fight another election, broadened into a critique of post-war Conservativism. At Upminster, in Essex, on 22 June, he said:

Our industry, economic life and society have been so debilitated by thirty years of socialistic fashions that their very weakness tempts further inroads. The path to Benn is paved with thirty years of intervention, thirty years of good intentions, thirty years of dis-appointments.

The reality is that for thirty years, Conservative governments did not consider it practicable to reverse the vast bulk of accumulating detritus of socialism.[11]

However, it was during the election campaign in October 1974 in a speech at Preston that Joseph delivered what was to become at once a seminal text. In it he challenged the very foundation of the Post-war Settlement – full employment. This was the speech in which the monetarist credo was first set out: inflation had been brought about by governments printing money in illusory pursuit of full employment.

> To us, as to all post-war governments, sound money may have seemed out of date: we were all dominated by the fear of unemployment. It was this which made us turn our back against our own better judgment and try to spend out of unemployment.

The speech was a political event. *The Times* published the text verbatim. Full employment, according to the post-war standard, had been effectively abandoned by the Wilson government after 1967 but nobody had dared to say so. Here was Joseph seemingly abandoning the very goal, tearing up the sacred Beveridge text. Denis Healey, who was currently Chancellor of the Exchequer, denounced the speech as: 'A disastrous prescription for a social breakdown on a scale unknown in this country.' Joseph had made the election issue clear, he said; the British people could 'vote either for a slump and class conflict on an unprecedented scale or for national unity in the fight for full employment and justice.'

In subsequent speeches, Joseph tried to correct the impression that he was a crude or vulgar monetarist who believed, or had suggested, that control of the money supply would alone cure Britain's ills. At Preston he had described monetary control as a 'pre-essential'. He was to elaborate on this later in his Stockton Lecture of 1976 which was titled, 'Monetarism is Not Enough'. 'Monetary contraction in a mixed economy,' he argued, 'strangles the private sector unless the state sector contracts with it and reduces its take from the national income.' Public expenditure must be cut therefore and also the taxes, a climate of entrepreneurship had to be created and restrictive practices broken down. 'We are over-governed, over-spent, over-taxed, over-borrowed and over-manned.' These were to become the familiar themes of Josephism, and of Thatcherism, for he was Mrs Thatcher's mentor. He repeated his prophet's message over and over, with hymns to the beauty of the free market and sermons against the evils of socialism.

Governments, he preached, were to blame for Britain's long decline, for it was they who printed the money. He attributed much of the mischief to war. War was the midwife of socialism. War not only resulted in greater intervention by the State but also excited expectations of a land fit for heroes when it was over. At the same time it burdened the country with expenditure and debt. In 1945 the euphoria of victory had reinforced the illusion that governments could do anything. He himself, he confesses – for he enjoys confessions – had been caught up in that climate. He had 'wanted to believe' that full employment, rapid growth rates, and price stability were simultaneously within grasp. He confesses also to class guilt. 'We found it hard to avoid the feeling that somehow the lean and tight-lipped mufflered men in the 1930's dole queue were at least partly our fault.' A failure to examine the implications of full employment, and of the Welfare State, had led to a failure to recognise the symptoms of the failure of these economic policies. For even though it was not immediately evident, artificially stimulated demand and high taxation were eating into the sinews of the economy. One of the first symptoms was slow growth. But the Keynesian cure had been applied, only to worsen the disease until, eventually, stop-go gave way to stagflation and, worse still, slumpflation.

Contained within this confession of personal error was an indictment of all Conservative governments since the war. In the course of it Joseph set about the systematic rewriting of history. Lord Blake, the High Tory historian, also a critic of the Heath government, dated the Fall to 1958 when in what Macmillan had called a 'little local difficulty' Peter Thorneycroft, Enoch Powell and Nigel Birch had resigned from the Treasury in protest against a lack of monetary stringency. Thereafter, the Tory Party had moved too fast and too far into the centre ground and had come 'too near to socialist policies'.[12] Joseph, however, went further. As Ian Gilmour puts it:

The sans-culottes of the monetarist revolution also wished to strengthen the party's new leadership by denouncing the alleged follies of the Ancien Régime. Ideally, perhaps, this could best have been achieved by a bell, book, and candle condemnation of the Heath government alone. The snag was that some of the leading monetarists had served without demur in that government. The

trail of heresy had, therefore, to be extended back to the thirteen
years of 1951 to 1964.[13]

Having endeavoured to rewrite the history of the post-war period
Joseph next embarked on a revision of its political geography. The
'middle-ground' which the parties rushed to occupy at election times
was no more than a chimera of the politicians' imaginations: it existed
only as an ephemeral compromise between them but bore no relation
to the true aspirations of the people. This so-called middle ground
was 'simply the lowest common denominator obtained from a calcu-
lus of assumed electoral expediency, defined not by reference to
popular feeling but by splitting the position between Labour's position and the Conservatives.' Not at all was it 'rooted in the way of life,
thought and work of the British people, nor related to any vision of
society, or attitude of mind, or philosophy of political action.' What
Joseph called, in contrast, the 'common ground', consisted of what
the people really thought and actually desired. 'The people', or so
Joseph claimed to know, 'were far closer to Conservative instincts on
many issues' than they were to the supposed consensus. He went on
to lambast his own party's 'obsession with the middle ground' which,
far from providing a secure base, was a 'slippery slope to socialism
and state control'. He arrived at this conclusion by a curious route.
The consensus was formed, he argued, by splitting the difference
between the Conservatives and the Labour Party; because the
Labour Party itself is a compromise which shifts constantly to the left,
the dynamic of the consensus – or its dialectic, he might have said –
is to drag the Conservative Party always to the left. Note how the
Labour Left used exactly the same argument in reverse to blame
electoral expediency for the betrayal of the working class by successive Labour governments. Joseph's argument is here hard to follow.
Wilson captured the centre ground in 1964 by trimming to the right.
By occupying the centre ground on their own terms the Conservatives
had held office for the previous thirteen years. When Heath defeated
Wilson in 1970 it was on the most right-wing programme presented by
the Conservative Party since the war. His 1972 U-turn had nothing to
do with the centrifugal pull of Labour but, rather, with his judgment
of the social and political consequences of the policy he was pursuing.
Labour's lurch to the left after 1970 was no reason for the Tories to
abandon the centre ground. As Gilmour said in his speech at Amersham on January 30, 1975: 'There is no reason in logic, history,
philosophy, or expediency why the Tory Party should join the
Labour Party in moving towards the extreme.' But for Joseph, and

for Thatcher, it was necessary to establish a Great Betrayal and the great betrayal was the *consensus*.

Because the policies emanating from the consensus were, he argued, doomed to fail, consensual politics could only breed still greater dissatisfactions. 'Far from achieving social harmony and strengthening the centre, it has created resentments and conflict, has moved the centre of gravity of the whole Labour Movement to the left, strengthening the left-wing, the irreconcilables, the revolutionaries.' By this argument the post-war Conservative Party, through its collusion with consensual politics, stood accused of actively promoting the cause of left-wing socialism.

Decline – although he did not here use the word – became the motor of party polarisation. For, 'paradoxically socialism advanced thanks to its own failures, not by successes.' He argued that the expectations for full employment and welfare excited by the war were not only extravagant but actually 'irrational'. Post-war promises were incapable of fulfilment by the adopted means because the mixed economy with all its interventionist ways was incapable of accelerating economic growth. The worse things became, the worse things were made. Joseph in this way diagnosed a crisis of Social Democracy which shares with the left-wing socialists' version the conclusion that the means are inadequate to the ends or, as the Marxists would say, are in contradiction. For a long while, however, there was a conspiracy to avoid examining the 'true causes' of slow growth (or relative decline) which were excessive State expenditure, nationalisation, job subsidisation and 'excessive State reactions to exaggerated expectations':

> The socialists were inhibited because it was their creation. We were inhibited because we had accepted these policies as the middle ground, so that to criticise them would be regarded as 'immoderate', 'right-wing', 'breaking the consensus', 'trying to turn the clock back', in short unthinkable taboo.

The indictment was complete. The collective guilt of consensus politicians was established. Post-war history was rewritten. The Post-war Settlement was exposed as a fraud. Heath's great betrayal was a culmination of a long saga of misguided interventionism.

4

A Moral Issue

Not only the intellectual but the moral foundations of the *ancien régime* were crumbling, or so the Thatcherites believed. In the way of all revolutionaries or counter-revolutionaries possessed of a simple truth, they embarked upon a crusade to restore lost virtue. See 'just how far we have fallen', she said, shortly after her victorious entrance to Number 10; there was a 'crisis in the nation'; society was 'sick – morally, socially and economically'. She instanced the events of the recent Winter of Discontent as a 'reversion towards barbarism'. She went on to attribute this moral malaise to a generation and more of collectivist thinking. 'The moral fallacy of socialism is to suppose that conscience can be collectivised.'

Decline was also a moral question. We have seen how the Ancients regarded this as a self-evident truth. Gibbon replanted the idea firmly in the modern mind. Every schoolchild knew about the bread and circuses. Note the implication that dependency and moral degradation are the two sides of the coin of corruption. In our times, 'welfarism' and moral decay go hand in hand. Thus Mrs Thatcher, addressing the Greater London Young Conservatives in 1976:

> A moral being is one who exercises his own judgment in choice on matters great and small . . . In so far as his right and duty to choose is taken away by the State, the party or the union, his moral faculties – his capacity for choice – atrophy and he becomes a moral cripple. A man is now enabled to choose between earning his living and depending on the bounty of the State . . .

It was in this speech that Victorian values made their first appearance in the repertoire of Thatcherism. Her moral agenda could have been written on a sampler. The individual owed responsibility to self, family, firm, community, country, God. She would put it in that order of ascent, for self-regard was the fount of all virtue; what else could have been meant by the injunction, 'love thy neighbour as *thyself*'?

Victorian values 'were the values when our country became great'. Implication: departure from Victorian values had something to do with decline. Decline she was pledged to arrest and reverse. 'Somewhere ahead,' she said in her final election broadcast of 1979, 'lies greatness for our country again.' Economic regeneration and moral regeneration were now to go hand in hand. Collectivism is the corroding culprit for both economic failure and moral decay. 'The truth is that individually man is creative; collectively, he tends to be spendthrift' she said in Cardiff in 1979. Earlier, from the pulpit of St Lawrence Jewry in the City of London[1] she had declared, 'The role of the State in Christian society is to encourage virtue, not to usurp it.' Inflation was both a symptom and a cause of the malaise. If the value of money was allowed to decline so would other values. Printing money was the equivalent of State-provided bread and circuses. Inflation was morally sapping, undermining all the Victorian virtues, and was ultimately the destroyer of liberty. Labour governments had:

> . . . impoverished and all but bankrupted Britain. Socialism has failed our nation. Away with it before it does the final damage . . . The very survival of our laws, our institutions, our national character – that is what is at stake today.[2]

But Victorian values implied something more than a nostalgia for lost civic virtue, for the entrepreneurial spirit, frugality and the authority of the family, all of them rooted in individual responsibility: it was the code also for repudiating the 'permissiveness' of the 1960s, that iniquitous decade. Others were explicit, Dr Rhodes Boyson, for example:

> Some people look with amusement or even horror at the self-help of the Victorian age, but its virtues of duty, order and efficiency have been replaced in the muddled thinking of our age by a belief in individual irresponsibility . . . The predictable outcome is seen in disorder, crime and lack of civic duty and in the palsied inefficiency so often visible throughout the public service . . .[3]

By blaming the 1960s for the 1970s the distempers of the time could be laid at the feet of socialism. The indictment was long: crime, especially juvenile crime; violence, personal and political; industrial militancy and public disorder; flouting of the rule of law; loss of parental control, of authority generally; the decline of learning and discipline in the schools; divorce, abortion, illegitimacy, pornographic display, four-letter words on television; the *decline of manners*. This fall from grace had occurred during the Wilson government, and in particular during the time at the Home Office of Roy Jenkins, who had presided over the abolition of capital punishment, legalisation on homosexuality and abortion, the liberalisation of divorce, and the abolition of theatre censorship. 'The End of Victorianism' is how the social historian, Arthur Marwick, describes this period. Exactly. Before long, however, the Swinging Sixties had joined the Naughty Nineties and the Roaring Twenties in the hall of notoriety. In his 'history of respectable fears', *Hooligan*, Geoffrey Pearson contrasts these generational alarms with what he discovers to be 'a seamless tapestry of fears and complaint about the deteriorated present'. He argues not that lawlessness and disorder are myths of our time, far from it, but that real and present fears are incorporated into a myth of moral decline.

> The twin mythologies of 'law-and-order' and 'permissive' rot . . . arise out of the way in which the facts of disorder are paraded within a historical idiom of decline and discontinuity. Whereas if we reinstate the facts of the past it becomes clear that the preoccupation with lawlessness belongs more properly to a remarkably stable tradition.[4]

By the same process, the myth of moral decline was incorporated into the Thatcherite account of Britain's all-too-real economic decline.

The myth was multi-layered. It was compounded of the explosion of youth, the flowering of pop culture, the 'permissive society' so-called, and the concurrent waves of industrial militancy and political protest. The youth explosion was, as Marwick has pointed out, at heart an economic phenomenom. Why this should be thought to belong among the annals of decadence is not clear, for the flowering of the pop culture of the early 1960s was at the same time a flowering of enterprise culture, and the boutiques and the Beatles were among the more successful export industries of the age. Perhaps it was because money buys freedom and independence as well as jeans and records. In 1951 there had been 14·5 million people under the age of 19; by 1968 there were more than 17 million. By then the sons and daughters of the newly 'affluent' workers of the 1950s had money to spend; the youth revolts of the early 1960s were not anti-materialist, far from it, but they undermined established authority to the extent that the middle aged and middle class were no longer the sole arbiters of popular taste: culture was now made from the bottom up. The sexual revolution was harder for the older generation to take. Philip Larkin spoke for middle age in the famous lines:

> Sexual intercourse began
> In nineteen-sixty-three
> (Which was rather late for me) –
> Between the end of the *Chatterley* ban
> And the Beatles' first LP.

But as Kenneth Leech has observed, attitudes change more rapidly than behaviour. The sense of new freedom generated by the 1960s was greater, perhaps, than its gratification, certainly if such surveys as there were are to be trusted. For example, at the University of Durham in 1970, according to a *New Society* survey, 93 per cent of girls coming up to the University were virgins and 49 per cent continued to be so in their third year. However, it was the idea of sexual freedom combined with the statistics of divorce, illegitimate birth, abortion, and single-parenthood which made up the indictment against the 'permissive society'. The Abortion Act came into force in 1968. A year later there were 53,000 abortions and in 1980 137,000. Thereafter it levelled out. How many illegal abortions took place before 1969 is unknown. Illegitimate births increased from 48,000 in 1961 to 81,000 in 1981. In 1961 however, 38 per cent were registered in joint names, and 58 per cent in 1981, suggesting an increase in stable extra-marital relationships. Divorces rose from 27,000 in 1961 to 80,000 in 1971. In that year the Divorce Reform Act of 1969 came into effect and by 1980 divorces had increased to 160,000. Single-parenthood, a function of both divorce and illegitimate births, increased from 367,000 in 1961 to 515,000 in 1971 and to 890,000 in 1981. By 1981 there were almost 1½ million children brought up in this fashion. The reforms in all these cases were designed to accommodate human behaviour rather than to shape it; the upward trends, admittedly, in divorces, abortions, etc., were steep but in each case levelled off after a while; the absolute numbers do not suggest that marriage as an institution is threatened. It must be said, however, that the new freedoms of the 1960s became the new servitudes of the 1970s and 1980s for large numbers of women whose 'liberation' consisted in bringing up children alone, having been divorced or deserted.

The 'counter culture' of the latter part of the decade was altogether more subversive than the commercialised pop culture of the early 1960s. The youth revolts of the 1950s and early 1960s had not been revolts against materialism; this counter-culture, although – or, more likely, because – it was a revolt of the affluent and the privileged, bit viciously at the hands which had reared it. Generational war broke out. According to Robert Hewison, in his excellent cultural history of the age, the use of drugs was the 'symbolic and actual *casus belli* between the authorities and the underground' and was one cause of the political explosions of 1968.[5] 'Sex and drugs and rock-and-roll' as the Rolling Stones proclaimed at the time, were 'in'. Authority became alarmed. The Wootton Report which had distinguished between 'hard' and 'soft' drugs and recommended the decriminalisation of cannabis was rejected. Homes of pop stars were raided. The counter-culture, in the words of Stuart Hall, came to be seen as:

> a moral conspiracy against the State: no longer simply getting and spending, clothes and records, fun and games – but drugs, crime, the withdrawal from work, rampant sex, promiscuity, perversion, pornography, anarchy, libertinism and violence. It became a source of moral-political pollution, spreading its infection in its every form; the conspiracy to rebel. In a profound sense, the dominant culture – face to face with this spectacle – felt itself out of control.[6]

This passage may over-dramatise the sense of confrontation at the time but, written in 1978, it catches the flavour of the *post hoc* view of the 1960s as a source of all that was decadent in the declining Britain which was to turn to Margaret Thatcher for salvation.

The counter-culture was founded on the idea of alienation. According to one fashionable guru of the day, Theodore Roszak, the source of the alienation was technology, which had provided society with a total power to manipulate its members and smother them with affluence. The affluent privileged young drew comfort from the discovery that they were the victims of repression as total as any of which the Nazi or Stalinist regimes had been capable. 'Repressive tolerance' it was called. Herbert Marcuse was the chief corrupter of that generation of youth. A philosopher of the Frankfurt School who had taken refuge in the USA, he turned the world upside down as a revolutionary should: it was affluence, not immiseration, which had beaten the working class into submission; welfare, rather than exploitation, had dried the sap of revolution; what passed for liberalism was in truth repression by another name; the permissive society was tantamount to a Fascist society. The next stage in this thought-process was to justify violence – 'demystify' was the cant word – by identifying the liberal State as the source of all violence. 'State violence' legitimised 'counter-violence'. The inhabitants of the affluent society owed their 'comfortable servitude', according to Marcuse, to the export of 'terror and enslavement' throughout the world. Encouraged by this thought, the students imported the techniques and style of Third World wars of liberation into the politics of the affluent society. Their white guilt about the Third World, and about their own affluence, was channelled into hatred of the West. In Vietnam they had a unifying cause and a bountiful supply of images of violence. 'Racism' within their own societies was a form of violence inviting counter-violence, and Black Power was a part of the struggle of all colonial peoples. Che Guevara was their romantic hero and he had made hatred an element of the struggle, 'relentless hatred of the enemy that impels us over and beyond the natural limits of man, and transforms us into effective, violent, selected and cold killing machines.'[7] The students, together with the blacks, were metaphorically – some believed literally – the guerrillas of the affluent society. Hence they dressed in jungle fatigues and marched upon the American Embassy in Grosvenor Square, and advanced on the offices of their Vice-Chancellors, chanting 'Ho, Ho, Ho Chi Minh.'

The intellectuals, among whom the students were pleased to number themselves, had been promoted to the vanguard of the revolution by Marcuse. For, with the working class no longer revolutionary, they were the one group within the affluent society who, 'by virtue of their privileged position, can pierce the ideological and material veil of mass communication and indoctrination.' It could not quite be counted a revolutionary class – the nostrum that the intelligentsia was the 'new working class' was 'at best premature' but, nevertheless, he told the Congress on the Dialectics of Liberation held at the Roundhouse in London in July 1967, the intellectuals had a 'decisive preparatory role' to play, as the catalysts of revolution.[8]

It was an immensely flattering role. It was also profoundly undemocratic. For no longer was it the role of the vanguard to anticipate the wishes, or the *consciousness*, of the working class but rather to overrule it in the name of history and 'liberation'. The events of 1968 in Britain were peaceful by the standards of those which took place in Paris, Berlin and Berkeley. There were big anti-Vietnam demonstrations in Grosvenor Square, one of them violent, and campus disturbances notably at the LSE and the newer plate-glass universities of Essex and Sussex, which the architects seemed to have designed for purposes of confrontation. The revolutionary project was well summed-up in the metaphor of masturbation with which Trevor Griffiths began his play *The Party*. There was never the slightest prospect of socialist revolution in Britain between 1968 and 1979. Nevertheless, the excitements and turmoils of the years from 1967 to 1974 – embraced by the notion of '1968 and all that' – left lasting legacies. The student revolts after 1967 and, perhaps too, the concurrent wave of shop-floor militancy in industry were in part expressions of disillusion with Labour government under Harold Wilson. A generation too young to have remembered the disappointments of 1945–51 were experiencing what passed for socialism in Britain for the first time, and their disillusion had all the passion of new discovery. After 1968 the Marxists gained intellectual ascendancy over the Reformists until the oil shock of 1973 put paid to Anthony Crosland's vision of socialism without socialism. Revisionism, as Crosland had said, was 'a doctrine about means as well as ends'. To the true believers, if socialism was not to come about by parliamentary means it would have to come about by extra-parliamentary means, for come about it would.

Thoughts of revolution, however delusory, were part of a new ambivalence towards democracy, the rule of law, and political violence. During the 1970s it became increasingly difficult to accommodate conflict within a growing general prosperity. Liberal society was torn apart as people were either pulled to the right or pushed into condoning activities which had no place in liberal society. This was another consequence of the snapping of the Social Democratic consensus; for if the reformist approach towards socialism was now bankrupt, the reformer was obliged to choose sides somewhat in the way that the constitutionalists in the last days of Tsarist Russia were obliged to choose between autocracy and revolution. Of course, the predicament was nowhere near as hopeless or extreme, but the same fascination with the Left could be observed among the liberal intelligentsia. For example, the cause of the Viet Cong was widely espoused. The Palestinian Liberation Organisation was regarded with sympathy and acts of terrorist violence, although not usually condoned, were regarded with a certain ambivalence. Closer to home, when five London dockers were committed to Pentonville Prison in 1972 for defying a court order under the Heath government's Industrial Relations Act, Labour's attitude was ambivalent in the extreme. Reg Prentice, a Labour MP who later became a Tory, was the only voice raised on behalf of the rule of law and he was castigated in consequence. Tony Benn congratulated those 'who would rather go to jail than betray what they believe to be their duty to their fellow workers' and Barbara Castle said that it was no solution 'to say that we must all obey the law. Lawmaking should be an expression of the democratic principle.' 'How long will it be before the cry goes up, "let's kill all the judges?"', Michael Foot asked a miners' rally. When Arthur Scargill and ten thousand flying pickets prevailed over the police at the gates of the Saltley coke depot in 1972 the event could be seen either as an heroic victory for trade unionism or as a triumph of political violence against the rule of law. No Labour leader sided with the police. When the councillors of Clay Cross, a mining village in Derbyshire, defied the 1972 Housing Finance Act, and were disqualified from holding office and were surcharged[9] in consequence, the Labour conference of the following year resolved to indemnify them retrospectively. Crosland, then the 'Shadow' Minister responsible, said, 'As a democratic socialist proudly committed to the rule of law, I could not condone, let alone encourage, defiance of the law.' Yet when Labour was returned in 1974 it enacted a measure to end the disqualification and indemnify all councillors against future surcharges arising from refusal to implement the 1972 Act.

It seemed to some that law and order was breaking down in all directions and that society was about to be engulfed in a general wave of violence. In addition to political violence, there was hijacking and terrorism. Protesters were protesting and marchers marching. Violent picketing was an increasingly frequent accompaniment of industrial disputes. Violence was sweeping the football terraces. Mugging was rife in the streets. While Labour was in power in the 1960s the Tories had been ready to link the rise in crime and disorder with the rise in unemployment, a view which after 1979 became the worst of heresies. But, in fact, crime had been on the rise, and not only in Britain, since the mid-1950s, perhaps because affluence had intensified the relative deprivation of those who could not afford the goods and pleasures which were everywhere displayed, advertised and enjoyed. Crime would seem to be among the distempers of prosperity. Conservatives were inclined to blame it on the deterioration in the cohesion and authority of the family and the associated lapsing of discipline in the schools. 'Many of our troubles stem from a lowering of family standards which were once the pride of this nation,' said William Whitelaw as 'Shadow' Home Secretary. Such explanations

were more easily accommodated within a general theory of decadence and decline. Yet complaints about the decline of the family had
been heard for a hundred years or more, especially 'from that
well-heeled section of the community which segregates its own
children away from the family in private schools and preparatory
schools as soon as it is decently possible to do so.'[10]

It may be that relative prosperity, working mothers (who were an
important source of that prosperity), changes in manners, education
(for the most part improved) and the general climate of opinion
concerning freedom and authority had together resulted in the family
becoming a less effective agency of control on behalf of society.
Bringing up children had been made a more difficult business because
they were more financially independent and were subjected to the
influences of the mass media, greater sexual freedom and the tempta-
tions of drugs. The sociologist and educationalist A. H. Halsey,
himself of working class upbringing, was struck when re-reading
Richard Hoggart's classic *The Uses of Literacy*, which describes the
working class world before the affluent 1950s:

> by the integration of ordinary families in those days with the moral
> traditions of the old class and Christian society which he so
> accurately and lovingly described. That moral structure had ebbed
> away fast under the assault of the classless inequalities and the
> secular materialism of the post-war world and, in the process, the
> familial controls over upbringings have steadily attenuated.[11]

The increase in crime which was the cause of such anxiety was real
enough, even when allowances are made for increases and changes in
the reporting of crimes. Violent crime had turned sharply upwards
from the mid-1950s and rose steeply through the 1960s. Reported
crimes against the person increased from 38,000 in 1969 to 95,000 in
1979. The rise was especially alarming among young persons. Law
and order was an issue in the 1966 General Election. It figured
prominently in the Selsdon Park programme of 1968. Nor was it the
only thong to the backlash. The coming of the permissive society and
the reaction against it were concurrent events. The clampdown on
drugs dates from 1968, the reaction against egalitarianism in education from the first Black Paper[12] in 1969. Mary Whitehouse's campaign against violence and sex on television dates from 1964. 'Let us
take inspiration from that remarkable woman,' Keith Joseph was
later to say. Another remarkable woman did. The backlash against
the 1960s, or, we should say, the myth of the 1960s, took on a new

force with the advent of Margaret Thatcher to the leadership of the Conservative Party.

Concern about law and order, however real in itself, is a symptom also of more general angst and there was much to be anxious about as the 1970s wore on. Inflation itself was a source of anxiety. Crime on the streets, and its vivid reporting in the newspapers, seemed to be part of an epidemic of violence. Colour television brought the atrocities of war, hijacks and acts of terrorism – such as the massacre at the Munich Olympic Games – into every home. Outside were a host of pickets and protesters – for example with confrontations at London rail termini between angry commuters and railmen because Southern Region trains seldom ran on time.

The Labour leaders, or some of them, saw which way the public mood was moving. Thatcher had made law and order (Dame Laura, the young 'wets' at the Conservative Central Office called it) a populist issue. Callaghan in his call for a 'Great Debate' on educational standards had already identified discipline in the classrooms as a matter of proper parental concern. At the conference of 1978 Labour hardened up its line on policing and crime. Labour had joined in the backlash, but to no avail. The Conservative Party Manifesto said:

> The most disturbing threat to our freedom and security is the general disrespect for the rule of law. In government, as in opposition, Labour have undermined it. Yet respect for the rule of law is the basis of a free and civilised life. We will restore it, re-establishing the supremacy of Parliament and giving the right priority to the fight against crime.

'Rome itself fell, destroyed from inside,' warned Sir Keith Joseph. Was that true of the *ancien régime* in Britain in 1979? Not, I think, in the sense of a moral decay emanating from the 'permissiveness' of the 1960s but true, perhaps, to the extent that the changes in attitudes and behaviour which had occurred made it more difficult to manage an accelerating economic decline. The 1960s are easily caricatured as some kind of 'happening' or fantasy, a last fling, a final spasm of delusion, before reality set in. But the 1960s, as I saw them, were a time in which a reforming Home Secretary did more for the sum total of human happiness than the combined endeavours of the Department of Economic Affairs and the Treasury. More than that, they were a period in which people did more for themselves than the government did, in which society changed – and changed quite profoundly – from the bottom up. And, in the end, the ceiling seemed a little higher. That Britain became more difficult to govern as a result does not mean that it changed for the worse – not at all. Some of the new freedoms brought new miseries and new anxieties, but freedom is freedom and freedom is good. The 1960s were boom years for freedom. As Britain's decline accelerated, life got better – more open, more varied, more fun, noisier, better designed, funnier, sexier, more exciting, adventurous, dangerous – better in almost every way. If we were not becoming a more classless society at least we thought we were, or at least the fashionable attitude towards the working class changed quite profoundly.[13]

Orwell had said that the English working classes were 'branded on the tongue'. The 1960s made working class accents into marketable brands. Growth, albeit sluggish by continental standards, was a motor of egalitarianism, although not quite in the way that Crosland had envisaged: consumerism was the equaliser, not the provisions of the Welfare State which was much exploited by the middle classes. Men are what they eat, that ultra-materialist Feuerbach had said, but the 1960s helped to make men and women into what they wore, what they drove, what they listened to, how they cut their hair and where they spent their holidays. What was so wrong with that? The equalities engendered by materialism are of greater importance than the inequalities which may be involved in its achievement. A man behind the wheel of his car or sunning on a Spanish beach feels both more equal and more free, and so he is.

Hope was the other mass market of the 1960s. Material hope, spiritual hope, revolutionary hope, all were in demand at the same time: people hoped for more goods, more love, more happiness, for transcendence and transformation. Perhaps prosperity itself raises non-materialist expectations. It would seem that societies cannot live by consumer goods alone and that some prospect for improvement or salvation must be entertained. For many centuries people expected nothing in improvement of their lot on earth but looked to heaven for a better life. Then with God so inconveniently dead, expectations were transferred from heaven to earth and, in the early years of the century, hope became an altogether more dynamic quantity. Science and socialism were its chief vehicles through the twentieth century.

Hope, of course, is inflationary and in all sorts of ways. The wages explosion which burst across all Europe after 1967 was, one suspects, an expression of raised expectations rather than a response to the endeavours of governments to dampen them. But wages were only a part of expectations and when the music stopped in 1973 the game went on, as people demanded more and more from a system capable of providing less and less. This was the essence of ungovernability. For expectations to be lowered again the power of the State would be needed, the State acting within its proper role, that is as policeman not as nanny. Repression, the Left called this. 'Fascism!' some said, to keep their revolutionary courage up. The National Council of Civil Liberties issued a poster which proclaimed: '"The streets are in turmoil. The universities are filled with students rebelling and rioting . . . We need law and order." They got it! (The words were Hitler's in 1932.)'

But more than a stick was required. A new religion was necessary, for one hope can only be knocked on the head by another. The money religion offered a means of social redemption provided people could be persuaded that the laws of economics were written in heaven and not the Treasury. But monetarism, as old Hayek complained from Vienna, was in truth no different from what had gone before in that it still excited expectations of economic management by the State. And so it was, for in 1979 the Thatcher government promised more by promising less. Expectations must be lowered, the satisfaction of wants postponed, hope contained. Yet a hundred years of decline was to be arrested and reversed! How? By a cultural counter-revolution, a transformation of attitudes. Decline, it seems, *was* at heart a moral issue.

2
THE MOULD BROKEN?

5

Unconventional Wisdom

As Margaret Thatcher stepped through the doorway of Number 10 Downing Street no doubt she considered herself to be making history. And so she was. She was the first woman to become master at that august address and, what was more, a local grammar school girl made good. Moreover, she was a woman with a mission: to arrest and reverse her country's ineluctable decline and to save it from a fate worse than death – socialism.

She paused on the way to evoke St Francis of Assisi. 'Where there is discord may we bring harmony,' she said. 'Where there is error, may we bring truth. Where there is doubt, may we bring faith. Where there is despair, may we bring hope.' The quotation has been held to be singularly inappropriate in the light of the style of government which was to follow but, apart from the bit about discord and harmony, these words (though not St Francis's but a Victorian attribution) serve as an accurate enough manifesto of her intentions. St Francis, after all, was a conviction politician of a kind.

Her 'conviction politics' were what came to be known as 'Thatcherism'. 'Thatcherism' is more usefully regarded as a style than as an ideology: an ideology is a consistent system of ideas whereas what she called her conviction politics were largely instinctive and very much the product of her own experience. These instincts were narrow in range, dogmatically voiced; that she came to be credited with an 'ism', a most un-Tory achievement, is a tribute to the force of her beliefs rather than to their coherence.

She did not need to read books by Milton Friedman or Friedrich von Hayek to learn the importance of sound money or that the power of the State was the enemy of freedom. She had learnt these self-evident truths at her father's knee. For her they were not the abstractions of an ideologue but the products of experience; what set her apart from the empirical and pragmatic Tory tradition was not the source of her convictions but their unchangeability in the face of all subsequent experience. Ralph Harris, the supreme ideologist of market forces, describes how he first recognised her as a co-religionist at a lunch at the Institute of Economic Affairs:

> I can remember her falling on one rather stupid Conservative MP who was asking why we thought that people should value choice. She got up and spoke like a Finchley housewife about the choice of going shopping, and being able to go to one shop and then to another shop, and being able to make a choice, rather than being registered with the butcher as some of us remembered during the war and having no choice.[1]

It is that phrase *registered with the butcher* which rings so true. The leaders who had come before her – Callaghan, Heath, Wilson – being men, had been formed less by direct experience of handling ration books than by the economic and political experiences of the 1930s, brought up as they were under mass unemployment and in the shadow of war. With her arrival at the top a profound generational change took place. Born in 1925, fourteen when war broke out, at Oxford 1943–7, her formative memories were not of the dole queue but of the queue outside the butcher's, not of the means test but of the ration book. Her crucial political experiences were gained under socialism at home and communism abroad; she was a daughter of the age of austerity, a child of the Cold War.

Her anti-socialism was deeply rooted not only in time but in place. I myself was brought up a shopkeeper's son in a small East Anglian town. I know Margaret Thatcher. For someone of her background the election of 1945 was a shattering event, as if anti-Christ had come to power. The Attlee government was regarded with fear, loathing and almost total incomprehension. How could something so alien have come to pass in England? Edward Norman, chaplain of Peter-house and Reith lecturer in 1979, has described how 'like most English lower middle class people' he was brought up 'with a savage view of working class life'.[2] It was a view based on an almost total lack of knowledge, due to the fact that in small towns in the southerly part of England the working class scarcely existed as a sociological entity. In my own town there was one council estate on which were segre-gated an alien race of people who frequented certain disreputable pubs and the dog track down by the gas works and whose children threw stones and attended the secondary modern school. For the rest there were the working people of the town – labourers, artisans, gardeners, delivery men and so on – sons and daughters of their fathers and grandfathers, who lived in their own streets and houses and treated their betters with proper respect and had nothing to do with trade unions and (or so it was fondly believed) with the Labour Party.

To the petty-bourgeois mind what was still more appalling than that the working classes should elect a socialist government was that they should be aided and abetted in this evil and unpatriotic enterprise by upper middle class people. In small market towns such as Grantham the upper class consisted of the 'county', titled folk and gentlemen farmers, Tory to the core. Then there were professional people, a cut above 'trade' ('business' was the preferred word), whose sons attended public schools, though usually minor ones, and a few of whom 'went on to the university', though rarely to Cambridge or to Oxford. Indeed, Oxford and Cambridge were words spoken in awe not merely of the scholastic achievement required to gain admission but for what they represented in terms of social class – the 'varsity', an idyllic world of blues and toffs and gowns and punts where servants still existed to make the beds and clean the shoes of the 'young gentlemen'. That the products of such pinnacled privilege, Balliol men no less, old Etonians even, should turn traitors to their class and, as members of a socialist cabinet – Mr Attlee was a Haileybury boy himself – preside over the demise of shopkeeping, middle class England was as incomprehensible as it was enraging.

The Roberts of Grantham were Methodists and I can speak to that too. 'Methodist means method', she told an interviewer. My own headmaster was always saying the same: 'There is method in our Methodism', a claim which he elevated to a par with God moving in mysterious ways His wonders to perform. East Anglian Methodism was of a very different temper from the Methodism to which the Labour Party, according to Morgan Phillips, its then General Secretary, owed more than to Marx. Occasionally at my school we would be visited by a fiery preacher from Lancashire, but in East Anglia Wesleyan enthusiasm had given way to a smug non-conformity. Methodism was the religion of prosperous shopkeepers and farmers, a pious celebration of the work ethic and discharge of the religious duty which accompanied the ownership of property. East Anglian Methodism was the petty bourgeoisie at song in a part of the country where the Church of England tended to be the 'county' at prayer.

Later, upwardly mobile, she abandoned the Methodism of her childhood and its memories of gloomy Sundays – her father was a lay preacher and strict Sabbatarian. She became C. of E. Religion merged into politics. Conservativism and Christianity were synonymous, and that was all there was to it. Socialism was the anti-Christ. But she seldom prays the name of God in aid. 'Rejoice' she commanded, at that tense moment of the Falklands war, not 'Thank the Lord'. Her intellectual friends at Peterhouse took her to task for this lack of religious interest; for them monetarism was too earthly a creed and, like Keynesianism, liable to excite secular expectations when the task of government should be to restore authority and a spirit of acceptance.[3] Religion offers no special clue to the make-up of the latter-day Margaret Thatcher, although the evangelical certainty of her parents' church may have contributed something lasting to the style which we are calling 'Thatcherism'.

More to the point is the contribution of her upbringing to the religion of herself. To take her at her own word as a 'conviction politician', to see her as an ideologue engaged upon some lifelong crusade, would be to miss entirely the force of her ambition. It is of the small town variety and there is none more ardent. According to one of her biographers, it was not until she had escaped from Grantham that she revolted against it. Perhaps it is true, perhaps she was too conventional a girl to revolt against the excruciating tedium of petty bourgeois life in a small provincial town, although we are told she was carried away by the excitement of a week with family friends in London which included a performance of the *Desert Song*.[4] Perhaps she too would never quite live down the excitement of arrival at one of the great London termini, in those days grimy cathedrals of steam and clatter, the taxi ride with luggage strapped in, past the dome of St Paul's or down the Mall towards the Palace where, perhaps, the guard was being changed. That feeling is never quite extinguished: it is the exhilaration of escape.

Whether or not escape was consciously on her agenda she was plainly most strongly motivated by the circumstances of her childhood. There are stories of deprivation of the kind which grow up around all fairy tales of self-improvement: modern prime ministers need, like American presidential candidates, their equivalent of the log cabin. In her case it was the outside lavatory. It sounds an unlikely tale; there was, I remember, some similar story about Harold Wilson having no shoes as a boy. Her father, Albert Roberts, could perfectly well have afforded a proper lavatory; nor is he likely to have seen any special virtue in an outside one, the prime status symbol of the working classes and not something which a self-respecting shopkeeper would want to own up to. His shop, by her own account, was 'quite a big shop. It had a grocery section and provisions section, with all the mahogany fitments that I now see in antique shops, and beautiful canisters of different sorts of tea, coffee and spices. There was a post office section, confectionery section and cigarettes . . .'[5] Her father came to employ five assistants and, later, he opened a second shop. It is hard to believe that there would have been a real problem about the fees of £13 a year in 1935 when she was admitted to Kesteven and Grantham Girls' School or even about her taking up her place at Somerville, with the aid of a college bursary, in 1943. Her father was a substantial man in the town, a councillor and Alderman. Shopkeepers for the most part did well out of the war, and even better under the Attlee government, when there was more money around than goods to spend it on. Rationing and shortages affected them less than others as they were in a position to help each other out in an informal barter economy. Margaret Thatcher's childhood may have been repressed but it cannot have been deprived.

She was driven on and upwards not by the spur of poverty but by ambition and a spirit of acquisitiveness. Chemistry was her first choice (her elder sister had settled for physiotherapy) but she was soon to regret it. She raised her sights to the Bar, the highest ambition for a small-town girl or boy, but read chemistry none the less on discovering that, combined with the law, it would enable her to make money at the patents bar. Professional politics became a possibility for her when a Labour government raised the salary of an MP from £600 to £1,000. She became a barrister in 1953. By then she had married a rich man, ten years her senior. Indeed, she passed her Bar Finals within four months of the birth of twins. In 1955, with the children not yet two, she began looking again for a parliamentary seat. She was adopted for Finchley in 1956, elected to Parliament in 1959. Her children were then just six.

Already she had come a long way from Grantham. Within ten years since coming down from Oxford she had begun a lucrative practice at the tax bar, married a rich man and obtained a safe parliamentary seat. The idea that the family is the true centre of her moral universe, that she was a paragon of motherhood and wifely virtue, does not fit easily with the speed and determination with which the Grantham girl made good. Even more preposterous is the view that representing Finchley somehow made her into a suburban housewife. On marrying she moved into Flood Street, Chelsea, and from that day she was untouched by financial worry of any kind, spared from the economics of housekeeping, and materially for ever removed from the shop-keeping world in which she had grown up. Her little shopping expeditions, the apron at the sink, Denis's special breakfast bacon, were aspects of the politician's image. Moreover, she had brought with her from her girlhood a whole armoury of homely virtues with which to justify and explain her good fortune, and the less good fortune of others, and to protect her from any pangs of petty-bourgeois guilt which might from time to time impinge upon the paramountcy of her ambition. For ambition, in small-town girls and boys, is like genius in a writer or a painter – a demonic force, harnessing all vices to one transcending virtue, in this case self-improvement and self-advancement, the creative art of success.

Workaholicism is the most common symptom of this condition in later life. At school she was notorious for the thoroughness of her homework. As a Minister she soon became famous for her attention to her boxes. Ministerial boxes are the politicians' drug, their escape from life into work, the expiation of familiar guilt. She would sit at hers into the night until every piece of paper was dealt with – sidelined, initialled, scribbled on – still the scholarship girl attending to her homework. It was in this way that the word 'wet' entered into the terminology of politics; it was her frequent comment on papers from colleagues and officials which she found lacking in true doctrine or true grit. Her addiction to homework may have saved her life, for she was still at her boxes when the bomb went off in the Grand Hotel, Brighton in 1984.

Her early political ambitions are often attributed to the self-educating, self-improving zeal of her father. There are touching descriptions of her family life in this regard – the insatiable borrowing from the library, current affairs eagerly discussed around the dinner table, her father's dissertations, ears tuned to the radio – a habit that stayed with her. But she did not derive from this the intellectual curiosity, or any of the originality of mind, which the self-improving drive of the Workers' Education Association excited in so many Labour leaders of an earlier generation. Rather, or so it seems – it equipped her with a neat set of prejudices, like a twin-set and court shoes, with which to pursue her ambition into politics.

At Oxford, the rags-to-riches version of her youth not withstanding, she was free with the sherry bottle in the service of her career. She became president of the Oxford University Conservative Association. The anti-socialist zeal she had brought with her from Grantham was appropriate to those times. When she turned to Von Hayek's *Road to Serfdom* it was not for revelation but rather to have her prejudices confirmed. She was much moved by Churchill's open-air speech at the great rally at Blenheim on 5 August 1947, in which he fulminated against the iniquities of socialism. That same year was one of Crippsian austerity, a heatwave summer after a worst-ever winter freeze up, a winter of fuel shortage and power cuts. The dollar loan was exhausted, Marshall Aid yet to come. The rations were cut again – meat from 1*s.* 2*d.* to a shilling's worth a week. The sugar ration was 8 oz a week, bacon, cheese and tea 2 oz.[6] Even the basic petrol ration was abolished, and the foreign currency allowance was cut from £75 to £35. The coal industry had been nationalised but the Yorkshire miners were on strike – over a demarcation dispute. At midnight on 15 August India became independent. Britain could no longer hold the line against communism in Greece; Palestine was in turmoil. *Picture Post* published a crisis issue. It portrayed Britain in decline. America had taken advantage of the First World War to industrialise. Markets had been lost. Now, after another war, Britain was a debtor nation while America prospered again. Why, *Picture Post* asked, were 40 per cent of directors drawn from the peerage and squirearchy? It was later that year that the British middle classes resumed the habit of wearing evening dress. In that year, too, Margaret Roberts came down from Oxford and embarked on her political career.

She had held junior office during the last days of Macmillan and was statutory woman in the Heath Cabinet. She became famous chiefly as 'Thatcher the milk snatcher' (Crosland's soubriquet) when, as Secretary of State for Education, she abolished free school milk. This was not an early 'Thatcherite' stroke but was done, ironically, at Iain Macleod's suggestion.[7] However, certain Thatcherite traits were at that time noted or, at least, with hindsight recorded: her immense capacity for work, a profound mistrust of civil servants, and a penchant for getting her way. But her biography is more of a piece if one proceeds from the young Margaret Thatcher, Grantham and Oxford, to the woman who in 1975 seized the leadership of her party in 1975. Keith Joseph as we have seen, flinched from the challenge. The Conservative Party by then wanted anybody but Heath, even if it were a woman. William Whitelaw, who had risen as his loyal lieutenant, was far too loyal – too public school, too cricket – to stand against him. There was a paucity of other challengers. Thatcher put up and humiliated Heath on the first ballot. The eccentric rules of the newly introduced procedure for electing Conservative leaders permitted new runners to declare for the second ballot, but by the time Whitelaw was into the starting gate Thatcher had stolen the race. It was a brilliant piece of opportunism, a successful *coup d'état*. Four years later she entered Number 10.

Addressing the House of Commons for the first time as Prime Minister on 15 May 1979 she proclaimed the election of that year to have been a 'watershed'. Was it? It was true that, for the first time since 1974, Britain had a government with a secure majority (43 over all) and the country had voted decisively for change. The campaign had made quite explicit the Conservative intention to make a deliberate break with the policies of the post-war era, and especially those which had been followed since 1964. But was it really a 'watershed' or 'critical' election, comparable to 1886, 1906 or 1945, an election which permanently altered the political landscape? The study of the election carried out by Nuffield College, Oxford, thought not. To be sure, the Conservative gain of 7 per cent in its share of the vote was the highest since the war but its 44 per cent was still the lowest percentage support for any post-war government save in 1974. The Tories had recovered from the débâcle of that year, but no more than that; there was no evidence of a growth in underlying support. Indeed, they seemed to be losing ground among the middle classes and any claim to have become the natural majority party once more would rest on the lasting allegiance of the skilled workers and trade unionists who had abandoned the Labour Party. Moreover, it was only with the Winter of Discontent that the Conservatives had moved into a decisive lead in the opinion polls on the key issues of prices and trade unions. In other words, the Labour Party had lost the 1979 General Election, as governments often do. As the Nuffield College study said:

> The Conservatives were well placed to catch the plum that fell into their laps. But it was the Labour movement that shook it off the tree. It is worth stressing that since 1959 no British government had won re-election at the end of a full term in office. In the country's declining position, the old rule about governments losing elections may apply more forcefully than ever. As one of Mr Callaghan's advisers complained, 'In today's world, it's jolly difficult for a government not to lose.'[8]

Callaghan shared the Nuffield College view. 'People voted against last winter, rather than *for* the Conservatives,' he said afterwards. And it seemed not improbable at the time that whoever presided over such high unemployment – 1·2 million – and over double-digit inflation would be punished by their electorates. Governments were going down all over Western Europe. The election came at the end of a decade of dissatisfaction. Real living standards had failed to rise during much of the Callaghan government's time; redistributive taxation had bitten hard on the working classes and the consequences for Labour in 1979 were exactly as Anthony Crosland had predicted (see Chapter 1). This analysis could be reinforced by the course and character of the campaign. In spite of all that had happened Callaghan remained the most popular of the contending leaders. 'We are winning in spite of an unpopular leader and an uncharismatic team,' said one Tory candidate from his constituency. 'Events have made Tory voters.' The Conservative policies were the most popular on the doorsteps – especially on taxation and law and order – but on other key issues, notably unemployment, Labour continued as the preferred party; there was no sign of any willingness to break with the Welfare State.

However, these electoral straws can be read in more than one way. The fact that it was Callaghan who fought his campaign using Conservative arguments – 'We are the party of roots, of tradition' – perhaps indicates that the country was in the mood for a radical break. If Margaret Thatcher was an unpopular leader, and Labour's unpopularity the temporary consequence of that winter's disasters, then, perhaps, all the more reason to suspect that the result of the 1979 election was the result of a subterranean earthquake.

Today we have the benefit of hindsight. We can see more clearly that the 1979 General Election *was* some kind of watershed. The re-election of the Thatcher government in a parliamentary landslide in 1983 made that clearer, although there were again special factors to cling to – the 'Falkland Factor' and the 'Foot Factor'. If the present helps us to explain the past, the past helps us to understand the present and, for that purpose, 1979 remains a seminal year in which the decline of the Labour Party opened the way to the realignment of British party politics.

There were some – Margaret Thatcher apart – who saw this at the time. Among the first to do so clearly was the Marxist Left, which lives in the expectation of ideological backlash. Writing in *Marxism Today* in January 1979, before the election in May of that year, Stuart Hall placed Mrs Thatcher in the context of a pervasive shift to the right which he dated from the late 1960s. 'It no longer looks like a temporary swing of the pendulum in political fortunes,' he wrote. He explained this in terms of reaction against the 'revolutionary ferment of 1968 and all that,' the populist appeal of Enoch Powell, the appearance of 'Selsdon Man'[9] but, above all, to the crisis of social democracy, or 'labourism', as it deepened through the 1970s. As befits a left-wing social commentator, Hall sees this in Gramscian terms as the establishment of class 'hegemony' in new form but, be that as it may, he spots Thatcher as the 'mould-breaker'. Thatcherism, of course, 'aims for the construction of a national consensus of its own. What it destroys is that form of consensus in which social democracy was the principal tendency.'[10]

Hall's sense of a re-alignment in progress in an ideological, or hegemonical, sense was confirmed in more precise terms by some of the studies of the 1979 election results. Although the Nuffield study was sceptical of the 'watershed' verdict, it nevertheless remarked on some far-reaching trends. One, which we shall come to, was the further tendency towards regional and demographic polarisation, the increasingly sharp distinction between north and south, city and countryside. More important still was 'the continued inversion in the relationship between class and party', a phenomenon observable elsewhere in Europe. While the middle class had been shifting to Labour, the Conservatives were increasing their strength among the working class.[11]

Marx had predicted that the inevitable result of universal suffrage would be the 'political supremacy of the working class' although Engels, commenting on the elections of 1868, complained petulantly, 'once again the proletariat has discredited itself terribly'. It went on doing so: out of 26 General Elections since 1885, the Conservatives have won 14; only on three occasions has the party of the Left won decisive victories, in 1906, 1945 and 1966. The Conservatives have been more often in power than their opponents and, when in power, have remained there longer.[12]

As some two-thirds of the electorate can be socio-economically classified as working class, it is to the working classes that the Conservatives owe this remarkable record of survival and success as a party of power. It is often said, with much truth, that the Labour Party is the party of the working class but it would be truer to say that there are two parties of the working class, Labour and Conservative.

Customarily about a third of the working class has voted Conservative, vastly outnumbering the middle class voters who have supported Labour. This, as Philip Norton and Arthur Aughey remark in the best recent book on Conservativism, 'is something that causes little surprise to a Conservative'.[13] Many theories have been advanced to explain this 'fact' of British politics. Deference was one explanation. The working classes, Disraeli's 'angels in marble', knew who their rulers and betters were and, with a touch of a forelock or cloth cap, would vote cheerfully and dutifully against their class interest. This theory was open to the criticism that such voters might be deferential because they were Conservatives, not Conservative because they were deferential. In any case, if ever this had been an explanation for working class Conservativism, the spirit of deference seemed singularly lacking in the Britain of the 1960s and 1970s; indeed, one commentator was to attribute Britain's increasing ungovernability in large part to what he called 'the collapse of deference'.[14]

Another explanation consists of a highly sophisticated version of W. S. Gilbert's famous verse:

> I often think it's comical
> How nature does contrive
> That every boy and every gal,
> That's born into the world alive,
> Is either a little Liberal,
> Or else a little Conservative!

According to this, the 'generational cohort theory' developed by David Butler and Donald Stokes in their seminal *Political Change in Britain*, children pick up their politics from their parents in much the same way as they learn their table manners. Moreover, they go on being socialised by their environment – neighbourhood, workplace, friends and so on – well into their adult lives. This theory helps to explain not only why voters vote according to their natural class circumstance but also why they do not; allegiances formed before the rise of the Labour Party continued to be handed down through the generation scale, postponing the fulfilment of Labour's natural class base. By the 1960s, with the pre-1918 generation slowly dying off and the post-1945 generation entering the electorate, Labour's socio-demographic prospects seemed good. When Labour then lost the 1970 General Election (the first edition of *Political Change* was published in 1969) many were eager to point out that the Butler–Stokes theory had been disproved. But it is just as likely that a generational effect was slowing the pace of Labour's secular decline and, if Butler and Stokes were right, Labour's class base may wither more slowly than the working class itself.

A tendency working in the opposite direction to childhood socialisation is that of *embourgeoisement*. According to this idea, working class families become more likely to vote Conservative as they become more middle class in their life styles, especially in the ownership of goods such as cars and labour-saving household appliances. This theory was particularly popular after Harold Macmillan had won the 1959 election, telling people they 'had never had it so good'. Washing machines, televisions, and holidays in Spain were thought to be eroding old class loyalties, and Labour – according to an influential attitude study of the time – suffered in this age of affluence from its 'cloth cap image' and reputation as the party of the underdog. Subsequent research cast serious doubt upon whether *embourgeoisement* in the kitchen translated into *embourgeoisement* in the polling booth; a study of affluent Luton car workers found no evidence of it. In any case, consumerism among the working classes had increased much more rapidly than Conservativism; and in spite of the continuing boom, the Tories lost the 1964 and 1966 elections.

The Conservative victory in 1979 was won against the background of a decade of recession in which materialistic expectations were disappointed and, in four years out of ten, average real living standards did not rise at all. Nevertheless, something very similar to what was thought to have happened in the late 1950s showed signs of happening in 1979. Labour suffered what Ivor Crewe called 'a massive haemorrhage of working class votes'. Its policies were out of tune with the aspirations of a significant section of its natural class base who wanted to own their own house and pay less of their income in tax; and the swings against Labour were particularly pronounced in high-wage working class areas such as the new towns, the Yorkshire and Lancashire coalfields, and the car-worker suburbs.[15]

Class voting, it seemed, was in decline. Butler and Stokes had spotted this at the same time as they were elaborating their generational cohort theory. It was in 1967 that another Oxford political scientist, Peter Pulzer, uttered his much-to-be-repeated dictum that 'Class is the basis of British politics; all else is mere embellishment and detail.' Yet already at that time it was ceasing to be true. Butler and Stokes, writing in 1969, noted the importance of housing tenure in influencing how people voted: owner-occupiers were more likely to vote Conservative than council house or private tenants. In part this was due to the socialising effects of neighbourhood; a Wates estate, it seemed, was an agent of *embourgeoisement* even if a modern kitchen was not. And as Butler and Stokes foretold, 'An electorate which saw politics less in class terms could respond to other issues and analyses.' And so, in 1979, it seemed the electorate did. Certainly class was out of fashion among the psephologists: issues were in. The most influential theory was by now Ivor Crewe's theory of 'partisan de-alignment'. In the early 1970s Crewe and his collegues at the University of Essex had taken over the British Election Study from Butler and Stokes, who had inaugurated it in 1963. Crewe pointed out that not only was the aggregate share of the vote commanded by the two parties steadily reducing but, more significant, voters' identification with parties was growing weaker; and, as loyalties weakened, this made them more likely to decide their votes according to the issues. The theory applied to both major parties but, in practice, its implications for the Labour Party were greater because the Labour Party was the class party *par excellence*. Until around 1974 working class voters had continued to think of themselves as Labour even if not voting Labour; but, from about that time, there was a weakening of party identification. The same tendency could be observed among Conservative voters but it was less pronounced and was more easily explained by temporary disillusion with the Heath government. In Labour's case a much more profound and ominous alienation was at work, it seemed, whether Labour was in or out of office. 'For a substantial number of Labour identifiers,' says Crewe, 'February 1974 appears to have been a "last straw" election, confirming doubts and fears that had originated in the preceding decade.'[16]

At every election since 1951, with the one exception of 1966, the Labour vote had declined – in total by about one-third between 1951 and 1979. The election of 1979 was the third successive occasion on which the Labour vote had fallen below 40 per cent of the votes cast, compared with 49 per cent in 1951, 46 per cent in 1955, 44 per cent in 1964, and 48 per cent in 1966. This, Crewe notes, had occurred in spite of the demographic factors favourable to Labour identified by Butler and Stokes and in spite also of a decade in which social and economic conditions ought to have favoured the Labour Party. Macmillan's 'Affluent Society' had given way to the worst recession since the 1930s and, after the events of 1968, the age of deference was no more.

Labour's seemingly-secular decline could be explained in part by the gradual contraction of the working-class base on which it traditionally relied. Manufacture was in decline and the service sector was growing, blue-collar was giving way to white-collar employment. The world in which the Labour Party had grown and flourished, the world brought about by the Industrial Revolution, was slowly disappearing. Between 1964 and 1979 the proportion of manual workers within the electorate had shrunk from 63 per cent to 56 per cent. But, according to Crewe, the news for Labour was worse than that: it was the erosion of support for Labour *within* the working class that was crucial. At the 1979 election manual workers, supposedly natural Labour supporters, were slightly more in favour of Conservative policies than of Labour's own policies. Crewe's researches showed a chasm opening up between Labour and the electorate, not least among its own traditional supporters. In 1979 manual workers were more in favour of reducing the highest rate of income tax (a Tory policy) than of introducing a wealth tax (a Labour policy). Crewe found among Labour ranks 'a spectacular decline in support for the collectivist trinity of public ownership, trade union power and social welfare'. In 1964, for example, 57 per cent of Labour supporters approved of more nationalisation while 59 per cent repudiated the idea that trade unions were too powerful. By 1979 these two opinions were held by about only one-third of its voters. Labour fought the 1979 election in opposition to the sale of council houses to their tenants but 85 per cent of the electorate, and 86 per cent of the working class, were in favour of this Conservative proposal. Only 39 per cent of the electorate, and 48 per cent of the working class, favoured Labour's plan to complete the elimination of the grammar school.[17]

Before the election of 1979 Crewe had written: 'It is difficult to conceive of a party avoiding a long-term electoral decline if the majority of its surviving supporters reject the majority of its basic policies.' The results gave support to his thesis that Labour was indeed in secular decline and to the belief among political scientists that class-voting, or the working class itself, was in decline. Among skilled manual workers there was an 11 per cent swing to the Conservatives, 6·5 per cent among semi-skilled, and 7 per cent among trade union members. In consequence Labour commanded less than half (45 per cent) of the votes cast by the working class (no more than 37 per cent, counting those who could have voted but did not) and barely 50 per cent of the trade unionists who turned out.[18]

'Watershed' or not, the 1979 General Election transformed the political geography of Britain. One reason for supposing that the Conservatives had done less well than Labour had done badly was their poor showing in the north. When Disraeli first said that the Tory Party was a national party he meant that it was the English party. He was referring to the fact that the Liberals nearly always owed their majorities at Westminster to the Scots, Welsh and Irish. Labour had inherited this Liberal ascendancy in Scotland and Wales and some parts of the north of England. Yet the Conservatives had never been an exclusively southern party. For example, there was a strong paternalist Tory tradition in Lord Derby's Lancashire, of which Lord Randolph Churchill was a part, and the progressive Chamberlain tradition in Birmingham. In 1979, however, the Conservatives were reduced to a mere seven seats in the cities of the north. In 1959 they had held 18. Altogether they finished with 20 fewer seats in the north (and 14 fewer in Scotland) than in 1955. But in the south and the

Midlands they had 34 more than in 1955 (and five more in Wales). The 1979 election saw the country divided along a line running roughly between the Humber and the Mersey, the northern part of it swinging by much less to the Conservatives than the southern part of it, and nowhere more than in Wales, which in 1979 joined the south for political purposes. However, to see this as simply a north–south divide would be to miss the polarisation which was taking place at the same time between town and country, and city and suburb. Like the growing divide between north and south, this also had been going on since 1959. In 1955 the Conservatives could win two out of five big city seats; in 1979 fewer than one in four. What was happening was that Labour was becoming the party of decline, the Conservative Party the party of growth. Slowly the political culture of the south was moving northwards (and this although the recession was moving southwards), colonising the Midlands, ghettoising Labour's strength in the inner cities and the urban centres of manufacturing decline.[19]

In 1983, if we may jump ahead for one moment, these tendencies accelerated and left the country even more sharply polarised along the lines we have indicated. Conservatives made further substantial gains in the Midlands in spite of that area having suffered badly from an accelerated decline in manufacture while in the south, outside London, Labour was virtually wiped out, holding only three seats – Bristol South, Ipswich and Thurrock. Yet, at the same time, the Conservatives for the first time since 1885 failed to win a single seat in Glasgow and in Liverpool. The political map of Britain corresponded still more closely to the map of unemployment and the contours of affluence and poverty. Labour, more than ever, had become the party of the poor and unemployed. Or, to look at it another way, Labour was in decline but its decline was not national. Rather, it was concentrated in certain parts of the country. In the south in 1983 it became the third party, with the newly formed SDP–Liberal Alliance[20] the chief challenger to the Conservatives; but in Scotland the Labour Party still enjoyed a huge lead, and in the north was only marginally behind. It was no coincidence that in Scotland the old manual working class accounted for nearly twice the proportion of the electorate than in the south, that 54 per cent were council tenants compared with only 20 per cent in the south. One result of this geographic polarisation and concentration was to cushion Labour's decline: its loss of seats was not commensurate with its loss of votes across the country as a whole.[21]

This regional voting pattern was one factor which helped to

obscure the significance of the 1979 General Election. A much more fundamental cause was that an influential section of Mrs Thatcher's own party continued to regard her as an aberration. She was a mistake of history, rather as the Stuarts are sometimes seen as an unnecessary break with the continuity of English history as embodied in the Tudors. She had become leader of the Conservative Party only because of its passionate desire to be rid of Heath. She was a usurper, who stood outside the true Tory tradition; some said that she was not a Tory at all but a neo-nineteenth-century Liberal. Had the party greybeards made the choice of Heath's successor it would not have been her; as the leading historian of the Conservative Party, Lord Blake, has pointed out, Disraeli, Bonar Law, Heath – previous outsiders – had all been embraced by the party establishment before rising to its leadership: 'She alone had captured it by direct assault.'[22] And outsider she remained. 'I am the Cabinet rebel,' she is reputed to have said. It was true, at least for a while, as we shall see; more important, it was how she saw herself.

Neither had she been the voters' choice; they were heavily for Whitelaw. Until the Winter of Discontent many in her party believed that she would lose the coming election and were preparing to blame her; she herself believed that she would have just the one chance, if only because her party would not give a woman a second chance. The most frequent complaint against her was that she appealed only to the suburban middle classes of the Home Counties and would be bound to lose the election north of Watford.

It was axiomatic that she stood to lose, because she had vacated the hallowed centre ground of politics where elections were won or lost. Moreover, she stood outside the Disraelian 'One Nation' tradition and would be a divisive force in politics; if she did win, her right-wing zeal would as likely as not open the way to its opposite extreme, Bennite socialism. Here is the not untypical view of one of her critics, a member of the left-wing Tory Reform Group, in 1978:

> Mrs Thatcher's grip on the party may prove short-lived . . . Some on the Tory Left, who dismiss her as an aberration, or a mistake, already regard the period of her leadership, which they expect to be brief, as an unfortunate although possibly necessary interlude: one which allows the party to get the bile out of its system before – regrettably, after another election defeat first – it can settle back into a normal, orthodox pattern once more.

For Ian Gilmour she was the epitome of 'What Conservativism Is Not', a chapter title in his book *Inside Right*, published in 1977:

> British Conservativism then is not an '-ism. It is not an idea. Still less is it a system of ideas. It cannot be formulated in a series of propositions, which can be aggregated into a creed. It is not an ideology or a doctrine. It is too much bound up with British history and with the Conservative Party.[23]

By definition, or at least by Gilmour's definition, 'Thatcher*ism* could not be Conservativism': 'conviction politics' had no place in the Tory tradition. In his speeches and writings at that time Gilmour extolled the virtues of moderation in all things, in terms unmistakably intended to brand Thatcher as an extremist who was defying the centripetal laws of political gravity. 'Others wish to divide the country,' he said in a speech at Amersham in January 1975, at the very moment at which Mrs Thatcher was declaring her candidacy for the leadership. 'Our mission is to unite it. And only moderation can do that. Extremism divides: moderation heals.' Because it relied on winning working class votes, and 'must recruit from the left', as Baldwin had said, extremism was out of the question for the Conservative Party, Gilmour wrote. For this reason, and because it is a 'national party' and not a 'class party', there was no place for ideology in the Conservative scheme of things. For Conservatives, 'talking about what Harold Macmillan calls "the old *laissez-faire* doctrine of classic Liberalism", in the way, say, that Mr Wedgwood Benn or Mr Foot talk about Socialism, is almost as bizarre as the idea that the Labour Party could win an election by threatening to carry Clause 4 of its constitution[24] into full legislative effect in the next Parliament.' Conservatives know that the country can only be well governed from the centre. The fundamental condition for a successful two-party system was that the parties should never be far apart. Conservative goals were not to be achieved by 'waging a holy war': indeed, 'the more Labour moves to the Left, the more relentlessly should the Conservative Party cling to moderation and the Centre.'[25]

When she did win the General Election it was easy for her critics to say that she had done so by default, just as she had won the leadership from Heath by default. Within months the 1979 election looked even less like a watershed than it had on polling night. In office she enjoyed only the briefest of honeymoons. By the autumn of 1981 her economic policies made her the least approved-of Prime Minister since Dr Gallup invented opinion polls.

The government did not recover its lead in the opinion polls until the Falklands war in 1982. In December 1981 the Conservatives stood at 27 per cent compared with 43·9 per cent at the election eighteen months before. This did not seem like the stuff of which permanent revolutions are made. The early failures of her government reinforced the expectations that she would trim, U-turn. The conventional wisdom had been that she would do so before the election, in order to win it; now the conventional wisdom was that she would have to do so in office, in order to govern. This expectation rested, partly, on the assumption that monetarism could not and would not work but, chiefly, on the belief that it was impossible to govern Britain outside the consensus which she had repudiated, indeed was busy smashing.

The conventional wisdom died hard. The country had come to assume that it could only be governed with the consent of the trade unions, which should be appeased not provoked. The social and industrial costs of monetarism were 'politically unacceptable'. The country wouldn't stand for two million unemployed, for cuts laid upon cuts. The conventional wisdom ruled still in most of Whitehall, and in half of the Treasury; it was shared probably by a majority in her own party, certainly by a majority in her first Cabinet. Her policies were viewed with growing dismay as unemployment soared and manufacture was thrown into steep decline. In November 1980 the *Financial Times* commented in an editorial: 'Whatever the monetary aggregates say the economy now is in an unprecedented tailspin.' The high exchange rate was contributing to a deterioration of competitiveness which, said the Bank of England, had 'no parallel in recent history, either in this country or among its major competitors'. Before the end of the year unemployment, at 1·3 million when she came in, had exceeded two million. 'How much responsibility do you feel for unemployment?' Sir Keith Joseph was asked in an interview. Sincere as ever, he replied, 'None. None.' In evidence to a House of Commons Select Committee the Treasury had explained that the object of policy was to reduce inflation 'through a reduction of the rate of monetary growth at reasonable interest rates'; the first effect of this policy was on the exchange rate, costing jobs and output, but in the longer run, prices and wages would adapt; 'it is only to the extent that these wage expectations do not adjust that you get the effect on output and unemployment.' Mrs Thatcher's most influential economic adviser at that time, Professor Alan Walters, later elaborated:

The idea, based on the concept of rational expectations, was that the announcement of these target rates of growth of the money supply etc. would induce entrepreneurs, investors and workers to adjust their behaviour to the new policy as though it were a *new* reality. Much – perhaps all of the pain of adjustment – could be eliminated by a sea change of expectations.[26]

But what was the connection – where was the transmission belt – between monetary targets policy and people's attitudes or expectations? The economist James Tobin told the same Select Committee that the trouble with disinflation was that 'that kind of threat to everybody in general is a threat to nobody in particular'. The conventional wisdom was that collective behaviour had to be influenced through the institutions of collective bargaining, that is by an incomes policy in some form. But the government had no incomes policy in any form. It had disclaimed responsibility for the 'real' economy, the economy of output and jobs. With the Medium Term Financial Strategy announced in the 1980 Budget the economy had been put on automatic pilot. The government had abdicated management of the economy to the forces of the market. That was the profoundest insult to the conventional wisdom. The conventional wisdom indicated that a U-turn was inevitable. When it would happen was the only question. The Cabinet 'wets' were permitted no influence over the conduct of economic policy; they could only await events as the agent of change. The U-turn would come when the Prime Minister was confronted with the full consequences of her policies.

In the run up to the Budget of 1981 she came under intensifying pressure from her colleagues to change course. In the previous autumn she and the Chancellor had been defeated in Cabinet over the spending cuts demanded by the Treasury. They had been allowed only half of what was needed to put the Medium Term Financial Strategy back on its course. In the Budget of March 1981 the Chancellor curbed his borrowing requirement by other means, by taking £4.3 billion out of the economy in raised taxes. He achieved this in large part by failing to raise benefits and allowances in step with inflation, which had peaked at 21·9 per cent the previous June and was still running in double figures. Walters, one of the Budget's chief architects, calls it 'the biggest fiscal squeeze of peacetime'. It was probably also the most fiscally regressive Budget of modern times.

The majority in the Cabinet was outraged. In a barely coded speech delivered in Putney, Francis Pym had in February warned: 'Common sense tells us that changed circumstances make adjustments necessary – in both tactics and timing – to meet altered circumstances.' In other words, the government should take account of the recession resulting from events in the oil-producing world and be prepared to borrow in order to sustain demand. The Chancellor had done exactly the opposite, and without consulting any of them. His Budget was the antithesis of Keynesianism: a massive deflation in the middle of a recession. By the Treasury's own projections output would now decline by another percentage point and unemployment rise to above three million the following year. It would remain above three million through the next election. How on earth, Ministers were asking, could the government hope to win a General Election with more than three million unemployed?

The 1981 Budget threw the Cabinet into semi-open revolt. There were leaks and counter leaks. James Prior pondered his resignation. The Prime Minister publicly reprimanded her wayward colleagues in a speech at the Mansion House:

> What really gets me, is that those who are most critical of the extra taxation are those who were most vociferous in demanding the extra expenditure. What gets me even more is that having demanded that extra expenditure they are not prepared to face the consequences. I wish some of them had a bit more guts and courage than they have shown, because I think one of the most immoral things you can do is to pose as the moral politician demanding more for everything, and then say no when you see the bill.

After such a public rebuke the dissidents had no option but to close ranks. Nevertheless, that summer the demands for a U-turn grew still stronger. The riots in Brixton, Toxteth and Moss Side were seized upon by the Prime Minister's opponents in the Cabinet as confirmation of their predictions that monetarism would destroy the social fabric of the nation. Lord Bruce-Gardyne, at the time a junior Treasury minister, says that at this time, 'For once the Prime Minister's nerve seemed momentarily to falter: it seems conceivable that had the critics round the Cabinet table mounted a united campaign for a change of course, their demands might at this moment have prevailed.'[27] But, as he correctly says, they didn't. They were agreed on no clear alternative policy and lacked the will to act.

In September it was she who acted. She purged her Cabinet, sacking Gilmour and banishing Prior to Northern Ireland. For the first time she became the undisputed mistress of her own house, no longer the minority Prime Minister. Gilmour, in a statement accompanying his formal letter of resignation, said, 'Every Prime Minister has to reshuffle from time to time. It does no harm to throw the occasional man overboard, but it does not much good if you are steering full speed ahead for the rocks. That is what the government is now doing.' In that month Gallup reported her the least approved Prime Minister since Neville Chamberlain. The bars and lobbies at the Conservative Party conference in Blackpool that October seethed with sullen revolt. Every reference to Disraeli and his ideal of 'One Nation' was understood as a rebuke to Thatcher for having so divided the nation. As Bruce-Gardyne recalls, 'it would have been hard to find a journalist at Blackpool willing to take bets on a Tory victory in the next election; but easy to find those prepared to speculate on alternative names to lead the party into it. Majority opinion among the commentators was that the party was heading for a defeat of 1945 proportions, or worse.' So much, it seemed, for 1979 as a watershed; so much for the Thatcherite realignment of British politics.

6

Moving Left

The 1979 election results sent the Labour Movement into fierce convulsions. Much the same had happened after the 1959 and 1970 defeats and at first the complacent view of some senior figures in the party was that they were witnessing no more than a display of Labour's endemic disunity in opposition. Nor was it the first time that internecine warfare had broken out against a background of doubt about the party's ability to get itself elected, for a good few premature obituaries had been written after 1959 and, yet, by 1964 a Labour government was back in power. This time, however, events moved swiftly in support of the prophets of doom. By the moment at which Margaret Thatcher became the most unpopular Prime Minister since the invention of public opinion polls, the Labour Party had (a) achieved its first formal split since 1931, (b) adopted a policy of unilateral nuclear disarmament as part of a generally left-wing programme, (c) overthrown the sovereignty of the party in Parliament, and (d) adopted Michael Foot as its leader. These were among the reasons why, in that autumn of 1981, it was not the official Labour Opposition which was benefiting from the government's unpopularity but, rather, the newly-formed breakaway Social Democratic Party in its electoral alliance with the Liberal Party.

There were thus three aspects to the question as to whether – in the cliché of the times – we were witnessing the 'breaking of the mould' of British party politics. One was the possibility that Margaret Thatcher represented a lasting break with the past and would be the agent of a new electoral majority in the land. Another was that the nascent third party might succeed, even within the confines of the British electoral system, in digging the grave of one of its established rivals. A third possibility was that the Labour Party was engaged in digging its own grave as a majority party and, further to that, that the age of socialism was nearing its end. These three hypotheses were far from being mutually exclusive, indeed none could be true without at least one of the others being in some part true. The most crucial of them, however, was the third, for if realignment there was to be, whether of voters or of parties, it was likely to be at the expense of the Labour Party.

Within the Labour Movement itself the inquest had been opened even before the votes were cast and counted in 1979. In the March of the previous year, in a lecture which was to become seminal, the eminent Marxist historian, Eric Hobsbawm, had declared the Labour Movement to be in a state of crisis and listed a whole number of historical factors which, he argued, had made the future of socialism problematical. Although he had appended a question mark to the title of his Marx Memorial lecture – 'The Forward March of Labour Halted?' – his analysis pointed to an affirmative answer. We may think he was saying nothing very new. It was not a new thought that the Labour Party might be locked in a secular, perhaps terminal, decline; Ivor Crewe, as we have seen, had reached this conclusion by psephological analysis and I myself had made a theme of the immobilised condition of the Labour Movement, unable to bring about its version of socialism while, at the same time, unable to abandon socialism in favour of a continental-style social democracy. Quite why Hobsbawm's somewhat muddled essay in nostalgic pessimism should have set off such a debate is not obvious from a re-reading of it today. He has interesting things to say about the extraordinary preponderance of the manual working class during the Victorian–Edwardian heyday of Britain's industrial pre-eminence and the continuing consequences this had for the structure and traditions of the British Labour movement. But it is not exactly clear why the profound changes since that time should have set in motion the political decline of the Labour Party which he 'suspects', although cannot say exactly why, set in at some time in the 1950s. The nostalgic mood of the lecture suggests that socialism is to be seen as a Victorian project which ceased to be practical with the disappearance of the Victorian working class. That may well be the case, but Hobsbawm cannot bring himself to say so. As a Marxist, he insists that he is not a determinist; he deplores the sectionalism of the working class and the narrow 'economism' of trade union militancy[1] of the 1970s, but blames all this on failures of leadership ('the Wilson years') and laments the tragedy of it all, seeing that – or so he asserts – 'we are today in a period of world crisis for capitalism, and, more specifically, of the crisis – one might almost say the breakdown – of the British capitalist society, at a moment when the working class and its movement should be in a position to provide a clear alternative and to lead the British people towards it.'[2]

The importance of Hobsbawm's lecture, given in 1978, lay in the fact that he, no less, should express such gloom about the socialist project, and do so in the Marx Memorial Lecture. The notion that the Labour Movement might be in historic decline took on a new significance after the 1979 defeat and the debate reopened on the Left, conducted chiefly in the pages of *Marxism Today*. It is important to remember that Hobsbawm's pessimism contrasted in 1978, and still more when he came back to the subject in 1981, with a good deal of what – in the Marxist parlance – is called 'triumphalism'. For example, Hobsbawm's critics had taken encouragement from the following points:

1   That in 1979 the working class had at least repudiated the old consensus and indicated that it could no longer be governed in the old Wilson–Callaghan manner.

2   A rising tide of industrial militancy during the 1970s had shown the political muscle of the unions in the destruction of the Heath government in 1974.

3   The leftward shift in the Labour Party and trade union movement had resulted in the virtual abdication of the Jenkinsite right wing.

4   The Bennite Left had emerged, with Benn himself seen as a break with 'the squalid annals of Labour's lost leaders'.[3]

Writing in 1981 Hobsbawm found it necessary to point out that, 'If people don't vote Labour, there can be no Labour government, a fact sometime overlooked by enthusiastic militants.' In the circumstances of the 1970s he had pointed to the great illusion that militant unionism is enough. The even more dangerous illusion of the early 1980s was that '*organization* can replace politics'. Struggling to find a new way forward in the absence of a numerically predominant working class, and in the face of a general decline in class consciousness, Hobsbawm rejected the then-prevailing notion on the Left 'that all that stands between us and the next Labour government is a good left-wing programme for Labour and the proof that the party programme will not be betrayed.' He put it bluntly, to those who took this view, that Labour governments had not been defeated because of secessions of Labour voters disappointed with their records but because of Labour's failures to enlist people who ought to have been Labour voters, but no longer were. The only solution that he could see lay with what he called 'a broad progressive front', which although not specifically including the breakaway SDP – anathema to the Left at that time – would have to enlist the support of the people it represented who, he thought, ought to support the Labour Party and without whom the Labour Party would be electorally weakened. It was these remarks which led some to suppose that Hobsbawm, the guru of the Marxist left, was advocating some kind of electoral pact between the Labour Party and the Liberal–SDP Alliance. Hobsbawm denied this. He was unable to tell us how or why a broad progressive coalition could be expected to form around the flag of socialism, which he showed no willingness to lower. As his conclusion was that Labour's long-term decline will not be reversed unless such a broad coalition comes to accept 'the leadership of the Left' we are entitled to conclude that Labour's decline was, in his view, unlikely to be reversed.

I have dwelt on the controversies around Hobsbawm at some length for two reasons. One is because they convey the intellectual flavour of the times and help to explain the crisis in the Labour Movement which accompanied the advent of Thatcherism. The other is because the theories of Labour's decline tend to be attributed either to Thatcherites or to Social Democrats and dismissed accordingly, whereas Hobsbawm puts forward a *socialist* version of the possible demise of socialism which is essentially similar in its diagnosis. For we are here dealing with a moment of great political turmoil and ideological excitement in which reasonable people could variously suppose that the crisis of capitalism had arrived and that Thatcherism was the expression of it. Some went so far as to say it was a putative form of Fascism, or that the Labour Party was in the last throes of a terminal decline, presaging the ending of the socialist era. Within these extreme possibilities, realignment was in the air, the political ground trembling under foot. Perhaps it would turn out to be the most fundamental realignment since the decline and fall of the Liberal Party or the coming-of-age of Labour in 1945. And at the heart of it, for socialists no less than for anti-socialists, the future of the Labour Party was the fundamental question.

The 1979 defeat produced a rich crop of alibis on the left of the Labour Party the chief of which, as usual, was that socialism had not been rejected but betrayed – betrayed by those who had ignored conference decisions, abandoned the Bennite alternative economic strategy, and insisted on the 5 per cent pay policy. Although this view was at gross variance with the evidence of the opinion polls it served well to support the thesis that accountability was the key to the future triumph of socialism. If MPs could be made answerable to their constituency parties, and the parliamentary leadership to the extra-parliamentary movement, then there could be no more betrayals, and when 'Thatcherism' eventually resulted in the return of a Labour government, which it would, it would be a Labour government armed with a socialist programme the implementation of which would be guaranteed.

The long march through the institutions of the Labour Movement had begun in 1973. The story of the organisational advance of the Left between 1973 and 1981 has been well told by David and Maurice Kogan in *The Battle for the Labour Party*. It was in 1973 that Wilson had made it plain that if the Labour Party conference of that year had adopted a resolution calling for the nationalisation of the twenty-five leading companies he would not have had the slightest intention of implementing it in office.[4] 'I see,' he wisecracked at the time, 'they want to bring Marks and Spencer up to the standard of the Co-op.' The next year there were two million votes for the mandatory re-selection of MPs, the Campaign for Labour Party Democracy's first chosen instrument of accountability. Re-selection was carried in 1979 in the wake of Labour's electoral defeat. In 1980 the conference narrowly failed – by only 117,000 votes (with Neil Kinnock, on the NEC, voting against) – to capture control of drawing up the General Election manifesto. However, it voted to remove the election of the leader from the hands of the parliamentary party and at a special conference held at Wembley in January 1981 an Electoral College was established in which the trade unions and the local parties became the dominant forces. The CLPD had achieved a triumph of organisation, tactical manipulation and single-mindedness.

The claim that conference should decide was not a new one. It had been a recurrent cry on the Left which touched on a basic ambiguity in the Labour Party's constitution. Richard Crossman, always prefer-ring *Realpolitik* to constitutional nicety, had described the position exactly:

Since it could not afford, like its opponents, to maintain a large army of paid party workers, the Labour Party required militants – politically conscious socialists to do the work of organising the constituencies. But since these militants tended to be 'extremists', a constitution was needed which maintained their enthusiasm by apparently creating a full party democracy while excluding them from effective power. Hence the concessions in principle of sovereign powers to the delegates at the Annual Conference, and the removal in practice of most of this sovereignty through the

trade union block vote on the one hand, and the complete independence of the Parliamentary Labour Party on the other.[5]

This was the convention now to be overthrown, with the trade union
block votes forming alliance with constituency Labour parties against
the independence of the Parliamentary Labour Party. There was
nothing new, as I have said, in the constituency rank-and-file seeking
to resolve the ambiguity of Labour's constitution in favour of the
conference; what was new was the general fashion for participatory
democracy in which the enterprise could be clothed. The events of
1968 in France had helped to bring participation to the fore. Participation became the major student demand of the late 1960s and early
1970s. It was at once a practical claim to share in decision-making and
a challenge to established authority with revolutionary implications.
At the political level participation was no more than a new word for
the age-old challenge of direct democracy against the forms of
representative democracy, forms which had been made more hollow
by the scale and complexity of modern government. Bureaucracy was
one of the villains of 1968 and all that. The classical liberal model of
representative democracy had long since given way to a system, in all
industrial societies, in which groups of one kind or another were
admitted as valid participants in the decision-making process. As one
commentator put it, 'power sharing . . . was the necessary technique
of government' in modern industrial society.[6] The incorporation of
special interest groups in bureaucratic decision-making, however,
had taken place at the expense of political parties and over the heads,
it could be said, of the people at large.

In industry, participation could mean anything from management's emphasis on improved shopfloor communications, through
co-determination in the German-style (*Mitbestimmung*), to workers'
control which was the new left-wing syndicalism of the day. The
Labour Party had inaugurated a study into industrial democracy
under Jack Jones in 1968 and for the next decade worker participation
was in dispute between corporatists, syndicalists and those who
championed the representative form of democracy. Participation
became an issue also in local democracy, particularly in relation to
planning decisions. The Labour Party launched a campaign called
'Participation '69' with the claim that 'we are a democratic movement, hammering out our policies by argument and debate . . .' but
also with the admission that 'what has been needed is the opportunity
to involve local groups in the working out of our policies.'[7]

In each case what was involved was an opening-up, a 'democratisation', of the decision-making process. Who could be against that? In the process, however, the word democracy took on a new meaning: it applied no longer to the sovereignty of the people, *all* the people, but asserted instead the sovereignty of the members of whatever organisation it was – university, factory, church, political party. In the case of the Labour Party, the claim was that the rank-and-file (conference) should actually make policy and no longer be content to choose leaders, or representatives, to make policy for it. But the claim was entered in the name of the party activists, who were few, and dubiously representative of the party membership at large, which was small, and still less of the electorate as a whole. The claims of inner-party democracy took precedence over the older conventions of representative democracy, the chief of which was that government should be with the consent of the governed. Of course, the argument was not really about democracy in the abstract but about power – who decides. For example, the champions of Labour Party democracy were resolutely opposed to its being exercised on a one-person, one-vote basis. This, it has to be said, was put forward at a late stage in the argument by the defenders of the autonomy of the Parliamentary Labour Party and was intended as an outflanking device. Nevertheless, it exposed the nature of the Left's case for party democracy. Participation could not be extended to people who had not come to the meeting or heard the arguments; that would be to subvent the decision-making process to the manipulations of the media. The same arguments were used against postal ballots in trade unions, in favour of workplace ballots more easily dominated by the activists. Participation, in the Labour Party, meant rule by the party activists.

The Labour Party could scarcely have been more ripe for takeover than at the beginning of the 1970s. The once broad church had become a bare vaulted choir deserted by its congregation. Television and bingo had lured them away; education and greater prosperity had opened better horizons than the party meeting or social. The Welfare State had made Labour largely obsolete as the informal welfare agency it had been. The Labour Movement became a victim of its own success. Individual membership had peaked in 1951 at around 800,000. By 1979 it had declined to probably between 250,000 and 300,000. Hobsbawm was entitled to remark that Labour 'is probably less of a mass party at the moment than the Conservatives'.[8] A spiral of decline had set in: the less Labour was organised on the ground the less it could do for its people; the less it did for them the less it became organised. The planners and architects had played their part in this. The tower blocks of the 1960s were hostile grounds for recruitment and the collection of weekly subscriptions compared with the tight-knit street communities in which the old Labour Party had thrived. Not only was membership in steep decline, it was also ageing rapidly. Here is a description of the Newham North-East Party in 1970:

> Prentice's constituency Party in 1970 was a torpid affair run by a gerontocracy. Its Executive and general Committee were domin-ated by men, and a few women, in their sixties and seventies. The dominant group was a small knot of old local councillors. Most of the ordinary Party members were old too. Many wards did not bother to hold meetings.[9]

By 1979 it was estimated that less than half the Constituency Labour Parties had more than 500 members on their books and only 13 per cent – fewer than 80 parties – had a thousand or more. Most of these parties could be, and were, run by 30 to 50 people; perhaps there were some 50,000 activists spread across the whole country.[10] As Michels' 'Iron Law of Oligarchy' had recognised: 'It is only a minority which participates in party decisions and sometimes that minority is ludic-rously small.'[11]

Labour's 'ludicrously small' minority of activists became, with time, increasingly middle class. They were not necessarily of middle class origin but many were people who had by education, occu-pational advance or housing location moved on from the working class. The Labour Party in this way became increasingly detached from its traditional working class constituency although, at the same time, the change in its composition did in some part reflect changes which were taking place in society at large. The growth of the middle classes was caused not by any increase in the rate of upward mobility but primarily by the rapid expansion of public sector employment. The salariat grew from 18 per cent of the electorate in 1964 to 27 per cent in 1983.[12]

The 'new class' consisted predominantly of teachers and adminis-trators, lower managerial and professionals or semi-professionals. Its rise was reflected in the burgeoning bureaucracies of local govern-ment and the health service authorities in the 1970s and also in the rapid growth of middle class trade unions. In the manner of all new classes the 'new class' which grew up in the 1960s and 1970s was interested in status and in power. It challenged existing authority with a view to gaining better access for itself. Because many of the individuals concerned possessed a status that was lower than that of the professions – their positions were more in the character of being employees – they were not inhibited or squeamish about joining trade unions in large numbers. There was also, between 1964 and 1979, a 10·5 per cent swing to Labour among the professional and managerial classes, a small compensation for the swing away from Labour of from 3·5 to 8 per cent among the more numerous categories of skilled, semi-skilled and unskilled workers.[13]

The archetypal Labour activists of the 1970s were the NUPE organiser, the polytechnic lecturer, and the student agitator. It was they who were interested in constitutional reform, just as it was they who were most interested in Cambodia or unilateral nuclear disarmament; the ageing working class membership of the Labour Party, or what remained of it, was chiefly interested in housing allocations, hospital queues and welfare benefits – it did not much mind who wrote the manifesto or elected the party leader. The new model activist also soon discovered that organisation was fun. The long march through the institutions of the Labour Movement was better than the old trudge around the doorsteps collecting a few shillings a week. Campaigning for Labour Party 'democracy' was more like revolutionary activity; it was conspiratorial, disciplined and occasionally violent. The first stage was to gain control of a local party. This is what happened to the 'gerontocracy' in Newham North-East:

> In 1971 and the first half of 1972 there was a change in the nature of the party caused by an influx of very left-wing newcomers who became active within the party. They were young men and women in their twenties, mostly middle class professionals. Within a short time of joining the local party they became members of the general management committee. At a meeting of that committee on 2 December 1971 there were two very left-wing activists present out of an attendance of twenty-nine. At a meeting on 24 May 1972 there were seven present out of twenty-seven. At a meeting on 27 September 1972 there were eleven present out of thirty-two. Thus, by the summer of 1972, the left-wing activists constituted about one-third of attendants at meetings of the general management committee.[14]

'Entryism' of this kind required dedication and long hours, for an important part of the technique was to keep the meetings going until all good moderate people had gone home to bed. The power of the political activist derives from being unlike other people with normal lives to lead, careers to pursue, families to attend to, other interests to distract. Thus it was, by one little *coup d'état* after another, that the grass roots of the Labour Party were captured in the name of democracy until, in the aftermath of 1979, the sovereignty of the parliamentary party could be overthrown from below.

The civil war which engulfed the Labour Movement after the election of 1979 was conducted as if it were an ideological war, at the centre of which was the battle for democracy, but in truth it was a struggle for power. The struggle was fought between the parliamentary party and the extra-parliamentary party. It was also a struggle for the succession to James Callaghan with Tony Benn now striding to the fore to claim the inheritance of the 1970s.

The Labour Party conference at Brighton in the autumn of 1979 was like a show trial. Members of Parliament, who are entitled to attend *ex officio*, were arraigned like traitors to their class on bleachers at the side of the hall, adjacent to the platform, where they were frequently harangued and abused by fist-shaking delegates from the floor. The party's general secretary, Ron Hayward, although a paid official, played the role of prosecutor-in-chief. To cheers and applause, he said:

> You have got to ask yourself: why was there a Winter of Discontent? The reason was that, for good or ill, the Cabinet, supported by MPs, ignored the Congress and the conference decisions. It is as simple as that.

For many it was just as simple as that. When wars are lost it is of comfort to the troops to believe themselves betrayed by their generals, lions led by donkeys. All of the disillusion and hate, built up since the Wilson years, was now let loose. But the truth was that there was little, if any, evidence to suggest that the policies advocated by the conference would have proved more congenial to the electorate than those put forward in the party Manifesto.

On the eve of the 1979 conference, Austin Mitchell, who had succeeded to Crosland's seat at Grimsby, published a Fabian tract which pointed out that 86 per cent of the electorate had wanted to see bans on secondary picketing, 75 per cent were in favour of the sale of council houses, and 60 per cent wanted to bring back the grammar schools. Labour had opposed these policies. On the other hand, only 24 per cent thought fee-paying schools should be abolished, only 20 per cent wanted to abolish the House of Lords, and only 38 per cent wanted to give trade unionists seats on company boards. All of these were conference policies.[15]

Yet for the Left the abolition of the House of Lords was the test case of parliamentary accountability to the conference. Callaghan was alleged himself to have struck the proposal from the Manifesto. Tom Litterick, a leftist MP who had lost his seat, described how while the NEC had been trying to work the conference's decisions into the Manifesto, Callaghan had turned up.

'That is what he did to your policies,' said Litterick, scattering a handful of papers from the rostrum. '"Jim'll fix it," they said. Aye, he fixed it. He fixed all of us. He fixed me in particular.'

However, the campaign for inner-party 'democracy' fed on the myth of betrayal. In 1979 it came into its own. There were by now three prongs to it. One was the mandatory re-selection of MPs. A second was the election of the leader. The third was control over the Manifesto. Re-selection had been on the agenda since 1974. It would have been carried at the conference of 1978 had not Hugh Scanlon, in typical AUEW-style, mislaid his union's card vote – accidentally-on-purpose it was widely suspected. There was no doubt that re-selection would carry in the atmosphere of the 1979 conference, and it did, by four million to three million votes. The principle that the Manifesto should be written by the NEC, and the NEC alone, was narrowly adopted, but the amendment to the constitution required to give effect to this was postponed, as a result of tactical manoeuvring, to the following year. The question of who should elect the leader of the Party – the parliamentary party or the extra-parliamentary party – had been first raised in 1976. A compromise proposal for an Electoral College, representative of the whole Labour Movement, had been voted down in 1978. In the recriminatory atmosphere of 1979 there was an increased enthusiasm for wresting the election of the leader from the parliamentarians, but no agreement as to how this should be done. Meanwhile, however, the matter would fall within the terms of reference of a Commission of Inquiry and would return to the agenda the following year.

The establishment of the Commission of Inquiry was a crucial development. It was the source of much future disaster for the Labour Party. There would flow from it Michael Foot's accession to the leadership and the breakaway of the SDP. It was the brainchild of senior trade union leaders, chief among them David Basnett, the general secretary of the General and Municipal Workers, shortly (with the addition of boilermakers) to become the inelegant GMBA-TU. We have no need to rehearse in full the saga of the ill-fated, and mishandled, Basnett inquiry.[16] Basnett, like former general secretaries of his union, had lived his life in the shadow of the Transport and General Workers' union. Now he saw it as his chance, with Jack

Jones retired, to become the dominant figure on the trade union scene. He had the ego and the vanity for the job but few of the other qualities required. In Healey's book he was 'as wet as water'. He was a man who needed to be seen coming and going at Number 10 but there the door had now been closed by Margaret Thatcher. The role that remained open to him was to be the saviour of the Movement. But as Alex Kitson, the left-wing leader of the Scottish transport workers, was overheard to say in one of the bars of the Brighton conference centre, 'With Basnett for a foe, we'll n'ae need friends.'

Never for a moment was he in control of the Commission of Inquiry. The party NEC was under complete left-wing tutelage. It was in a position to determine the membership of the Commission and ensured it a built-in left-wing majority. It had 14 members but the parliamentary party, whose autonomy was at stake, was represented only by Callaghan, Foot and Norman Atkinson, who sat on the NEC *ex officio* in their capacities as leader, deputy-leader and treasurer. Atkinson was, in any case, a left-winger.

At various points of the proceedings Callaghan was urged to dissociate the parliamentary party from the Inquiry, insist that the unions withdrew from it, or to stand down from the leadership to make way for Healey while there was yet time. He did none of these things. 'I have as little authority in the PLP as I have in the NEC,' he told one of his aides, who added: 'The Left are the masters now.' 'Let me take the shine off the ball for a bit,' said Callaghan to Healey, who by early 1980 was urging Callaghan 'to fight or go'. Callaghan did not wish to go yet; he was enjoying his new role as international elder statesman, he was looking forward to a visit to China that year.

Moreover, he believed that he could 'work from within' to defend the prerogative of the parliamentary party and that, in the end, as on so many previous occasions in his long, long experience, his union friends would come to the rescue. That was his mistake. It was characteristic of him, endemic in everything he was and stood for and believed. He had been around for too long to be expected to realise that the unions, far from being the upholders of the Labour Movement, had become one of the chief agents of its destruction. Even the experiences of the Winter of Discontent, which had left him feeling deeply betrayed, had not shaken the underlying belief, inculcated in him by history and his whole life experience, that the trade unions and the Labour Party were as one, 'This great Movement of ours'. His view, at bottom, was the trade union leaders' own view. 'It's our party. It always has been,' said Basnett. This proprietary sense runs through the history of the Labour Movement, it guided Ernest Bevin after the débâcle of 1931, Jack Jones after the 'In Place of Strife' confrontation, and now, after the calamity of the Winter of Discontent, it was the instinct of a lesser breed of men at Congress House.

As the trade union establishment now saw it, the Labour Party was 'on the blink' and needed sorting out. Who else was to do that if not the unions? They had little if any sense, however, that something historic or disastrous was in the making. 'A misunderstanding among gentlemen over *crème de menthe* should not be made into a fundamental division over Marxism,' said one. That was a large part of the problem. The union leaders felt, instinctively, that they owned the Labour Party but their proprietorial responsibility tended to be spasmodic and erratic; their attention span for Labour Party matters was brief. Trade union general secretaries are, in the first instance, territorial barons, preoccupied with their own organisations, pursuing their own aggrandisements, and prosecuting their own feuds. At the TUC they play politics on a larger scale, as statesmen of the trade union movement, but to the Labour Party executive they send their deputies, or their deputies' deputies. At the Labour Party conference once a year it is the great men themselves who brandish the voting cards before the television cameras, but for the remainder of the year precious little of their time is devoted to Labour Party affairs. The way the block votes are cast is determined, in most cases, by the way their own conferences voted months beforehand; these conference decisions may themselves be the outcome of intra-union politicking, the product of deals without very obvious connection with the interests of the nation or even the Labour Party. In 1980, for example, the AUEW was in the throes of crucial elections and locked in power struggles between its various constituent elements. Moreover, the two most powerful natural political allies on the Right, the AUEW and GMBATU, were engaged in a bitter industrial dispute concerning laggers on Canvey Island. The autonomy of the PLP was at stake but, for David Basnett, who should organise the laggers was a more constant preoccupation.

The union leaders of the Right had no desire to see the conference being allowed to elect the leader of the Labour Party. For that would mean, in practice, that the union block votes would elect him or her. Such an arrangement would invite opprobrium both within the Movement and in the country at large. In any case the union leaders preferred power without responsibility. They wanted to be the king-makers but not the king. The best solution would be to leave procedures as they were but, unfortunately, the supporters of the status quo had been manoeuvred into a minority position on the Commission. The Commission had been their idea, or at least Basnett's idea, and a failure to agree would be embarrassing. In any case, the trade union way is always to compromise: in a dispute between God and Satan, the instinct would be to split the difference. Another factor was that Basnett, and some of the others, had not forgiven Callaghan for leading them down the garden path to the General Election which never was in the autumn of 1978. Still more bitterly did they blame Healey for the 5 per cent pay policy which, as they saw it, had caused the Winter of Discontent.

It was considerations of this character which, in the summer of 1980, were allowed to determine the fate of the Labour Party. Later, the union leaders' vindictive feelings against Healey played their part in the elevation of Foot to the leadership and, in the following year, in Benn almost capturing the deputy-leadership. But we are anticipating. The Basnett Inquiry was to complete its report at a week-end conference at the ASTMS college in Bishop's Stortford in mid-June. On the eve of the meeting attempts were made in the Shadow Cabinet to ensure that Callaghan and Foot would in no circumstances betray the autonomy of the parliamentary party and make it the poodle of the conference. These moves had led to sharp exchanges. Callaghan was resentful of the mistrust implied. How could he go to a conference with his hands bound, unable to negotiate? How could a leader of the Labour Party refuse to negotiate with union leaders? It was his duty to do all that he could to hold the Movement together and his colleagues would simply have to trust him.

As it turned out, their fears were amply justified. It was agreed at Bishop's Stortford that the election of the leader should be vested in an Electoral College representative of the whole Movement, although no one had been able to agree on the composition of such a college. It was also agreed that the Commission should recommend that responsibility for drawing up the Manifesto be removed from the Shadow Cabinet and vested solely in the National Executive Committee, although the Electoral College should have the final say. In addition, mandatory re-selection of MPs was endorsed by seven votes to six. Callaghan had been outwitted and outvoted. He might hope, as he did, that the party conference at Blackpool in October would reject the Commission's recommendations, but the principle of an Electoral College had been conceded. He and Foot returned from Bishop's Stortford like Chamberlain and Halifax from Munich.

One view at the time was that how the leader was elected did not matter terribly. Certainly there were those who believed that mandatory re-selection of MPs and control over the Manifesto were more important battles for the parliamentarians to fight against the extra-parliamentarians. It was pointed out that in many other countries, Sweden, Germany, The Netherlands and Denmark among them, all respectable havens of Social Democracy, the leader was elected by a franchise wider than that of Parliament alone. Be that as it may, the merits of the case for or against the Electoral College which had been agreed in principle within the Commission of Inquiry were no longer the point: a Holy War had been joined which neither side could afford to lose. It is not unusual for great contests to come to their head around issues of secondary importance (take the Reformation for example). In any case, in retrospect it is by no means clear that the changes in the Labour Party's constitution made in 1980 were not every bit as important as their protagonists believed. Neil Kinnock, for example, according to his biographer, had no doubt that history was being made when at Blackpool, in that October, the conference at last voted for the College:

> The conference broke into prolonged applause. Callaghan, who had opposed the motion, looked grim. The most remarkable platform demonstration was given by Neil Kinnock. 'To this day,' recalls one MP, watching from the floor of the hall as the delegates cheered, 'I can see Kinnock leaping around with his hands clasped above his head. He went crazy. He knew what it meant for him.'[17]

This must be so; for it is hard to imagine Kinnock, no great House of Commons man, who had held no office of any kind, becoming leader under the old system whereby the choice rested solely with MPs voting in secret. It is equally hard to imagine that MPs would have supposed in 1980 that Michael Foot was the man to lead them into the next General Election, and into the future, had not the sword of re-selection dangled over their heads and had not the prospect of the Electoral College undermined the legitimacy of their proceedings. For these reasons alone, the turning which the Labour Party took at Blackpool in 1980 was a fateful one.

The conference took place on the 600th anniversary of the Peasants' Revolt.[18] By the time the delegates and the attendant hordes of hangers-on converged upon the Winter Garden in Blackpool, two things were clear. One was that Callaghan was about to go and that there would be a struggle for the succession. A new priority had arisen on the Left: it was 'Stop Healey'. The second was that the launching of a new party, talked about all year, was now a real possibility. The 'Gang of Three' – David Owen, Shirley Williams and William Rodgers – had in August published in the *Guardian* a manifesto which, in effect, set out their terms for remaining in the Labour Party. These plots now unfolded against the background of the Chinese-style Cultural Revolution which raged through Blackpool. The foyer of the once-exclusive Imperial Hotel was like a Soviet permanently in session; the environs of the conference hall were ankle-deep in leaflets and revolutionary newspapers; on the floor of the ornate and gilded ballroom, a fine theatre for politics, the new Labour Party, the product of a decade and more of desuetude and decay, of entryism and militancy, was now on display. Class hatred was rife. Speakers who attempted to stand against the tide were subjected to venomous hissing. Healey, particularly, was denounced as the man 'who led the advance against working people', under the Callaghan government. On the fringe the Left drew huge crowds. Tony Benn moved from meeting to meeting, as if blessed with ubiquity, to be greeted with revolutionary adulation. In a keynote speech to the conference, tumultuously received, he promised that the next Labour government would obtain powers to nationalise industries, control capital and introduce industrial democracy 'within days', would restore all powers from Brussels to Westminster 'within weeks', and – to loudest cheers of all – would abolish the House of Lords, first by the creation of a thousand peers and then by the abolition of the peerage.

If Benn's speech was triumphal, and shamefully demogogic, Callaghan's speech as leader had the air of a Farewell Address, spoken by a beaten man in sorrow. 'We're all comrades,' he declared plaintively: 'for pity's sake stop arguing,' were his last words of advice. The power struggles in the party had left him powerless to stem the tide of policy. He could not fight on more than one front; scarcely had he been able to fight on one. That summer the Campaign for Nuclear Disarmament had marched unimpeded through the union conferences and now, at Blackpool, Callaghan was obliged to watch the party declare itself for unilateral nuclear disarmament. Whereas Gaitskell in 1960 had pledged himself to 'fight, fight and fight again', Callaghan now was powerless. Moreover, the conference declared itself for Britain to be taken out of the European Community, this time with no nonsense about a referendum.

'There is no doubt at all that the British Labour Party conference is the most democratic body of its kind in the world,' said Benn at the end of the week. In my *Guardian* column I wrote:

My nightmare of the week is that political liberty is now at threat in Britain, for I cannot feel confident that it would long survive the coming to power of the people who have taken hold of the Labour Party . . . Not many of the lay delegates who spoke this week seemed to be speaking out of working class experience; more often they mouthed the jargon of paperback Marxism. The participatory revolt which has rocked the Labour Movement is the revolt of the *lumpen polytechnic* . . . [The] three tests of a viable democratic socialist party – its commitments to a mixed economy, to internationalism and to representative democracy – were failed at Blackpool this week.

It depended, perhaps, on what you meant by democracy. For many, quite evidently, the 1980 conference in Blackpool was an exhilarating and liberating experience; for others it was deeply appalling and truly frightening. For some it marked the triumph of Bennism, for others the end of the Labour Party they had known and loved. One must be careful, especially from a growing distance in time, not to exaggerate the excesses of popular democracy. Today most would endorse Joseph Chamberlain's response in 1877 to the critics of his own espousal of extra-parliamentary democracy, the *caucus* as it was then called:

Those who distrust the people and do not share Burke's faith in their sound political instincts – those who reject the principle . . . that the best security for good government is not be found in *ex cathedra* legislation by the upper classes for the lower, but in consulting those chiefly concerned and giving shape to their aspirations wherever they are not manifestly unfair to others – these all view with a natural apprehension a scheme by which the mob, as they are ever ready to term the great bulk of their countrymen, are for the first time invited and enabled to make their influence felt.

Benn might have spoken in very similar terms in Blackpool that week as the 'mob' rampaged through the Winter Garden. But Chamberlain's 'mob' was a pejorative expression for the people, whereas this Blackpool mob represented the people only to the extent that it was the vanguard for the historical march of socialism. The people themselves, asked by Gallup where, for example, they stood on unilateral nuclear disarmament, had on the eve of the conference declared 21 per cent in favour and 67 per cent against. Among Labour's own supporters 26 per cent were in favour, 61 per cent against. Moreover, in its frenzy of democracy the conference had voted for the compulsory repurchase, at below market prices, of the council houses of which their working class tenants had become the owners. Whom did that decision represent? Not the 75 per cent of people who had in 1979 approved of this policy but the 19 per cent who had been against it. The more accountable to its various factions the Labour Party became the less representative it became of the wider public. At Blackpool in October 1980 the Labour Party, in the name of democracy, finally parted company with the people.

All else flowed from that. The way was now open for Michael Foot to become leader when 70 per cent of the public thought Healey was the man for the job. Among Labour voters the preferences were Denis Healey 38 per cent, Tony Benn 17 per cent, Shirley Williams 8 per cent, Michael Foot 7 per cent, and Peter Shore 2 per cent. The choice still lay with the parliamentary party, for at Blackpool the conference had failed again to agree the modalities of the Electoral College and that was to be done at a special conference at Wembley in January. To the Left's great fury Callaghan had stood down all the same, precipitating an election under the old rules. If he still wanted Healey to succeed him he had left it far too late. Benn was ordered by his zealous cohorts not to stand but to await the legitimacy of the College. Foot had decided also not to stand but was prevailed upon by his own vanity, his wife, and the determination of his friends (who included Neil Kinnock) to stop Healey at all costs. Some of the union leaders who had helped matters to reach this pass now put their weight behind Foot as the man who could bring peace in their time to the warring Labour Movement. Fearful now of re-selection, many MPs were reluctant to declare openly for Healey, although for the last time the ballot remained secret. Healey reminded them of the Christian Democratic slogan in the Italian elections of 1948: 'In the secrecy of the polling booth God can see you but Stalin can't.' There was a fear that if Healey were elected the legitimacy of the contest would be challenged and a new contest called in the Electoral College, which Benn might win. Foot was the lesser of two evils. Some, on the hard Left, made no secret of regarding Foot as a suitably ineffectual stop-gap until Benn could mount his challenge. At the age of sixty-seven Michael Foot became leader of the Labour Party.

The spoilt baby of his distinguished family, he had remained an *enfant terrible* until in 1974 at the age of fifty-eight he had condescended for the first time to accept the responsibilities of office as Secretary of State for Employment. Until that time he had preferred the luxuries of opposition, to which his temperament was suited, and studiously avoided acquiring any of the skills of modern government; he was ignorant of economics, unversed in nuclear strategy or the affairs of the European Community, a stranger to Washington. His interests were literary and rhetorical and it is likely that he knew more about the eighteenth century than his own. Loved by his friends, captivating when talking of books and bookmen, he was a House of Commons man although, in my opinion, a somewhat stagey speaker more suited to ranting in Trafalgar Square. A lover of Parliament, he was a great respecter of tradition and opponent of all parliamentary change. He did not bother himself with the detailed drudgery of committee work but, most afternoons, was to be seen in his place below the gangway, the leader of the Tribune Group, heir to the mantle of Aneurin Bevan, whose hagiographer he was. He attributed Bevan's attachment to the expensive Ivy restaurant to the 'good anti-Fascist record' of its Italian proprietor.

During the first Wilson government he had refused all office and railed against all encounters with reality. By then an amiable, and for the most part harmless rebel, he insulated Wilson against the full venom of the Left and in this way was a useful accomplice. In 1974 his first task as Secretary of State for Employment was to buy off the striking miners, which he did by meeting their every demand in full. Thereafter Congress House was treated as if it were a department of government, even having papers circulated. In 1975 he was obliged to bring himself to terms with the need for pay restraint – inflation was at an annual 27 per cent – and this was regarded as a great act of statesmanship on his part. Why growing up at the age of almost sixty should have been thought a matter for special congratulation is not clear. However, Foot's acquiescence in the government's accommodations with the hostile world of the 1970s were important for its stability. For on the backbenches he had been the left-wing conscience of the party.

He contributed to Labour's débâcle in 1979 by his role in talking Callaghan out of going to the country in the autumn of the previous year. But his most profound disservice to his party was reserved for the year 1980 when, having played Halifax to Callaghan's Chamberlain at Bishop's Stortford, he took it upon himself to become its leader. Quite unfitted for the office of Prime Minister and hopelessly ill-equipped to fight an election in the television age, he led his party to catastrophe. The eccentricities which his friends found so endearing in him – the flowing mane, the shabby clothes, the stick – were an image-maker's nightmare. His appearance in a casual duffel coat at the nation's annual Service of Remembrance at the Cenotaph, as if he were attending the CND's Aldermaston March, did him powerful and lasting damage. His invocations of the 1930s and of 1945 stirred old folk memories but meant little to the electorate of the 1980s. Probably few young voters had heard of Aneurin Bevan. Foot appeared to the country as the walking past. It was a shameful betrayal. In the self-indulgence of pure principle, patrician sentimentality and an old man's vanity, the working people of Britain for the first time since 1945 lacked a proper champion.

At Wembley the Labour Party put the finishing touches to the job done at Blackpool. Much energy and cunning was invested in a battle about whether the parliamentary party should have 50 per cent of the votes in the Electoral College, which is what the PLP wanted, or less than half. Foot backed the PLP formula and lost. So much for Foot as the man who could unite the party. The sovereignty of the parliamentary party was ended. The Electoral College was constituted on the basis of 40 per cent of the votes belonging to affiliated unions and 30 per cent each to the parliamentary party and the constituency labour parties. This represented a tactical triumph for the Left although it owed a great deal as well to disunity and incompetence on the Right.

The next day the first public step was taken to launch the new Social Democratic Party. In the words of the declaration issued at Limehouse by the 'Gang of Four' (Roy Jenkins, David Owen, Shirley Williams and William Rodgers):

> The calamitous outcome of the Labour Party Wembley Conference demands a new start in British politics. A handful of trade union leaders can now dictate the choice of a future Prime Minister. The conference disaster is the culmination of a long process by which the Labour Party has moved steadily away from its roots in the people of this country and its commitment to parliamentary government.

There then began the final and most bitter stage in Labour's civil war. This was the symbolic struggle between Denis Healey and Tony Benn, the old guard against the vanguard. Ostensibly they were contesting the deputy leadership of the party but in reality they were engaged in a fight to the finish for possession of the Labour Party.

The deputy leadership itself is an office of no great consequence, more often used as an honourable repository for passed-over leaders than as the last stepping-stone to the top. With it, however, went an *ex officio* seat on the National Executive Committee, a matter of some importance in the context of the power struggle raging within the party. The Left was in complete control of the NEC, with Benn in a powerful position as chairman of the home policy sub-committee. In recent times no right-winger had stood the slightest chance of election by the constituency section, with the bizarre result that, in government, Labour's senior parliamentary figures played little role in party affairs. On the famous occasion, for example, on which Healey as Chancellor of the Exchequer had announced to the 1976 party conference that he would be making application to the IMF for a traditional loan, he had had to make do with four minutes at the rostrum, like any other rank-and-file delegate, much of it lost in boos and catcalls.

Healey had been elected deputy leader without contest after he had lost the leadership to Foot in November. Like Foot he owed his position wholly to the parliamentary party. Now, the leader and deputy leader were to be elected annually by the whole Movement through the Electoral College as constituted at the Wembley conference. So it could be argued that Healey no longer had legitimate title to his office and should be opposed in the name of democracy. But the same could be argued exactly of Foot's position. However, if Benn were to challenge Foot he would lose without doubt. A challenge to Healey therefore was his only next move. This could be rationalised in all manner of ways. One argument was that the new constitutional machinery must be put to use or the Right would soon set about dismantling it. Another was that by forcing the Right to rally around Healey the Left could protect the organisational and policy gains made since 1973. A tactical reason was that the trade unions were now the chosen arena for left-wing advance and a contest in the Electoral College would provide the opportunity for mounting organisational campaigns within the unions. But the overwhelming reason was that Benn by now was the undisputed hero of the Left and that the time had come to show Foot and the parliamentary party who was the true master.

As we have said already, no one – Margaret Thatcher apart – embodied the spirit of the times better than Benn. He was an authentic voice of post-imperial Britain and an exponent of the politics of decline. He was a product of the new age of nationalism and a formidable opponent of Britain's membership of the EEC. He was a mature student of the class of '68, and no one more than he personified the cultural revolution which had swept through the

Labour Movement. An outsider himself, not by birth or origin but through some demonic aspect of his personality, he became the scourge of a failed ruling class and a champion of the aspiring new élites who had been liberated and enthused by the experiences of 1968 and thereafter.

He was never at ease with what he took himself to be. When first elected to Parliament for Bristol in 1950 he announced that he intended to lose the stigma of being an intellectual, to which Crosland (who liked him) rejoined, 'You had better acquire the stigma before worrying about losing it.'[19] Although he could be wildly funny, and occasionally self-deprecating, there was always an earnest, holier-than-thou side to his character. Class guilt was deep in him as in many Englishmen of his generation and background, which was similar to Michael Foot's in that he came from a distinguished, well-off, radical family. Sometimes he would apologise for his privileged circumstances while stressing the 'radical, dissenting and socialist tradition' to which he belonged. At other times he would disown his background, expurgating Westminster School and New College, Oxford from his *Who's Who* entry, as if in an official Soviet biography. Somewhere along the way the Honourable Anthony Wedgwood Benn became plain Tony, and Citizen Benn.

This suggests some personality change but it was not so. 'Wedgie', as his friends called him, was given to enthusiasms no less than the later Tony Benn. One of his earlier ones was public relations. There was the air of a keen public schoolboy about him; he was often to be seen in bicycle clips. In the 1960s Wedgie liked to be 'with it', especially with the gadgetry of the times. There was something in him of Toad, who – you will remember – fell in love with the motor car in the wreckage of his Romany caravan, sitting by the roadside saying, 'Poop, poop. Poop, poop'. One craze gave way to another in Benn's case, and his ideological enthusiasms of the 1970s grew out of the wreckage of the technological enthusiasms of the 1960s. He lost interest in lasers and took up the Levellers. Chartists replaced computers in his affections.

Like Gladstone, he moved leftward as he grew older. He liked the idea of having set out from the House of Lords to finish on the barricades. He could not bear the idea, it was said, of being out-flanked by his own children who were of the 1968 generation. An accomplished dialectician, a brilliant debater from his Oxford Union days, he was never short of arguments in which to clothe his radical progress. But we may suspect that his 'conversion' in the early 1970s was not so much a blinding moral insight into the iniquities of capitalism, or the belated intellectual discovery of its contradictions, as a passionate falling-in-love with the working class.

His romantic attachment to the workers was matched by a growing hatred of his own class and, perhaps – although we can only guess this – of himself. At first his affectations seemed harmless enough, if somewhat foolish – the miners' banner aggressively displayed in his ministerial office, his labourer's tin mug transported around the country with him like a royal chamber pot. But by the mid-1970s he had become increasingly unable to resolve the conflict between the Outsider and the Insider within himself. His outsider role by now made him an impossible colleague but as an insider, to the manner of the Despatch Box born, he lacked the daring, or the confidence, to stake all upon his own Destiny. Had he done so by resigning in 1975, when Wilson vetoed his industrial strategy and banished him to the Siberia of Millbank,[20] his unsullied credentials as the alternative leader would after 1979 have been hard to gainsay.

As it was, he had by then the air of a man of destiny come too late and in too desperate a hurry. He declined to stand in the 'Shadow' Cabinet elections of 1979. But this was a retrospective dissociation of himself from the Wilson–Callaghan governments, the first of many such acts, infuriating to his colleagues, especially those such as Kinnock, who had declined to serve under what Benn now called 'labourist' governments. The decision also enabled him to transfer his energies fully from Westminster to the country and may have represented – although we do not know exactly what was in his mind – a decision to adopt an extra-parliamentary strategy in a more precise sense. A customary first step by a man of destiny is to take his case to the people, over the heads of parliaments, parties and politicians. While he was within the Wilson and Callaghan governments, although increasingly dissident, he had never entirely burnt his boats. At the farewell dinner given for Wilson at Number 10 it was Benn who had provided the wittiest turn of the evening, mocking himself by reading extracts from an obituary of Wilson he had written for *The Times* in the 1950s. While in government he had kept his lines open to the capitalist press and, some of us suspected, his options open too. He was as always courteous, and eager to listen – wherein lies much of the secret of political charm. His ability to distinguish the real from the ideal was at that time unimpaired.

After 1979, however, he increasingly, and in the end entirely, severed his contacts with the orthodox world and moved in an ever-more sectarian world of his own. He aligned himself with various 'hard' Left groups, including the Rank and File Mobilising

Committee (known as the Dank and Vile Mobilising Committee), an umbrella organisation which included the Militant Tendency. The amiable pottiness of his earlier life was beginning now to take a more sinister form, although the old 'Wedgie' in him was occasionally evident, as when he extended his open-house principle to the Posadists, a sect which believes that socialism will be brought to earth from outer space by extra-territorial beings who have achieved a higher level of technological development and, *ergo*, must be socialists.[21]

Like Lenin, he would admit to no enemies on the Left. He happily accepted support in his bid for the deputy leadership from people who had no place in any democratic socialist party. Michael Foot observed sadly how he was to be seen these days intently studying obscure revolutionary newspapers. His vocabulary became more and more extreme, and more strikingly paranoid. Constant vilification goes to the head in much the same way as celebrity; as early as 1975 the *Daily Express* had published a picture of him wearing a Hitler moustache. Now, he was happy to equate Thatcherism with 'Fascism', a word which in semi-private he would throw out in a studiedly casual and matter-of-fact way.

It is easier in retrospect to see how Benn's career became a pilgrimage of self-destruction which led him, like Enoch Powell, whom he in several ways resembles, beyond the fringe and beyond the pale of British politics. Men of destiny seek proof of their greatness by exercising a licence to go too far, and as the fear grows in them that destiny may have played a terrible joke on them, so they double and redouble the stakes on the wheel of their own fortune. In this way they destroy themselves. In Benn's case, at least for the purpose of explaining what happened in the Labour Party after 1979, the task is not to identify his fatal flaw but, rather, to locate the sources of his huge charisma. For he inspired devotion in his followers far greater than the contempt in which his colleagues had learnt to hold him. He packed great halls, the length and breadth of the land, arousing more excitement than any one-man cause since Chamberlain.

He preached mainly to the converted. Or, rather, he converted mainly his own party, transforming it ideologically and organisationally. This was a major feat and a matter of great importance. It was essentially on his programme that the 1983 General Election was fought, and calamitously lost. The constitutional changes which he powerfully helped to bring about registered a substantial leftward shift in the gravity of the Labour Party and opened the way to the succession of Neil Kinnock. In more indirect fashion Benn contributed to the schism of the party in 1981, for it was his maverick scheme for a Common Market referendum which he forced upon the Labour Party in 1972 which provoked the resignation of Roy Jenkins and formalised the split with the old Gaitskellite wing of the party in a way that was never to be healed. In these ways he was, after Thatcher, the most powerful agent of political realignment.

Benn was the apostle to the 'new class', numerous enough to make a revolution within the Labour Party but not numerous enough to constitute a majority in the land. To capture the party and to lose the country was the entire nature of the Bennite phenomenon. It was well illustrated during the by-election at Glasgow, Hillhead in March 1982. Benn arrived during the last few days and packed a large school hall and two overflow rooms with a crowd of some 1,500. He was in cracking inspirational form but his audience, bussed in to working class Scotstoun from all over greater Glasgow, consisted of the new Labour Party, predominantly middle class (in the sense of being educated) people, from the universities and polytechnics, the local authorities and trade union offices throughout the conurbation. The next lunchtime, outside the gates of the Yarrow shipyard, fewer than a hundred workers were gathered to listen in dispirited fashion to the Labour candidate. The seat was lost to the SDP, to Roy Jenkins no less.

The message which Benn brought to his mass audiences was highly congenial to the new classes. He told them that the old system was corrupt and finished, the consensus broken and Keynes dead. They, and the energy in them released by the events of 1968 and thereafter, represented the future. It was they, he told them, who had broken through 'the façade of ritualised parliamentary exchanges about which leadership could run the system best'.[22] He appealed to the resentments of an excluded and aspiring élite; he told them they had been betrayed by an effete and treacherous ruling class which had placed Britain in colonial tutelage to the Pentagon, the Common Market and the IMF. Bennite populism appealed to class resentment and hurt national pride, which were the essence of the politics of decline. And as always with fundamentalist preachers or demagogues, the remedy was blindingly simple and consisted in the coming of the socialist light. The Blackpool conference speech, cheered to the gilded roof of the Winter Garden, had come near to saying that Jerusalem could be built in weeks not months.

Benn was obliged to conduct an extra-parliamentary campaign for the deputy leadership, for he could not expect much support from his parliamentary colleagues. That was the more so after the polarisation of the Tribune Group around his personality into 'hard' and 'soft' Left factions and John Silkin had entered the race as the 'soft' Left candidate. An outspoken indictment of Benn's intimidatory style and tactics by Neil Kinnock in Hull had an important influence in the creation of this split on the Left. Kinnock, referring back to the Blackpool speech, accused Benn of 'offering a fantasy that insults adult intelligence, invites derision and guarantees disappointment.'[23]

As the unions commanded 40 per cent of the vote in the Electoral College it was necessary for him to campaign vigorously at their seaside conferences all through the summer. In any case, it was the next tactic of the Rank and File Mobilising Committee, which ran his campaign, to politicise the unions. Some organisational inroads were made as a result but the chief consequence was to split the trade union movement at all levels along the same ideological flaw as the Labour Party. Another consequence was to expose the shortcomings of trade union internal democracy. No thought had been given as to how individual unions would discharge their new responsibility to elect the parliamentary leader of the Labour Party and thereby, in effect, perhaps the Prime Minister of the country. The scandals which arose around the wielding of block votes in the Electoral College gave the Conservative government its opportunity to propose a third trade union Bill, this time to regulate the conduct of inner trade union democracy. The unions had invited this outcome by the casual and half-hearted way in which they had extended their suzerainty over the Labour Party, increasing their power but not their responsibility.

Healey won the election by the narrowest fraction: by 50·426 per cent to Benn's 49·574. Kinnock in the end abstained, together with a number of other Tribunites, and this was enough to deny Benn his victory. From that moment the split on the Left was irrevocable and bitter. The result could be seen as a moral victory for Benn. He had commanded, remarkably, more than 80 per cent support among the constituency rank-and-file and two-fifths of the union block votes. It was a humiliating outcome for Healey and for Foot. Yet at the same time, or so it turned out, the deputy leadership contest marked the turning of the leftist tide. The pre-emption of the Electoral College by Callaghan's resignation before the Wembley conference could take place had denied Benn the chance of contesting the leadership in the only forum in which he could have hoped to win. Thereafter his bid for the deputy leadership was bound to be seen by some, such as Kinnock, who had no use for Healey, as an unnecessary and divisive act. This was especially so after Foot, who commanded affectionate loyalty if not much else, had appealed to Benn either not to run at all or to run against him for the leadership itself. The tactics employed by Benn's supporters, and the ultra-leftist company he seemed happy to keep, gave further offence.

That autumn Foot sought to rehabilitate Benn within the Shadow Cabinet but he behaved in such recalcitrant fashion that no reconciliation was possible. The following year the Right, by then somewhat more organised, regained a tenuous control of the NEC. Benn was purged from his key position as chairman of the home policy sub-committee. He became more and more *outré*, following his Enoch-like path to the very limits of the political wilderness. In 1983, partly as the consequence of the programme he had wished upon the Labour Party, although chiefly due to boundary revisions, he lost his seat in Parliament. This made him ineligible to contest the succession to Foot. The Electoral College which he had played so prominent a part in bringing into being now conferred the leadership on Neil Kinnock, the chief instrument in halting the forward march of Tony Benn. Within two years of his near-triumph Benn was down and out, finished, politically dead.

His legacy remained, however. The Campaign for Labour Party Democracy had achieved most of its goals. The parliamentary leadership had been made more accountable to the extra-parliamentary party. Meanwhile, socialist policies were in place. A broadly Bennite economic and industrial strategy had been adopted. The conference had espoused unilateral nuclear disarmament and had stated its intention to take Britain out of the EEC. The conditions had been created for a victory for socialism. All that was now required was a victory for the Labour Party.

7

The Birth of the Social Democrats

The Labour Party was the victim of economic decline and social change. The Social Democrats were their offspring. The crisis which engulfed Labour after the General Election of 1979 was the midwife which brought the new party into being in the spring of 1981 but the SDP was a child of the times in more fundamental ways. During the 1970s British politics may be described as consisting of a two-party system from inside which a third party was trying to get out. There had been a Liberal revival in 1962 with the advent of Orpington Man[1] but the return of a reforming Labour government in 1964 had put a damper on it. The Liberal revival resumed with the Heath government of 1970 and in the General Election of February 1974 the Liberals, who in 1950 had scored only 2·5 per cent of the votes, won 19·3 per cent (21 per cent in England), although this brought only a meagre harvest of 14 seats. Through the 1960s and 1970s the Liberal vote tended to move up, ratchet-like, although somewhat erratically, rising under Conservative governments and falling under Labour governments. From 11·2 per cent in 1964 it had increased to the dizzy 19·3 per cent in February 1974, from 7·5 per cent in 1970 to 13·8 per cent in 1979.

The recovery of the Liberal Party was only one aspect of a general malaise of the two-party system in the 1970s. In Scotland the Scottish National Party experienced a meteoric ascent. From a sensational by-election victory in Hamilton in 1967 the nationalists won 11·5 per cent of the votes in Scotland in 1970 (giving them one seat), 21·9 per cent in February 1974 (7 seats) and 30·4 per cent in October (11 seats). In Wales nationalism was less rampant but it had been on the increase since 1966 when Plaid Cymru won the Carmarthen by-election. In the 1966 General Election it took 4·3 per cent of the votes in Wales, in 1970 it scored 11·5 per cent and more than 10 per cent in both 1974 elections.

Nationalism was a phenomenon with its own roots, chiefly linguistic in Wales, but in Scotland with the wealth of the North Sea ('Scottish oil') stirring historic memories of nationhood. Essentially it was a form of protest, by the periphery against the centre, and a part of a pattern of protest in which the Liberals had a share. While the by-election successes of the Liberals implied a rejection of the two-party choice nationally, the nationalists in Scotland and Wales were rejecting it locally. A revulsion against the two largest parties was an aspect of the ungovernability of the 1970s.

In the 1951 election the two main parties had between them monopolised 96·8 per cent of the votes cast. In 1970 they still had the support of 91·5 per cent. In the two elections of 1974 their share had fallen to just over 75 per cent. From 1945 to 1974 there were on average 13 minor party MPs; the two elections of 1974 returned 37 and 39.[2]

The volatility of the electorate was another sign that allegiance to the two-party system was breaking down and in the two elections of 1974 nearly a third of the electorate voted for parties other than Conservative or Labour. By-elections in the 1960s and 1970s frequently resulted in huge swings against the government, which had not happened in the 1950s. Opinion polls in the 1960s and 1970s discovered around three times as many 'don't knows' as in the 1950s. There was the marked decline, noted by Ivor Crewe, in voter identification with both established parties.

The hankering by the electorate for a third party was not new but it grew stronger in the 1970s. Over the post-war period opinion polls had consistently discovered some 40 per cent of the electorate to be sympathetic to the idea of coalition (in 1967 Gallup put it at 52 per cent) but this may represent not much more than vague desire to escape from party politics. Voters were also telling the pollsters how they would be ready, in considerably greater numbers, to vote Liberal if only they could believe that the Liberals had some real chance of winning. This was the 'wasted vote' syndrome, a heavy handicap on a third party in a two-party electoral system.

In September 1972 an ORC poll commissioned by *The Times* reported that 35 per cent of respondents claimed that they would vote for a 'left-of-centre' party composed of an alliance between the Liberals and Labour moderates such as Roy Jenkins and Shirley Williams, who were at that time at war with their own party over the Common Market. Some 40 per cent said they would vote for an alternative, centrist alliance between the Liberals and Tory moderates. When similar questions were put by ORC in January 1980, after Roy Jenkins had mooted the notion of a new party of the 'radical centre' in his televised Dimbleby Lecture, 55 per cent favoured such a party. However, only 23 per cent professed themselves ready to vote for the left-of-centre alliance of Liberals and moderate Labour, and only 16 per cent for a simple breakaway party. While both these polls cast doubt on how much 'cashable' electoral support there would be for a realignment in the centre they clearly revealed a high level of disaffection with the existing party system and a wide sense of disenfranchisement through the choice on offer.

The notion of realignment had been around for a long while. The maverick voice of Woodrow Wyatt had proposed a Lib–Lab pact after 1959 as a means of dislodging the Conservatives from what at that time had begun to look like a permanent ascendancy. In 1965, when the Wilson government had an overall majority of only three (later to be reduced to one), the then leader of the Liberal Party, Jo Grimond, proposed a coalition the purpose of which, he insisted, could not be simply to maintain Labour in power but, rather, to bring about a radical realignment:

> We must mobilise the great central body of opinion for a long campaign of reform. I am more than ever certain that what Britain needs is a vehicle for Liberal or radical progress, not for a year or two, but for a decade at least.[3]

The *Guardian* took up the cause and went so far as to urge a merger of the two parties into 'a single reforming movement on the Left'. In offering this advice, however impractical, the *Guardian* was reverting to an old tradition, for its most famous editor, C. P. Scott, had from 1912 consistently championed a progressive alliance between Liberals and Labour. Scott could not believe that the British worker, individualistic and acquisitive in spirit, would ever embrace socialism. In one of his very last editorials he wrote:

> The time may not be very far distant when real political affinities may assert themselves and a great middle party be formed out of the existing progressive forces of the country.[4]

Wilson's landslide victory in 1966 dished Grimond's dream of what he called a 'non-socialist radical party'. The realignment he had hoped to see was postponed for another fifteen years. He wrote later in his autobiography:

Our strategy depended upon the Labour Party or some part of it being convinced that, as a socialist party committed to public ownership of all the means of production, distribution and exchange, it had a poor future. The state of public opinion pointed to a realignment. There was a hope that the full-blooded socialists would split off to the left leaving a radical party on the left of centre of British politics but free of socialist dogma.[5]

Realignments in party politics of the kind that Grimond had in mind are rare phenomena and usually associated either with war, which hastened the demise of the historic Liberal Party after 1914 and ushered Labour to majority power in 1945, or an extension of the franchise, as after 1867,[6] or with the rise of a new class or interest in the land, the Peelite middle classes of the 1840s and the trade unions in the 1880s and 1890s. Was there any comparable development in the 1960s and 1970s which would be capable of sustaining a realignment less ephemeral than the politics of by-election protest? Not unless the new 'post-materialist' middle class proved adequate to the task. This phenomenon had been identified in the late 1960s with the help of elaborate multinational surveys by the American political scientist, Ronald Inglehart. His thesis was that the 'formative affluence' of the post-war period, combined with an unusual absence of war, had resulted in a generational change in attitudes to give higher priority to post-material, or 'post-bourgeois' values and a lower priority to material needs or aspirations. These values did not fit easily into the conventional spectrum of Left–Right issues.

> The strongest indicators of whether one is on the Left or the Right are the new political issues, such as support for liberalising abortion and support for the peace movement, at the leftist pole; or support for nuclear power plants, belief in God and patriotism at the other pole. In short, the *issues* that define Left and Right for Western publics today are not class conflict, so much as the polarisation between the goals emphasised by post-materialists, and the traditional social and religious values emphasised by materialists.[7]

In part post-material politics were a revolt against parental affluence, which at its extreme took the form of middle class terrorism as practised by the Baader-Meinhof gang and its successors. In this respect it was likely to be temporary and may already have been superseded by what we might call *post*-post-material politics as here described by Peter York:

Today's teenager has discovered something a little more pleasant than poring over the garbled philosophy of third-rate continental novelists, than trying to look gaunt and angst-ridden. And what is it, that glorious land over the adolescent rainbow? Is it the Land of Oz, the yellow brick road, Dorothy and Toto? No, it's dinner for two at the Chelsea Wharf, a Porsche and an American Express card, even if we can only gaze at them in the pages of *Harpers* and *Queen*. It is having money, the money our babyland parents would not give us . . .[8]

However, post-materialism could be seen as something more than reaction against too-comfortable affluence; it could be seen as the ideological expression of the emerging 'post-industrial society'. That phrase, originally coined by the American sociologist Daniel Bell, referred to a society in which knowledge played the central role in determining power and wealth, a society which therefore placed a premium on higher education and advanced technical skills. It was characterised by the decline of manual work and the predominance of the service sector. In such a society the middle classes became more radical, the working classes more conservative. The theory, if true, would help to explain a number of related phenomena which stretched right across the spectrum of Western politics – enthusiasm for participation and freedom of information, the growth of the peace movements, the emergence of 'Green' politics, the new importance of sexual politics, the anti-statism of the Right and of the Left. It is part of the other side of the coin of the decline of class-based politics, the polarisation of politics around issues which cut across class and party lines.

Inglehart and his colleagues found post-materialist values to be less prevalent or, at least, less relevant to the political process in Britain than in many European countries. The reasons are not surprising. Britain's politics in the late 1960s and in the 1970s were the politics of decline. If the post-industrial society was characterised by its educational attainment then Britain was not a post-industrial society. One American commentator has suggested that one mark of the post-industrial society is that at least 40 per cent of its school leavers should enter college education. The United States achieved that level in about 1963. Even by 1984 only 15 per cent of British school leavers entered higher education. Nevertheless, there does seem to have been some kind of generational change after 1968 or thereabouts, a change which contributed to a different mood and a different political style. Inglehart's thesis helps to explain middle class protest in all its forms – the march of the Bennites through the Labour Party, the anti-collectivism of the New Right, the resurgence of the Liberal Party and the birth of the SDP. In Britain's case these developments were constrained largely within the two-party system but in the multi-party societies on the Continent the most striking phenomenon of the 1970s was the rise of Green politics at the expense of the New Left. In Britain, a similar though less pronounced realignment may have been taking place within the new middle classes, at the expense of the Labour Party and to the benefit of what was to become the Liberal–SDP Alliance.[9]

At the same time, the imposition of middle class values and priorities on the Labour Party helped to alienate still more its traditional working class supporters. This had happened to the Democratic Party in the United States when it became the party of peace and pot in 1972, when George McGovern was its presidential candidate. It happened to the German Social Democratic Party (SPD) as it became increasingly involved in ecological, libertarian and peace campaigns. The process reinforces the tendency of the middle classes to move left and the working classes to move right in the context of post-industrial society.

However, we shall not make too much of this as a factor contributing to a realignment in the centre of British party politics. When Roy Jenkins delivered his Dimbleby Lecture in November 1979 he could point to no new block of voters entering the electorate, nor to any new class or interest arisen in the land, but only to a widespread dissatisfaction with party politics as presently organised and conducted. As president of the Commission of the European Economic Community in Brussels, Jenkins was at that time in political exile, the king across the water or – as the joke was – Le Roi Jean Quinze. He called his lecture 'Home Thoughts from Abroad'. It addressed not merely the shortcomings of the political parties and the politicians but what he took to be a crisis of the system. The party system had worked well enough for a while after the war but as Britain fell progressively behind the countries which had participated in the formation of the EEC the politicians had made more and more extravagant promises of faster economic growth. Their failure to achieve this had bred disillusion with the system for which his remedies – scarcely exceptional – were greater continuity of policy and moderation of language. But turning then to the institutional framework of party politics he declared that the case for proportional representation had become 'overwhelming'. This was important for, although the prospects of proportional representation being introduced were virtually nil, it signalled to the Liberals – by pre-arrangement with David Steel – that there was a basis on which they and the Jenkinsite elements in the Labour Party could form common cause. His remedy for decline was in essence the adoption of continental-style Social Democracy, a goal which had eluded the right wing of the Labour party since Hugh Gaitskell's ill-fated attempt to emulate the German SPD and repudiate doctrinaire, Clause 4 socialism. 'We need,' he said, 'the innovating stimulus of the free market economy without either the unacceptable brutality of its untrammelled distribution of rewards or its indifference to unemployment.' This, he went on to say, somewhat cautiously and modestly, could be 'assisted by a strengthening of the radical centre'. That was it, apart from the inevitable quote from Yeats about how, otherwise,

> The best lack all conviction, while the worst
> Are full of passionate intensity

and thus:

> Things fall apart; the centre cannot hold.[10]

A 'radical centre', was this not a contradiction in terms? In the then atmosphere of British politics, so it seemed to many, Margaret Thatcher had expropriated radicalism for her 'conviction politics', Tony Benn for his campaigns for inner-party democracy and left-wing socialism. To be sure, a great many people disliked this intense partisanship and ideological polarisation. The people were consistently more moderate than the parties.[11] But that did not mean that they would vote for a moderate centre party. There was a paradox here. The centre was simultaneously sought after and despised. 'All centre and no circumference,' said Harcourt of Randolph Churchill's plan to form a new party.[12] His was a typical attitude. Similar jokes were made about Jenkins's project. 'Thought of joining myself,' said Lord Thorneycroft, then the chairman of the Conservative Party. 'After all it isn't a party; it hasn't a programme and I'm told the claret is very good.'[13] It was discovered that Jenkins himself had said in Oxford in 1973:

> There has been a lot of talk about the formation of a new Centre Party. Some have even been kind enough to suggest that I might lead it. I find this idea profoundly unattractive. I do not believe that such a group would have any coherent philosophical base.

People might not like a great deal of what the two major parties stood for but that did not stop them complaining perennially that the third party did not seem to stand for anything either. The more policies it published, the more they would complain. A party in the centre was 'neither fish nor flesh, nor good red herring.' Moderation was a bit like a health food, good for you but rather dull: when it came to it, people preferred meat to muesli. Who went to moderate plays or looked at moderate paintings? Even moderates seemed to prefer immoderate newspapers. It is striking too how moderation in politics is frequently championed by immoderate men. Cicero is the best example. Danton is another. It is the usual fate of the heroic moderate to become caught in the crossfire of revolution and reaction.

It is, perhaps, an endemic feature of class-based, two-party politics that voters have great difficulty in recognising any other kind of party as being a real political party at all. In British politics the centre was not an idea but simply a place, the no-man's-land between the trenches of the class war. One reason why third parties had failed to prosper was that the two major parties, for all their Manichaean rhetoric, had remained singularly adept at contesting the centre ground between the trenches. That, according to the conventional wisdom, was where elections were won or lost. Now perhaps the conventional wisdom had been cast aside with Thatcher and Benn. Jenkins plainly thought so.

A passionate man beneath his fastidious surface, he had always been of the moderate tendency. His father, Arthur Jenkins, was a miner who had risen within the South Wales Miners' Federation to a safe seat at Westminster, where he had become Attlee's Parliamentary Private Secretary. Arthur Jenkins had been sent to prison for nine months for an incident during the General Strike. This had been kept from the young Roy, who was five at the time, and he learnt about it only by accident years afterwards. Great pleasure was taken in the Labour Party at the thought that the Jenkins family regarded the matter as a social disgrace rather than a noble martyrdom in the workers' cause. It is true that Roy's background was more lower middle class than working class. He saw little of the inside of the chapel and had little of a Welsh accent to lose by the time he reached Oxford, although it was said that even the slight impediment to his speech was an upper class affectation. The union had sent his father up to Ruskin College where he had become a linguist, continuing his education in Paris; the young Roy's early gastronomic experiences were in Paris. At home in Wales his mother kept a maid. The family could afford to send Roy to Balliol as a fee-paying commoner. He took to Oxford with effortless superiority. He was, he said later, 'a great believer in not working excessively long hours.'

His friendship with Hugh Gaitskell was more personal than political but he became one of the group dubbed by Aneurin Bevan as 'revisionists'. He was welcome in the salons of New York and Washington and admitted to the Kennedy circle. Like Gaitskell, he had a talent for friendship but, in general, preferred the company of women to that of men. When in London he seldom dined alone. He wrote an elegant life of Asquith with whom, perhaps, he identified as a latter-day Whig. He was a social and literary success before he became a political one.

Europe was his first cause. It resulted in a painful, although temporary, estrangement with Gaitskell and more lasting estrangement with his own party. Under Wilson he became a reforming Home Secretary and then a successful Chancellor, although he was blamed for losing the 1970 General Election through fiscal probity. As heir to Gaitskell he was regarded by Wilson with the utmost suspicion. He invited some suspicion by his liking for cabal and he was invariably surrounded by a group of devoted acolytes and protégés – Roy's boys.

His position became somewhat more comfortable when in 1967 Wilson, with a show of great enthusiasm, espoused the Common Market. The enthusiasm lasted only until the election. Jenkins, for his part said, 'I believe that what was right in 1967 is at least as right in 1971.' He found himself now the leader of the pro-European faction of the Labour Party and felt obliged, on 28 October 1971, to lead 68 MPs against a three-line whip into the lobby in support of a motion approving Britain's belated entry into the European Economic Community. Later, he resigned the deputy leadership of the party in protest against the referendum on continuing membership of the Community to which a future Labour government became committed, at the instigation of Tony Benn.

These were fateful events. The 1971 split over Europe prefigured the schism of 1981. One result was that the pros and antis broke party ranks to fight the referendum in 1975. Jenkins quickly learnt to prefer the company he kept in the 'Britain in Europe' campaign to the company he was obliged to keep in the Labour Party. His dedication to the European cause made him increasingly isolated within his own party. When Wilson resigned the leadership in 1976 Jenkins could muster only 56 votes on the first ballot against 90 for Michael Foot and 84 for Callaghan. In the deputy leadership contest in 1970 he had beaten Foot by 133 to 67. This was a measure of the party's leftward shift. From time to time he complained. In 1975 he said: 'Unions are and should be an important part in our national life. But they should not usurp the functions of the government. They should certainly not be asked to tell the government what to do.' The next year he said: 'I do not think you can push public expenditure significantly above 60 per cent and maintain the values of a plural society with adequate freedom of choice. We are close to one of the frontiers of social democracy.'

The former Gaitskellites now commonly described themselves as social democrats. It was a long while since Jenkins had thought of himself as a socialist. His European enthusiasm had made him increasingly aware of the virtues of Social Democracy in the German style. That is where Gaitskell had hoped to go with his campaign in 1960 to expunge Clause 4 from the party constitution. In 1959 at their Bad Godesberg conference German social democrats had come to terms with the market economy and had abandoned statist socialism. Gaitskell had tried to follow suit after the 1959 defeat but had failed. Now prospects of making the transition to Bad Godesberg from inside the Labour Party were even more forlorn. Beleaguered on the European front, the Jenkinsites were discredited and inhibited from fighting on the ideological front. It was during this time that the social democratic cause within the Labour Party was lost.

Ironically his European convictions debarred Jenkins from the Foreign Office in the eyes of the Labour Party. When Callaghan refused it to him, he accepted the presidency of the European Commission in Brussels and retired from British politics. The President of the Commission is an office not without honour but largely without power. It is a job more suitable for a Permanent Under-Secretary than a Cabinet Minister. Jenkins's skills were not of the bureaucratic kind, his style was to rise laconically to the great occasion. The influence which a President can exercise on member governments is not commensurate with the salary they afford him or the pomp which goes with the job, the white-gloved butler and the large black limousine. Roy Jenkins lived well but not happily in Brussels.

He had left England believing himself a political failure. That was one reason why he was now eager to return. 'My adrenalin is flowing again,' he said. 'The sap is rising in my old bones.' Perhaps what had been lost from within the Labour Party could be regained from without. What had now to be done, he said in his Dimbleby Lecture of 1979, was 'not to slog through an unending war of attrition, stubbornly and conventionally defending as much of the old citadel as you can hold, but to break out and mount a battle of movement on new and higher ground.'

The invitation was plain enough. It was by no means welcome to all who heard it. Most of Jenkins's friends had tried to dissuade him from saying what he said. The timing was premature, the game not yet lost in the Labour Party, or so they thought. But Jenkins had told them, 'You don't get asked every year to give the Dimbleby Lecture.' The leading Social Democrats in the Labour Party fell over each other to disassociate themselves from the notion of a centre party. Shirley Williams declared that such a party would have 'no roots, no principles, no philosophy and no values'. David Owen described Jenkins's initiative as 'a dastardly act' and told his friends, 'It is important for people to realise that some of us who are staying to fight are doing so not simply because we think that Roy's party won't take off.' Owen, in fact, believed that it might well take off. William Rodgers, although the closest of them to Jenkins, also believed the best hope still lay with fighting to save the Labour Party from inside although he did, in a speech on 30 November, warn that the Labour Party had only one year in which to save itself.

These statements are of some importance because they remind us of people's intentions at the time. Following Jenkins's lecture, and as the crisis in the Labour Party deepened, talk of a new party became incessant; slowly the assumption built up that, in the end, something would happen. But what? Jenkins had not committed himself to a new party, he had spoken of 'strengthening the radical centre'. It was not ruled out that he and his political friends, who were mostly now out of Parliament, might join the Liberal Party. This was not David Steel's wish. Since becoming leader of the Liberal Party in 1976 his aim had been to lead it out of protest into power. To the first Liberal Assembly which he addressed as party leader he said:

We must not give the impression of being afraid to soil our hands with the responsibilities of sharing power. If people want more broadly based government they must vote Liberal to get it. And if they vote Liberal we must be ready to help provide it.

Power-sharing became his consistent theme; patiently Steel set about educating his unruly and recalcitrant party in the virtues of governmental responsibility and the tactical necessity of coalition. The Lib–Lab pact, which between March 1977 and August 1978 sustained the Callaghan government, was a one-sided arrangement but it enabled the Liberals to brush shoulders with power. With the Conservatives now back in office Steel could rely on the cycle of protest resuming; the Liberals could hope to harvest a few more seats but there was no hope of a breakthrough into power. His life would be wasted in the futility of permanent opposition. If the mould was to be broken a new departure was required, something capable of firing the imagination of the electorate, a force more credible than the Liberal Party which he led, the limitations of which he knew too well. The best hope that he could see lay with a social democratic break-out from the Labour Party; in electoral alliance with the Liberals that might stand a real chance of cracking the system; the total, he reckoned, would be greater than the sum of its parts. Jenkins's commitment to proportional representation would help Steel to sell this project to his party. Meanwhile, he urged Jenkins – with whom he was in frequent touch – to stay his hand and await events in the Labour Party which, Steel hoped, would drive the social democrats into his arms.

The timing of the Dimbleby Lecture had been unwelcome to the Labour Party dissidents because there was nothing they could say or do until the battles inside the Labour Party had been fought to the end and lost. That outcome was not yet certain. At least they would have to wait until the conference at Blackpool and for Callaghan to step down. Much therefore depended on Healey. He was their last best hope. The trouble was that his own best hope was of succeeding Callaghan quietly. His chances of becoming leader rested entirely with the parliamentary party. If the election was thrown open to the Movement he would be bound to lose. The trade union leaders had not forgiven him for the 5 per cent pay policy and Basnett, in particular, was ready to wage vendetta against him even at the cost of making Foot the leader; he was the *bête noire* of the constituency parties to the same degree that Benn was their darling. The sooner Callaghan stepped down, the greater Healey's chance of inheriting the leadership and digging in; but if he played it rough with the Bennites, or put public pressure on Callaghan to fight or go, he risked opening the way to Foot as the man who might least split the party. So, through most of 1980, Healey complained in private and in public kept his head down and his mouth shut.

The Bishop's Stortford meeting was his downfall. His fatal error was to allow himself to be compromised by Callaghan and Foot. He took no stand on the principle of the autonomy of the parliamentary party or, at very least, the election of the leader according to one person, one vote. He clung still to the hope that by attaching himself to Callaghan he could succeed him. When members of the Gang of Three (Owen, Williams and Rodgers) inquired of his position before the Blackpool conference he admitted that his attitude was that he would accept an Electoral College if it could be constituted on a basis which would endorse his leadership. So much for principle, they thought. Now no one trusted him: the Left believed that he would split the party, the Right that he would flinch from doing so. The Footites now could argue that for the PLP to choose Healey would be to invite a challenge to him in the Electoral College and open the way to Benn. The Bennites calculated that they could make Foot their prisoner while Healey might somehow contrive to overthrow or defy the organisational advances they had made. The social democrats believed they could no longer rely on Healey as their champion although, had he won, and in spite of his take-it-or-leave-it attitude towards them, the schism would at least have been postponed.

After the Wembley conference, and the subsequent breakaway to form the SDP had occurred, Healey considered very seriously putting himself at the head of it. He had no doubts as to where the future of the Labour Party must lie if it was to have one. The transition to Bad Godesberg could no longer be delayed. The Thatcher government's liberal economic approach made it all the more urgent for Labour to abandon its old-style socialist dogmas and adopt the social market approach. Gaitskell had been right, but he had taken a hammer to the party tablets; Healey had hoped to succeed where Gaitskell had failed. Austria was his favourite model. In a lecture delivered shortly before Jenkins's Dimbleby Lecture, but scarcely noticed, he had said:

> Austria came to terms with its political and economic disadvantages after the war, jettisoned those parts of its Marxist ideological inheritance which were obviously no longer relevant, and turned a country which in the inter-war years had been suffering from an ex-imperial hangover into a model welfare state, without sacrificing any of its cultural attractions in the process.

He was offering no New Jerusalem, he went on to say, 'simply a country with stable prices, jobs for those who want them and help for those who need it.' If he was to offer more who would believe him? To achieve his Austrian dream would be to achieve more than any post-war British government had managed.[14]

In the same lecture Healey quoted some words of the émigré Polish philosopher, and the historian of Marxism, Lesjek Kolakowski. I want to requote them at some length not only because they are noble words but because, eighteen months later, at the launch of the SDP they were used by David Owen to convey what he took to be the quintessence of social democracy:

> The trouble with the social democratic idea is that it does not stock and does not sell any of the exciting ideological commodities which various totalitarian movements – Communist, Fascist or Leftist – offer dream-hungry youth. It is no ultimate solution for all human misery and misfortunes. It has no prescription for the total salvation of mankind, it cannot promise the fireworks of the last revolution to settle definitely all conflicts and struggles. It has invented no miraculous devices to bring about the perfect unity of man and universal brotherhood. It believes in no final easy victory over evil.
>
> It requires, in addition to commitment to a number of basic values, hard knowledge and rational calculation, since we need to be aware of and investigate as exactly as possible the historical and economic conditions in which these values are to be implemented. It is an obstinate will to erode by inches the conditions which produce avoidable suffering, oppression, hunger, wars, racial and national hatred, insatiable greed and vindictive envy.

These were Healey's values. With Roy Jenkins out of Parliament he would have made the obvious and natural leader of a party which, unlike the Labour Party, might hold them dear. Ancestral loyalty held him back. So did his knowledge of international politics, for wherever the Left was divided on sectarian or religious lines the hegemony of the Right prevailed, while wherever the Right was divided between Catholics and Protestants, Conservatives and Liberals, or farmers and industrialists, a united Left became the natural majority. Healey could see no future for a social democratic party cut away from its trade union base.

Holding him back also was an indomitable optimism, the vast resilience of his spirit and the huge stamina of his frame. He was frequently accused of being a politician of no fixed belief – ideas yes, plenty of them, but no settled convictions. This was neither fair nor true, for he was a cultured man imbued with civilised values, who trod his way undaunted through a wicked world armed with the incrementalist creed described by Kolakowski. An ounce of such values is worth a pound of ideological belief. However, Healey was a true believer in one respect: he had an unshakable faith in the proposition that it would all be all right on the night.

Partly this was born of an immense confidence in his own abilities, a confidence which was well justified. A powerful brain, agile intelligence, combined with a good memory and a driving energy, had made him into a political polymath. He was an expert in international relations who could hold his own in the dismal sciences of strategic theory and economic practice. He could sing German drinking songs and tell dirty jokes in his Eighth Army Italian, he could give interviews in French on monetarism or nuclear strategy. At home the cloakroom in his hall housed an eclectic collection of gramophone records numbering thousands; his library included shelves of poetry and the *avant garde* novels he had read at Oxford. He claimed to have introduced Iris Murdoch to Beckett's *Molloy*. He was a great name-dropper, usually of international statesmen – Robert McNamara and Helmut Schmidt were among his favourites – but if it was not them it would be 'Claudio' (Abbado) or, if he was trying to fix something with the unions, Charlie Kelly of ACATT. He liked to be one up. He was the most enjoyable politician of his day.

In his own party he was regarded as an intellectual bully. True, he would often begin a remark with the words 'With respect' and then proceed to flatten the recipient without the slightest respect. However, he could take as good as he would give, was of thick skin and cheerful disposition and bore no grudges. Fastidiousness is usually the inhibiting vice of the intellectual in politics but not in Healey's case. Rather he believed himself to possess a special understanding of power and its uses. This made him a bit of a thug. Like Machiavelli, he was neither surprised nor shocked when he found principle to be at variance with practice and he regarded the truth as no more than one good to be set against another as necessity required. He may have acquired these habits of mind as a youthful recruiter for the Communist Party and, later, as an apparatchik at Transport House.

Yet when the time came for him to bid for power he had no cabal of political friends to call upon. He did not even possess an indexed book of their home telephone numbers. Denis Healey had always walked alone. His mother has recounted how as a boy, out walking with his family on the moors above Leeds, he would walk ten paces or so ahead of everyone else. Now he was the despair of his campaign managers. Many of the MPs whose votes he now sought were numbered among the fools he had failed to suffer gladly down the years.

In the first Wilson government he had been Secretary of State for

Defence throughout and presided, though reluctantly, over Britain's withdrawal from east of Suez. That was when he had learnt to think about the unthinkable and he had played a part in equipping NATO with a new strategic doctrine, that of Flexible Response. In the second Wilson administration and in Callaghan's he had been Chancellor of the Exchequer throughout and, as we have already said, equipped the Treasury with its new strategic doctrine: monetarism – a doctrine some would say of inflexible response. In truth his mix of monetarist and fiscal policy struck a good balance between curbing inflation and not curbing production but his own party would not soon forgive him for having compromised with what, in economic terms, was to them the equivalent of Satanism. In terms of experience, knowledge and intellect he towered high above his rivals. He was a big man in every sense. He was the only man equipped to become Labour's next Prime Minister. But his party no longer required these qualifications in a leader.

Healey was effectively one of the founding fathers of the SDP. Had he become leader of the Labour Party there would have been no breakaway, or at least not until he had been given a chance to restore the position of the parliamentary party, reverse the policy decisions on nuclear weapons and the Common Market, and abandon the Bennite economic strategy. Had Healey stood and fought when he could, Callaghan and Foot might never have sold the pass at Bishop's Stortford and then, too, the political map might have been different. But what happened happened. In their Open Letter to the *Guardian* on 1 August 1980 the Gang of Three in effect set out the terms on which they could remain in the Labour Party. These could be interpreted as, first, the leader of the party must continue to be elected by the parliamentary party or, failing that, on a one-person, one-vote basis; second, Britain must not disarm unilaterally and must remain a member of the European Economic Community; and third, the next leader of the party must uphold these positions. 'We are not prepared', they said, 'to abandon Britain to divisive and often cruel policies, because the electors do not have an opportunity to vote for an acceptable socialist alternative to a Conservative government.'

Their experiences at the Blackpool conference made up their minds for them. By the end of that horrendous week in which the Labour Party appeared to have succumbed to what Shirley Williams had called 'the Fascism of the Left', they were prepared to go. Only if Healey won might they have been deterred. Essentially what had happened was that the broad church of the Labour Party, into which the broad Left had moved, would no longer serve as a sanctuary for moderates. The social democratic project had ceased to be realistic within the Labour Party. As one of the Gang of Three saw the prospect: 'An endless succession of Kinnocks and Hattersleys and never again a Gaitskell.'

It happened that during the conference I dined with the three of them together in a small Italian restaurant. Neil Kinnock and some friends were at another table and there were shouts of 'Claret, claret' as we came in. I was asked my advice on what they should do next. I said that for some while I had seen no prospect of the Labour Party becoming an effective social democratic force but that I was a journalist, with nothing to lose or gain, while they were politicians in the prime of their promising careers and it was no use their supposing they would be back in their Rover cars with their red despatch boxes at the next election. The last realignment in British politics had taken from 1918 to 1945 and what they were envisaging would take at the very least ten years to come about. I added that there must have been a good few rising politicians in the last Asquith administration whose names were now lost to us. I was told that I was unduly pessimistic.

Between Blackpool and Wembley there were doubts and hesitations, second and third thoughts, backsliding and slipped disks, but on the day after the Wembley fiasco the Gang of Four, as they had become with Roy Jenkins's arrival at Dover, issued the Limehouse Declaration which said, *inter alia*:

> We do not believe in the politics of an inert centre merely representing the lowest common denominator between two extremes. We want more, not less radical, change in our society, but with a greater stability of direction.

The three who were leaving the Labour Party, tearing up the roots of a lifetime, were not interested in 'a strengthening of the radical centre' as proposed by Roy Jenkins, already deracinated, in his Dimbleby Lecture. Their project was to replace, and eventually to bury, the Labour Party. We must make allowances for emotional attachments, for the rationalisation of life-long convictions, for the horrors of apostasy. When men and women make dramatic departure they do so usually in the name of consistency, believing that it is not they but the world around them which has changed. Those who broke with the Labour Party in the charged atmosphere of early 1981 did so in the name of such consistency of purpose. It was their values which would march on. Shirley Williams, for example, wanted an 'absolute commitment to equality and classlessness'. It was not democratic socialism they were abandoning but the Labour Party which had abandoned democracy. Owen, who from being the most opposed to a break had become the driving force behind it, had had no doubt that if a new party was to be created it was to be a *social democratic* party. Even at that time he was cool towards the Liberals. He saw no role at all for David Steel in what was being projected; eventually there would have to be some kind of electoral arrangement but the first task and absolute priority was to get the SDP off the ground.[15] (Shirley Williams's attitude at that time was 'to hell with the Liberals'.) Like her, Owen continued to speak the language of socialism. The first chapter of the book he published to coincide with the official launch of the SDP was headed, 'The Values of Socialism'. For Owen at that time the terms socialism and social democracy were interchangeable:

> For all socialists, whether they use the label social democrat, democratic socialist, or whatever position they may occupy in the political spectrum of socialism, there is common ground in one particular set of beliefs, the need to redress poverty and to reduce inequality.[16]

There were many such statements at the time. In part they reflected old habits of mind, in part perhaps an emotional need to reaffirm old commitments, but they leave no doubt that the SDP was originally conceived – although not by Jenkins – to stand within the socialist tradition. Furthermore, although an alliance with the Liberals might be a necessary electoral convenience, there was no thought of any marriage of minds. The Liberals were amateurs, the SDP was a party being launched by professional politicians; the Liberals were all things to all voters, the SDP was emphatically to be a party of the Left.

But what did these refugees from the Labour Party mean by social democracy? Essentially they still meant what Gaitskell and Crosland had meant: equality and the redistribution of wealth created by economic growth. But equality had its price in liberty and the joining together of the words socialism and democracy had always begged one of the fundamental questions of political philosophy. For a while Crosland, with the powerful assistance of Keynes, appeared to have solved it: socialism could be, as Gaitskell had said, 'about equality' provided there was growth. But socialism had never really been about wealth creation. It had been about wealth distribution. Of course, the old revisionist approach could be made to seem eminently reasonable when set beside the Bennite socialism adopted by the Labour Party. By 1981 to call for the reinstatement of Keynes and Crosland was to beg some large questions. As Ralf Dahrendorf joked, they seemed to be 'promising a better yesterday'. We have seen how the recessions of the 1970s, Britain's accelerating decline, trade union militancy and the increasingly onerous burden of public expenditure had conspired to undermine the post-war order. Keynes and Crosland had both in their ways endeavoured to increase the role of the State without the need for the coercive statism required by socialism. Keynes had attempted to cure the disease of unemployment 'whilst preserving efficiency and freedom' and by this means he had hoped to side-step the class war, changing behaviour without having to change the political and social system. Crosland had, in effect, declared the class war over and hoped that in future economic growth would enable the redistribution of income without the need for State ownership. As Keynes's biographer puts it:

> Keynesian management became generally acceptable because it was manipulative, not coercive. If Keynesianism moves to coercion it loses its basic political function, its ability to provide consensus; or, more precisely, to obviate the need for consensus.[17]

The same could be said of Croslandism.

However, conversely, in each case, successful performance depended on the efficacy of the technique – deficit financing to correct recession and prevent high unemployment, economic growth to enable equality without tears. Neither appeared any longer to do the trick. Keynes and Crosland had armed social democrats with a political theory but not with an economic strategy. The social democrats had no new recipes of their own for curing unemployment or for creating the wealth with which to gratify their passion for equality. What is more their attitude towards the State, which was instinctively Fabian, required rethinking. David Marquand, an academic politician turned politico-academic, was the one who saw most clearly the necessity for revising revisionism. He now believed that:

> the policies through which post-war Social Democracy has sought to realise its fourfold commitment to personal freedom, social justice, resource redistribution and economic growth have rested, in practice, on a number of over-optimistic assumptions about the nature of the State, about the possibility of changing society by

acting through the State, and about the risks involved in trying to act through the State.[18]

If the State was no longer able to serve as the agent for Croslandite redistribution, or even to perform its Keynesian managerial functions, then not only was socialism dead but so was social democracy, or at least social democracy in its British revisionist form. The mould had been broken more thoroughly than the mould-breakers realised. Keynes and Crosland were among the pieces.

The post-war success of continental social democracy was owed in large part to the pursuit of liberal-market economic policies. In Germany it was called social market policy and under Adenauer and Erhard it had been the elixir of the German 'economic miracle'; it was this approach to which the SPD became reconciled at Bad Godesberg, jettisoning much of socialism in the process. It is true that the Bad Godesberg declaration speaks of socialist values, asserts a role for planning within the social market regime and reserves a residual, last-resort role for public ownership. But, to all intents and purposes, it turned the SPD into a non-socialist progressive party. Moreover, ideological intent was effectively subordinated to electoral necessity and the SPD came to power, first, through a Grand Coalition with its right-wing opponents and, subsequently, in alliance with the liberal Free Democrats. Planning and public ownership were soon forgotten. In 1979, as new radical pressures were building up within the SPD, Willy Brandt was to deny that Bad Godesberg had implied a renunciation of socialism[19] but for twenty years that was how it had seemed: social democracy in Germany had successfully combined broadly liberal economics with social reform. Free of the Labour Party, the British social democrats were now to move in this same direction. Some more rapidly than others, they shed their socialist impedimenta. The notion that the SDP could or should become a Labour Party Mark II receded, not least because of the failure of the new party to gain much of a foothold in the Labour strongholds. The logic of its position, ideologically and electorally, pushed the new party towards becoming an explicitly non-socialist party of the Left-centre. The word socialism was dropped from the SDP vocabulary, as Roy Jenkins some while since had dropped it from his. When the second edition of Owen's *Face The Future* appeared, the chapter head 'The Values of Socialism' had become 'The Values of Social Democracy'.[20] After the 1983 election Owen was to embrace explicitly the 'social market' economy and was accused of embracing

Margaret Thatcher at the same time. In truth there was little difference between her approach to wealth creation and that of the continental social democrats and, in a speech at Chicago, the Mecca of monetarism, she had held up Helmut Schmidt as a paragon of economic virtue. We were, it seemed, all social marketeers now – all, that is, except the Labour Party.

8

The Thatcher Factor

In the autumn of 1981 Margaret Thatcher's fortunes reached their lowest ebb. The newly formed SDP–Liberal Alliance was riding on the crest of its wave. Labour, in the aftermath of the Benn–Healey struggle, was floundering in the polls. The MORI poll, averaged over the last quarter of the year which had seen the great schism in the Labour Party and the launching of the SDP, put the Alliance at 38 per cent, Labour barely in second place at 28 per cent, with the Conservatives, as unemployment rose inexorably towards three million, one point behind. Following Shirley Williams's sensational victory in the Crosby by-election,[1] the Gallup poll for December reported the Alliance set to win a General Election, 'if held tomorrow', in a landslide with 50 per cent of the vote against 23 per cent each for Labour and Conservative.

In moments of euphoria Alliance politicians began constructing their first Cabinet. A leading psephologist said on television that he would be 'very surprised' if the Alliance did not take at least 30 per cent of the vote at the next General Election. With 60–80 seats in Parliament – which was pretty much what the Alliance's own strategists had in mind – a significant breakthrough would have been achieved. At Buckingham Palace and in the Cabinet Office contingency studies were conducted into the constitutional and political implications of a Parliament in which no party had a clear majority. Coalition became the gossip of the day.

With the Warrington by-election in the previous July Labour Party's strategists had begun to wake up to the threat posed by the SDP. In public at least, they had purported to pooh-pooh it as a serious electoral force; 'fluff' was what Callaghan had called it. At Warrington, the 60th safest Labour seat in the country, Roy Jenkins came close to winning with 42·4 per cent of the vote. The Labour candidate, a supporter of Tony Benn, scraped in with his majority humiliatingly reduced from over 10,000 to 1,759 – 14 per cent down on 1979. Had Shirley Williams put up the seat could have gone. As it was Jenkins could describe the result as 'my first defeat in thirty years in politics, and it is by far the greatest victory that I have ever participated in.' It was an exciting moment. The Alliance went on to scoop up the Tory marginal Croydon and then the ultra-safe Crosby. Local election returns meanwhile supported the impression that the Alliance phenomenon differed from previous Liberal revivals in that it was winning over large numbers of Labour voters.

They had, at that time, ample cause to desert. Benn, having so nearly captured the deputy leadership, had spurned an olive branch proffered by Foot and was continuing on his defiant wrecking course. His defeat in the Shadow Cabinet elections was among a series of setbacks for the Left which, it was becoming clear, had achieved the pinnacle of its fortunes at the Wembley conference. From now on its advance was impaired by the deepening split between the 'hard', or Bennite, and the 'soft', or Footite, Left. But for the public, and the voters, this was not the impression: Benn was still in the news and Foot was manifestly feeble; moreover, the spectacle of disunity did little to inspire confidence in Labour as an alternative government. Foot was further embarrassed by the selection of Pat Wall, a leading supporter of the Militant Tendency, for the constituency of Bradford North, and doubly so when Wall preached the overthrow of the State at a rally organised by the revolutionary Socialist Workers' Party. His embarrassment was compounded when Peter Tatchell was selected for the ultra-safe Labour seat of Bermondsey. Tatchell was on record with the opinion that:

> Debates and parliamentary divisions are fruitless cosmetic exercises, given the Tories' present Commons majority. And if we recognise this we are either forced to accept Tory edicts as a *fait accompli*, or we must look to new, more militant forms of extra-parliamentary opposition which involve mass popular participation and challenge the Government's right to rule.

January 1982 was the point of no return for the first Thatcher government. Her reshuffle of the previous September had made her the mistress of her Cabinet to an extent that her colleagues, and the governmental machine, were slow to grasp. But now she was in the position to decree that there was to be no going back. She hoped to be able to say, 'I held firm and things are getting better,' but, as a senior official put it at the time, 'they all know things can't get very much better.' For the question now facing the government was: could it hope to win an election with more than three million unemployed?

The official projections accompanying the 1981 Budget had shown production falling by a further 1 per cent (2 per cent below 1980 levels) and unemployment rising inexorably to above three million and, most alarming of all, remaining there for the duration of the Parliament. The history of the first Thatcher administration could in large part be written around the 1981 Budget. Confronted by the wage explosion of 1979–80 it was an article of monetarist faith that this would not, and could not, cause inflation unless it was accommodated by a government ready to print money. The monetary posture which the government had taken necessitated high interest rates which helped to force up the exchange rate, as did the oil wealth of the North Sea. The high exchange rate weakened industry, especially manufacturing industry, and industrial decline forced unemployment up. In 1981 it had to be admitted that this devastating exchange rate was neither God-given nor decreed by the market but was the consequence of a too-tight monetarist policy. In order to bring down interest rates, and thereby devalue the pound, the 1981 Budget combined a relaxation of monetary policy with a fierce fiscal squeeze. As the Cabinet had refused to impose the expenditure cuts demanded by the Treasury the previous autumn, the Public Sector Borrowing Requirement (PSBR) would be reduced by other means – by a sharp increase in taxation; meanwhile, interest rates would be cut, causing the pound to depreciate and – it was hoped – output to revive. However, the immediate effect of the Budget was to pile deflation upon deflation. Keynes was now stood on his head. The Prime Minister's economic adviser, Alan Walters, arch-monetarist and a chief author of the new strategy, takes much pride in the fact that: 'In spite of rapidly increasing unemployment and output the government introduced the toughest peacetime budget in memory.'[2]

When the monetary squeeze was relaxed, and a narrower target substituted for the broader M3, some saw this as a U-turn by the monetarists but for Walters the 1981 Budget marked the serious implementation of the Medium Term Financial Strategy to which he attributes chiefly what he calls 'Britain's Economic Renaissance'. By another way of looking at it, the monetarists in 1981 resorted to good – or, rather, bad – old-fashioned, 1920s' style deflation. In a letter to *The Times*, 364 economists, previous economic advisers to previous governments among them, warned that: 'Present policies will deepen the depression, erode the industrial base of our economy and threaten its social and political stability.' Already manufacturing output was down by more than 15 per cent. Activity in the 'metal-bashing' industries of the West Midlands, once the workshop of Britain, was down by more than a quarter. The CBI had proclaimed a slump and its president, Sir Terence Becket, rashly promised the Prime Minister 'a bare-knuckle fight'. At the July meeting of the Cabinet when the Prime Minister and the Chancellor stood alone, demanding yet more cuts, there were accusations of monetary madness and political suicide.

According to the Keynesians, whose beliefs were neatly set out in their round robin to *The Times*, there was:

> no basis in economic theory or supporting evidence that by deflating demand they will bring inflation permanently under control and thereby induce an automatic recovery in output and employment.

But the economy did begin to grow again and to grow while inflation continued to fall, although unemployment continued to rise. Was the recovery of output due to the policy adopted in 1981, as Walters is pleased to believe, or due simply to the revival of world trade? The question is fiercely disputed between rival schools of economists and, in any case, is incapable of final resolution until we see whether Britain's severely reduced manufacturing base proves sufficient for the day when the North Sea oil runs dry.

Whatever its economic consequences, the 1981 Budget was for Mrs Thatcher the triumph of her will. She had defied the conventional wisdom. There were riots in the cities that summer to add further to the alarm of those who believed that she was pressing beyond the limits of social and political tolerance. That autumn, as we have seen, she broke all records of unpopularity. Odds were being laid against her survival in office. Yet by the end of the year the polls were recording a recovery in the government's fortunes and, eighteen months later, she was to sweep back into office in defiance of the three million unemployed. The war to recover the Falklands had intervened and the 'Falklands Factor' contributed to the remarkable victory of 1983. So did the 1981 schism on the Left and the 'Foot Factor'. Yet these are insufficient explanations for the 1983 triumph and obscure its meaning. For in the meanwhile something more extraordinary had happened: the country had lowered its expectations and consented once more to be governed.

The success of the government in this respect is not to be measured by the achievement, or non-achievement, of arcane money targets. It is more likely that inflation was brought down in spite of monetarism than because of it, chiefly by general deflation and falling commodity prices. But monetarism, perhaps, was important as a cover for what had to be done. The mumbo-jumbo of M3, M1, M0, and NIBM1[3] gave a scientific air to a policy which was wanting in simple humanity towards its victims, enabling ministers to attribute what were, in reality, political decisions to the sovereignty of the market. Or, as a senior Bank of England official put it:

> [overt deflation] would have meant disclosing objectives for, *inter alia*, output and employment. This would have been a very hazardous exercise and the objectives would have either been unacceptable to public opinion or else inadequate to secure a substantial decrease in the rate of inflation, or both.[4]

Moreover, setting targets and sticking to them had the smack of Thatcherism about it. It was like living within the housekeeping money. The Chicago school and the Grantham school had much in common. Indeed, for the public, monetarism, whatever it was, became synonymous with Thatcherism. Moreover, it symbolised a break with the past. By 1983 many were ready to blame unemployment on the international situation, not on the government of the day. Moreover, they were ready to blame it on the prodigalities of the past, on prolix over-manning, on trade union militancy and bloody-mindedness. Their daily experience told people that a great deal of what Margaret Thatcher was saying was true. Blaming unemployment on external factors, or on forces beyond the government's control, was a stage in the process of blaming unemployment on nobody. The appeal of market economics lies in precisely this: it is a means of avoiding social responsibility. There is no economic logic, no logic of any kind, in saying that because Keynesianism no longer achieves its purpose, the 'laws of the market', whose deficiencies Keynes had addressed, have miraculously been restored. 'Thatcherism' was a way of filling an intellectual and a moral vacuum.

However, a high price had been paid for the conquest of inflation. Calculations have been made which attribute up to half of the rise in unemployment after 1979 to the deflationary policies of the government, although we may suppose that if the recession bit deeper in Britain than elsewhere it was also because the economy had been progressively enfeebled by decline. By 1983 there was not much to show for the pain endured. There was little evidence that the lower rate of inflation would of itself result in the faster growth which might arrest and reverse Britain's relative decline. Taxation, which the government had promised to cut, had increased. True, the basic rate had come down from 33 to 30 per cent but all but the rich were paying more of their incomes to the State: nearly 40 per cent of the national wealth was being collected in taxes compared with under 34 per cent when Margaret Thatcher came to power. The increased tax burden was one measure of the government's failure to cut public expenditure overall, another of its central pledges. Partly this was due to the high cost of the recession in terms of unemployment benefit and partly to planned increased spending in the fields of defence and law and order. Other social spending, indeed, had been cut in real terms, chiefly in education and housing. The result was a litany of protest about 'the cuts' without commensurate benefit in rolling back the frontiers of the State.[5]

At best roll-back had given way to containment. In the autumn of 1982 the government ran up against the political limits of Thatcherism. Projections made by the Treasury showed that the performance of the economy would be unlikely to prove adequate for sustaining the Welfare State in the face of demographic pressures upon it. The 'Think Tank' then confronted Ministers with the kind of measures which would be required to bring spending into line with performance. They included decoupling social benefits from inflation, private health insurance in place of the National Health Service, an end to State funding for higher education. A great furore resulted when these measures were leaked to *The Economist*. The Welfare State was an aspect of the old order which voters had shown no sign of rejecting in 1979. It continued to be supported across the classes. Moreover, the Prime Minister had made a specific pledge to maintain the real value of social security benefits and NHS spending. At the Conservative Party conference later that autumn Mrs Thatcher felt obliged to declare, 'The National Health Service is safe with us.' The price, it was turning out, of getting the government off the backs of the people in the field of welfare was to set the people at the throats of the government.

The frontiers of the State had not been pushed back far in other directions either. For the Thatcherite 'enterprise society' to be brought about in Britain required, paradoxically, a State strong enough to roll itself back and open the space for free markets. But apart from the sale of council houses there had been little in the way of privatisation by 1983. That arch-non-interventionist, Sir Keith Joseph, in his capacity as Secretary for Trade and Industry, had become the agent of massive cash injections into loss-making nationalised industries, British Leyland and the British Steel Corporation. The Prime Minister herself had become an enthusiast for the encouragement by the State of new technology, although this willingness was combined incoherently with an aversion to the public sector and a refusal to develop an industrial policy to shape the restructuring of basic manufacturing industries such as chemicals and engineering.

The most important change achieved on the supply side was the curbing of trade union power. The government had pledged to redress the balance of industrial power between union and employer and this it had done. The Trades Union Act of 1980, piloted through by James Prior, had outlawed secondary picketing and removed immunity for most secondary actions (sympathy strikes, blacking). Norman Tebbit's Act of 1982 exposed union funds to claims for damages resulting from unlawful acts and removed immunity from political strikes. Both Acts had placed restrictions on closed shops. As important as these laws themselves, however, seems to have been the government's demonstration that the trade unions were no longer running the country. Trade union leaders, to their great chagrin, were no longer to be seen coming in and out of Number 10. Kept at arms-distance by the government, they came to be in less demand by television producers. The days when Jack Jones's opinion was sought on almost everything were gone; there was little interest in David Basnett's opinion on anything. This was one reason why trade union leaders came to invest so heavily in the return of a Labour government and became increasingly embroiled in the internal power struggles of the Movement. On one of the rare occasions on which the Prime Minister condescended to receive a delegation from the General Council, the TUC general-secretary, Len Murray, emerged to complain, 'we're in two different worlds'.

It was true. The union ethos no longer pervaded the country. The curve of militancy was now sharply downwards. As the Left advanced within the Labour Party it was in retreat across the land. Partly, of course, this was due to the recession and rising unemployment but there does seem also to have been some kind of change in attitudes, a sense of release perhaps from the prisons of the past. Erstwhile militants, the British Leyland car workers for example, were refusing their shop stewards' calls to strike. The TUC's Day of Action against the trade union laws was a flop, a day of inaction. By 1983 the number of days lost in industrial disputes was the lowest since the war. The great confrontation which many had predicted never came about, although Thatcher in 1981 – haunted as always by what had happened to Heath in 1974 – beat a tactical retreat in face of a threat from the miners. That battle was to await another day.

The country she governed was a more divided place: the rich had got richer but the poor had got poorer and the gap had grown wider between north and south, city and suburb, town and country. But what was remarkable was how she was able to win re-election in 1983 in the absence of a general improvement in the condition of the people. Real living standards had begun to improve again in 1983, with the rate of inflation down to below 5 per cent, but the expectation of a significant annual increment to real wealth which had prevailed since the 1950s had been scarcely gratified since 1979. Real disposable income in 1983 was about the same as it had been when Mrs Thatcher came to power in May 1979. Production was still more than 3 per cent down, manufacturing production by more than 15 per cent. Unemployment, at well over three millions, had almost tripled since the government had come to power.

This was not the sort of record on which governments could expect to be returned to office. Moreover, the Thatcher government could not claim with much plausibility that discipline and self-sacrifice had arrested or reversed the relative decline of the British economy. Britain's share of world trade had continued to diminish and 1983 was the first year since the Industrial Revolution in which the one-time workshop of the world had run a deficit on trade in manufactured goods. It is true that since 1981 the rate of growth was above the average of the industrialised world, but that was most likely due to Britain's being first into and first out of the recession. More hopeful was the trend in productivity, which had increased at a faster rate than in competitor countries, and at a considerably faster rate than the underlying post-war trend; but it was not clear whether this represented some real and lasting change or was merely the temporary concomitant of lower output, of drastic labour-shedding and the closure of inefficient plant. There was little sign of improvement in that other symptom of the British disease, which was the propensity of wages to run ahead of prices and at the expense of unit costs. In spite of some devaluation of the pound since 1981 the British economy was substantially less competitive than it had been in 1979.

How then was it that the government could be re-elected in 1983? Certainly no one could any longer say with plausibility that the country was ungovernable. The power of the unions had been curbed. It was no longer true to say as Norman St John Stevas had done in 1976: 'No Government in Britain can hope to succeed today without the goodwill of the unions.'

The country had suffered a tripling of unemployment and a more than decimation of its manufacturing industry, but the authority of the government was under no serious challenge. For left-wing writers, such as Hobsbawm and Hall, Britain was experiencing a crisis of capitalism, no less, something comparable to the 1930s; and yet the militancy of the 1970s seemed largely spent and there was no sign to be seen that the forward march of labour would be resumed.

What had been a crisis for government in the 1970s had become a crisis for those in opposition. The schism of 1981 in the Labour ranks had meant that in so far as there could be said to exist an anti-Thatcher majority in the land its forces were divided between the Labour Party and the SDP–Liberal Alliance. The Alliance might be incapable of forming a government in the foreseeable future but its flash in the pan in 1981 had been bright enough to signal to the electorate that Labour's days of power were over. Labour, meanwhile, seemed determined to disqualify itself from office. Michael Foot, whose approval-rating was to slump to rock bottom, had been put where he was, into a position for which he was wholly unfitted, by the people who had known him best. They had put him there for sentimental reasons mitigated only by inner party expediency, and he personified in every way both Labour's unfitness to govern and the extent to which it had lost touch even with its natural constituency. For its part the Alliance, after the heady moments of its birth, had confirmed many of the forebodings about the fate of centre parties. It suffered special disabilities in that it consisted not of one but of two pigs in the middle. Due to the defections from the Labour Party the SDP was, pending the election, the larger party in the Commons while the Liberals were the stronger on the ground, with a base in local government. The SDP was the senior member of the partnership in the special sense that its leaders had sat in Cabinets while no Liberal politician alive had ever done so; but the Liberal Party was the senior historically and in being the more experienced in campaigns and in the specialised, and sometimes dubious, arts of third-party politicking. The device of anointing Roy Jenkins as 'Prime Minister designate' and David Steel as 'campaign leader' neither capitalised on this division of labour nor resolved the bemusement of the public's mind. It served to blur further the already blurred image which is the occupational hazard of centre parties.

The old adage about oppositions not winning elections but governments losing them was stood on its head: in 1983, or so it seemed, the opposition lost. But in what sense did the government win? In an interview with the *Sunday Times* in 1981 Margaret Thatcher had said:

> What's irritated me about the whole direction of politics in the last thirty years is that it's always been towards the collectivist society. People have forgotten about the personal society. And they say: do I count, do I matter? To which the short answer is, Yes. And therefore, it isn't that I set out on economic policies; it's that I set out really to change the approach, and changing the economics is the means of changing that approach. If you change the approach you really are after the heart and soul of the nation. Economics are the method; the object is to change the heart and soul.[6]

This statement contains the essence of what we might call 'religious Thatcherism'; her project was the conversion of the British no less. To what extent she had begun, by 1983, to bring about a cultural change, or ideological counter-revolution, it is hard to say. The statistics of economic performance did not suggest that the 'enterprise society', which was her equivalent of the American dream, was struggling to be born. Perhaps, in a limited sense and for the time being only, she had won the argument about the economy, won it negatively in that the electorate was largely persuaded that there was, truly, 'no alternative'. Of course, the alternative consisted in rejecting false alternatives and lay somewhere between the extremes of Thatcherite deflation and Labour's exorbitantly inflationary spending plans. Nevertheless, the public was correct in its conclusion that a return to the ways of the past offered no alternative if Britain's problems were ever to be solved. A return to full employment, as promised by Labour – within the lifetime of a Parliament! – was no longer seen to be a feasible goal.

Essentially, however, the Conservative victory of 1983 marked the political triumph of Thatcherism, not its economic or ideological triumph. The earthquake which had cracked the surface and sent tremors through the system in 1979 now transformed the political landscape of Britain.

What of the Falklands Factor? One may doubt its salience in any literal sense by the time voters came to enter the polling booths, one year after Port Stanley was retaken from the Argentinians. At least that is what they would have had the pollsters believe. The Falkland Islands were of no concern to the electorate before the war and it would not be surprising if they became of little concern once more soon after it was over. Indeed, an important cause of the war was that a small but single-minded pro-Falklands lobby had been able to take advantage of governmental timidity and huge public indifference to prevent some negotiated arrangement with Argentina which would guarantee the status of the islanders while ending a territorial dispute which had been going on for longer than anyone could remember. It had been the policy goal of successive governments to liquidate a post-imperial commitment which Britain, at a distance of 8,000 miles, no longer had the means of honouring except by expensive distortion of her other defence requirements.

For some months before the Falkland Islands were thrust upon the national consciousness the government had been regaining popularity, chiefly at the expense of the SDP–Liberal Alliance, whose bubble had reached bursting point at the time of the Crosby by-election in December 1981. In that month the standing of the parties (according to Gallup) was: Conservatives 23; Labour 23; Alliance 50. By March the parties were running virtually neck and neck. The figures were 31: 33: 33.[7] Nevertheless, the war did transform the political scene. In July, with the war won, the government had a 19 point lead: Cons. 46: Lab. 27: All. 24. On the eve of the 1983 General Election the figures were 49: 31: 16. The actual result was 43·5: 28·3: 26. The mould was thus set by the Falklands War but that does not mean that it might not have been set in the same way for other reasons. That we can never know.

The Argentinian invasion of those remote and unimportant islands threw the nation into a patriotic fit. Parliament set the lead. When news of the invasion was first rumoured this commentator failed totally to grasp the significance of the matter. The Falkland Islands were a post-imperial leftover of no strategic or economic value and far removed from the real problems facing the country, at home and abroad. I left London that Friday for the country and the next day, annoyed at the disturbance of my Saturday, listened to the emergency debate in the Commons on the radio. Had I been in my place in the Press Gallery perhaps I, too, might have been carried away by the excitement of the moment but as it was, listening at my kitchen table, I could scarcely believe my ears. That the Commons was sitting for the first time on a Saturday since the Suez crisis of 1956 was an invitation to exaggerate the importance of the occasion. One speaker went further and solemnly compared the invasion of the Falklands with the fiasco of the Norwegian campaign in 1940, one of the darkest moments of the war which led to the fall of the Chamberlain government. The most jingoistic speech of the morning came from

Michael Foot, who having proclaimed Britain's role as 'defender of people's freedom throughout the world' and asserted the 'absolute right' of the Falklanders to British protection, called upon the government to 'prove by deeds – they will never be able to do it by words – that they are not responsible for the betrayal and cannot be faced with that charge.'

It seemed to me then, and it seems to me now, extraordinary that it should be supposed that Britain could be responsible for 1,800 people and their 600,000 sheep in the remoteness of the South Atlantic. That we should hold ourselves responsible was honourable, noble in the extreme, but foolhardy. It had been irresponsible to continue with such a commitment without the capability of discharging it. The defence of the Falklands had for some time rested on bluff. Now that that bluff had been called the proper course was to seek to discharge our responsibility to the islanders as best we could through negotiations to guarantee their status as British citizens or to repatriate and compensate them as need be. It was preposterous, it seemed to me, to assert their absolute right to self-determination. Rights could not exist without the means of upholding them and it was quite unrealistic to expect Britannia to rule the South Atlantic in the year 1982.

Karl Marx had said that history repeated itself as farce but then had gone on to say that when it repeated itself for a second time it did so as tragedy. In 1956 the folk-guilt of the ruling class had led an out-of-touch generation to mistake the nationalisation of the Suez Canal by Gamal Abdul Nasser for another Munich. Suez had been a post-imperial farce, a tilting at windmills; but now, it seemed, young lives were to be sacrificed tragically in the Quixotic cause of making a world safe for South Atlantic sheep-shearers. For it was questionable to claim – as Mrs Thatcher did throughout the affair – that liberty was indivisible to the extent that if aggression were allowed to succeed in this case licence would be given to aggressors everywhere, in Afghanistan and Cambodia or wherever. We were deluding ourselves if we supposed that the rest of the world, even our American allies and Common Market partners, would regard a dispute over an insignificant outpost of a lost Empire as an event on the same footing as the Nazi invasion of Poland. Thus:

At the State Department, in the early hours of the crisis, most of the staff shared the amusement of the press and public over what was perceived as a Gilbert and Sullivan battle over a sheep pasture between a choleric old John Bull and a comic dictator in a gaudy uniform.[8]

In his memoirs General Haig, then the Secretary of State, disassociated himself from this mockingly contemptuous view of the matter but when shown maps he was alleged to have said at the time: 'Gee, it's only a pimple on their arse.'

Indeed, there seemed to me, and here I consulted theologians, something disproportionate about the British response to the Argentinian invasion, reprehensible though it was. St Thomas Aquinas had laid down three conditions for a 'just war' – it must be authorised by the sovereign, the cause must be just, and the belligerents of valid moral intention. Recent Catholic moralists have stressed a fourth condition, most relevant to modern times: a war, to be just, must be waged by proper means (*debito modo*). Could this be said of the despatch of a large naval Task Force (which on its way would sink a cruiser and drown 308 young men) to avenge an act which, if the truth were admitted, was more costly of national pride than of true national interest? The Falklands, as we know, were recaptured in glorious fashion and the Union Flag flies once more over Government House, Port Stanley. The death toll all round was about a thousand, plus some 1,700 wounded – for 1,800 islanders and 600,000 sheep. *Debito modo*?

There were two flaws to this analysis, more apparent in hindsight than at the time perhaps. The first was that it pointed to no clear alternative course of action. It would have been disproportionate equally to have done nothing. The Junta in Buenos Aires were a nasty lot ('a gang of thugs' Haig told the Cabinet) and their aggression could in no way be condoned; even the Security Council of the United Nations had condemned it. Resolution 502 required Argentina to withdraw but, if she did not, Britain had the right under Article 51 of the Charter to repossess her territory by the use of reasonable force. Diplomacy backed up by the threat of force, it seemed to me, was the appropriate and proportionate strategy.

The Prime Minister's intention from the beginning was to get the islands back and undo the humiliation which had been done. The Foreign Office was in such disrepute as a result of the invasion that it was, literally, *hors de combat*; a peace strategy never really received a hearing. Nevertheless, the Cabinet was from the outset united on the total war objective. The services had many options but no clear plan. The Americans stepped into the diplomatic action. The 'war cabinet' in London in fact went a long way in co-operating with the Haig mission but it was his reports on the character of the Junta in Buenos Aires, anecdotes of drunkenness and imbecility, which convinced the doubting members of the inner group that the 'Argies' would be neither willing to make peace nor capable of it. And, as it turned out, it was the Junta which rejected, first, terms to which Mrs Thatcher had reluctantly agreed, and subsequently – to her huge relief – terms which she would herself have declined to put to Parliament had Galtieri had the wit to accept them. Meanwhile, as the Task Force approached its destination, the options narrowed until the only choice was between all or nothing. Her military strategy achieved its goal; looking back, it is hard to see how a diplomatic approach could have succeeded.

Be that as it may, we are concerned here with the politics of the matter, with the contribution of the 'Falklands Factor' to the realignment in British politics brought about by, or under, Mrs Thatcher. The second flaw in the position of those of us who at the time were critics of the war is that we underestimated, perhaps, the psychological needs of the nation. I do not mean by that a need for crude chauvinistic distraction, for one thing which was striking about those ten weeks was how rare it was to hear of the spirit of high patriotism degenerating into hatred or crude 'Argie' bashing. It might have been otherwise if the horrendous sinking of HMS *Sheffield* had preceded the tragic sinking of the *Belgrano*. Nor do I mean simply that the country was willing to have its attention diverted by an external adventure, the oldest trick in the book, from three million unemployed at home, although diverted it was for a while as the places of public entertainment emptied and all eyes became riveted to the nightly television news bulletins. No, the psychological need was for a success, a success of some kind, an end to failure and humiliation, to do something well, to win. Nostalgic knee-jerk reaction it may have been, vainglorious posturing in a post-imperial world of Super Powers, but it made people feel better not worse.

Moreover, it aroused genuine admiration around the world and, where not that, reluctant respect. There is a slight note of astonishment in Haig's account of how:

> In a reawakening of the spirit of the Blitz that exhilarated Britain, warships were withdrawn from NATO, civilian ships, including the liner *Queen Elizabeth II*, were requisitioned and refitted, troops were embarked, and in an astonishingly short time a task force of over 100 ships and 28,000 men was steaming under the British ensign toward the Falklands.[9]

Perhaps no people were more surprised than the British, accustomed to being told they did not know how to run a motor car factory. By jingo they knew how to launch a Task Force. The point was not lost upon the Prime Minister in her heady hour of victory. On 3 July a great throng assembled on the race course at Cheltenham – where better? – and she said:

> It took the battle in the South Atlantic for the shipyards to adapt ships way ahead of time; for dockyards to refit merchantmen and cruise liners, to fix helicopter platforms, to convert hospital ships – all faster than was thought possible; it took the demands of war for every stop to be pulled out and every man and woman to do their best.

On she went, dishing out the medals to British industry, the British people – the British worker! Of course, Churchill had to be quoted at such a moment – he had said something somewhere about the need to work together in peacetime as in war, a banal enough sentiment, and now – thirty-six years on – the truth of it at last was dawning on the British people, or so she said.

> We saw the signs when, this week, the NUR came to understand that its strike on the railways and on the Underground just didn't fit [we can hear the voice] – didn't match the spirit of these times.

And on she went. Printing money was no more.

> Rightly this Government has abjured it. Increasingly this nation won't have it . . . That too is part of the Falklands Factor.

Not only was the Falklands Factor making the trains run on time, it was – it seems – rallying the nation behind the Medium Term Financial Strategy. And as the climax is approached, the sentences grow shorter:

> What has indeed happened is that now once again Britain is not prepared to be pushed around.
>
> We have ceased to be a nation in retreat.
>
> We have instead a new-found confidence – born in the economic battles at home and tested and found true 8,000 miles away.
>
> That confidence comes from the rediscovery of ourselves, and grows with the recovery of our self-respect.

Britain found herself again in the South Atlantic and will not look back from the victory she has won.

Such oratory is not to be taken too literally; it is indicative of a state of mind, not of the state of the nation. War is a celebrated midwife but it is improbable that the loss and recapture of the Falkland Islands in 1982 will prove to have been the rebirth of Britain, or the apotheosis of Thatcherism. What it may have done, however, is to help link in people's minds their images of her with this powerful image of success. She was a winner. Luck was on her side. What she said she would do she would do. She was a sticker whose determination paid off. What had worked so brilliantly abroad, would work at home. And she was quick to reinforce these thoughts in people's minds: 'I think people like decisiveness, I think they like strong leadership,' she told an interviewer. In this way the Falklands Factor became the Thatcher Factor.[10]

The schism on the Left gave the Conservatives their parliamentary landslide in 1983. A 42·4 per cent share of the vote, fractionally down on 1979, yielded them 61 per cent of the seats, a majority overall of 144 compared with 43 in 1979. There are two interpretations of this result: it can be noted that this share of the vote is smaller than the share with which Churchill lost in 1950 and Lord Home in 1964; or it can be remarked how support for the government had held almost steady in the face of the challenge from the SDP–Liberal Alliance and in spite of three million unemployed. I prefer the second view; the first, it seems to me, is an observation about changes in the party system and not about the relative showing of the parties. Another way of looking at the 1983 result is to say that with more than three million unemployed Labour should have won and that it lost only because of its defence policy and its spectacular disunity, or that the Tories won only because of the Falklands Factor. Alternatively, it can be said that the continuance of the social and political trends which had contributed to Labour's loss in 1979 virtually doomed it to lose again in 1983 and, probably, thereafter. Of these I strongly prefer the second view.

That is not to suggest that Labour's defeat was inevitable, although there is no doubt that most of the changes taking place in society were making it more difficult for it to win. Between 1979 and 1983 the working class, itself further diminished in size, swung 3 per cent to the Conservatives – in spite of 'Thatcherism', in spite of the unemployed, the welfare spending cuts, the union laws – or, perhaps, not in spite of but because of some of these things. Only 38 per cent of manual workers and 39 per cent of trade unionists voted Labour while 32 per cent of trade unionists voted Conservative. The Tories led Labour by 12 per cent among the skilled working class, but trailed 15 per cent among the unskilled. In 1983, still more than in 1979, Labour became not 'the party of the working class' but rather the party of the underclass.

In part this was due to continuing demographic change. The trend of a quarter of a century or more towards polarisation between north and south, city and suburb, town and country, had continued. Outside London, Labour in 1983 held only three of 186 southern seats while the Tories had only five remaining strongholds in the Metropolitan County conurbations in the north.[11] Not only was Labour becoming the party of the underclass but in 1983 it became, more than ever before, the party of declining Britain, geographically driven back into the decaying inner cities and the depressed industrial regions of the north.

However, there were new or special factors at work. In 1979 Labour appears, roughly speaking, to have punched its class weight. In 1983 it did a good deal worse than socio-economic or demographic changes can explain. By one calculation Labour's 'natural' constituency is now around 35 per cent of the electorate. In 1983 Labour's share of the vote was only 27·6 per cent, compared with 37 per cent in 1979. In 1983 Labour presented an unelectable face to the electorate, in terms of its leaders, many of its policies and in its general demeanour as a party aspiring to government, and this must explain a good deal of its unnaturally poor showing. Yet at the same time there would appear to have continued, and perhaps accelerated, the ideological shift which had been a part of the reason for Labour's defeat in 1979, indeed for its decline over two-and-a-half decades. The Oxford study of the General Election for 1983 endeavours to make some measure of this shift but its general conclusion is that what damaged Labour more than the specifics of its policies was the unattractiveness of its image as a party. 'It is the fit between the general character of the party and the voter's own general ideology which, we believe, best accounts for electoral choice.'[12]

Just so, Labour and the electorate in 1983 made a poor 'fit'. Labour had moved Left and the electorate Right; or, as I would rather put it, the spectrum of Labour's preoccupations and the electorate's had grown increasingly apart. For the first time since the war, in 1983 more voters identified with the Conservatives than with the Labour

Party, although identification with any party at all had continued to grow weaker.

These were not haphazard developments to be cited in support of an argument that, even in 1983, Margaret Thatcher's victory was some kind of aberration to be explained by special or temporary factors. For the ideological gap between Labour and the voters, including a great many of its own erstwhile supporters, was not an accidental matter but, as I have tried to show, in part an endemic consequence of the structure, composition and character of the Labour Movement. And even if we regard the Party as having been hi-jacked by predominantly middle-class ideologists and activists, the reasons why this could happen, and was allowed to happen, themselves weigh against Labour's claims to have remained a representative party of the masses. That it could put forward Michael Foot as its prospective Prime Minister in the year 1983 says nearly all. But hi-jacking is too facile; the 'Cultural Revolution' which engulfed the Labour Party, as I have tried to show, was a consequence of disillusionment with socialism, of the shortcomings of social democracy, of the rise of a new class and, above all, one of the responses to the painful experience of decline which was reshaping British politics during the 1970s and 1980s.

Neither was the schism of 1981, which ensured Margaret Thatcher her parliamentary landslide in 1983, an accidental occurrence. The split was rooted in the ideological division of the Labour Party which had grown increasingly acute after the ending of the 'long boom' in 1973 and with the intellectual collapse of Croslandite socialism. Moreover, the new self-assertion of the political centre was another expression of the growth of the middle class, and the rise within it of a 'new class' of educated professionals and technicians, or, perhaps we should say, the rise not of a new class but of *a new classlessness*. It was an expression also of that ideological shift which, with the changing composition of the classes, was rendering obsolete many of the old preoccupations of Labour as a working class party with ostensibly a socialist programme. The Alliance is a child of the 'Cultural Revolution' in the Labour Party. It is also an aspect of the politics of decline.

Hence, in so far as these events and trends are seen as among the explanations for Margaret Thatcher's victory in 1983, they reinforce, rather than qualify, the thesis of realignment. A process that had begun some time after 1966, and had manifested itself in 1979, was taken a big step further in 1983. To be sure, the elections of 1979 and 1983 did not give Mrs Thatcher a 'new' or 'natural' majority in the land, or any kind of majority at all. But that is hardly surprising if she too is seen as a feature of a shifting political landscape. As class politics break down, whether due to the decline of class itself or the weakening of class allegiances, so the electorate by definition becomes more volatile, more fickle, more open to argument, more suggestible by the media. Voters come to be increasingly of no fixed ideological abode.

The Conservative victories in 1979 and 1983 were not socially determined, they were brought about partly because Margaret Thatcher was the most successful player of the new game. She seized advantage of Labour's decline by making populist appeal to working class or erstwhile working class voters. It was she who was most attuned to the changing spirit of the times. The Thatcher style of politics – and I have suggested that 'Thatcherism' is more a style than it is an ideology – may not have commanded majority support in the country in 1983 but it was more applauded by Labour voters than by Conservative voters![13]

It was her purpose to bury socialism which she saw as chief perpetrator of the decline which she was pledged to arrest and reverse. Hers was the first Conservative administration since 1945 which saw its task not to postpone or mitigate the advance of collectivism but to reverse it. This she set about by means which were as political as they may have been ideologically inspired. She aimed her attack at the bastions of Labour's power – the trade unions, the council estates, the Socialist local authorities, and the nationalised industries. She curbed the unions at law but, more important, banished them from centre stage until, by 1983, it was no longer held to be axiomatic that the country was ungovernable without their consent. She sold council houses to their tenants, contributing to the increase in owner-occupation from 55 per cent of households in 1979 to 60 per cent. And she won 47 per cent of their votes. Labour won 49 per cent of the votes of council tenants – but these constituted only 29 per cent of the electorate. According to some commentators tenure had some while since replaced class as the prime determinant of voting behaviour and if the Thatcherite Conservative Party can be said to have a core majority it consists, perhaps, of the 40 per cent of the electorate who are non-trade-unionist houseowners. Of them 60 per cent voted for her in 1983.[14]

The assault on municipal socialism was yet to come. It was promised in the Manifesto, a target for the second term. Nor had privatisation yet more than dented the public sector. Shares were sold in British Aerospace, Britoil, and Cable and Wireless. However, support for privatisation among the voters had increased from 22 per cent to 42 per cent in 1983. That was beginning also to show populist potential as a vote-winner.

One view of the 1983 General Election is that the Thatcher government was re-elected in the face of an anti-Thatcher majority. Another view is that she and the Labour Party between them had conspired to create an anti-socialist majority in the land. The SDP–Liberal Alliance was a part of that majority willy-nilly. But its support was spread thinly and evenly across the land. In this regard the new Alliance had not progressed significantly beyond the position of the Liberal Party. The authors of the Oxford study identify the makings of an Alliance 'heartland' in the form of the more educated and liberal wing of the salariat, or what I have more loosely called the 'new class'. Potentially this is an important constituency, for on the Oxford reckoning the salariat as a whole is almost as large as the working class and continuing to grow. It is a constituency that the Labour Party cannot do without if it is to become once more a broad progressive force.

The Alliance's putative socio-ideological base, however, was no match for the huge disadvantages imposed by geography. The concentrations of Conservative and Labour strength in their regional bastions made it more difficult than ever for a third party to win seats. None of the Tory targets in the south was toppled by the Alliance, no gains were registered in the Labour heartland. The Alliance cut across the two political nations, cut across its class divides and demographic boundaries. In Tory Britain the Alliance became the second party in two-thirds of its seats; across the country more than one-third of Labour's 1979 supporters defected to it; but nowhere save in tiny pockets or at the very fringe of the nation did the Alliance possess territory of its own.

Geography saved the Labour Party in 1983. With 28 per cent of the votes it obtained 209 seats. In 1931 Labour won 31 per cent of the votes and only 52 seats. The geographic polarisation of Britain was the product of many factors. Labour Britain, the urban north, was where the working classes were most concentrated; Tory Britain, the south outside London, was where the middle classes lived in greater numbers. The spread of owner-occupation had been greater in Tory Britain; in Labour Britain more families lived in council houses. Where the working classes were congregated together, as in the north or London, they were more likely to vote Labour than where they had become dispersed into more mixed communities, as in the south and the countryside. The manufacturing industries of the north were in decline, the new service industries were growing chiefly in the south.

Tory Britain had more of everything – more people, more jobs, better schools, more cars, telephones and dishwashers. Nearly twice as many working class people voted Tory in Tory Britain than did in Labour Britain.[15]

The anti-socialist majority was very largely the south against the north. The 1983 General Election established a hegemony whereby a Conservative government could govern, or at least hope to be re-elected, without much deference to the other and less prosperous half of the nation. Tory Britain ruled. Margaret Thatcher was its ruler.

3
PICKING UP THE PIECES

9

Prime Ministerial Government

The tasks facing Margaret Thatcher at the beginning of her second administration were those left unfinished from her first. She had yet to arrest and reverse the nation's decline, yet to confine socialism to the attic of history. To achieve these goals there would need to be, she believed, a profound change in national attitudes, some kind of moral regeneration which would replace the collectivist mentality which had ruled since the War with a thrusting spirit of enterprise. She had frequently insisted that the task she had set herself would take ten years or more – at the very least two full terms of office. Here she was embarking upon her second term, the first Prime Minister in this century to win a second after a full first term in office, in her case by a landslide, and yet she had no strategy for completing her revolution, scarcely a programme enough to keep Parliament busy. The General Election of June 1983 had been called in a hurry while the going was good. She had been urged by campaign advisers, notably the Conservative Party chairman, Cecil Parkinson, to strike while the 'Falklands Factor' was still hot. There was insufficient time, and insufficient thought, to compile a radical Manifesto. Said one disgruntled colleague, 'She thinks that her own re-election is all that is necessary to save the country.'

The 1983 Manifesto prescribed more of the same but in bland and reassuring terms. It had been launched in the blue womb of the conference hall at Conservative Central Office to the accompaniment of musak. Inflation would be brought lower, public expenditure and borrowing firmly controlled, the taxes cut. This time there was a list of industries to be privatised but nothing to indicate the role which privatisation would come to play in the second phase of Thatcherism. Union members were to be given the right to secret ballots – 'giving the unions back to their members', this was called – but nothing was proposed for curbing the right to strike in essential industries. Mrs Thatcher herself, it was said, had insisted upon the inclusion of a pledge to abolish the Greater London Council and six other Metropolitan Authorities. She had described these as 'the last vestiges of feudal power'. She had also insisted on a renewed commitment to rate reform, having herself promised to abolish them in 1974 when she had been the Shadow spokesman on the matter.

These reforms of local government – which were to occupy an inordinate amount of parliamentary time – were scarcely the most urgent problems facing the country, although they were relevant to her goal of destroying the remaining bastions of socialism. The reform of the Welfare State, from which she had flinched during the expenditure review of 1982, was not at the top of the agenda. (As always, however, there were allegations that a 'secret agenda' existed.) The published manifesto pledged the government to maintain the real value of the retirement pension and other benefits. It turned out that getting on for two-thirds of the vast cost of social security was protected by election pledges. All in all, the manifesto did not read like a prospectus for permanent revolution.

However, manifestoes are as nothing to the authority which electoral victory confers upon a government and a Prime Minister. Mrs Thatcher had gone to the country as herself, her style of doing things and her ideological intentions as clear as could be. Her victory had been overwhelming, at least in terms of seats. If it was argued – and, of course, it was – that 57 per cent of the votes cast had been against her, she could riposte that 72 per cent had been cast against the Labour Party and socialism. She had all the authority she needed to do what she would, if she knew how.

Her first move was to sack her Foreign Secretary. Had she fallen as a consequence of the Falklands expedition, Francis Pym very likely would have succeeded her. Now he was out. He had annoyed her during the campaign by observing – correctly, it soon was to seem – that 'Landslides on the whole don't produce successful governments.' But, in any case, she had never liked him, simply couldn't get on with him – nor he with her. Pym was an officer and a gentleman from Cambridgeshire stock going back to the Civil War. She disliked his gloomy disposition, even the way he sat at Cabinet table, shoulders hunched in despondency. To her he represented the defeatism which had for too long pervaded the natural ruling class.

She was the mistress now. With two of her protégés, Nigel Lawson and Leon Brittan, promoted to the Treasury and the Home Office and the ever-obedient Geoffrey Howe transferred to the Foreign Office, the Cabinet now became the complete instrument of her will. James Prior remained banished to the Irish bog while Peter Walker was transferred to the Department of Energy – our nearest equivalent to a Siberian power station – where he occupied the very same room in which Tony Benn had languished under Wilson and Callaghan. Her most adored favourite, Cecil Parkinson, the architect of her victory, was promoted from the Central Office to her least favourite spending department, Trade and Industry. This was to the great chagrin of Norman Tebbit, Parkinson's chief rival for her favours. Indeed, he had believed the job to be his and had his bags packed at the Department of Employment.

The reason for Tebbit's last-minute disappointment was not to transpire until some months later when the Parkinson Affair, or rather Parkinson's affair with Sarah Keays, became a public scandal. His mistress had become pregnant in April and on the night of the great Conservative triumph at the polls he had been obliged to inform the Prime Minister of the tangle in his personal life. For all her public moralising Margaret Thatcher was no prude; she herself was married to a divorcé. Her advice to Parkinson was to stay with his wife; she saw no need for him to resign from the government. However, she did now abandon her plan to reward her campaign manager with the Foreign Secretaryship no less. That would have left no doubt about his status as her heir apparent. Instead she accommodated Parkinson at the DTI, at the expense of Norman Tebbit's ambition. Miss Keays revealed her highly-damaging side of the story to *The Times* on the eve of Mrs Thatcher's keynote speech to the Conservative Party conference in Blackpool that October. Parkinson was obliged to resign. Norman Tebbit moved in to the Department of Trade and Industry.

The Parkinson Affair was the first of many mishaps which plagued Mrs Thatcher's second administration from its earliest days. Prime Ministers in their second term seem to become accident prone. In 1959 Harold Macmillan had led his party to a spectacular victory, its third in a row, within three years of the Suez débâcle which had destroyed Eden and brought him to power. Yet within three years everything had gone wrong for Macmillan and after sacking half of his Cabinet in 1961 – the wrong half was Wilson's joke – his administration ended in the Profumo scandal. John Profumo, the Minister of War, had an affair with a pretty call girl, Christine Keeler. Profumo lied to the Commons and was forced to resign. In June 1966 Harold Wilson turned the tiny majority he had scraped together in October 1964 into a near landslide. Yet it was then that his real troubles began. Gripped for a while by a strange lassitude, perhaps exhausted by the tactical exertions of his earlier survival trick, he lost his grip on events and his government stumbled from crisis to crisis until, in November 1967, there was no escaping a devaluation of the pound. Unlike Wilson in 1966 Margaret Thatcher had had four grinding years in what has increasingly become a destroying job. Like Wilson, perhaps, she had expended more emotional energy than she knew and suffered something resembling a post-electoral depression.

The government backbenches were crowded with new faces, men – and a sprinkling of women – many of whom had not expected to be there. Very quickly they grew to like the House of Commons – proverbially the best club in London – and had no wish to lose their marginal seats at the next election. Pym had been right. With a majority of 144 the Parliament was much more difficult to manage than with the 1979 majority of 45, which had seen her comfortably through the previous one. A smallish working majority keeps a party, and a government, on its toes; a landslide is bad for party discipline, enabling rebellion with impunity. Radical Thatcherites by conviction, instinct or in tone of voice as many of the new intake were, they were conservative enough – conservative, that is, with a small c – about anything which might lose them votes in their constituencies. They were more frightened of their postbags than of the Whips. Through 1984 and 1985 a series of backbench revolts occurred on such matters as university fees, which it was suggested the middle classes might in part pay for themselves, and the proposal to withdraw tax subsidies from private pension schemes. These revolts culminated in early 1986, following the Westland Affair, in the prevention of the break-up and sale of British Leyland and the defeat of a government Bill to permit trading on Sundays. Ironically, the size of her majority became one of the brakes on radical Thatcherism.

In the early sessions of the Parliament she was also in trouble on her own backbenches over the choice of the new Speaker, on banning trade unions at the GCHQ, housing benefits, rate support grants and the reform of local government. The dispute over the future of the Westland helicopter company provoked a major Cabinet crisis which shook the government to its foundations. In some cases these were revolts of the faithful in fear of their seats and inspired by middle class protest, in others they were rearguard actions by the High Tory wing of the party against what it took to be the excesses of Thatcherism. At one point, briefly, the flag of rebellion was hoisted by Pym himself. He announced the formation of a new inner party grouping to be called Conservative Centre Forward which, it was said, might on occasions defy the party Whip en bloc in favour of its own. The move contained the hint of a split in the Conservative Party. Pym had no intention of putting up against Thatcher for the leadership, if only because he knew that such a bid would be forlorn, but he was in effect declaring himself as a candidate for the succession. Some 32 Tory backbenchers, a good few from the old squirearchy of the party, had originally signed up for Conservative Centre Forward but some quickly backed out under pressure from the Whips or the big-wigs of their local parties. Pym himself was in trouble down in Cambridgeshire.

'Pym's rebellion' may have sounded like a Peasants' Revolt but in fact it was more of a patricians' reaction. Like most rebels, the supporters of Centre Forward regarded themselves as the defenders of true tradition; it was Thatcher, as they saw it, who had departed from the central stream of the Tory Party which they took to be the Disraelian tradition of 'one nation'. In part they were motivated in this by the fear that David Owen, who was making his mark as new leader of the SDP, would appropriate the Disraelian banner. In a recently published book, *The Politics of Consent*, Pym had written: 'my concern is that the flag of traditional Conservatism is kept flying, and that people are reminded of its values and worth, so that one day a standard bearer can pick it up and put it back at the centre of our affairs where it belongs.'[1]

By this time, which was May 1985, the miners' strike was over and the Falklands War had faded in the public's memory; there was no 'Scargill Factor' or 'Falklands Factor' to buoy up the Prime Minister's popularity. MP's were beginning to wonder whether, without such special factors, Thatcher and Thatcherism provided a winning combination for the future. The party had done badly in the recent local elections in the English shires. The grandee wing of the Tory Party disliked Mrs Thatcher for a number of reasons. Partly it was snobbish disdain for the politics of a shop-keeper's daughter; partly it was aversion to ideology, an 'ism, which lay uneasily upon what John Stuart Mill had named 'the stupid party'; and partly it stemmed from patrician concern for the 'condition of the people'. This last was the product in part of social conscience and in part of *noblesse oblige* and sheer prudence, their response to Joseph Chamberlain's rhetorical question: 'what ransom will property pay for the security it enjoys?' With three million unemployed in the land and the cities recently in riot, that question seemed real enough to some.

Thatcher, however, was having no nonsense about Disraeli. 'I am much nearer to creating one nation than Labour will ever be,' she declared. 'Socialism is two nations. The privileged rulers, and everyone else. And it always gets to that. What I am desperately trying to do is create one nation, with everyone being a man of property, or having the opportunity to be a man of property.'[2] That went for the 'wets' in her own party as well. There was much in what she said. Disraeli's famous remark – it comes in his novel *Sybil* – was: 'I was told that the Privileged and the People formed Two Nations'; but in 1985 it was the people who were, for the most part, the privileged, while the poor, the other nation, consisted chiefly of an underclass of the unemployed, underpaid, uneducated. That underclass had grown during the Thatcher years but so had the prosperity of the people. One of the profound changes underlying the Thatcher Revolution was the coming of age of the majority of the 'haves' over the minority of the 'have nots'. It had been the Labour Party which had claimed to speak for 'the people', while the Tory Party had – in Labour eyes – been the party of the ruling class, of landed interest and property. But now property was spreading among the people. The old model was no longer valid and Mrs Thatcher, the first wholly to grasp and exploit the change which was occurring in society, had converted the majority of the 'haves' into a political majority cutting across old party lines. That she had achieved this, and had – as Disraeli would have put it – 'dished the socialists', was not yet understood either by the Labour Party or by the old patrician guard of her own party.

Disraeli had had something to say also on the subject of local government, which was at this time a cause of trouble in the Tory Party. 'Centralisation is the death-blow of public freedom,' he had said.[3] Here again traditional roles had been reversed. It was the Conservatives who were now the centralisers, Labour the decentralisers. Indeed it was one of the ironies of Thatcherism, another way in which it departed from the mainstream tradition of the Conservative Party, that the power of central government needed to be invoked on an unprecedented scale in order economically to 'set the nation free'. As the Marxist commentator, Andrew Gamble, had well put it: 'The state is to be rolled back in some areas and rolled forward in others

. . . The real innovation of Thatcherism is the way it has linked traditional Conservative concern with the basis of authority in social institutions and the importance of internal order and external security, with a new emphasis upon free market exchange and the principles of the market order.'[4]

Local government reform divided the Conservative Party between those – Pym was one – who adhered to the traditional view of local democracy rooted in the shires and the boroughs, sustained by local squires and burgesses (Alderman Roberts of Grantham, for example), while others were of the opinion that reversing Britain's decline was too serious a business to be left to the sort of people who these days got themselves elected to the town and county halls.

The government had embarked upon reform for three reasons. One was that Mrs Thatcher had rashly pledged to abolish the rates as long ago as 1974 and even more rashly renewed it in the 1983 manifesto. A second was that she had been provoked by the left-wing antics of the Greater London Council under Ken Livingstone and decided to close it down, together with six other second-tier Metropolitan Authorities which had arisen out of the Heathite bureaucratisation of the early 1970s. The third was that the spending of the local authorities was inconsistent with the government's borrowing targets which were a part of the mumbo jumbo of monetarism.

Local authorities accounted for about a quarter of all public spending. Central government provided more than half of their income but had no control over their expenditures. Successive governments, Labour as well as Conservative, had found this highly unsatisfactory. Rates absorbed between 2 to 3 per cent of personal incomes, compared with 14 per cent in expenditure taxes and 12·5 per cent in income taxes, but were more painful to pay because they had to be handed over as a lump sum.[5] For both these reasons, it was widely agreed that the rating system was in need of reform. But nobody had been able to come up with an acceptable solution to the problem. The rapid inflation of the early 1970s had sparked off rates revolts and had led to Mrs Thatcher's promise of abolition. Labour in 1974 had appointed the Layfield Committee, which reported in 1976. It recommended a reduction in the government's share of local government finance from the then 67 per cent to nearer 50 per cent. Otherwise, it warned, local democracy would continue to be undermined by the unsatisfactory division of responsibility between central and local government.[6] But Labour did nothing.

After 1979 it was not ratepayers in revolt but zealous monetarists who kept the issue to the fore. 'Two very legitimate concerns of central government', Nigel Lawson had said, were 'the overall burden of taxation and the total of public expenditure.' Another problem was that many voters did not pay rates. In an electorate of 35 millions, there were 18 million ratepayers compared with 21 million income-tax payers. Moreover, some 6 million people received full or partial rate rebates under the social security system. In Sheffield, for example, as many as 26 per cent did not pay, in London's Tower Hamlets 28 per cent. Thus the rate burden fell heavily on business. During the government's first term rates had risen on average 91 per cent, other prices 55 per cent. In consequence business was fleeing from the cities, or so it was claimed. Heseltine had attempted to deal with the problem by cutting the funds from the central government but instead of cutting their spending accordingly many authorities had simply pushed their rates still higher. Twenty local authorities had overspent to the tune of £750 million in the four years since 1979. The government argued that since it was Parliament which had delegated democratic power to local authorities they had breached the conventions of the Constitution by such overspending. This was true in a strict constitutional sense, although it had been a purpose of the Local Government Act of 1888 to diminish the power of the central government.

The government now proposed to bring the big spenders to book by capping their rates, that is, making it illegal for them to levy rates above a certain prescribed level and thereby forcing them to reduce their expenditures. This was the issue which posed the question of whether the power of central government was growing too great and ought to be diminished. A former Tory Minister, and a former mayor, Geoffrey Rippon, told the Commons that rate-capping would confer upon the central government, 'wide, sweeping general powers of a kind that have not hitherto been regarded in this country as being in accordance with the rule of law. We stand for the Town Hall not Whitehall,' he declared, echoing the traditional Tory view.

Similar doubts were felt about the proposal to abolish the GLC and the other Metropolitan Authorities. They had never been popular in the Conservative Party and were regarded as of doubtful utility. Nevertheless, they were democratically elected bodies. The only legitimate way to remove them was through the ballot box, argued Pym. Edward Heath warned that to close them down would invite reprisals of a similar nature if Labour returned to power. 'It seems to me,' said Gilmour, the Highest Tory of them all, 'that the lack of political scruple being shown is, at least, stupid.' All Tories wished to spare the country from socialism but some believed that this would best be achieved by governing in a spirit of moderation and generosity. The Prime Minister believed that the best way to destroy socialism was to eradicate it in its strongholds. She was not in the business of putting off the evil day, her aim was to prevent it from ever happening. As Norman Tebbit put it, 'The Labour Party is the party of division. In its present form it represents a threat to the democratic values and institutions on which our parliamentary system is based. The GLC is typical of this new modern, divisive version of socialism. It must be defeated. So we shall abolish the GLC.'

On both Bills the government lost the argument but won the day. As Edward Heath pointed out, 'The fact that the Government have lost the argument has not been due in large measure to the efforts of the Opposition.' The more effective opposition to the march of Thatcherism was coming not from the Labour benches but from the government's own backbenches.

Thatcherism had some unpleasant implications for the middle classes which espoused it or, at least, espoused Mrs Thatcher. The middle classes gained considerable benefit from state subsidies, in the form of tax breaks, and made extensive use of the Welfare State, both of free education and the National Health Service. Although already by the autumn of 1984 ministers were alert to the danger of 'banana skins' – the favourite cliché of the time – Sir Keith Joseph managed to elude their grasp. In the course of that summer's public expenditure review in which, as a means of extracting money from the Treasury, spending ministers customarily make lavish bids in the hope of being scaled down only to their true requirements, Sir Keith – characteristically – volunteered cuts in his own budget. Too pure for politics, he deemed it immoral to ask for more when the logic of doing so was in conflict with the strategy he supported.

In consequence he now proposed to levy charges to recoup a portion of the cost of tuition at universities and other institutions of higher education. This would have saved the Treasury some £39 millions a year, £24 millions of which would be re-allocated to scientific research which had been badly impaired by government cuts and was the subject of an articulate and vocal lobby. What he proposed would have involved some 50,000 families with incomes of around £22,000 a year paying £725 a year towards their children's university fees while 180,000 would be worse off in some lesser degree. Families with higher incomes would have to pay more, up to a limit of £4,000 a year, and the scheme would be particularly severe for those on around £25,000 a year. In the previous year there had already been a tightening up on the housing benefits which students were entitled to claim.

Students' maintenance grants had long been means-tested but it had been a principle that tuition fees should be paid in full by the State on a universal basis. The Thatcher government was no respecter of such principles. Joseph queried the justice of the predominantly better-off minority whose children attended university being subsidised by the less-privileged majority of taxpayers, for that is what it amounted to. Moreover, he did not allow that education was solely a public good for it was also a highly desirable form of private consumption. In addition he pleaded 'the desperate plight of scientists' in support of his scheme, although their desperate plight was the result of government parsimony and many considered that cutting scientific research was hardly the best way to go about reversing Britain's industrial decline. However, the fees proposal was vigorously protested against by Conservatives in the constituencies who were not interested in such theorising. One complained to *The Times* in typical terms: 'Life assurance premium relief abolished, VAT imposed on home building improvements, and now punitive charges for higher education, all aimed squarely at those who hold to the principles of self-help and family betterment.' Cascaded with mail from their constituents, besieged at Westminster by students, 180 backbench Tories signed motions of protest. It was the largest backbench rebellion yet to occur. It was also the broadest. It brought together High Tory and Thatcherite, united those who cared about learning and the advancement of science and those who cared chiefly for the pockets of their £25,000-a-year constituents.

Although ill-judged, Joseph's plan had been consistent with the general thrust of Treasury policy. The Chancellor, Lawson, was eager wherever possible to save money on tax subsidies to enable him the more to reduce the basic rates of taxation. For example, in his Budget – as the correspondent to *The Times* complained – he had withdrawn tax relief from private life insurance policies. He now wished to do the same on the private pension schemes of companies, which would have yielded him a huge saving. He would also have liked to end the payment of child allowances regardless of means. The trouble was that the logic of the government's financial strategy was leading it once again into the no-go areas of the Welfare State, the areas from which it had flinched in 1982. Moreover, it was severely constricted by pledges made at election times. It had variously promised not to introduce hotel charges in hospitals, not to charge for GP services or make changes in the exceptions to prescription charging, and not to abolish mortgage tax relief. That was another reason why the privileged tax position of occupational pension funds was of such interest to the Chancellor. Later this too had to be abandoned. So did a move to decontrol rents. So did the plan to abolish the State Earnings-Related Pension Scheme (SERPS). The imperious style of the Thatcher prime ministership was in sharp contrast with her ability to push through reforms unpopular with her middle class supporters.

She saw herself as activist, not as arbiter of disputes. She had said on taking office, 'It must be a conviction government. As Prime Minister I could not waste time with any internal arguments.'[7] Her style in Cabinet was a tendency to lead rather than to take the voices. In any case, hers was the most insistent voice. Her Cabinet proceeded by argument rather than by discussion.[8] 'I take your point about frankness,' she wrote in reply to James Prior's letter of resignation. 'That's what Cabinets are for, and lively discussions usually lead to good decisions.' Francis Pym saw her as embodying the 'absolutist spirit of the age'.

Her dominance of the government was achieved partly through the force of her personality and partly by the technique of side-stepping the Cabinet whenever she could. 'I am the Cabinet rebel,' she once said. The number of Cabinet meetings a year was reduced to about half the post-war norm.[9] Ministers were mostly scared of her. To request an interview was to invite a detailed grilling on departmental policy. Only Sir Keith Joseph was masochist enough to enjoy that sort of thing. 'My eyes light up at the sight of her even though she's hitting me about the head, so to speak.'[10] Keeping the head down was the wiser course. She ruled through a web of ad hoc committees manned by trusties. For example, Prior and Pym were kept off the key economic policy committee and John Biffen, when he fell from her favour, was virtually excluded from the government although still occupying the important position of Leader of the House of Commons. When the decision was taken to ban trade unions from the intelligence headquarters (GCHQ) the first most Cabinet Ministers knew was when Sir Geoffrey Howe announced the decision in the Commons. It was a style well-suited to crisis management – the Falklands War, the miners' strike – but less so to crisis prevention.

Myths surround the subject of Cabinet government. In retrospect the previous age seems always a golden age of collective responsibility while the present is invariably taken to be the apotheosis of prime ministerial or presidential government. But according to the former Permanent Under-Secretary to the Treasury, Douglas Wass, 'The extent to which prime ministers behave like presidents and the extent to which they behave like chairmen of committees, varies almost randomly.'[11] Wilson was both in his time, Callaghan perhaps the best chairman since Attlee. The notion of 'first among equals' has long been a fiction. The prime minister of the day controls the agenda of the Cabinet and it is the prime minister who sums up. 'A majority of us think,' Mrs Thatcher would say, meaning, 'I think,' or, perhaps, 'Geoffrey and I think'. In addition the prime minister has the last word concerning the minutes. One reason why prime ministers keep business out of Cabinet is that nothing brought before Cabinet stays secret for long. Some 200 people see the most restricted Cabinet papers. But the power of a prime minister resides not in the institutions of the system but rather in the political standing of the incumbent. When prime ministers are up they are very, very up but when they are down they can be virtually powerless. Moreover, Mrs Thatcher's imperious style cut two ways: when matters did reach Cabinet she was defeated on more numerous occasions than any other post-war prime minister.

Her outsider mentality led her to regard government as a personal conspiracy against her. Her technique was to conspire against it. This she did by bringing in outsiders, by dealing directly with officials who took her fancy, by operating a network of trusties strategically placed in the departments. 'I think she instinctively dislikes anybody who is not helping in the wealth creation process,' said Sir Frank Cooper, then PUS at the Ministry of Defence. 'I'm not sure she dislikes civil servants in their own right. I don't believe she does. But I don't think that she regards them as a group of people who are contributing to the wealth of the nation.'[12] Hers was a highly personal and frequently arbitrary style of governing. Her private office at Number 10 hectored and bullied the private offices of her departmental Ministers. 'I was quite amazed at the rudeness of the letters that came round,' said one. The leak was also an instrument of her personal power. Pym first learnt he was for the chop from the newspapers, actually during the 1983 General Election campaign. The word was out against him. It happened to others. When Prior was endeavouring to establish a new assembly in Northern Ireland her own parliamentary secretary, Ian Gow, lobbied against it among backbenchers.

The outsiders she brought in or the officials she promoted were by no means invariably 'yes' men. Anthony Parsons, whom she installed at Number 10 as her foreign policy adviser (to Pym's annoyance) on one occasion dared even to tell her once to shut up. That had been at

Chequers during the Falklands War. 'Excuse me, Prime Minister, but would you mind allowing me to finish,' he had said. Often the people she took a fancy to came from similar backgrounds to her own and were not of the Establishment. They were grammar school not public school, men like Peter Middleton, an irreverent monetarist whom she made PUS at the Treasury in succession to the unreconstructed Keynesian Wass.

But she did not transform the role of prime minister in any institutionalised sense.[13] Richard Crossman had argued many years before that the tendency towards presidential or 'prime ministerial government' could not be resisted and would better be institutionalised. Wilson for a while had talked vaguely of making 'a power house' at Number 10. But as Douglas Hurd had discovered while serving as Heath's political secretary, Number 10 remained more of a private house than an office. Thatcher was an imperial Prime Minister in style but, like her predecessors, did little to increase the power of her office. Her attitude was that it was better to get on with the job than to waste time worrying about the tools. Her staff at Number 10 consisted of half-a-dozen senior officials. One of them on arrival reported, 'Any idea that you have a power house running things from Number 10 is entirely misplaced. I soon discovered that it was done with brown paper tied up with string.' Only the most trusted cronies or advisers were admitted to the flat upstairs. There she would kick off her shoes and cook bacon and eggs for her officials. Lloyd George is not known to have cooked. Hers was the first literal 'kitchen cabinet'.

The style in which she governed became an issue in the Westland Affair, which was by far and away the most serious of the difficulties of her second term. It was the nearest she came to nemesis. In a television interview during the 1987 General Election David Frost challenged her gently with the suggestion that on 27 January 1986, she had said, 'I may not be Prime Minister by six o'clock tonight.' She could easily have denied it. Instead she said, 'You suddenly come out with these things. I would not necessarily take them as if they had any very great deep significance.'

Exactly how close to the brink she did come has never been properly established and perhaps never will. Some say she did, some say she didn't, but some know or saw more than others and no one was witness to the whole story. It is said that by the end of the affair she was reduced to tears and it may have been in a moment of misery or depression that she made that desperate remark on the day she was to face the emergency debate in the House of Commons which was tantamount to a motion of censure against her.

The Westland Affair destabilised the government and left it profoundly demoralised. Yet, as one Cabinet Minister said afterwards, 'It was about nothing, absolutely nothing.' Ostensibly it had been about helicopters. Westland was Britain's only helicopter manufacturer and it had been in financial difficulties for some while. By 1985 it was facing bankruptcy and unless a solution was found for its difficulties would by mid-December become insolvent. The American company Sikorsky was prepared to take a minority stake in Westland sufficient to save it. But this would mean Britain becoming dependent on the United States for helicopters, which had come to play an increasingly important role in modern warfare, as in Vietnam for example. An alternative would be some form of European association or consortium.

It was suspected that Sikorski was interested in Westland only because it wished to secure a foothold within the common market of the European Community and because it wanted to sell its Black Hawk helicopter to the British government. The defence chiefs didn't want it. The European manufacturers had an interest in keeping Sikorski out of their markets if they could. Collaboration might enable them better to compete in American markets.

As the problems of the company became more urgent the government looked increasingly to the quickest available solution, which was Sikorski. Its market philosophy prejudiced it in this direction. Leon Brittan, who was the Secretary of State for Trade and Industry, had begun with an open mind about the European alternative – if such there was – but at an early meeting of the committee of the Cabinet which was handling the issue he had said: 'I don't give a toss if Westland goes to the wall and I'm not going to spend a penny of DTI money.'

The Secretary of State for Defence, Michael Heseltine, was an ardent European and as a junior Minister in the Edward Heath government had championed European aero-space collaboration. He came to see the government's growing partisanship for Sikorski as a mark of its anti-Europeanism. Later in the affair he was to tell a friend that he had been sickened by the poison which poured from the Prime Minister's lips concerning Europe.

These were the familiar tensions of the Thatcher government, between free marketeers and interventionists, between enthusiasts and unenthusiasts for Europe, and there was no reason why they should now produce a major Cabinet crisis. But they did. The problems faced by Westland provided Margaret Thatcher and Michael Heseltine with their opportunity to lock horns, something they had been waiting to do for some time.

She regarded him with suspicion, as she did all potential rivals. When his name was mentioned, 'Michael,' she used to say, 'he is not one of us.' Back in February, long before a helicopter had appeared on the horizon, she had suspected him of looking for a resignation issue which would enable him to set up against her from the back-benches. Paranoia is one of the many occupational hazards of a prime minister. However, she was not far wrong in this case. Heseltine was becoming increasingly disaffected by her style of governing. He believed that if she continued as she went she would lose the next General Election. He hoped that the Conservative Party might look instead to his own more traditional, more paternalistic brand of radical Conservativism. By the time of the Conservative Party conference at Blackpool that autumn he certainly had resignation in mind – although not over helicopters.[14]

The argument within the government over Westland came to a head in December 1986. On 9 December Sir John Cuckney, the chairman of the company, was invited to attend a meeting of a Cabinet committee under the chairmanship of the Prime Minister. For the chairman of a commercial company to attend such a meeting was in itself unusual. He urged the government to leave the decision to the Westland board, which was what Brittan and Thatcher wished to do. Heseltine once more pressed the European suit. He succeeded in winning time. He was allowed a week in which to put together convincingly the European consortium he had been talking about.

The Prime Minister later saw this as her big mistake. She should there and then have slapped him into line. She should have insisted on collective responsibility for a Cabinet decision to allow Westland to decide its own future. She should have accepted his resignation if necessary. But she did none of these things. She was too afraid of him.

Heseltine's understanding following the 9 December meeting was that there would be a further meeting of the committee the following Friday. The Prime Minister's understanding was that it had been decided in any case that the decision was for the Westland board not for the government. When the full Cabinet met the following Thursday Heseltine discovered to his rage that there was to be no meeting the following day, no further meeting at all. He claimed that the meeting had been cancelled. The Prime Minister claimed that none had been arranged. The reason it had been cancelled, he believed, was that his European initiative had succeeded. He had been permitted to go ahead with it, he was now convinced, only because his opponents were sure that he would fail. Now it was plain that the Prime Minister and Leon Brittan were wedded to the Sikorski deal come what may. He demanded that his protest about the cancelling of the meeting be recorded in the Cabinet minutes. It was not.[15]

The following day the Westland board, as was to be expected, rejected the European proposal. Heseltine from that point set out to campaign for his solution to the problem. What ensued now was an increasingly open inter-departmental row between the MOD and the DTI. It was an unscrupulous affair on both sides. When such civil wars break out in Whitehall a standard weapon is the press leak. There is nothing particularly reprehensible about leaking to the press. In the relatively closed British system of government it enables a policy argument to be conducted in public or semi-public. In more open systems bureaucratic battles are fought in semi-public. There would have been nothing in the least remarkable about the way Heseltine set about trying to reverse the government's policy had London been Washington. He waged a war of leaks.

But London was not Washington. His activities increasingly became an embarrassment to the government and an annoyance to the Prime Minister. In the last week before Christmas she did consider sacking him. Some told her she should, some told her she shouldn't. John Wakeham, the Chief Whip, was one who favoured keeping him on board.

The name Heseltine was not far from her mind during the family festivities at Chequers that year. No sooner was Christmas over – what a relief to be back at her desk – than she launched a new move to bring Heseltine to heel. It was arranged that Sir John Cuckney should write to the Prime Minister requesting clarification of the European consequences of going ahead with the Sikorski tie-up. Heseltine had been alleging it would mean the virtual exclusion of British helicopters from the European market. Thatcher's draft reply to Sir John reached Heseltine on New Year's Eve. He considered the letter to be tendentious and inaccurate. He consulted the Solicitor General, Sir Patrick Mayhew, who advised that the government ought to warn Westland that there had been some indications of anxiety from Europe about the arrangement with Sikorski. Heseltine wanted to specify these threats in some detail. Eventually Downing Street added a vague health warning to its original letter and sent it off.

Heseltine then contrived an opportunity to put his own version on record. He inserted all of the language the Prime Minister had

1 Student revolutionary leaders sing the 'Internationale' at the tomb of Karl Marx, 1968. *Left to right*, Karl Dietrich-Wolff (Germany), Tariq Ali (Britain), Daniel Cohn-Bendit (France) and Yasuo Ishii (Japan).

The Establishment everywhere was a target for demonstrators in 1968. Here police try to contain crowds outside the Embassy of the German Federal Republic in London.

3 and 4 The Winter of Discontent. *Above*, NUPE pickets outside the Great
Ormond Street Hospital for Sick Children, February 1979; *below*,
rubbish piles up in central London while the dustmen are on strike.

5 A CND demonstrator climbs into the Greenham Common US Air Force Base to protest about the siting of nuclear missiles there.

6 Confusion and dissent at the Labour Party conference, 1980.

7 and 8   Arthur Scargill, president of the NUM, and the police see two sides
of each other: *above*, at a Yorkshire pit strike, and *below*, outside
the National Coal Board headquarters in London.

9 Margaret Thatcher takes on Edward Heath for the leadership of the Conservative Party.

10 After her victory, with Sir Keith Joseph.
11 A show of unity: Edward Heath (*centre, left*) with Margaret Thatcher
and William Whitelaw and, between them, Sir Keith Joseph.

12 On the way to fight the Falklands War.
13 After the Falklands victory, Margaret Thatcher in Whitehall. 'We knew what we had to do . . . and we did it. Great Britain is great again.'

14 Before the General Election in 1983. Mrs Thatcher with (*seated, left*) the Home Secretary, William Whitelaw, and (*seated, right*) Cecil Parkinson, Chairman of the Conservative Party. Standing (*left to right*), Norman Tebbit, Minister of Employment, Sir Geoffrey Howe, Chancellor of the Exchequer, Francis Pym, Foreign Secretary, and Michael Heseltine, Minister of Defence.

15 Mrs Thatcher, with her husband Denis, returns to No. 10 Downing Street, for her third consecutive term of office after the General Election of June 1987.

16 *Above, left*, Michael Foot at a TUC rally in 1982.
17 *Above, right*, James Callaghan.
18 Tony Benn, Arthur Scargill and Ken Livingstone (*right*) at the Labour
Party conference, 1982.

19 Militant Tendency leaders Tony Mulhearn (*left*) and Derek Hatton.
20 Michael Foot after the Wembley conference which resulted in a victory for the left wing of the Labour Party.
21 The outgoing leader, Michael Foot, embraces his wife at the Labour Party conference in 1983, while Neil Kinnock, leader-elect, looks on.
22 Neil Kinnock and Denis Healey visit Washington in 1987.

Neil Kinnock rallies supporters during the 1987 General Election campaign.

The birth of the Social Democratic Party, 1981. On the platform (*left to right*) are Roy Jenkins, David Owen, William Rodgers and Shirley Williams. Grouped on the left are the MPs who joined the new Party.

25 and 26 Two faces of the Alliance: Dr David Owen (*left*) and David Steel, leaders respectively of the SDP and the Liberal Party.

27 Roy Jenkins wins the by-election at Glasgow, Hillhead for the SDP. With him is Shirley Williams.

28 After American Air Force bombers had attacked targets in Libya an
American serviceman makes a security check, while a protester
demonstrates with a placard which reads, 'Go home US terrorists. No
sanctuary here.'
29 Mrs Thatcher with President Reagan at Camp David.

30 *Glasnost:* Mrs Thatcher meets Mikhail Gorbachev in Moscow.
31 Towards a share-owning democracy. Privatisation of the Trustee Savings Bank causes an avalanche of applications from the public.

32 'You've never had it so good' – 1987-style. Norman Tebbit with a Conservative Party General Election poster.

33 Making her point.

declined to include in her letter to Cuckney in a letter he wrote to
Lloyds Bank, who were acting for the European consortium. The
letter had been discussed with no one outside the MOD and had not
been cleared with the Solicitor General. Heseltine leaked it to *The
Times*.

The Prime Minister was now furious. A Cabinet Minister was
engaging in open warfare against her. The Fleet Street headlines
proclaimed the government was out of control, a shambles. Moreover, Heseltine was running circles round Brittan. She said this to
Brittan, angrily, in the presence of officials. 'Get Heseltine!' was from
now on the order of the day.

It was she who suggested that Heseltine's letter now be referred to
Sir Patrick Mayhew for his opinion. Obviously the hope was that he
would consider it over the top and insist that the true position be
accurately stated. Brittan made the call to Mayhew.

At Chequers again that Sunday (5 January) the question was how
to prevent Heseltine from – as she had said – running circles around
Brittan. Among those present were Lord Whitelaw and John Wakeham. Nothing, however, could be decided until the Mayhew trap had
been sprung. Meanwhile, Mayhew and Heseltine were in touch.
Mayhew was not especially agitated by Heseltine's letter and Heseltine assured him that on Monday his office would be able to substan-
tiate every statement made in it. However, Mayhew was of the
opinion that the letter as it stood – and he had only the version which
had appeared in *The Times* to go on – was misleading. By that
evening Brittan's officials had learned that Mayhew would refer to
'material inaccuracies' in Heseltine's letter.

Monday, 6 January was the first fateful day in the affair. It was the
day on which the letter containing Mayhew's opinion was selectively
leaked to the Press Association by the Chief Information Officer of
the DTI, Colette Bowe. The remainder of the Westland story turns
on who authorised this leak. Was it Leon Brittan acting on his own
authority? Was it, as Brittan was to claim, Number 10? If so was it
Bernard Ingham, Mrs Thatcher's press secretary, acting on his own
authority? Or was it Mrs Thatcher herself?

What happened was that the text of Mayhew's letter reached the
DTI that morning. It did say that Heseltine's letter – or, rather, one
sentence of it – contained 'material inaccuracies' but added that this
view was based only on documents available to him (i.e. he had not
taken account of any further evidence that Heseltine might provide).

Whether or not it had always been the plan to leak the letter
(Heseltine had leaked his) the purpose of commissioning it had been

to discredit Heseltine. It was also to serve as the basis for the ploy which at the Cabinet that week would either gag Heseltine or force him to resign. The letter could have had no other purpose. The Department of Trade and Industry was on red alert that Monday morning awaiting its arrival. Colette Bowe was standing by, which, as the Select Committee on Defence later commented, 'suggests . . . that officials had in mind that some public use of the information contained in the letter was indicated.'[16] When the letter arrived Brittan's private secretary, Roger Mogg, telephoned him at lunch in the City. By coincidence or otherwise his luncheon appointment was with Morgan Grenfell, the merchant bankers who were acting on behalf of Westland. According to Brittan – or rather according to Sir Robert Armstrong, for Brittan himself remained silent, in public at least – he told Mogg that he thought the Solicitor General's opinion 'should go into the public domain and that it should be done in specific terms but that No. 10, the Prime Minister's office, should be consulted.' There followed two telephone calls between the DTI and the private office at Number 10 which resulted – in the fastidious words of Sir Robert – in 'a difference of understanding'. The Number 10 officials insisted that they were being told of something the DTI was going to do in any case; the DTI officials insisted they had sought and obtained Number 10's approval. All that could be agreed subsequently was that the officials at Number 10 had refused to make the disclosure themselves.[17]

Phase one of the Westland Affair had been about helicopters, or ostensibly so. Phase two had been about bringing Heseltine to heel. Phase three was to be about cover up. In the Watergate scandal which preoccupied Washington from 1972 to 1974, eventually destroying the presidency of Richard Nixon, the original misdemeanour was soon almost forgotten. The unacceptable crime was the cover up of the original crime. The selective leaking of a privileged letter to the press scarcely compares with presidential complicity in a burglary.[18] Nevertheless, the danger Mrs Thatcher faced was now similar. It was that she would be drawn deeper and deeper into trouble through seeking to conceal her part in what was, in essence, an unscrupulous and improper conspiracy to discredit and defeat a Cabinet rival.

But before we come to that the second phase of the affair must be played out to its *dénouement*. Much was made subsequently of the logistics of the leak. Although denying that he had authorised it Ingham did not deny that he advised Colette Bowe on how best to go about it. If the object of the exercise was to make Mayhew's corrections to Heseltine's warnings available in time for a Westland press conference due at 4 o'clock that afternoon, he told her, it was no use her spreading the word around the Lobby for the next morning's papers; the only way was to get the story running on the Press Association tapes. But – as the Select Committee wondered – why did they not simply tell Cuckney, who already knew in any case? Moreover, the Westland board had already taken its decision to recommend acceptance of the Sikorski offer. There was no conceivable commercial urgency requiring the leaking of the letter. Cuckney later told the Select Committee that the information made no difference to what he said at the press conference.[19]

The real reason for leaking the letter, of course, was to discredit Heseltine. It was part of a scheme either to silence him or bring him down. That explains why the letter was leaked as it was, unattributably of course. The Select Committee commented: 'It is clear that the passages chosen for selective disclosure . . . were calculated to do the maximum damage to Mr Heseltine's case and to his personal credibility.'[20] The work was well done. The next morning the headline in *The Times* declared: 'Heseltine told by Law Chief: Stick to the facts', while the *Sun* put it more bluntly: 'You Liar!'

Heseltine was aware over the weekend of 5 and 6 January that he might be heading for resignation. Hints of this appeared in the *Financial Times* which he was briefing. But by the eve of the fateful Cabinet on Thursday, 9 January he had no intention of resigning. His judgment was that nothing more could happen before the Westland shareholders' meeting the following week. He expected the Cabinet meeting to be a fairly routine affair. He told his wife Anne, he told his political friends, and he told the *Financial Times* that the possibility of his leaving the government had receded since the weekend.

But a plot had been made. At the Cabinet the Prime Minister, all innocence, asked Leon Brittan if he would be so good as to bring the Cabinet up to date. Brittan then launched into a somewhat anodyne reprise of the affair but one which annoyed Heseltine for being, once again, in his view, an entirely pejorative account of what was involved. At the end of this Brittan provided the Prime Minister with her cue. The government simply could not continue in this open disarray. There was only one thing for it, all further statements on the matter of Westland must be cleared through the Cabinet Office. Was that clear?

Heseltine appears to have worn this. Perhaps he was quick enough to reckon that all he would need to do to sustain his campaign was to file all of his previous statements with Sir Robert Armstrong. Then he could repeat them at will. But, in any case, it was not his wish to resign. The business moved on until Nicholas Ridley intervened. Ridley's effete and laconic Old Etonian manner disguises a quick and clever mind which he is prone to speak, often to disastrous political effect. On this occasion we do not know whether a point of logic had suddenly flashed into his brain or whether he spoke deliberately to respring a trap that had failed to work. Whichever it was, he asked to be clear whether the Prime Minister's ruling applied merely to future statements or also to reiterations of past positions. Oh, the latter too, was the answer. Its effect was dramatic. Heseltine lost his cool. He rose to his feet. He gathered up his papers. 'I can no longer remain a member of this Cabinet,' he said and swept from the room.

This was the man who had once seized the Mace from its holy place on the Order Table in front of Mr Speaker's Chair in a moment of impetuosity and parliamentary impiety. It was this kind of talent for melodramatics which had given him his reputation for untrustworthiness, an unspecific vice in the lexicon of the Tory Party but a damaging word to be muttered about a chap. Otherwise he possessed all the talents required for success as a Conservative politician: he was rich, handsome, married to a beautiful wife, a fine speaker, and not suspected of being an intellectual.

That he wore his ambition on the sleeve of his flak jacket (dressing up was another aspect of his flamboyant character) was not widely held against him in his own Party. His performances at the annual Party conference, however, were considered to be in poor taste. The grandees, who were becoming fewer as the Thatcher years wore on, disliked this kind of enthusiasm rather in the way that their eighteenth-century predecessors could sniff a papist in a parson a mile off. The Thatcherites, for their part, did not much care for the Disraeli-worship in which he indulged on these occasions. The conference, however, and especially the women, loved it and he was rare among Tories in possessing a base of his own not at Westminster but in the country.

He was probably the richest man in the Cabinet from which he resigned that Thursday morning. A few may have been worth more in acres but none in terms of annual income. His was reputed to be more than a million a year. That did not prevent a colleague describing him as 'the sort of chap who had to buy his own furniture'. However, there was less of that kind of snobbery in the Thatcher Cabinet, indeed snobbery of the opposite kind was more common: to be 'one of us' it was preferable to be an outsider of some kind, against the Establishment; Ridley, for example, qualified through being the younger son of a lord.

Being so rich was very important with Heseltine. It gave him his independence as a politician, common in earlier centuries but rarer in this one. Ministers when suddenly deprived of office are often like lost children, bereft of their Rover cars and their officials. After the 1964 General Election, when Lord Home summoned a meeting of the defeated Cabinet, Lord Hailsham demanded from Claridges: 'How can I come? They've taken my car.' After his resignation Heseltine could continue to travel by helicopter or executive jet, he could afford any staff he needed. In this way, at least, he was equipped for the wilderness.

He had made his fortune from publishing and property speculation. There had been some early ups and downs. He had come from what we might call good colonel stock. He had been brought up in a posh suburb of Swansea where his father was by then a brass-hat in the Territorial Army. In the way of the Anglo-Welsh he was sent across the Severn to public school. I knew him slightly as a boy and remember him cutting a great dash on the beach at Langland Bay in electric-blue swimming trunks. He was also the only boy we knew with his own canoe. Now he says that he built it himself. But he was never one to lecture others on the virtues of self-help, rather he preferred (as in the first speech he made following his resignation) to laud the eighteenth-century aristocratic ideal and speak of the duties owed by what he called 'the great trustees of modern wealth'. In other words, he was romantic about money.

At Oxford he became President of the Union. He saved it financially (for a time) by opening a night club in the basement. Here he showed the bent which was to shape his later political career. Administration was what interested him most, running things; he was a doer, not a thinker. When Lord Carrington described him as the best Defence Secretary Britain had had in a very long while he had in mind Heseltine's interest in collaboration and joint-procurement. Policy interested him less; personnel was his passion, reorganisation, efficiency. Appropriately, his entire ministerial career had been spent in huge conglomerate departments, as a Cabinet Minister at Environment before he went to the MOD.

It was at Environment that his affair with Liverpool began. Shortly after the Toxteth riots he dropped everything and spent three weeks on Merseyside. He bussed in thirty tycoons for a day-trip in which they saw some of the worst housing conditions in Britain, probably in Western Europe. Over tea at the Adelphi Hotel he achieved histrionic effect by declaring (to their relief) that he wanted no money from them. Pause. 'I want one thing: I want one of your brightest managers to come and work in my department for a year and to examine with us all the extremes of polarisation and the ineffectiveness of the public machinery which you have seen today.'[21] But money he did want from the Treasury. He got only enough to save his face, not Liverpool.[22]

His reputation at the MOD was mixed. The service chiefs saw him as a politician on the make who would put his career before the nation's defences, but they think that about most politicians. However, it did seem to be his view that if he put off awkward questions about the defence budget he would be gone from the MOD by the time they caught up with him. He was not the first Secretary of State to proceed on that principle. His civilian officials thought better of him. They sometimes thought that destiny had touched him but he was an elusive man, capable of odd and provocative behaviour. Early in 1985 he had snubbed Caspar Weinberger, the US Defense Secretary, when first he declined an invitation to an Anglo-American conference on 'Star Wars' at Ditchley Park, then arrived late, then failed to appear at all the next day, claiming to be snowed up in his country home. He was jealous of his privacy and, once out of the office, retreated deep into it. Asked about his ambition he would often reply that it was to create the best landscaped garden since Capability Brown, or whoever. The picture he chose for the back cover of his book, *Where There's A Will*, shows him dressed like a Royal Duke. Accompanied by his wife and two large sporting dogs, he is wearing green wellies, corduroys, a waterproof shooting jacket and a checked cap.

Outside the Cabinet Room at Number 10 there loiter officials or junior Ministers waiting to be summoned for particular items of business. It is said that when Heseltine stormed out he strode towards the front door, stopped and went into the loo where there is a mirror. Then, with the famous golden locks adjusted, he was ready to burst upon the world and the television cameras. On the steps of Number 10 he said, 'I have resigned from the Cabinet and I shall be making a full statement later.'

His car was not expecting him so he had to walk across Whitehall to his department, accompanied by reporters. Had the car been there, and had the cameras not, his private office might have been able to unresign him, or so his officials thought. But it is in these impetuous ways that men and women decide their fates.

Heseltine's resignation rocked the government. In his statement later that day he said in a sarcastic aside that he expected the usual leaks inquiry to be mounted into the leaking of the Solicitor General's letter. The Attorney General, Sir Michael Havers, had been away, recovering from open heart surgery, when Mayhew's letter had been commissioned, written and leaked. Now he was summoned to return, although far from fully convalesced. He found Mayhew, his junior colleague, fuming with indignation at the way he had been treated. Mayhew considered he had been set up to do someone else's dirty work. It had been a gross abuse of a Law Officer's position. Not only was Mayhew talking about resigning, Havers was himself in some difficulty. He had taken a consistently stern view of breaches of official secrecy and so had the Prime Minister. As Attorney General he had made more than a dozen prosecutions under the Official Secrets Act. Sarah Tisdall, a foreign office clerk, had been sent to prison for alerting the *Guardian* to the arrival of the cruise missiles at Greenham Common and Clive Ponting, an MOD official, had been tried at the Old Bailey (though acquitted) for communicating to an MP information about the sinking of the Argentinian cruiser, the *General Belgrano*, during the Falklands War. With this record he could hardly now condone the leak of a confidential paper emanating from a fellow Law Officer, all the more so when the finger pointed to high places. There could not be seen to be one law for the humble official and another for the powerful.[23]

Whether Havers from the very first suspected Brittan we do not know. But he soon discovered that he was the likely culprit. On the day after Heseltine's resignation the Attorney General met the Secretary to the Cabinet. Armstrong said that he had no reason for taking the matter any further as he understood that the leak had been authorised. Authorised by exactly whom, Havers wanted to know? It was his duty, he said, to ascertain whether there had been a breach of the Act and grounds for prosecution. However, it became plain from the conversation that the Prime Minister wanted no inquiry. Havers then said – or so it was later said – that unless there was an inquiry he would have Commander Hobbs from New Scotland Yard at Number 10 Downing Street the following morning and Commander Jones round at the DTI. Armstrong then called in the Prime Minister's Principal Private Secretary, Nigel Wicks, to hear this for himself.[24]

Inquiry there was. Armstrong would investigate the circumstances of the leak and report, privately of course, to the Prime Minister. It was subsequently her story that she had not known what had passed between her own officials and the officials at the DTI on that Monday of 6 January, or discovered that Brittan had directly authorised the leak until she received Armstrong's report on Tuesday, 21 January.

However, she must have had dealings with Brittan between the arrival of Mayhew's letter on the Monday and the Cabinet meeting on the Thursday for the purpose of setting the trap for Heseltine of which Mayhew's letter was an essential component.

But if she really did not know exactly what Brittan had been up to Armstrong must have known before he even began his inquiry. The reason he must have known is as follows. On the day of the leak the Permanent Under-Secretary at the DTI, Sir Bryan Hayes, had been out of the office. Had he not been, what happened there that day might not have happened. Colette Bowe, unhappy about what she was being made to do, and the way she was being made to do it, had tried to reach him but he had been in a car without a phone. The moment he was back she reported all to him. He went at once to Armstrong. Armstrong was fully apprised therefore of the DTI version of events, namely that Brittan had authorised the leak in the belief that he had obtained clearance from Number 10.

Armstrong's inquiry, therefore, although ostensibly for the purpose of discovering the culprit, was in reality concerned – if it had any purpose at all – with discovering who were the accomplices. In effect he had been charged by the Prime Minister to investigate her own role in the affair. No more delicate a task can ever have been set to a Secretary of the Cabinet. But no mandarin's talents could have been more appropriate than Armstrong's to undertake such a task.

His education and experience had smoothed him to perfection. The Dragon School, Eton, Christchurch, Butler's private office at the Treasury, Heath's and Wilson's at Number 10. In the meanwhile there had been a stint in the Cabinet Office. He had never in his career been more than a memo's shove from power. A Treasury man, needless to say, he went to be Permanent Under-Secretary at the Home Office under Roy Jenkins and eventually, with effortless inevitability, became Secretary to the Cabinet and Head of the Home Civil Service.

He arrived at the top quite unruffled by such high-flying, not a hair out of place on his brilliantined head, not a cell out of place in his brilliant mandarin's mind. He came to his position of immense power and influence – the most powerful in the British system of government – at the same time as Mrs Thatcher came to hers. She was new in her job, and so was he in his. In any case, she was suspicious of the Establishment, and who more personified it than Sir Robert? She was ill-disposed to place herself in safe hands. At the same time, she was thoroughly conservative about the civil service and, apart from abusing it from time to time, did nothing to enhance the power of her own office or diminish that of the Cabinet Office. Thus their careers shaped each.

According to the textbooks the Cabinet Office serves the government as a whole and the Prime Minister as *primus inter pares*. But the power of the Cabinet Office grew with the power of the Prime Minister. The Cabinet Secretary came increasingly to be in effect the Permanent Under-Secretary to the Prime Minister. Things had come a long way since eyebrows were raised when Harold Macmillan took Sir Norman Brook with him on a trip to India. In the 1970s a succession of weak governments faced with economic and industrial crises had required the official machine to take a firmer grip on running the country. Between 1973 and 1979 Sir John Hunt had built the Cabinet Office into an immensely powerful instrument. Armstrong inherited this under a woman who now intended to become an immensely powerful Prime Minister.

Unlike his predecessors, who had served more than one master, he was to serve only one mistress, and not an easy one at that. Happily, he was blessed with the courtier-like qualities necessary to the task. He was a man of all the qualities. Theirs was not an intimate relationship or a smooth one, especially as she grew more assertive and confident in herself. It is difficult to imagine Sir Robert being shouted at but he was obliged to endure it. It is the courtier's role to endure, to appease, to employ guile and stealth, to manipulate power – always behind the throne. In such abilities Armstrong excelled. For example, against all her instincts and, perhaps, her better judgment he steered her towards the Anglo-Irish Treaty signed at Hillsborough in 1985. Perhaps his most subtle achievement was to assist her to overcome her physical and moral revulsion against the advertising campaign and other steps required for combating the AIDS epidemic. An Englishman not given to overstatement, he saw this as potentially the greatest challenge facing any government in his lifetime. On other occasions he failed, however. For example, he had failed to persuade her to see that the no-strike agreement conceded by the trade unions at the GCHQ would serve her purpose as effectively as the confrontational course she insisted upon adopting. For Armstrong, who had served Butler, government was the art of the possible, and Mrs Thatcher could be pretty impossible.

He found refuge for his soul in music. He had had a musical upbringing. His father had been Principal of the Royal College of Music. He played the piano, sang tenor, and had conducted the Treasury choir. When he became Cabinet Secretary the Prime Minister had encouraged him to continue as treasurer to the Royal Opera, although eventually he found he had to give it up. Sir Thomas Beecham had urged that everyone should listen to Mozart for half-an-hour a day. Armstrong found it hard to go a day without music.

Secrecy was said to be his other passion but this was not quite true. He was on record as being in favour of open government, at least up to a point.[25] However, he was completely the traditionalist on the subject of the confidential relationship between officials and their Ministers. He saw this as the foundation stone on which the system rested. Discreet is a better word than secretive for his attitude of mind and the way he went about things. It was a word he used in a television interview, itself a rare event for a serving Secretary of the Cabinet and for someone as publicly anonymous as Robert Armstrong preferred to be. 'I don't want to be out there in front,' he said. 'I feel much happier, much more sure that I'm in a role that suits me when I am in a kind of backroom.'[26]

The Westland Affair was to drag him from that backroom. He was to become chief witness before the Select Committee on Defence. Later, and as a result of that performance, he was sent out to be teased and goaded in the Supreme Court of New South Wales where a rougher style of justice prevails. It was there he made his famous remark about being 'economical with the truth'. This was taken to be a euphemism for official lying whereas it was intended to mean the opposite: that a civil servant could tell the truth without being obliged to tell the whole truth. Here was another facet of the courtier's art. His judicious economy with the truth enabled Armstrong, in private, to be a remarkably open man.

That he was too much the courtier was the chief criticism of him, too adept in the arts of survival, too much the Tallyrand of the Thatcher regime. For during the years in which he had held court to her the morale of the civil service, of which he was the head, had declined quite drastically. She had made no secret of her low opinion of it. It had become more politicised at the same time, as we have seen. The Prime Minister saw herself as at war with bureaucracy in all its manifestations. People were for her or against her. It was this atmosphere, this way of proceeding, that was partly responsible for the Westland Affair.

The events which he was now obliged to inquire into cannot have brought delight to so fastidious a mandarin. In fact, he must have hated what had happened and deplored that it could have happened. It was not his idea of how a civil service should behave. However, Sir Robert Armstrong was born to duty. His duty now was to save the system.

He presented his report to the Prime Minister on the evening of Tuesday, 21 January. The officials involved in the leak had helped him with his inquiries – Ingham and Powell from Number 10, Mogg, Bowe, and John Michell, an assistant-secretary, from the DTI. No Minister gave evidence, nor did the Prime Minister. His report told her what she could and should have known already, namely that Brittan had authorised the leak himself over the telephone to Mogg. However, she was to insist that this was the first she had heard of it. At the meetings which now took place she is reported to have said four times, 'Leon, why didn't you tell me?' 'Either she's a remarkable actress or she really didn't know,' said one who was there. But Brittan hadn't told her because he understood that she had already known, for he insisted that what he had ordered had been cleared by his officials with Number 10.

However, if she really did not know she could very easily have found out. Ingham, for one, could have told her because his conversation with Colette Bowe had made it perfectly plain that she had been authorised to leak the letter. Indeed, he had advised her on how to go about it. The Attorney General could have told her because, as he later made plain to the Commons, he had been confident enough that Bowe had been authorised to grant her immunity before she gave evidence to Armstrong. Armstrong could have told her because Sir Brian Hayes had told him, days even before the inquiry was instituted. Indeed, when he minuted her in favour of an inquiry (following his conversation with Havers) it would be remarkable if he had not acquainted her with the facts as then available. Moreover, I learnt on the day after the inquiry was announced (13 January) that the leak had been authorised at the highest level in the DTI, and if a newspaper columnist knew it seems scarcely possible that the Prime Minister did not. Yet on 27 January she told an incredulous House of Commons:

I discussed the matter with my office the following day [7 January] when I also learned of the Law Officers' concern. I was told that the Solicitor General's advice had not been disclosed by my office . . . I was also told, in general terms, that there had been contacts between my office and the Department of Trade and Industry. I did not know about the then Secretary of State for Trade and Industry's own role in the matter of the disclosure until the inquiry had reported.[27]

When later questioned by the Select Committee on how it was that no one had mentioned the matter to the Prime Minister, or that she had failed to find out for herself, Armstrong could only say that he found it 'strange'.[28]

Brittan himself refused to enlighten the Select Committee on any point of substance. However, he is reputed to have told close friends subsequently that not only had she known perfectly well what had happened but that, on the day following the leak, had expressed her satisfaction to him at the way things had been handled. Remember, at that time the downfall of Heseltine had yet to be achieved.

Now that Armstrong's report was in her hands the Prime Minister's next task was to decide what she should say to the House of Commons. This was no easy task for there were five interests at stake, all of them represented in the Cabinet Room on the morning of Wednesday, 22 January when work began on the statement she would have to make the following day. Her own interest was plainly to exonerate herself from the charge of complicity in an unseemly and improper business. But in whatever she said she had to satisfy her officials, Powell and Ingham, whose careers and professional reputations were on the line. She could not afford to make a statement which they would feel obliged to repudiate. She needed also to satisfy Hayes, who was present in order to see that his officials did not take the rap. She had also to satisfy the Law Officers, for Havers was not prepared to go along with any statement which gave the impression that she was condoning the leak of his colleague's classified letter; he had initiated too many prosecutions for that. Then there was Brittan himself. Unless what she told the Commons was acceptable to him he might come forward with another story. He might try to point the finger at her. Potentially he now had the power to destroy her.

Brittan arrived while this Wednesday morning meeting was in progress. He objected to the statement as drafted. He continued to insist that he had received clearance for what he had done from Downing Street. When it was hinted to him, by Lord Whitelaw, that he should resign he said that he had no intention of resigning; if anyone was to resign it should be Bernard Ingham.

Predictably a statement required to preserve so many reputations could not satisfy the House of Commons. Indeed, during its final drafting Mrs Thatcher had been warned that what she proposed to say might well provoke disorders which would oblige the Speaker to suspend the sitting. It did not come to that but her statement was received with a good deal of incredulity. 'An enormous number of facts were not known to me until yesterday when I received the results of the inquiry,' she said.[29]

She fudged as much as she could the question of whether Brittan had obtained 'cover' from Number 10 – he had insisted on the inclusion of the word – but if her own professions of innocence were to be believed the only other conclusion to be drawn from her account was that Brittan had let her down. That was the conclusion his own Party now drew.

He had never been popular in the Party. He owed his position entirely to the Prime Minister's favour and had no base of his own either in Parliament or in the country. He was regarded as a toady. He had made few friends when wielding the axe for Mrs Thatcher at the Treasury when, as First Secretary, he had been responsible for public expenditure. After the 1983 General Election he had become at 43 the youngest Home Secretary since Winston Churchill in 1910. Instinctively and, on his past record, a liberal on penal matters, he won little respect, and fewer friends, when first he compromised his opposition to the restoration of capital punishment (which the Prime Minister favoured) and then endeavoured to appease the Conservative Party conference by, among other things, limiting the right to parole of prisoners convicted of violent offences or drug-trafficking.

To his chagrin he was moved from the Home Office to the DTI in the reshuffle of September 1985. Ostensibly a sideways move – he was allowed to hold his place in the pecking order – in practice it was a demotion. Wakeham had insisted that if the reshuffle was to restore the government's confidence and credibility after the recent harvest of banana skins there would need to be one symbolic change at the top. That meant moving either Howe (Foreign Secretary), Lawson (Chancellor) or Brittan (Home Office). In practice, therefore, it meant Brittan. The Whips' Office, in any case, had it in for him. He was considered a clumsy politician, poor on television.

There was a nasty undertone of anti-Semitism as the Westland Affair closed in on Leon Brittan. He came from an Orthodox Jewish family of Lithuanian origin. His father had studied medicine in Berlin and came to England in 1927. There had been unpleasant ripples of anti-Semitism in 1983 when he had been obliged by the redrawing of constituency boundaries to find himself a new seat. Now, with the future of the Prime Minister at stake, the poison reached the surface. Very senior Conservatives were guilty of quite disgraceful remarks – one described Brittan as 'behaving like a cornered rat.'

The Chief Whip, Wakeham, had decided that he would have to go, so had John Biffen, the Leader of the House. So had Whitelaw and, from very early on, Havers. Brittan had refused. But now the Black Spot was issued by Cranley Onslow, the chairman of the powerful Tory backbench 1922 Committee.[30] That was it. The support of his Party was withdrawn. Brittan was finished, bullied out. He resigned the following evening. The Westland Affair had claimed its second victim.

Would there yet be a third? That weekend Ministers met in case the worst should happen. At the Foreign Office Sir Geoffrey Howe was noticed straightening his collar in case the call to the Palace should come. Mrs Thatcher was in a very low state as she prepared her speech for the emergency debate which had been called for Monday, in which she would have to defend herself all over again. She was near the edge, sometimes in tears. 'Leon has been very difficult,' she told a friend. It was in that sort of mood that she had said, as she confessed to David Frost, 'I may not be Prime Minister by six o'clock tonight.'

But she was. She survived the debate quite comfortably. Her Party rallied behind her. Brittan kept his public silence, before the Select Committee and to this day. Heseltine, got at by Wakeham, chose not to attack her (she had unwisely attacked him the previous Thursday) but instead to lay the foundation for his rehabilitation by the Tory Party. At this time he believed that she would be out by the autumn and the Party would be looking for a leader who could win a General Election in 1987. Later the Party managers arranged with the Select Committee that it would not insist on calling the five officials to testify before it. That meant it had to make do with Armstrong's version of events. In its report it censored him, not the Prime Minister.

So how near to the edge had she truly come? 'Robert Armstrong saved her and saved the government,' said one Cabinet Minister. Another was of the opinion that she had never been in serious danger, although 'Leon was very difficult, insisting on being given what he called "cover"'. The Select Committee in due course reported: 'The evidence is that the action of the Prime Minister's office on 6 January in relation to the disclosure was without her direct authority. She has stated that she had no knowledge on 6 January of what was taking place. We accept this.'[31] But it was made obvious that the committee found it almost impossible to believe that she had not become aware of what had happened. Or, if she had not been told, why not? 'Because they all knew that the deed was her wish,' said one of its Tory members. 'Robert got her off the hook,' said one Permanent Under-Secretary. 'Everybody knows what happened but nobody can prove it. They were out to get Heseltine. Brittan was fitted up, made the fall guy. She did not want to know and their game was not to tell her.'

It was probably something very like that. She was accustomed to her will being done, especially by someone like Brittan. Although by nature a meddler she may on this occasion have had the shrewdness to place her telescope to her blind eye. She didn't know what she didn't need to know. Brittan's mistake was not to have gone to her direct for authorisation of the leak if he felt he needed 'cover'. It wasn't his document to leak. Poor Leon. He hadn't realised that the game was being played according to what John Le Carré calls 'the war rules'. When he was caught Control abandoned him, the Circus disowned him, he was out in the cold.

The Westland Affair seemed all very exciting at the time, at least it did to Westminster and Fleet Street. It was a high drama involving the great and mighty. For all the cant about politics being about issues, politics is more fun when it is about people. The drama of the Westland Affair flowed from the character, as good drama should; it was about the character of the Prime Minister. Her single-mindedness, blinkered determination and lack of proportion – the traits which had helped her to win back the Falklands and suppress Arthur Scargill – were now seen to disadvantage. She became engaged in a feud and could think of nothing else. She could think of nothing else but Heseltine. For a while she lost control of herself and the government.

For a while the Westland Affair destabilised the government but its lasting consequences were few. It is of interest now chiefly for what it tells us about the ways of government under Margaret Thatcher. It drew attention to her style of governing, to the absence of the Cabinet as a stabilising force and to the politicisation of the civil service, especially at Number 10. The Select Committee found it 'extraordinary' that none of the officials involved was disciplined. (Not long afterwards Roger Mogg was promoted.) The Committee pointedly criticised Armstrong for failing to give a lead.[32] This view was widely shared in Whitehall. Several senior officials thought that by acting to protect the system in the way he had Armstrong had done it a profound disservice. At the time of the Affair one Permanent Under-Secretary called in all of the private secretaries and press officers and told them that if anything like that happened in his department they would be out and don't let them think that the Minister could save them.

Fascinating though all this was to some, the Westland Affair did not hold the public's interest for very long. It was arcane throughout.

It had originally been about a small helicopter company of which people knew little. Then it was about leaking a letter from someone called the Solicitor General of whom few had heard. The public's attitude may have been close to that of the Cabinet Minister who said, 'He's our solicitor. Why shouldn't we publish his letter? If my solicitor sends me a letter and I want to show it to you, that's my business.' In general all such questions of constitutional or parliamentary procedure or propriety interest the governors more than they do the governed. Leaks in particular are a subject of endless fascination to politicians and the press but of little interest to the public. The Westland Affair was an in-house scandal and in that way a very British scandal, except that for once it lacked sex.

It also lacked the essential ingredient of 'who dunnit'. Probably most people assumed throughout that Margaret Thatcher had dunnit. But done what? Lied to the House of Commons? It is easy to exaggerate public cynicism about politicians, and wrong to suppose it is any greater than ever it was, but it is the case nevertheless that people for the most part are unshocked by the thought of the House of Commons being misled. They find it hard to distinguish between the parliamentary lie and the sort of lies they expect to be told by politicians on television. They do not regard this as especially reprehensible; they regard it as politics.

The great Westland row engulfed the government at a time when people were growing disenchanted with Margaret Thatcher. She had been around a long while. She had been Prime Minister for nearly seven years. The seven-year itch was setting in. At the end of 1985 her satisfaction rating was already low at 39 per cent, by May it was to be down to 28.[33] The Westland Affair reinforced the impression that in her second term the Prime Minister had lost her touch. Moreover, it portrayed her as being weak, the government out of control. Why had she not sacked Heseltine in the first place? 'Oh yes,' she said when asked this, 'then you would have called me bossyboots.' But the people expected her to be bossyboots. She had never been loved, or thought to 'care' or possess the common touch, but she had been respected for all those masculine qualities which had won wars and strikes. Now she presided over disarray.

The lasting political effects of the Westland Affair were few and the government's recovery swift. However, the Heseltine meltdown continued for some months. Thoroughly unnerved, the government proved unable to carry through its plans to privatise the British Leyland motor company or to repeal the laws restricting trading on

Sundays. The Conservatives sagged in the opinion polls and Labour moved into a lead. Tory morale was further sapped by the now widespread anticipation that the government would lose its parliamentary majority at the next General Election. That was how the opinion polls were to be interpreted. This in its turn excited speculation about Mrs Thatcher's continuation in the leadership. By this time she was widely regarded as a liability and not an asset to her Party.

Controversy over the future of British Leyland broke within three days of Leon Brittan's resignation when it was revealed (to the new Secretary of State for Trade and Industry, Paul Channon, among others) that the government had been engaged in secret talks with the Ford Motor Company as a potential buyer of Austin Rover. At the same time negotiations for the sale of the Leyland truck division to General Motors were at an advanced stage. These developments produced a spasm of anti-Americanism, latent in the Westland Affair, which became even more intense two months later when the Prime Minister consented to the use of British air bases for the American bombing raid against Libya.

Austin Rover was the last remaining wholly-owned British car producer. Its sale to Ford would mean the final Americanisation of an industry which for many, or so it now appeared, was one of the essential badges of an industrial nation. The future of Leyland Trucks touched less directly on such atavistic feelings of national pride but General Motors had insisted that Land Rover be thrown in as part of the deal. This produced an astonishing public reaction.

The story of the motor industry was a sad parable of Britain's industrial decline. Long years of mismanagement, investment deficiency and notoriously bad industrial relations had substantially reduced Austin Rover's scale of operation and done long-term damage to its international reputation. By 1986 it commanded only 17 per cent of the domestic market and 4 per cent of the European. It had become too small to support the full model range required to hold its own in the British market. Producing some 450,000 cars a year, it was estimated that to become profitable it would need to sell a million cars a year. That would mean capturing 25 per cent of the home market and 10 per cent of the European.

To finance that improbable project would cost the government at least another billion pounds. Since British Leyland had been nationalised twelve years before it had swallowed up several thousands of millions of public money. In 1975 the Labour government had put £1·5 billion behind an over-ambitious seven-year expansion plan. The Thatcher government, although ill-disposed towards all State enterprises and eager to privatise Leyland, had continued to fund it. This was chiefly because of the appalling employment consequences of not doing so. In spite of its decline the car industry remained Britain's largest manufacturing industry. Not only did Leyland employ 276,000 workers but it supported hundred upon hundred of suppliers mainly centred in the West Midlands, where there were a great number of Conservative-held marginal seats. Whereas British Leyland bought 90 per cent of its supplies from British suppliers the American trans-nationals contributed a substantial net deficit to the British balance of payments.

Since the 1979–81 recession Austin Rover had recovered remarkably. Productivity was at record levels (three times up on 1979), and the wildcat strikes which had plagued the company had become an unhappy memory of the past. But in a saturated market lay-offs were continuing. The company's export sales had not been helped by the unnaturally high exchange rate which was in part due to North Sea oil but in part to the government's financial strategy. However, the European car industry as a whole was suffering from serious overproduction. The American giants were busy rationalising their production on an international scale. Motor assembly was shifting to the less developed European countries such as Spain and to the newly developed countries of Asia. It was doubtful whether a medium-sized nation such as Britain should or could remain in the volume car production business.

The problems facing trucks were even worse. The oil crisis had caused a slump in demand for heavy trucks. Across Europe there was unused capacity of 40 per cent and rationalisation was the only solution. Leyland trucks had lost £60 million in 1985. General Motors were offering £230 million for the group but only if Land Rover was included. Land Rover was losing market share and was badly in need of new models. General Motors had the resources for this and would be able to provide it with dealer outlets throughout North America.

What the government had in mind thus made much industrial good sense. But it meant the end of independent car production in Britain. A sense of humiliation at becoming an off-shore assembler of American knock-downs had touched surface with the prospect of Sikorski taking over Westland. That feeling was much stronger when it came to motor cars. 'It is appalling,' said the Labour industry spokesman, John Smith, 'that the government is even willing to contemplate the disposal of the largest part of the British truck and bus manufacturing industry to an American competitor. Is there no part of British industry which is safe from the destructive purposes of this government? Is there nothing not for sale?' A West Midlands MP, Anthony Beaumont-Dark, declared he was 'not prepared to be pall bearer at the British motor industry's funeral,' which, he went on, would leave the industrial heartland of Britain with 'nothing but Meccano sets'. A Labour backbencher, Dale Campbell-Savours, accused the government of 'dropping the Union Jack and raising the Stars and Stripes over British industry'.

However, it was the idea of selling Land Rover which really touched a chauvinistic nerve. Conservative MPs were bombarded with angry mail, lifelong Tories swore they would never vote Conservative again if Land Rover became American. Exactly why the Land Rover should arouse such patriotic passions we may only guess. Perhaps it was because it was the nation's favourite Dinky toy. It was a distinctively British vehicle, as British as the Jeep was Yankee. Perhaps, for the Tories of the shires it was associated with agricultural shows, shooting, hunt following and the Pony Club, and thus was seen as an essential part of the British way of life. Perhaps, even, it excited romantic visions of Arabian sands, imperial folk memories of governor-generals and district officers. But, for whatever reason, the public wasn't having it. A MORI poll in the *Sunday Times* showed that only 19 per cent thought the government should sell British Leyland to the Americans.

The same poll reported that 62 per cent of the British people thought that the United States paid too little attention to British views. Moreover, more than half of those questioned believed either that the United States posed a greater threat to world peace than the Soviet Union (20 per cent) or an equal threat (34 per cent). An even sharper reaction followed the Libyan bombing in April when more than two-thirds of the public said the Prime Minister had been wrong to allow the American planes to fly from British bases.

At that time President Reagan had sent the veteran soldier-diplomat, Vernon Walters, on a mission to seek co-operation from the allies. It was he who had put the request to Mrs Thatcher to despatch the F-111's from their British bases. While in Europe he complained about the upsurge of anti-American feeling. 'What you've got in Europe,' he said, 'is a complex that Americans are ignorant, they are naïve, they are stupid,' and added that the anti-Americans were the very same people who had never forgiven the United States for Marshall Aid. But this was not the cause. The new anti-Americanism was not of the old 'Yanks go home' variety. That had flourished in the years after the war for two reasons which no longer applied. One was that the powerful Communist Parties in

France and Italy, and a few on the left wing of the British Labour Party, had looked to the Soviet Union as a friend and ally. The second was that Western Europe at that time was still ravaged by the war, everything in short supply, while the Americans, with their bountiful nylons, Nescafé and gum, were 'overpaid, oversexed and over here'.

The sources of the new anti-Americanism were quite different. The MORI poll had reported that 64 per cent said they liked Americans while only 16 per cent that they did not. The same number said they would like to holiday in the United States if they could. Nor did they regard the American President as a warmonger in the sense of believing that he did not wish for peace. Sixty-eight per cent recognised that he did. It was rather his judgment, not his intentions, which they did not trust.

Europe perennially fears either that the United States will fail to defend her or will drag her into nuclear war. With the election of Ronald Reagan this second fear came to the fore. People were alarmed by his hostile and abusive tones towards the Soviets and also by the talk among some generals and academics about nuclear war-fighting strategies. Sharing a continent with the Soviet Union, the European countries feel most secure when nuclear deterrence is complemented by détente. But the Soviet invasion of Afghanistan in 1979 had put an end to détente. Dialogue between the Super Powers was at an end, and what Lord Carrington called 'megaphone diplomacy' had replaced it. And this was at a time when new medium-range American missiles – the Cruise and the Pershing II – were being deployed in Britain, Germany, Italy and Belgium in accordance with a NATO decision reached in 1979.

That Reagan was a movie actor did not inspire confidence in him as the leader of the Atlantic Alliance. The Europeans found it hard to take him seriously as a President and difficult to comprehend his popularity with Americans. In the Tory Party he was known as Hopalong. The cowboy image was unfortunate for it suggested shooting from the hip. It seemed to many in Britain and Europe that an alien breed of President had taken over from the line of Roosevelt, Truman, Eisenhower, Kennedy. They found it hard to relate to Jimmy Carter from the South and Ronald Reagan from way-out West.

For some while the Atlantic had been growing wider. It was inevitable, perhaps, that as wealth became more equal on the two sides of the ocean Europe would come to feel more independent of America and America to feel less responsible for Europe. I had sensed this drawing apart when I came home from living in America in 1974. It was a very different feeling from the one I had had when I first returned from a year at an American university at the end of the 1950s. Then I had said to myself that in future it would make no difference to me whether I lived and worked in the United States or in Britain. I was interchangeable. I was of the mid-Atlantic generation. Where earlier generations had adopted France or Germany or Italy as their second countries, for us it was a case of 'go West young man'. But later, in some part due to Vietnam, people came to feel differently. The young generation of Europeans which came of age in the 1960s and 1970s were the children of détente. They had known nothing but peace on their own continent. At the same time, the gravity of American politics was shifting westward and southwards towards the sun. As Europe became more European the United States became less Europe-orientated, looking more towards its own backyard in Central America or westward towards the booming Pacific basin. The shared experience of the War, which had flowered in the 'Truman Era' (which lasted until the assassination of John Kennedy) was very slowly giving way to something more historical, a renewed sense of an Old World and a New World. Except that we need new vocabulary to define the nature of this relationship. It is as misleading to categorise the stirrings of nationalism in Europe as 'anti-Americanism' as it is to dub America's dissatisfactions with Europe as 'isolationism'. The latter derive not from isolationist sentiment in the United States but rather from Europe's unwillingness to define alliance solidarity in globalist, as opposed to regional, terms. For Europe's part, it seemed not unreasonable – or 'anti-American' – to construe loyalty or even gratitude as involving something less than submitting her own interests, for example in East-West trade or relations with the Arab world, to the overriding preoccupations of American foreign policy.

In Britain's case there were also specific local factors to take into account. On the one hand, the British still believed themselves to enjoy a 'special relationship' with the United States and were more inclined than, say, the French to equate their fundamental interests with those of America. This was especially so in that Britain's status as a so-called independent nuclear power depended on the United States. In short, the relationship was that of client. And, by the same token, the British had still the weakest sense of European identity among the members of the 12-nation European Community. But, on the other hand, the British had been made prickly by the experience of their long, slow decline. A frustrated sense of national pride lurked not far beneath the surface and had been summoned forth at the time of the Falklands War. Moreover, Margaret Thatcher, while personifying these stirrings of patriotism, was at the same time regarded as too subservient to her friend Ronald Reagan. 'Poodle-ism' was the Foreign Office's name for the condition.

While it was true that Britain's relationship with the United States was essentially that of a client it was not true that Margaret Thatcher was President Reagan's poodle. It was not in her nature to play that role. Her relationship with him had begun as an ideological love affair. 'Thatcherism' and 'Reaganism' had much in common; they subscribed to the same liberal economic nostrums and took similar views of the Soviet Union. Ron was 'one of us'. She liked to think that Thatcherism was the precursor of Reaganism. In 1979 when she was already Prime Minister and he merely a presidential candidate, she received him warmly at Number 10. The then President of France, Valéry Giscard d'Estaing, stood on protocol and declined to do so. Reagan remembered that. He admired her gutsy, single-minded 'conviction politics'. One of his favourite slogans was, 'It ain't easy but it is simple.' She admired Reagan for his immense talent as a persuader and she was fond of him as a man. They were both of them champion charmers.

Nevertheless, she knew perfectly well that she wouldn't have tolerated him in her own Cabinet for a moment. 'Poor dear, there's nothing between his ears,' she once said to one of her officials. Nor did she delude herself about the true power relationship between him, the President of the United States, and herself, the Prime Minister of a Great Britain struggling to arrest its economic decline and regain some of its lost standing in the world; or, at least, she deluded herself no more than previous exponents of 'special relationship' diplomacy. She proceeded from the simple conviction that Britain and Europe's dependence on the support and protection of the United States was paramount. Nothing whatever should be done to jeopardise that. She saw in Europe nothing that could possibly substitute for the Atlantic relationship. Therefore she used every ounce of her determination and persistence, every wile she could command, to persuade, nag or cajole the President to her point of view. She found herself at odds with him on many important matters – on 'Star Wars' and nuclear deterrence, on economic sanctions, on East-West trade, on the US budgetary deficit and the high interest rates made necessary by it, on the invasion of Grenada. But what she would never do was to endanger her influence with him by indulging in open criticism or public posturing. Rather she went out of her way to flatter him in public, showering him with fulsome praise. But in private she would press hard on behalf of British or European interests as she saw them.

With the request to allow the raid against Libya to be launched from American bases in Britain she was placed in an impossible position. She was against the raid. It was being mounted for reasons of American domestic politics. It would be unlikely to deter future acts of terrorism. It would have adverse repercussions in the Arab world. It would be an act of dubious legality and morality. From Britain's point of view, it would excite controversy about the American bases from which the Labour Party was pledged to expel all nuclear weapons. But neither she nor the other NATO allies were being consulted about the wisdom of the raid. She was merely being asked to consent to the Americans' use of their bases under the terms of the agreement by which they were in Britain. There was a danger that if she said 'no' the Americans might construe the agreement as entitling them to act anyway. But the greater danger by far, as she saw it, was that refusal would be seen in Washington as proof absolute that the allies were craven and wimpish, ready to shelter comfortably under American protection but unwilling to join in common cause.

The circumstances in which the raid was being planned were particularly poignant in this regard. A series of Libyan-perpetrated outrages – at Vienna and Rome airports, on board a TWA jet – had produced a mood of rage and humiliation in the United States. The President was under public pressure to do something, to hit back. For him it had been made a question of pride and guts. However, the final outrage had occurred on 5 April when a bomb explosion in a disco in Berlin had killed an American GI, Sergeant Kenneth Ford. There was no doubt that Libya was responsible. The symbolism of this affair was vivid. The American garrison in Berlin was one of the tokens of the American commitment to the defence of Europe. Sergeant Ford had been in the course of duty while defending Europe. That was how Americans were bound to see it. That was how Mrs Thatcher saw it.

The European allies had been procrastinating since January on American demands for sanctions against Gaddafi. The Prime Minister judged that the costs of refusing the American request to fly from Britain would be greater than the costs of acceding to it. She believed herself to be acting in the best interests of Europe and of NATO in this. It was a lonely decision for her to take. The affair was handled by a group of four – herself, Whitelaw, Howe and the Defence Secretary, George Younger. This was partly because they happened to be in Downing Street when the telegram arrived from Washington. That was on Tuesday, 8 April. She received Admiral Walters at

Downing Street on the Saturday. On Monday she took the precaution of involving the Defence and Overseas Committee of the Cabinet which is a large and representative body. The planes took off later that day. The next morning, following the raid, a special Cabinet meeting was called. The list of Ministers who wished their names to be dissociated from the raid was a long one. Younger had said in a radio interview the previous day, 'My colleagues and I are very dubious as to whether a military strike is the best way of doing this. It's too liable to hit the wrong people and it creates tensions in other areas.' That indeed was the view of the government and, indeed, of the Prime Minister. But the question now was whether she had been correct to acquiesce in the use of the bases none the less. Ministers who thought not, or who at least insisted that there should be no repeat performance, included the Home Secretary, Douglas Hurd, the Lord Chancellor, Lord Hailsham, the Education Secretary, Kenneth Baker, the Leader of the House of Commons, John Biffen, and, most significantly, the party chairman, Norman Tebbit.

The raid produced a sharply hostile reaction in the Conservative Party. Coming after the Leyland–Land-Rover affair it touched on raw nerves. Two out of three people thought the Prime Minister had been wrong to allow the Americans the use of their bases. Half of them agreed with the proposition that her relations with President Reagan had badly served Britain's long term interests. A number of Conservative commentators – Ronald Butt of *The Times* and Ferdinand Mount of the *Daily Telegraph* among them – considered that the Libyan raid could well lose Mrs Thatcher the next General Election.

On the same night as the bombs fell on Tripoli the government was defeated in its endeavour to reform the laws concerning Sunday trading. Sixty-eight Conservative backbenchers voted against the measure which had been opposed by an unholy alliance of Ulster Unionists and trade unions, of sabbatarians and socialists. The Sunday laws were a notorious mess, riddled with stupid anomalies; it was legal to sell a pornographic magazine but not a Bible, to sell Chinese take-aways but not fish and chips. In part the Bill was lost through parliamentary mismanagement; the Prime Minister wondered that night if her backbenchers might not have performed a mercy killing, for the measure promised nothing but trouble and trouble she had enough of, with now Libya on top of all else. Nevertheless, it was a significant and indicative defeat. The Shops Bill had been conceived as a part of the Thatcherite modernising, privatising thrust. Although no libertarian, she had been eager to liberalise the English Sunday. She had been opposed by all her old enemies including the bishops, whom she regarded as, on the whole, a 'wet' and leftish lot. Traditionalists, conservatives of all kinds, and the vested interests represented by the trade unions had ranged themselves against her. The incident illustrated the difficulties of modernising Britain. It revealed once more the power of producer interests over the silent majority of consumers. It showed how easy it was for small numbers of people determined to oppose change to frustrate the will of the reformer, especially when they were equipped with word processors. MPs had never been so bombarded with adverse mail. The 'Keep Sunday Special' campaign was the most successful single-issue campaign of recent times. It was also a sign of the times, another indication of how party loyalties and disciplines were breaking down. But the Shops Bill was at the same time another casualty of the Westland Affair, another scalp for Michael Heseltine. Tory MPs with marginal seats now lived in fear of losing them. They had become highly susceptible to their postbags and felt vulnerable to local lobbies. Moreover, they no longer had much confidence in the government's parliamentary managers, indeed in the government.

Nor, it seemed a month later, did the people. On 8 May the Conservatives suffered sharp setbacks in local government elections, mainly in the shires, and in two parliamentary by-elections held on the same day. The Yorkshire constituency of Ryedale, which was lost to a Liberal–SDP Alliance candidate, had been one of the hundred safest Tory seats in the country. Projected into a General Election the results indicated a Parliament in which Labour would be the largest party although without an overall majority. Some of the blame for these setbacks was directed at the abrasive style of the Party chairman, Norman Tebbit, some of it was attributed to the 'Thatcher Factor'. It was reported from the doorsteps that many voters were giving 'that bloody woman' as a reason for not voting Conservative. Moreover, the complaints from local party people about the Tebbit style were in some part coded signals of disaffection with the Prime Minister herself. Tebbit, after all, had been her protégé, her appointment, a chairman very much in her own image. And that was part of the problem: Tebbit's abrasive Red-bashing – what Biffen was to describe as the 'raucous tendency' – and her reputation for uncaringness, now firmly fixed in voters' minds, reinforced each other.

On the Sunday following the elections of 8 May John Biffen was put up on the weekly television programme, 'Weekend World', to make the best he could of the government's poor showing. Instead of putting a brave face on it he described it as 'Black Thursday'. He made a series of scarcely-veiled criticisms of the Prime Minister's style. 'To assume that because a party has one dominant figure it thereby benefits is not necessarily true at all.' What the country wanted to see, he suggested, was 'a bit of "calculated humility".' He continued: 'The Prime Minister will make her most effective contribution by being what she is – others will have to provide the balance in that situation.' He went on to suggest that the General Election would have to be fought on a 'balanced ticket'. This implied, first, that Tebbit was the wrong man in the wrong job and, second, that the Prime Minister was no longer a sufficient asset to win a General Election. For good measure, Biffen threw in the thought that she might well not continue through the whole of another Parliament.

Biffen was a Tory, not a revolutionary. He was a High Churchman, not an evangelical. He admitted to 'a brisk sense of ideology', yes, but deplored zealotry. True Conservatism, as he saw it, involved both change and continuity. 'The conviction politics of today should become the political consensus of tomorrow,' he believed. As a true Tory he was an innate pessimist. He knew the art of government to be difficult; man was in his fallen state and the world was wicked; the working class was a dangerous beast to be assuaged with a combination of authority, patriotism, and social amelioration; governing required a subtle hand.

He had come into Parliament in 1961. Ironically his first opponent had been the man who was interviewing him now, Brian Walden, who was to be the unwitting agent of his destruction. Biffen was the son of a smallholder, a grammar school boy who had got to Cambridge, an army private during national service. There was Somerset in his voice. By social background he was 'one of us'. He had been a monetarist before she was, for in Parliament he had sat at the feet of Enoch Powell. At first he had bought the whole Powellite package, including the repatriation of immigrants. He saw immigration as the biggest social transformation since the Industrial Revolution. It had taken place against the will of the people and was at the root of the alienation of the cities, as Powell had foreseen and foretold. In those days John Biffen was known at Westminster as 'John the Baptist'. Later his Powellism was to mellow.

From the master he had learnt to attach importance to working class opinion – on immigration, Europe, Ireland. Powell's style of Conservativism aimed at appealing directly to the working classes. In this Enoch had been the true forerunner of Sir Keith Joseph and of Thatcher.

She had plucked John Biffen from the backbenches where he had distinguished himself only as a rebel. He had been opposed to Heath and all his works. He was most passionately opposed to Britain's joining the European Community. 'I am not prepared to be marched Prussian-style through the Westminster lobbies by the Common Market drill sergeants: I value British independence too highly.' Biffen was an English nationalist. The loss of Empire, as he saw it, had made the country more difficult to govern, had 'bruised working class Tory sentiment'.[34] Europe was no substitute for Empire, an upper middle class project of little working class appeal.

In office he had first been Chief Secretary at the Treasury in charge of cutting public expenditure. He was not tough enough for the job. He lacked, it was said, 'stamina'. Nor was he much of a success during his brief spell as Secretary of State for Trade. Some said that he was a bit on the lazy side. However, he had found his *métier* entirely as Leader of the House of Commons. For one who had suffered all his parliamentary life from tension and chronic lack of self-confidence his mastery of the Commons was all the more remarkable. The House would eat from his hand. Laid back and nicely self-deprecatory, always suitably pessismistic about the government's hopes and plans, he was well liked on all sides.

Butlerian in style, he became increasingly Butlerian in content. He mentioned Butler twice during the Walden interview. The meaning of that was clear. At an early stage, during the first term, he had declared himself a 'consolidator' which was a coded way of saying that enough was enough, social spending should take future priority over tax cuts. He stated his position most explicitly in his Disraeli Lecture – an appropriate vehicle – in 1986 when he said:

> There are always a handful in politics – across the divide – who favour endless and restless political action. These people see politics as an essential element in social engineering. Some libertarian radicals on the Far Right seem inspired by that frenetic phase of Red China politics described as 'Perpetual Revolution'. They are, as it were, Tory Maoists. Their quest for further far-reaching reform is vigorous and uninhibited. I clearly dissent from that view.

The priority, as he saw it, was to make the Thatcher Revolution stick. Pressing it further risked losing the gains which had been made – sound money, trade union reform, wider home ownership. He did not underestimate the conservative appeal of the Labour

Party but he saw even greater danger in the Alliance. He expected eventually to see some form of moderate realignment on the Left. He saw no point in scare tactics about socialist extremism. That was not the real danger. The real danger, as he saw it, was a reversion to the Wilson–Callaghan years. That he wished his country to be spared. By consolidation, the gains made could be made safe for a generation and, perhaps, a new consensus formed around a liberal market economy.

He was accustomed to think aloud in these terms, over a bottle of wine or a Chinese meal. Thinking aloud on television that morning was the end of him. She was livid. Whitelaw and Wakeham had to restrain her from sacking him on the spot. For the next whole year he was excluded from the inner circle of the government. From that day she scarcely spoke to him. In its usual way Downing Street put out the word on him. He was to be regarded as 'commentator' rather than as active participant; Biffen was an 'intellectual' and therefore not to be taken seriously. He was given no role to play in the 1987 General Election campaign. The moment it was safely over he was sacked.

The summer of 1986 was the low point for the second Thatcher Government. Everything had seemed to go wrong. Some senior officials wondered seriously whether the government might not finally fall apart under the strain of it all. One after the other, Westland, Leyland, Libya and the Shops Bill had exposed the lack of cohesion within the government, had cast doubt on its competence. The government was reaping the unpopular fruits of its expenditure cuts. Instead of making substantial economies in certain areas of the Welfare State, as it had been advised to do by the 'Think Tank' in 1982, it had done what it had said on taking office it would not do, namely resorted to the traditional salami method of expenditure control, cutting it across the board. The result was a general deterioration in the quality of services. The schools were an example. Sir Keith Joseph, who was that summer to be replaced by Kenneth Baker, was engaged in long-drawn-out confrontation with the teachers over pay and conditions of work. He had been attempting the impossible, a radical reform of the State school system within the confines of Treasury policy. There was no such thing as a free lunch, he used to say – after Milton Friedman; but there was no such thing as a free improvement in the deplorable standards of the secondary schools. To be fair, he had put a sum of money up front for the task, in effect, of buying out the restrictive practices of the teaching profession. But it was nowhere near enough. While the teachers disrupted the schools with 'industrial action' children in some parts of the country were obliged to share text books, some of them to be taught in schools scarcely fit for human habitation.

Yet in spite of all of this, on closer analysis, the local and by-election results proved not as bad for the government as in its low state of morale it had been ready to assume. Considering the mess it had made of things, its vote could be interpreted as having held up remarkably. How was Labour going to win a General Election if it could not score 40 per cent in the polls during the depths of the government's mid-term unpopularity? The Prime Minister continued to enjoy the priceless advantage of a divided opposition. Moreover, the news in people's pockets was a good deal better than the news in the headlines. The economic recovery was gathering speed and strength and this mattered more to people, and to the fortunes of the government, than the Cabinet rows or parliamentary defeats.

While the Westland Affair had raged the government had virtually ceased to function. During that time the world price of oil had plummeted and with it the value of the pound. But while sterling was being devalued against the Deutschemark and other hard currencies, the dollar was being devalued at the same time. Britain bought the greater part of her raw materials in dollars, and sold the greater part of her exports in hard currencies. The result of these uncontrollable events was a substantial improvement in the terms of trade. The revenues from North Sea oil would be diminished but industry had been given the competitive boost it had long been urging from the government. In this fashion, at the moment of impotence and disarray, when the Prime Minister's very future seemed in doubt, events far beyond her control provided the elixir of the economic success which would later win her an unprecedented third term of office – in spite of Westland, Leyland, Libya – in spite of everything.

10

Comrades at Arms

Neil Kinnock was Michael Foot's chosen successor. Within forty-eight hours of the humiliating débâcle of June 1983 Foot stood down from his disastrous leadership of the Labour Party and Kinnock was rushed to the fore. If it was his last act Foot was determined to deny the succession to Hattersley. Benn, having lost his seat in Bristol, was disqualified from running. With Kinnock's own union, the Transport and General Workers, behind him and several other major block votes quickly lined up, the race was over before it began.

Kinnock was to be the first Labour Party leader to be chosen by the electoral college as set up in 1981. This from the outset gave him an unprecedented authority within the whole Movement. He had received 72 per cent of the trade union votes, more than 90 per cent of the constituency votes, and very nearly half the votes of the MPs. He was effectively the choice of the whole Labour Movement. In contrast to this was his authority in the country. His party had recently suffered a catastrophic defeat. To win a majority in the next Parliament Labour would need to win 117 seats from the Conservatives on a quite unprecedented swing of 10 per cent.

Kinnock himself had had no ministerial experience of any kind. He had never served in local government or pursued a career outside the Labour Movement. Very briefly he had been Foot's Parliamentary Private Secretary, a junior dogsbody job which he had found too restricting; he was too accustomed to the rebel's role. He claims to have been caned more times than any other boy at the Lewis School, Pengam, a grammar school which some have called the Eton of the Valleys. If so he was the Swinburne of the Valleys.

Born into the Labour Movement, brought up in it, and married into it, he had lived his whole life within that closed world. He had been a professional politician virtually since boyhood. A student leader at the University of Cardiff (where he did as badly as he had done at school) he had met his wife, Glenys Parry, while handing out leaflets on behalf of the Socialist Society. For a brief while he had a job of sorts as lecturer for the Workers' Education Association, a traditional stamping ground for politicians, pending his adoption for the safe seat of Bedwellty in time for the 1970 General Election which returned him to Parliament at the age of 28.

Raised in Aneurin Bevan's old constituency of Tredegar he saw himself in the mould of his childhood hero, although he had only met him to shake hands with.[1] In the tradition of Bevan, and contrary to the tradition of the House, he used his maiden speech to make a vitriolic attack on the callousness and hypocrisy of the Tories. 'I am in this House, and I hope that other Hon. Members of this side are, to knock the salt off the table.' But he was always more of a Party man than a House of Commons man.

Labour's return to power in 1974 had extended his scope for opposition. He could now oppose his own side as well. A speech at the Tribune rally at the 1975 Labour Party conference, in which he attacked the Labour government, did more to propel him on his way than his attacks on the Tories in the House. He had grown up to regard betrayal of socialist principles as the occupational disease of Labour Party leaders, although he was later to deplore this view of the world in Tony Benn. Wilson he regarded as the chronic case of his times. In 1973 Kinnock had become one of the original members of the Campaign for Labour Party Democracy. He was thus one of the founding fathers of the revolution that was eventually to carry an inexperienced rank-and-filer to the leadership of the Party.

Yet, while a rebel, he was at the same time a traditionalist, a Welsh traditionalist, an old-fashioned Bevanite at heart. For example, he was not happy with the notion of mandatory re-selection of MPs, believing that a good socialist owed his constituents his judgment. Even as a rebel his style had more to do with words than deeds. He turned down junior jobs in the Callaghan government and became more and more the darling of the party. He was a popular turn at annual party dinners around the land. Being good at telling jokes can take you a long way in politics. In a conference cabaret he scored a great success with 'Ole Man Callaghan, He must know somethin', But he don't do nothin'.'[2]

Increasingly he preferred to be out in the country than in the House. He had never liked the place much. 'The House of Commons is like a factory,' he once said. 'That's where I happen to work.'[3] He was also becoming a success on television, by that time far more important to a budding politician than a House of Commons reputation. He was elected to the NEC in 1978. His first act in that capacity was to appeal to the conference to take 'a major, giant step towards democracy' by allowing to the unions and local parties a role in the election of future leaders. Thus again he paved the way for his own eventual succession.

He had taken the first instinctive steps in that direction after the 1979 débâcle when, first, he stood in the 'Shadow' Cabinet elections and then, having narrowly failed, accepted from Callaghan (at Foot's urging) the job of education spokesman. He had come inside. Nevertheless the conference platform, not the Despatch Box, remained the scene of his triumphs. At Brighton that year his speech was compared by those who could remember with that of Nye Bevan. In the NEC elections he ran Benn a close second for top of the pops. One or two commentators began to talk of him as future leader.

At the same time he was trimming on inner party democracy. He had always opposed mandatory re-selection. Now he used his NEC vote to block the reformers' move to wrest control of the manifesto from the parliamentary leadership. Yet he had little love or admiration for the Parliamentary Labour Party. Nor did the PLP think much of Neil Kinnock. On the Left many by now suspected him of careerism, saw shades of Harold Wilson in his ideological agility, while at the same time many on the Right saw him as a rebel with only one cause, his own advancement, and a lightweight to boot. The one constitutional change he remained enthusiastically committed to was the election of the leader by the party at large. Without that the dice would be loaded always against him. He was jubilant when the reform was carried at the 1980 conference.

Sentiment, laced with opportunism, overcame whatever realisation he may have had that Michael Foot at the age of 67 was scarcely the leader required by the party at that time. He had played upon the old man's vanity and helped to push him forward. Now he closed ranks around him to protect him from the Bennite assault. He had become increasingly estranged from the hard Left. The 'cultural revolution' had now gone quite far enough for him. He was a Bevanite not a Bennite. Moreover, he did not like Benn. Kinnock's Labour Party was a working class party, not a party of middle class intellectuals; the Bevanite Left, he believed, had been excited by the challenge of the real world while the Bennite Left was excited by delusion, it was – he said in a speech at that time – 'offering a fantasy that insults adult intelligence, invites derision, and guarantees disappointment'. He launched into even more ferocious attacks and while, as a man of the Left, he could not vote for Healey in the deputy-leadership election, in the end he would not and did not vote for Benn.

That had been a traumatic moment for him, perhaps the most decisive in his career. It had meant a break with the past, with his image of himself, with some of his friends, and it had meant a bitter inquest in his own party at Bedwellty which had been for Benn. He who had cried 'traitor' would now be called one. Later Kinnock saw it as the decisive turn in Labour's civil war, the beginning of the realignment of the 'soft' Left around himself and a crucial stage in the demise of the Bennite 'hard' Left which Scargill and his miners' strike was to complete. It was true, Neil Kinnock had saved the Labour Party from Tony Benn.

This then was the man who succeeded. Note how his political biography has been entirely the story of his rise within the party. Everything in his experience equipped him to lead and manage his party; nothing in his experience equipped him to address the needs and wishes of the country. He was a party insider through and through, a man who knew a thousand Christian names, at home in every twist and turn of the sub-culture of the Labour Movement, impenetrable to outsiders, a man secure in the world into which he had been born. While Margaret Thatcher had captured her party by a coup at the centre, Kinnock had captured his at the grassroots. They had this in common, however: he was as true to his origins in the old-style socialism of the Welsh valleys as she was to the middle class ethos of Grantham.

For example, while for her the grammar school was the ladder of opportunity for shopkeepers' daughters, for him the eleven-plus (which he had failed) was the mark of Cain put upon working class children by the capitalist system. In his first speech from the Despatch Box as education spokesman he had said, 'Nobody who has observed a community that operates a selective eleven plus can doubt that on the morning of the results there are not faces of children wreathed in smiles but there are floods of tears in many homes. The guilt for those tears will remain on the back of the Right hon. and learned Gentleman.'[4]

Kinnock was a child of the Macmillan years, the affluent 1950s. He had known neither the suffering of the 1930s nor the post-war deprivations of austerity Britain. However, that had done nothing to blunt the class hatred in his soul. 'When I was about thirteen or fourteen,' he once explained to me, 'people started having carpets in their homes, cars, foreign holidays, television – although we didn't have one till I was sixteen – but it never for a moment occurred to me that having a washing machine was a reason to depart from basic beliefs.'

'If socialism can't relate to affluence – if it deals only with poverty – it carries the seeds of its own destruction. In any case, in order to help the poor you first have to win power. That's why we need to be enthusiastic about success, say "bloody great, terrific," but success means collective provision for the purpose of individual advancement.'

These became familiar Kinnockian themes and are the key to much about him. For him socialism is a given, an immutable value, applicable in all ages and all circumstances; the task, therefore, was to apply it. That is what he set out to do as leader of his party, never for one moment pausing to reconsider or revise his faith, but ready to revise his strategy for achieving it. For he attributed the Labour Party's reverses, including the 'catastrophe' of 1983, not to the shortcomings of socialism but to the shortcomings of the Labour Party. Even in his own Welsh and mining constituency, of all places, the SDP had picked up 8,000 votes. Why? 'They wanted to teach us a lesson, that's why.' And the lesson was that, 'if we can't run ourselves people won't think we can run the country.' That remained basically his view.

Everywhere he went he preached victory. 'What we need to do,' he told the Durham miners in 1985, 'is to ensure that every word, every action, every statement, everything we do to educate, agitate and organise is geared completely to victory . . .' But his scheme for victory had no architecture, it was a construction of words. It suited him to regard Labour's problems as being primarily presentational and managerial. He saw no point in fighting resolution by resolution to change party policy, rather he hoped to dispose of embarrassing commitments by according them low priority; for socialism, after all, was the 'language of priorities', Nye had said so. His persistent theme was that the dispossessed, the have-nots, did not comprise a sufficient electoral base and that in order to win Labour must appeal positively to the better-off sections of society, families who owned their own homes, ran cars, and took foreign holidays. But it sometimes seemed as if he believed that if he said this enough times it would come to pass.

We must not underestimate the power of words. It is words which excite hopes and dreams, inspire people to action, send men into battle. They are the politician's only weapon. But words, to wield their power, must relate to common experience and address reality.

Kinnock had a taste for simple aphorisms, such as Bevan's 'socialism is the language of priorities'. One can imagine the young Neil copying it out, underlining it in red ink. Words were his solution to everything. 'We are the party of production,' he declared. 'Social ownership', 'Freedom and fairness'. Slogans spun from his tongue. Later it was to be 'Socialist individualism'. He seemed to believe that all ideological difficulties, perhaps even practical choices, could be disposed of by hyphenating words with 'socialism'. Democratic-socialism he said was about 'individual freedom' (Gaitskell and Crosland had said that it was about equality) but, said Kinnock, 'the means which democratic-socialism has chosen to protect that freedom are equality and democracy.' But equality has its price in liberty and liberty in inequality and the problem is to decide how that tension is to be resolved.

Now, as Kinnock came into his inheritance, he would also reap the whirlwind of the 'cultural revolution' he had helped to make. The Bennite Left was no longer in the ascendant but its grip on the apparatus of the party was enough to prevent the lessons of defeat from being learnt. Moreover, the spectacle presented still was one of warring factions, some of whom presented a repellent face to the electorate. Meanwhile, the Left as a whole had been split by the breakaway of the Social Democrats, a defection in part provoked by the destruction of the autonomy of the Parliamentary Party in which Kinnock had gladly assisted. Moreover, the Militant Tendency remained at large and with Arthur Scargill on the class warpath, Labour's constitutionalism was in doubt for the first time since before the war.

The Left had been in decline since Benn's defeat in the contest for the deputy-leadership to Denis Healey in 1981. At Westminster it had split into rival factions. The Tribune Group, with some 60 members, constituted the 'soft' Left while the 30 or so of the 'hard' Left were gathered in the Campaign Group of which Benn was a member. In 1986 Sarah Benton in the *New Statesman* described a forlorn gathering of the hard Left in Hampstead. No television cameras were in attendance, none of the Fleet Street heavies. The Left was no longer news. Benn, once the national bogeyman, these days seemed more like a harmless pipe-smoking peripatetic from the WEA. The broad-left alliances of the 1970s and early 1980s had crumbled. The CLPD had briefly served as a single umbrella, even for the Militant Tendency. But after Wembley they had gone their sectarian ways. Tribune had split over Benn's candidacy. Later that year the ultras split to form the Campaign Group. Benn laid hands upon Militant Tendency. In 1983 Heffer came nowhere against Kinnock for the leadership. In the contest for deputy Michael Meacher was beaten by Hattersley even in the constituency parties. In 1982 the Left had lost its majority on the NEC and Benn's power base as chairman of the home policy sub-committee was destroyed. The realignment of the Left had taken place around Neil Kinnock.

So, by the time he became leader of the Labour Party, the power of the Left, or at least the hard Left, was on the wane. Nevertheless, for two years the Labour Party lived in the ideological shadow of the miners' strike and the local government problems of Liverpool. These were traumatic events. We need to grasp the meaning of these events but equally we need to grasp what the Labour Movement was unable to grasp, namely that they meant much less to the country as a whole. It was a common error of the times to suppose that these psycho-dramas, these heroic last stands of the working class, were seminal and historic events for everybody else. It was part of their tragedy that they were not.

The year-long strike by the miners is part of the story of the Thatcher government's endeavours to arrest the economic decline of Britain but it is even more central to a chronicle of the decline of the Labour Movement. The coal industry was among the unfinished business of her first term. It was at the heart of Britain's decline in a number of ways. Coal had been the foundation on which Britain had built her nineteenth-century wealth. Now it was a vivid example of the triumph of the past over the present at the expense of the future. The nationalisation of the coal industry had been one of the foundation stones of the post-war order which the Prime Minister was in the process of dismantling. The Coal Board headquarters at Hobart House was one of the last bastions of that *ancien régime*. The spirit of Thatcherism had not crossed its threshold, rather the ethos of the place harked back to that great dawn of 1947 when Emanuel Shinwell had stood, hat raised, at the gates of Murton Colliery, County Durham, before a notice which proclaimed: 'This colliery is now managed by the National Coal Board on behalf of the people.' From that time the Board had been permitted to weigh the economic costs of mining coal against the social costs of not doing so and had been required to show a profit only on the basis of taking good years with the bad. Mrs Thatcher had put a stop to that in 1980. Then in 1983 she put in as chairman Ian MacGregor, a Scot by birth who had been re-imported from the United States – at a gigantic transfer fee – to rationalise the steel industry. He was 'one of us'; from the other side of the Atlantic, where he had lived and worked since 1940, his vision of Britain was of a country sinking slowly into the sea under the weight of bloody-minded trade unions and namby-pamby managements. At 71 he was at the age when old men's minds turn to thoughts of saving their country.

Part of MacGregor's brief was to insist that management must manage. A society which compromised on management's right to manage, the Prime Minister was to say during the strike, would soon become 'a mausoleum society'. It was not true, although it was sometimes said, that the National Union of Mineworkers ran the coal industry but neither was it exactly true that the Coal Board managed it. Since nationalisation the industry had experienced a vast contraction and massive migrations from one coalfield to another. In the 1960s this had been achieved patiently and peacefully but in the 1970s – with energy suddenly in short supply – the industry had been racked by violent disputes. For all that, something of the industry's old ethos had survived. Its labour relations machinery, for example, had been constructed according to the enlightenment of the 1940s and provided for elaborate consultative procedures. This applied to pit closures and, in practice if not in theory, pits were closed only with the consent of the NUM.

Now more and more collieries had to be closed and more manpower shed if there was ever to be any end to the piling up of unwanted coal or the pouring of taxpayers' money into uneconomic pits. But the National Union of Mineworkers, under the militant leadership of Arthur Scargill, was also on the Prime Minister's list of unfinished business. The miners had flexed their industrial muscles against her in 1982 and she had beaten a hasty but prudent tactical retreat. Now she was ready.

The ghosts of 1974 were powerful actors in the strike of 1984. Heath had been brought down by the miners; Mrs Thatcher had to show that she could bring them down. Heath had asked, 'who governs Britain?' She would show who did and lay the ghost of ungovernability, restoring once and for all the primacy of constitutional authority over the pretensions of trade union power. For no organisation more embodied the power of the unions than the NUM, the vanguard of the Labour Movement, the crack division of the working class.

From that humiliating day in February 1981 when William Whitelaw, Lord Carrington and James Prior (the last two, ironically, the 'hawks' of the 1974 confrontation) had cautioned her to retreat in the face of fire, the government had been preparing to fight another day. It had been helped by a glut of world energy. Mounting coal stocks were quietly moved from pithead to power station; the electricity generating industry made contingency plans to burn oil in coal-fired stations; a special Cabinet committee drew up all manner of plans for dealing with civil emergency.

That is not to say that the government provoked the 1984 strike, although it has frequently been accused of doing so. The start of the strike was more like the outbreak of the First World War: nobody exactly intended it to happen but a complicated series of accidents and misperceptions set it in progress. On this occasion the Sarajevo was the Yorkshire pit of Cortonwood. The pit was uneconomic in the sense that there was no market for its coal; at the same time, a large investment had recently been made in it and miners had been transferred there from a recently closed pit near by. Five days after the Yorkshire Coal Board announced the closure of Cortonwood the National Coal Board in London more or less confirmed the truth of Scargill's persistent allegation that there was a secret plan to close some 20 pits.

Arthur Scargill had prayed for MacGregor's appointment.[5] They were made for each other, born to confront. For Scargill also wished to pull down the old order. He was not in the business of class collaboration. He would no longer consent to the closure of pits on any grounds whatsoever short of geological exhaustion. If Mrs Thatcher had learnt some lessons since 1982, so had he. Since his election as the miners' president in that year he had twice burnt his fingers on the ballot box. The political structure of the NUM enabled the prosperous coalfields who were not threatened with closures to outvote the militant coalfields who were. Scargill was determined this time to engineer a national strike without a national ballot. He set about this by giving a blanket blessing to whichever of the largely autonomous areas of the union called local strikes against closures as the Yorkshire Area had done as a result of Cortonwood.

The English have mixed feelings about Yorkshiremen. They are regarded as a bloody-minded, cussed lot, convinced of their own superiority. The cricketer, Geoffrey Boycott, was a good example. The greatest living English batsman, some would say the greatest living Englishman, he amassed runs at a snail's pace and by the force of his obstreperous, obstructive genius, came near to destroying one of the greatest county cricket clubs in the land. Arthur Scargill did the same for his union. He and Boycott were born geographically close to one another in the area of the West Yorkshire coalfield. Scargill had become a headline name – and shortly thereafter a television personality – in 1972 when his 'flying pickets' scored their famous victory at the gates of the Saltley coke depot in Birmingham. This hitherto unknown industrial establishment soon became the equivalent of the Bastille in the mythology of modern militancy. 'Flying' or mobile mass pickets had been Scargill's invention in an earlier local strike in Yorkshire. They did for class struggle what the cavalry or the tank had done for military struggle. On this occasion Scargill arrived at the head of a 10,000-strong column of men. Later he would vividly invoke the decisive moment when the AUEW banner came over the hill, as if in an Eisenstein movie.[6] The police retreated in the face of superior force, and Scargill claimed victory from the roof of a public lavatory.

He was born in 1938 in a traditional one-up, one-down miner's cottage with no electricity or hot water and an outside lavatory. It was not much of an improvement on the sort of house in which D. H. Lawrence had been brought up. But most of his childhood was spent in a post-war council house with modern conveniences.[7] Down the pit at fifteen, the young Arthur soon found his vocation as a trouble-maker. He joined the Communist Party through its youth section. The circumstances of his leaving it towards the end of the 1950s have never been satisfactorily explained. Certainly he was not protesting at the Soviet invasion of Hungary or reacting to Khrushchev's revelations about the Stalin era; if anything, he disapproved of de-Stalinisation. The most probable explanation is that he wanted to pursue his vocation as militant and revolutionary free from the heavy-handed, bureaucratic discipline of the party. If he had a hero at that time it was Fidel Castro. His philosophy was one of pure class struggle; he was a latter-day syndicalist who believed, it seemed, that the sheer pursuit of wages was the road to British socialism.[8] 'Jam today and jam tomorrow', was a typical Scargillism.

At the time of the Saltley coke depot incident Scargill was no more than a minor official of his area union. His fame did not extend beyond Yorkshire. From that point his ascent was swift and sure. That year he worked his last shift underground. By 1973 he was the youngest-ever president of the Yorkshire Area NUM, the largest constituent of the federalised national union. When he became national president nearly ten years later one of his first acts was to move the union's headquarters out of London to Sheffield. He ran the union in modern managerial style. He was a sharp dresser with a penchant for fast cars. He was a genius of self-promotion, a master of the pithy short paragraph which is the medium of political communication in the television age. He was the first trade union leader to exploit the power of television.

Like Lenin he understood the value of blinkers. There is no such thing as an uneconomic pit, he said, over and over again. Perhaps he believed it. Compromise is not a Yorkshire word. Uneconomic for Scargill was a capitalist word. For as long as there was geologically gettable coal in it, a pit was a pit was a pit. He had been tutored in economics and politics by leftist dons at the University of Leeds. He could blind his opponents with science, pouring out what purported to be the facts and figures of coal production.

Scargill fascinated his opponents.[9] From a distance it was easy to pour scorn on his leadership of the strike, as many TUC leaders did. But those who had to face him were scared of him, mesmerised by his sheer gall. They would emerge dazed from encounters with him. There was demonic force in the man. He was an exponent of the big lie. He went on saying that the coal stocks would run out, that soon there would be power cuts.

He was venerated by young Yorkshire miners. A cult formed around him. He was worshipped with incantations borrowed from the football terraces. In Arthur Scargill their resentment and class hatred were made flesh. King Arthur he was. 'Arthur Scargill, Arthur Scargill, we'll support you ever more,' they sang to the tune of 'Cwm Rhondda' and 'Arthur Scargill walks on water,' to the tune of 'Deck the Walls'. 'Here we go, here we go, here we go,' was the battle cry of his élite corps of flying pickets. It became the battle cry of pickets everywhere.

It was impossible for him to grasp that the miners' struggle was not synonymous with the struggle of the working class. He could not comprehend that the picket line was sacrosanct no longer. Still less did he begin to understand the changes in the power structure of society which had tipped the balance decisively in favour of the State. The striking miners were the past challenging the present. Scargill had placed their banner on the top of a slag heap. His fatal blunder was to try to 'picket out' the Nottinghamshire miners against their will. With the rich, modernised Nottingham coalfield continuing to mine coal, and Nottinghamshire railwaymen continuing to move it, the strike was lost before it had begun.

When the end came Scargill himself would not sign the armistice. Others could do that. He was triumphalist to the last, even in the moment of defeat. 'Above all,' he said, 'we've seen workers in struggle demonstrate to the working class that if they're prepared to take a stand . . .' Defeat was only victory in disguise, a stage in the education of the working class, for what was history but a series of lessons in the triumph of class? As Benn said: 'The miners' strike was the greatest piece of political radicalisation I've seen; there have never been so many socialists in the country in my lifetime. We're only half way between Dunkirk and D-Day.'[10] The reverse was true, the miners' strike was an ending, not a beginning. It was the last hurrah of the old Labour Movement, the closing of a chapter which had opened in the nineteenth century, the explosion of a proud myth founded in the struggles of the General Strike of 1926, and another landmark of the Thatcher Revolution.

Once Scargill's gauntlet was down it was for the Prime Minister as it had been with Galtieri: defeat was unthinkable. The State could not afford again to be a loser in a confrontation with trade union power. Certainly no Conservative government could afford to be vanquished another time by the NUM. As one of her closest advisers put it: 'To lose might not be the end of civilisation as we know it but it would be the end of Thatcherism as we know it.'

Defeat, however, never seemed probable except for one brief instant in November when it seemed as though the deputies – the coal industry's equivalent of foremen – might stop the Nottinghamshire pits. That might have tipped the balance. Otherwise the forces of the State were all the while superior. Coal was mined and moved from the prolific pits of Nottinghamshire. There were massive stocks at power stations and imported coal was moving through the ports. There were more police than pickets. Scargill continued to hope that he could provoke the State into acts which would provoke the wider trade union movement to support him. He hoped that his pickets could provoke the police into such excesses of violence that the working class would rise up on his behalf. He hoped that the government would need to employ troops to move coal from pits to power stations. None of these hopes materialised.

He blamed not the workers but the leaders of the TUC for the betrayal of the miners, but the truth was that the working class of his revolutionary imaginings no longer existed. The men who sat upon the General Council of the TUC were generals without troops. The call to action went out but answer came there none, or very little. The unions could fight, if they wished, to the last full-time official but the members themselves, the rank-and-file, the infantry, had no intention of going over the top for Arthur. Many of those now asked to give support had themselves been made redundant in the course of 'Thatcherism', and they would have leapt at compensation terms half as generous as those now on offer to the miners. Some had been the victims of Scargill's aggressive tactics, for example his demands that coal replace oil or nuclear energy in the generating industry. Others reasoned that there was no cause for them to go on strike when

Arthur could not get his own members out in Nottinghamshire and had not dared to ballot them.

So coal continued to move through the docks, once themselves great bastions of class solidarity but now many of them monuments to class struggle, the victims of the restrictive practices which had driven trade away to smaller and less-unionised ports. The great ports through which the Empire's trade had passed had become ghostly places left to the seabirds or handed to the developers for conversion to marinas. And coal moved around the country chiefly by kind permission of the Transport and General Workers' Union, not withstanding its executive's declarations of total support for the miners in their struggle. In a parody of the small boats which in Britain's darkest hour had put to sea to relieve the stranded armies at Dunkirk, a fleet of tippers, cowboy heroes of the market economy, now took to the road to move the coal and brave the pickets on their way. In the first week of November 1984, as winter closed in, a million tons of coal reached its customers throughout the land. Was this Thatcherism's finest hour?

The strike had split the Labour Movement from top to bottom. After the General Election of 1983 the TUC had been edging towards what it called the 'new realism'. This involved recognising that the Thatcher government was no aberration, that the world had changed and that the trade unions would have to come to terms with it. This fragile détente was shattered by the GCHQ affair which the unions took as an indication of the Prime Minister's unrelenting hostility to the very principle of trade unionism. The miners' strike, when it began a few weeks later, put an end to all thought of rapprochement. The hard Left minority on the General Council, which had been opposed in any event to the 'new realism', preached all-out support for Scargill. The soft Left could not allow itself to be outflanked on such an issue. Scargill was regarded as a dangerous clown, a tearaway, an industrial and political disaster. His methods were deplored and few of the more moderate trade union leaders could see how he could possibly win. But wish as they might that Arthur would take a jump down the deepest pit in Yorkshire the politics of the Labour Movement required a display of solidarity. Nor was it in their interest that he should lose. For it would be they who would then be singled out as the traitors to the Labour Movement. And the government would be encouraged to behave towards the unions in still more overweening manner. The miners occupied a very special place in the folk history of the Labour Movement and anything to do with them was charged with emotion. 'We can't afford to let the miners lose this strike; it would mean back to 1926,' said Jim Slater, the seaman's leader. That simple view lurked in many tortured hearts.

Shortly before the Christmas of 1984 I spent a few days in the Yorkshire pit village of South Elmsall in the home of a striking miner. What called itself a village had been all but eaten up by the urban sprawl of Doncaster. Yet that intense sense of community born of isolation had survived as if South Elmsall were miles from nowhere. My host was employed not at the colliery in the village but at another some four miles down the road. There 1,400 men produced not quite a million tonnes a year. By contrast, at Selby, one of Yorkshire's new super-pits, 2,200 men could mine some 10 million tonnes a year. With production costs of £123 a ton, Hickleton Colliery was hopelessly uneconomic. But what the government called economics offended deeply against what these miners called morality. To them the moral assumptions of 'Thatcherism' were utterly alien and totally repugnant. Working underground had made it seem self-evident to them that life was about mutual dependence. They set no store by economic individualism. Their saying is that 'good seams make good colliers'. The bonus systems which were introduced to increase productivity they see as evil devices for 'setting men against men'. At the same time they have no use for 'idle buggers and dole-wallahs'. Theirs is an old fashioned world all round.

The geography of a pit village serves as a child's guide to socialism. The pit is sunk in the valley, the rows of grimy houses nestle in the shadow of the slag heap, but the eyes lift up to the countryside as God made it – and the manager's house on the hill. Miners have one foot in the urban class structure of the Industrial Revolution but the other in the aristocratic class structure of the pre-industrial age. The ownership of coal and land went together and for miners to this day a bit of poaching remains a continuation of the class struggle by other means.

In South Elmsall people were convinced they were fighting for something much more than their pits and their livelihoods. They saw themselves as fighting for a whole way of life, a heritage which had been entrusted to them and which it was not theirs to surrender. The miners who were taking the redundancy money were 'selling their sons' jobs'. When they talk about capitalism they are not speaking of an abstraction, picked up from books, but of the corruption they see eating the heart from their community. 'Capitalism' and 'the South' are indistinguishable foes. The South is some kind of Sodom and Gomorrah where the meaning of the word community has been forgotten. That theirs is the superior ethic they have no doubt. People come first, before profit, before everything; you help one another, stick together. 'It's brought us closer, this strike, it's done a Falklands on us,' you hear people say.

It is beyond comprehension that it could be thought courageous or noble to cross a picket line. A scab is the lowest of the low. The oldest men in South Elmsall can point out the sons of the scabs of 1926. When one of them had died the other day he had gone to his grave a scab still. It angers these people deeply to be classed as criminals. They worry about how their children may come to see their fathers. Some parents would not let their children see the violent clashes on the television news. They will never forgive Mrs Thatcher for her 'enemies within' speech at the Carlton Club. 'We weren't enemy within when we was digging for fucking victory in the war,' said one old miner.

The miners' strike was a blind clash of moralities. Not once during it did the Prime Minister manage a generous word about the strikers and their families, some recognition of what their country owed to them, or imaginative understanding of the force of their folk memories of hardship and struggle stretching back into Victorian times. A more imaginative woman than she might have seen that the values which inspired such passionate loyalty in these people, such fierce clinging to tradition and such stoic acceptance of hardship were not so very different – the other side of the same coin, perhaps – from the Victorian values by which she set so much store. 'The finest body of men he'd ever known,' Harold Macmillan, now the Earl of Stockton, was to say in his maiden speech in the Lords, the men who'd seen the Kaiser off and then sent Hitler packing. But unlike Harold Macmillan, Margaret Thatcher bore none of the mental scars of the period between the wars, apparently knew nothing of the social suffering of the people, was devoid of all class guilt. The best she could say at the end of it was that it had been 'a tragic strike but good will emerge from it'.

The strike was a contest between a group of workers and the State in a novel and ominous sense. The miners were at the same time State employees and threatening services essential to the State. As in 1974, an industrial dispute in those circumstances was tantamount to a political confrontation. What was novel about this strike was that the outcome depended in large part on the outcome of a trial of strength between police and pickets. The violence of these clashes gave the strike an insurrectionist character exacerbated by Scargill's rhetoric. As Raymond Aron had once said in riposte to Jean-Paul Sartre, 'The revolutionary myth bridges the gap between moral intransigence and terrorism.'[11] Seen from the other side of the barricades, the strike exposed the State for what it was – or had become under Mrs Thatcher – the police force of the capitalist class. As seen on television – where scenes of violence became a nightly fare – the dispute represented an alarming breakdown of public order. Most people, according to opinion polls, sided with the police but that did not mean that the sights that they saw were relished in Wiltshire or Berkshire. The police might be winning, in the sense that the pickets were not succeeding in preventing working miners from entering the pits, but the government, for all that, seemed powerless to restore law and order, or to put a stop to such disgraceful scenes as took place at the Orgreave coking plant, near Sheffield, where that June some 10,000 pickets suffered cavalry charges from mounted police.

Orgreave was the pickets' Waterloo.[12] A month of battles demonstrated the superior force of the police. The lessons of Saltley had been learned; Scargill's famous victory was at last avenged. The police had prepared for the struggle now in hand. They had learnt some lessons also from Northern Ireland, where the policy had been to equip and train police to carry out the public order functions which had at first fallen invidiously to the army. Something similar had happened on the mainland where, faced with the challenges of urban disorders and of terrorism, the police had quietly developed a para-military capability. In 1984 there were some 140,000 police in Britain trained in 'tactical operations' and the use of riot control equipment including the long and short shields, resembling those of Zulu warriors, which were to become so familiar to television viewers during the strike.[13] The so-called National Reporting Centre set up at Scotland Yard at the beginning of the strike was to all intents and purposes a national command centre, the thin end of the wedge – as some chose to see it – of a national police force. Whatever it was, it drafted police around the country in considerable numbers. A good many of the complaints of police misbehaviour were against members of other forces drafted into the coalfields, especially those from the Metropolitan Police.

Violence, Albert Camus had said, was the contagious epidemic of our times. He was right. Images of violence have become the stuff of politics in the television age. Television heightens, selects its images, provokes narcissistic responses, makes violent disorders seem exciting. Those set-piece confrontations outside the pit gates in the eerie pre-dawn light were, perhaps, many of them, less violent than they were made to appear by the lurid shifts of colour produced by hand-held spot lights, the reeling images of jostled cameramen, the jumble of noises picked up by their umbilically-linked soundmen. 'We shove, they shove, and at the moment they're winning,' said a good-humoured picket after one such encounter. At some pits the morning shove became a daily sporting event. But there was nothing sporting about some of the battles, the flying truncheons and the boots put in, the charges by the horses. Much of the violence that occurred went unseen, for the media were not ubiquitous – the cameras could not be everywhere to record the brick through the window at dead of night, the family car scoured or slashed, the beatings and intimidation, the bullyings in the school playgrounds. Violence bred violence, as it does. In the miners' dispute it bred violence on both sides of the picket lines. We may guess that the year-long strike as-seen-on-tv added to the contagion of violence in our already violent society.

The miners' strike set back Labour's recovery for the best part of a year. The violence of the picket lines rubbed off on Labour's image. Kinnock was unable or unwilling wholly to dissociate himself from Scargill and Scargillism or to satisfy his critics that his condemnations of violence or lawlessness were wholly unequivocal. He was not helped in this by the simultaneous campaign of sixteen Labour local authorities to break the new rate-capping law.

At the same time the strike paralysed the trade union movement and retarded it in its snail-like coming to terms with the changed world in which it was obliged to live and work. The TUC's official position towards the new trade union laws remained one of defiance. Under the Thatcher government the trade unions had become a declining industry. Their membership, which had peaked at over 12 million in 1980, was reduced to below 10 million by 1985. The tide of militancy which had swollen their ranks in the 1970s and raised them to new pinnacles of political importance had subsided into the trough of recession and reaction. Three Acts of Parliament had curbed their powers and at last brought them within a framework of labour laws similar to those which ruled in most other countries. Incomes policies were a thing of the past and this also reduced the importance of the unions at the centre. The government was no longer their recruiting sergeant. The demotion of the TUC leaders from their role as an Estate of the Realm had been signalled by their exclusion from the 'corridors of power' in which, during the Callaghan–Foot years, they had strutted as if they owned them. These days they were never to be seen at Number 10 and increasingly seldom interviewed on television. The limelight was no longer theirs.

They were inclined to visit all these woes at the door of Mrs Thatcher but in truth more fundamental factors had been at work since their arch-enemy had come to power. Similar changes were taking place across the industrialised world of Western Europe. Everywhere manufacture was in decline in relation to services. In Britain, manufacture was in absolute decline. The decline had taken place in the most-unionised sectors of employment; the compensating growth was taking place in the least unionisable. By 1986 employment in manufacture had declined by 13 per cent, union membership by 24 per cent. Jobs in the service trades had increased by almost 10 per cent but few of these jobs were unionised. For example, it was estimated that in the hotel trade no more than 6 per cent of employees were members of trade unions. Much of the growth in employment consisted of part-time jobs, predominantly for women; in 1985 there were an estimated 6 million such jobs; in 1980 one in five jobs had been part-time, by 1990 it would be one in four. This also was bad news for the union recruiters. So were the swelling ranks of the self-employed who had increased by one-third since 1979 and now numbered 2·6 million or almost one in ten of the work-force. Altogether of a work-force put at some 32 million some 10 million, nearly one-third, were for the most part beyond the reach of the union organisers.

Moreover, the great expansion of public service trade unionism had also been brought to an end. This had been the great growth sector of the 1960s and 1970s, exemplified in the membership explosion of NUPE. Now public expenditure was under curbs and some services were being privatised. With incomes policies no longer in force there was less incentive for public service workers to join unions. In the private sector, much of the employment growth was centred around small-scale high-tech industries. In Scotland's 'Silicon Glen' a study found that 63 per cent of electronics plants were non-union, and 86 per cent in the still faster growing high-tech health business. Yet Scotland had been traditionally a stronghold of trade unionism. The trade union culture hardly existed along the route of the M4. In general, union membership had been more heavily concentrated in the north than in the south and it was the north that was in decline, the south growing.

Projections into the future told an even more alarming tale. There would be further declines in employment in most of the traditional areas of union strength while future growth would be chiefly in the service sector, in health services and insurance sectors, in hotels and catering, the garage trade and so on. There would be more supervisors and managers, health professionals, scientists and engineers. These increases in employment would be heavily centred on the new towns and market towns of the south. Even in some of the traditional areas of union organisation the unions were losing ground. The Japanese and American employers in Wales and the north-east wanted either non-union or single union plants, and in others the advantages of trade union membership were no longer as evident to workers as once they had been. At the 1985 Trades Union Congress an officer of the EEPTU told delegates, 'We are fighting yesterday's battles with yesterday's methods and, worse still, in yesterday's language. Class war talk won't earn you a yawn up and down the country.' The only kind of trade unionism workers were interested in, he claimed, was the kind exemplified by the 'total agreements' negotiated by the electricians, with their middle-class fringe benefits and no-strike provisions. He was booed.

The emerging demography of Mrs Thatcher's Britain did not look promising territory for either the trade union movement or the Labour Party. The emergence of a 'new servant class' was how one trade union leader saw it. John Edmonds, Oxford-educated professional officer of the GMBMU, saw this as the nature of the challenge facing the trade union movement. He estimated the burgeoning underclass of badly paid and exploited at between 8 and 9 million workers earning (in 1985) less than £115 per week, or its part-time equivalent. In drawing attention to this phenomenon – which he saw as the greatest challenge facing the trade union movement – Edmonds touched upon another profound change which had overtaken the Labour Movement: it could no longer claim to be the champion of the underdog as it had once done. As the secondary labour force grew and as its unionised core diminished, the unions' claim to be the authentic spokesman of workpeople and their families would become less convincing. As André Gorz had put it in *Farewell to the Working Class*: 'The traditional working class is no more than a privileged minority. The majority of the population now belongs to the post-industrial neo-proletariat.'[14] It was not easy to see how the Labour Movement could organise this underclass – or, as Gorz would have it, 'non-class' – while at the same time serving the sectional interests of its declining core membership.

In their weakened state the trade unions had become at the same time less of an asset and less of a liability to the Labour Party. It remained an embarrassment that they continued to insist on a total repeal of the Tory labour laws and this the Party was pledged to do. The counterpart to that commitment was the co-operation of the unions in enabling economic expansion without inflation. But all claims that Labour alone knew how to work with the unions were once more exploded by the miners' strike. Throughout the strike Kinnock was powerless; he was unable to end it, unable to control it, unable to condemn it. His influence with the NUM executive was non-existent. Yet, inevitably, a good deal of the opprobrium incurred by the NUM under Scargill's leadership rubbed off on the Labour Party. It always does in unpopular industrial disputes. This one was different in that it raised, for the first time since before the war, questions about Labour's bona fides as a constitutional party.

Privately Kinnock's opinion of Scargill was scathing. According to his first biographer, Robert Harris, he had said, 'He's destroying the coal industry single-handed. He's the Labour Movement's nearest equivalent to a First World War general.'[15] He had rowed with him publicly in the Panorama studio after his abstention in the Benn–Healey deputy-leadership contest in 1981. He had reluctantly shared a platform with him at the Durham Miners' Gala in June but was not to do so again until 30 November. In that month he had asked Scargill six times to reveal his strategy for winning the strike but could obtain no answer from him. By then he was under considerable pressure from within his Party to show more vigorous support for the miners. It was not until 3 January 1985 that he first visited a miners' picket line in his own constituency, although he had visited many around the country in 1972. He angered left-wingers by absenting himself from a series of five rallies staged that autumn, pleading previous engagements. Eventually, he did join Scargill on a platform in Stoke-on-Trent on 30 November. That morning a taxi driver in South Wales, driving a working miner to work, had been killed by a concrete block dropped from a motorway bridge. 'We meet here tonight in the shadow of an outrage,' Kinnock said, to the accompaniment of abusive heckling.[16]

At the Party conference that autumn he had said, 'We have to be visibly, unequivocally and triumphantly the party of democracy – respecting the law and realising that in a free society bad laws have to be changed, not broken.' But that should not have needed saying in the year 1984; moreover, it was a difficult reputation to sustain in the face of the law-breaking activities of Labour-controlled councils, their attacks on the police, and Arthur Scargill's persistent refusal to condemn picket line violence or even to admit to its existence. When he came to condemn violence himself in that conference speech Kinnock did so in blanket terms which stretched the meaning of language. By condemning violence in all its manifestations, literal and metaphoric, economic violence, State violence, judicial violence, legal violence, the condemnation of picket line violence – when he came to it – lacked certain force.

Of course, Kinnock condemned violence. What Scargill stood for was a million miles from his Welsh-valley vision of democratic socialism. He also knew how damaging was the whole affair to Labour's climb-back to power, what a waste of precious time. But the fact that he was obliged to equivocate somewhat on the subject of picketing showed how constrained he was by shibboleths of the Labour Movement, how little room its past allowed him for man-oeuvre in the present.

The conference went on to pass a motion condemning 'police-violence against the miners'. Scarcely a voice was raised in even-handed condemnation. Tony Benn delivered an inflammatory speech in which he portrayed 'the hopes of millions' as focused on the miners' struggle. Earlier he had said, 'As far as violence is concerned I attribute it one hundred per cent to the government. They have prepared for it, they have recruited and paid the police for it, they have issued the plastic bullets . . . [none in fact was used] . . . and so on.' The electricians' leader, Eric Hammond, was booed to the gilded ceiling of the Blackpool Winter Garden when he said: 'The cult of violence will harm this Movement for many years to come.'

None had been more vocal in solidarity with the miners than the left-wing councils, who were themselves engaged in a campaign designed to bring them into confrontation with the government. The municipal Left saw the miners' struggle as part of a pincer movement which, combined with their unlawful refusal to set rates or balance their budgets, would force the government into retreat. During the government's first term, high-spending local authorities, most of them with severe social problems on their hands, had been forced, in effect, to choose between slashing cuts or swingeing rate increases. The left-wing councils refused to make cuts and bumped up their rates. The government's answer to this in its second term was rate-capping. It was made illegal to set rates above a certain level. The Rates Act 1984 was due to come into effect in the spring of 1985. At Labour's local government conference in Sheffield in 1984 a policy of 'non-compliance' was agreed. How this was to be carried out was a matter for debate. The hardliners, led by the leader of Lambeth Borough Council, Ted Knight, were in favour of refusing to set rates at all. Another school favoured fixing legal rates but introducing no-cuts budgets all the same. One was a formula for openly breaking the law, the other for financial irresponsibility. At the Sheffield conference the hard line was preferred and the stand taken was subsequently endorsed as official Labour policy by the National Executive Committee. The Party was thus committed to a policy of unlawful resistance.

At a meeting of Labour councillors in Birmingham the following February, however, Kinnock argued against the left-wing strategy. 'Better a dented shield than no shield at all,' he said. 'Better a Labour council doing its best to help than Government placemen extending the full force of Government policy . . . We don't want to weaken the broad coalition by wrangles over legality or public dramas or exciting excursions. Our basic concern is – and must remain – jobs, services and democracy.'[17] This effectively split the sixteen rate-capped authorities into moderate and militant camps. There was also no doubt a good deal of reluctance among many of the councillors involved to press their rebellion to the point at which they could be removed from office and incur heavy penalties against their own pockets. Solidarity crumbled as, one by one, the rebel authorities drew back from open defiance of the law and discovered the possibilities of 'creative accounting' within the prescribed limits to their rate revenues.

It was fashionable at this time to suppose that the new frontiers of socialism were being mapped out by local authorities such as the Greater London Council and Sheffield. David Blunkett saw 'the local state used as an example of what we could do as a socialist government at national level.'[18] For the first time in many years local government was projecting its leaders on to the national scene. In place of the old time-serving aldermen a new breed of local leader, typified by Livingstone of London and Blunkett of Sheffield, had burst upon the scene. In the early days of Labour's history municipal socialism had played an influential role, but as the emphasis had shifted to parliamentary socialism local government lost much of its interest and glamour. Part of the desuetude of local Labour parties, which by the 1970s had left them so vulnerable to take-over by the bed-sit brigade, had to do with the dead hand of the long-serving councillors who tended to dominate local parties. Corruption was another part of it; it was not unique to Labour but it flourished in the local 'one-party states' of Labour's heartlands in the north-east, Yorkshire and South Wales. Moreover, the 1970s saw a worsening of the social conditions of the cities and, in the context of economic recession, brought local authorities increasingly into conflict with the central government over their finances. Anthony Crosland had declared 'the party's over' in 1976, insisting that it was imperative for local authorities to bring their spending into line with overall government plans even if that meant cuts, which it did.

The new municipal socialism was an expression of the disillusion with parliamentary socialism which had spread through the Labour Movement as a result of the Wilson years. In essence what happened was that the 'broad Left' moved into the town halls. It was an aspect of the rise of middle class activism in the Labour Party, assisted by the 'gentrification' of certain parts of London, and the growth of public service trade unionism. It was also another aspect of the 1970s long march through the institutions of the Labour Movement. Local authority areas became arenas for extra-parliamentary politics in which all manner of activist groups – women, blacks, tenants, peace campaigners – could link up with trade unions and local parties to broaden the front of socialist advance. This style of left-wing politics derived in part from the 'participatory' anti-war campaigns and student revolts of the late 1960s and early 1970s; Cynthia Cockburn's *Red Bologna* was their new handbook. The new style owed something perhaps also to the 'community politics' practised with some success by the radical wing of the Liberal Party. It also owed something to the 'new Left' thinkers – Marcuse, Gorz and others – who had addressed themselves to the decline of the old proletariat and the need to replenish it with new radical elements, chief among them women, ethnic and sexual minorities. Nowhere was the disappearance of the working class more evident than in London, its manufacturing base meagre, the docks deserted, the printing industry entering its last days.

The creation of two-tier local authorities in the early 1970s had made it easier for the employees of one local authority to work for another. This opened the way to teachers, lecturers, and local government officers themselves becoming councillors.[19] A jobs-for-the-boys system grew up: people who were in reality professional politicians obtained for themselves well-paid part-time positions, or sinecures, with neighbouring authorities. In the London borough of Camden, 48 per cent of Labour councillors were dependent directly or indirectly on other councils for their livings, in Lewisham 55 per cent. Others were employed by unions representing council workers or council-funded voluntary groups.[20] Thus grew up a new nexus of power and patronage.

Whether it was any more, or any less, representative than what had gone before is another question. The periodical literature spawned by local left-wing socialism reveals a closed and introverted world of meta-politics in which debate proceeds according to assumptions shared only by the participants in the game. In more senses than one they were endeavouring to create socialism without the working class, for the socialism they preached and practised bore no relation to the wishes and needs of most ordinary people. To this new breed of activist ideologist the working class became an abstraction. As John Gyford puts it, 'The public are seen as a cross between an audience and a reserve army, not as actors in their own right who may have legitimately different opinions of their own.'[21]

The first of the new breed of local socialists to command national attention was Ken Livingstone, the leader of the Greater London Council. In the 1982 'Man of the Year' poll conducted by BBC Radio 4 he came second only to the Pope. His fame had grown to this within eighteen months of his becoming leader of the GLC. Labour had won control of the GLC in May 1981 with a Left-enough majority to oust by caucus coup the moderate leader, Andrew McIntosh, under whom the party had fought the election. Livingstone was installed in his place. He was the first post-war figure to graduate to the national scene. Born a few days after the ending of the war in Europe, he came of age in the 1960s. That meant that he grew up in the Wilson years. His interest in politics developed chiefly around the anti-war and other protest movements of the 1960s. He was twenty-three by the time he bothered to join the Labour Party. The year appropriately was 1968.[22]

The Labour Party at that time was at a low ebb, wide open to talent. Charm can take you far in politics and he had plenty of it. He was also a natural debater and good platform speaker in spite of – or, perhaps, because of – an unattractive voice. 'I didn't realise until I read *Private Eye* that I've got this boring monotonous nasal drone,' he was to say later. His career as Labour politician prospered rapidly. By 1971 he was a member of Lambeth borough council. From 1973 he sat on the GLC as well. He was well ensconced in conventional local politics by the time the 'class of '68' came flocking back into the Labour Party.[23] Their heads were full of ideology; Livingstone meanwhile had learnt something about power.

In the Norwood constituency Labour Party, and on the Lambeth council, Livingstone had come under the Trotskyist influence of Ted Knight, who for a while had been expelled from the Labour Party and became an open member of the Socialist Labour League.[24] However, apparently nobody saw Livingstone as particularly left-wing at that time.[25] His talents were organisational rather than ideological. Throughout his career, ally and foe alike have suspected him of being an opportunist. His style was to put together broad alliances of a tactical kind, not caring much about where the participants fitted into the spectrum. He was a peripatetic agitator, moving from borough to borough on his way, living off his attendance allowances and expenses as a councillor, a new kind of politician altogether.

It was he who spotted the potential of the GLC as a political base and after 1979 set about organising a London-wide caucus around the eclectic ultra-leftist magazine *London Labour Briefing*. The GLC had few powers beyond the provision of public transport. Such role as it had been assigned when set up in 1964 as London's second-tier authority had been largely whittled away by the central government on the one side and the boroughs on the other. But it had more rate revenue than it knew what to do with and enough discretionary power to enable it to engage in propaganda warfare on a broad front, to inject feminism, anti-racism, anti-heterosexism, and anti-war into many areas of administration and policy. Because its detailed responsibilities were few, the GLC could be turned into a debating society for the big questions. 'Space' was what the 'class of '81' were looking for – room in which to manoeuvre within the confines of capitalist society – and 'space' they found at County Hall. Livingstone's declared aim was 'to use the council machinery as part of a political campaign both against the government and in defence of socialist policies.' The GLC would lead the 'mass opposition' to Thatcherism, setting an example across the land.

Fleet Street made him. From day one after his successful coup he excited lurid press coverage. The royal wedding in London, a few weeks after he had taken over, gave him the opportunity to achieve overnight national notoriety. He had asked specially not to be invited. 'No one elected us to go to weddings, we were elected to run the buses on time,' he said. On the eve of the event he welcomed a delegation from the H-Blocks Committee of Armagh Gaol and the wedding day itself was spent releasing black balloons over London from the steps of County Hall.[26] Thereafter indiscretions poured from his lips, by 1982 they could and did fill a book.[27] Some were shocking, some were funny, some plain loony. He said, 'I fear that within ten years there will be a coup and that all gays, trade union activists and left-wing politicians will be led off to the gas chambers.' Asked about his line on civil defence against nuclear attack (he was against it) he said, 'I am not at all sure they want me to survive a nuclear war.' But it was the IRA which got him into the most serious and persistent trouble. After the bomb outrage at Chelsea Barracks in which an elderly woman passer-by was killed by flying nails, he had characterised the terrorists as 'not criminals or lunatics running around . . . [not] just criminals or psychopaths . . . they have a motive force which they think is good.' He subsequently denied that he had said or meant that the bombers were not criminals but for this the *Sun* appointed him 'the most odious man in Britain'. The rest of the popular papers joined the chorus of opprobrium.

Livingstone became living proof of the old saw that all publicity is good publicity. Whether this had been achieved through naïvety or brilliant self-promotion nobody was quite sure.[28] However, the onslaughts from Fleet Street led to television appearance in celebrity slots where his charm and eccentricity came through. From being a bogeyman he now became a card. He had always been something of an original. As a child he had engaged in imaginative games and solitary fantasies. He read strange and adventurous books – especially science fiction – and collected reptiles of which he was fond. Later his six salamanders were to become famous. 'We brought some tadpoles back from France and they turned into salamanders. It isn't bizarre. Many people have unusual pets. I feed them on slugs and woodlice. They just live under a stone, come out at night and are highly poisonous. People say I identify with my pets.'

He invented a politics of style. For the socialism he practised was mostly a socialism without substance. What the GLC under Livingstone did was to make propaganda and give away money. It didn't do much else. The House of Lords had put a stop to the popular 'Fares Fair' campaign[29] and later London Transport was removed from its political control. That left it with little real administrative responsibility for 'running London'. Spending money was Livingstone's antidote to monetarism. During his reign the GLC spent some £8,878 millions. That represented an increase of 170 per cent in expenditure during a period in which the rate of inflation had been 29 per cent. By giving money to special interest groups, and funding all manner of leftie and loony causes, a motley coalition of minorities was assembled. Blacks, feminists, Irish, gays, disabled, one-parent families, welfare claimants, homeless, peace campaigners – all were identified as potential recruits to the new ersatz proletariat which would reinforce the thinning ranks of the workers. The GLC hired more and more people to give more and more money to more and more people. In 1983–4 it handed out £42 million, in 1984–5 £47 million. To give away the money it hired the same sort of people it was giving the money to, although in truth only a small proportion of the money went to the exotic causes which got into the newspapers. Anne Sofer, a GLC councillor at that time, has brilliantly chronicled the Livingstone era at County Hall. 'The cornucopia of grants, combined with a high profile . . . has created an atmosphere at County Hall that is a cross between a students' union and a campaign headquarters.' Its 'pompous, oak-panelled, marble-columned halls' were now thronged with Rastas and Punks, young people in badge-festooned safari jackets, trainers and jeans. 'They intended to change the world, and ended up having a ball,' she said, when the end came.[30]

Abolition gave Livingstone his last cause. Mrs Thatcher had served his career wonderfully, first with the cuts and then with rate-capping. She had made him what he was, enabled the Left to construct a power apparatus that was now to take over much of London. Livingstone's 'Save the GLC' campaign was a slick and expensive operation aimed at arousing the patriotism of Londoners. During its last two years the GLC spent £10 million on propaganda, most of it on fighting for its own life. Livingstone himself fought the battle with great panache. He was the star turn at fringe meetings held at all the party conferences including the Conservatives'. For the duration he became Mr Nice. For once he kept his mouth shut about Sinn Fein. The 'most odious man in Britain' had succeeded in becoming something of a popular folk hero. He conned Londoners into believing that he and the GLC had been 'running' London. It was widely felt that a city of London's stature and fame should have some sort of government of its own. There was something not quite right, it was thought, about the government closing down an elected body in this way. But on 31 March 1986 the GLC surrendered. The flag was hauled down to the accompaniment of Elgar's 'Nimrod'. It spend £250,000 on its farewell party. It went out as it came in, with a bang – London's most expensive ever firework display.

Livingstone could not save the GLC but he had found one last mobilising issue. For a brief moment Labour was popular in London, superficially at least. Abolition helped it on its way to victory in the Fulham by-election that month, which in turn helped Labour to gain seats in the borough council elections in May. The elections swept in a new wave of young left-wing councillors with no experience of local government. Partly this was because many of the moderates had decided that they had had enough and gave up the 'struggle'. Others were de-selected by their local parties. Many candidates at that time were required to give written undertakings that they would not vote for cuts in jobs or services even if that meant surcharge and bankruptcy. As a result the left-wing London boroughs now became still more extremist and extravagant.

Legend and myth instantly developed around the Livingstone years.[31] He had shattered the old labourist image and shown that socialism need not be boring, indeed could be fun. Many of his opponents now came to see it as all having been good fun. Ken had had panache, style. His own view was that he had helped to create a power base in the Labour Movement which would be strong enough to prevent future betrayals of the kind he held Wilson and Callaghan to have been guilty of. On that basis he was content to see Labour win under Neil Kinnock. His eyes now turned towards Westminster across the river from County Hall. He had been foiled in a re-selection coup in the safe seat of Brent East before the 1983 election but for next time had things sewn up. In his last days at the GLC he trimmed towards the softer Left, parting company with Ted Knight and the old gang. They had always known he was of no fixed ideological abode. For the purpose of creating for himself a power base within the Labour Movement in London his coalition of minor-ities had worked brilliantly. For the purpose of winning a General Election for the Labour Party it was a disaster. It was a recipe for alienating the un-young, the un-black, and the un-gay. Of the 123 seats which Labour needed to win a majority in Parliament, 23 were in London.

The Conservatives now played the 'loony Left' card for all it was worth. The 'loony Left' did everything it could to oblige. Haringey ruled that only Nicaraguan coffee should be purchased. Hackney ended its twinning arrangements with France, West Germany and Israel, and entered into new ones with the Soviet Union, East Germany and Nicaragua. A spokesman explained, 'This will enable us to concentrate on our new friends.' Hackney staged an 'Open Day for Gays and Lesbians'. Lambeth banned the use of the word 'family' from council literature on the grounds that it was discriminatory. Ealing ordered a purge of all 'racist' and 'sexist' books from its libraries. Haringey introduced courses on homosexuality into its schools, including primary and nursery schools. At an ILEA school in Kennington competitive games were discouraged and writing protest letters was made part of the time-table. Television viewers saw a report in which boys and girls played non-competitive cricket with paddles and puff balls. Brent appointed 90 new officers to eradicate racism from its schools. An ILEA teaching pack called 'Auschwitz: Yesterday's Racism' instructed children that Hitler's policies should be compared with anti-union legislation in Britain today. In Lambeth the police were debarred from using all council facilities. The Lam-beth leader Linda Bellos (Ted Knight had been duly surcharged and disqualified) said, 'I think the police are bent on war.' Lewisham voted £64,000 for gathering complaints against the police. When representatives of Sinn Fein addressed Hackney Council a revolver was fired (by a Liberal) and fisticuffs ensued. Riots and disturbances in council chambers were shown on television.

People may have laughed at some of these excesses but the word 'loony' did not do justice to the sinister nature of some of them. Parents were appalled at the idea of their children being instructed in homosexuality. They were outraged by some of the political propaganda that passed for teaching. Workers employed by some of the councils were reported by informers for making 'racist' jokes or remarks and were disciplined or sacked. In some cases their unions refused to represent them. Life-long supporters of the Labour Party were alienated and lost in these ways. The 'London effect' it was dubbed by one of Neil Kinnock's aides, after an extreme left-wing candidate had succeeded in losing for Labour the previously safe seat of Greenwich on the eve of the 1987 General Election. But it was not just a 'London effect'. Livingstone had made London famous for this sort of thing, had put loony Leftism on the map. The price of socialism in one city was the continuance of Thatcherism at Westminster. That was Ken Livingstone's true legacy to London, and to Labour.

In Liverpool Kinnock had other troubles. An entirely different strain of Trotskyism had taken hold, that known as the Militant Tendency. Its appeal was the same as that of all fundamentalisms. As Islamic fundamentalism spread like the fire of hope among the Shi'ites of the Moslem world, as the Pentecostal religions exploded among the poor blacks of the northern American cities, and Rastafarianism among the alienated West Indian youths of Brixton and Brent, so this latter-day socialist fundamentalism caught hold among the poor whites of Liverpool and some other desolated cities. All of these were expressions, perhaps, of a common desire for certainty in an age of disbelief, instances of the old adage that when people believe nothing, they will believe anything.

The Militant Tendency was the cover for the Revolutionary Socialist League, one of several Trotskyist splinters from the international Communist movement. Ostensibly it was only a tendency within the Labour Party consisting of supporters and readers of the weekly newspaper *Militant*. In practice it was a highly organised party within a party, organised on strict Leninist lines. It employed more full-time organisers than the Labour Party.

From being a tiny sect of revolutionary cranks the Militant Tendency from the early 1970s grew to become what Michael Foot by

1982 called a 'pestiliential nuisance' to the Labour Party. It was in the 1970s that the tactic of 'entryism' prescribed by Trotsky was widely adopted by members or former members of revolutionary groups, among them the Revolutionary Socialist League. In 1975 the Labour Party's then national agent, Reg Underhill, investigated its activities and concluded that it was operating as a party within a party in defiance of Labour's rules. But the NEC was under left-wing control and no action was taken. After 1980 Militant took advantage of the new re-selection process to attempt to install its own candidates in some Labour seats. Its activities within the party became generally more overt and more embarrassing. Having regained tenuous control of the NEC, Foot managed to instigate a new inquiry and in February 1983 the five members of the *Militant*'s editorial board – in fact the key members of its central committee – were expelled. However, this was no more than a token purge. Indeed the Militant Tendency thrived on persecution. In 1979 its membership had been 1,800, by 1986 it was more than 8,000.

Leon Trotsky, the tragic hero of the Bolshevik revolution, had founded in his exile a tradition of dissident Communism marked for its propensity to almost infinite sectarian schism. Trotskyism in Britain was of no political significance during the 1930s and its flame burnt exceedingly low after the murder of the prophet in 1940 until, in the 1960s, it revived in an extraordinary fashion. Partly this was due to the ideological disintegration of Stalinist Communism in the West following the 20th Party Congress and the Soviet invasion of Hungary in 1956, partly to the revival of Marxism around the events of 1968 and the war in Vietnam.

Trotsky had originally prescribed the tactic of 'entryism' in the early 1930s when he despaired of the Communist Parties of the West. He urged his followers to proceed with the revolutionary education of the masses from within the more popular social democratic parties. But when 'entryism' became the tactic of the Revolutionary Socialist League in 1954 it was as a parasitic means of survival through hard times pending the coming of the revolution. From the late 1960s, however, revolutionary socialists of many hues entered the Labour Party for the purpose of playing a vanguard role. Most of them could do so openly, but the Militants continued to be disciplined members of a Leninist party working within the social democratic fold and hence were obliged to operate covertly.

Militant's vanguardist tactics derived in large part from Trotsky's 'transitional programme' put forward in 1938. Its purpose was to prepare the working class for revolution. It consists of consciousness-raising slogans, the chief of which is the demand for the immediate nationalisation of the 200 largest companies, and other 'impossibilist' demands designed to demonstrate the repressive nature of the system. The role of the Labour Party is not to advance the cause of socialism but rather to advance the struggle, by demonstrating the futility of reformism and parliamentary socialism. Then, when the final capitalist crisis comes, the workers will be ready for real revolution.

The Militant Tendency took its most tenacious hold in Liverpool, the industrial Carthage of the north, a place where cults flourished, home of the Beatles and football. At the same time there was a whiff of Chicago about the way the city was captured and governed, or a Brechtian parable of gangster socialism; and where more appropriate for that to flourish than on the windy waterfront of the Mersey with its spectacular skyline, and hollow warrens of humanity below. Liverpool had all the necessary ingredients: it had a tradition of sectarian Marxist politics, a long history of corrupt, boss-ridden Labour Party control, and above all as a city it personified the decline which, the Militants believed, would culminate in the capitalist apocalypse. Where better to put impossibilism into practice?

Liverpool had swung against the Tory tide to Labour in 1983. For the first time in 10 years a Labour council was elected. Militant had been able to fill a vacuum in Liverpool's Labour politics caused by the disintegration of the old right-wing machine and the absence of a new Left of the kind which grew up in London, Sheffield, Manchester and elsewhere.[32] Industrial decline, depopulation, and some of the most deplorable housing conditions in Western Europe meant that a crisis in the city's finances would have been likely under any administration. Liverpool's councillors ran circles round the Secretary for the Environment, Patrick Jenkin. When he compromised in order to avoid a confrontation with the city over its budget, Derek Hatton embarrassed the government, and helped to destroy Jenkin, by publicly proclaiming a great victory over Thatcherism for Militant tactics. But Liverpool was to become Labour's problem rather than the Tories'.

Hatton was a media Militant. A fireman turned community worker, he owed his rapid rise chiefly to a genius for self-advertisement. Officially he was no more than the deputy-leader of the council but effectively he was its driving force. This was all the more remarkable in that the Militant Tendency by no means controlled the council. Of the 51 Labour councillors who took office in 1983 only 16 were Militant members.[33] They manipulated the Labour

Group by operating as a disciplined caucus within the caucus which politically controlled it. In this way the minority wielded the power of the majority. Lenin would have approved. Power was also wielded in a more traditional Liverpool way, through patronage. Jobs for the boys, the technique of the old bosses, was used to extend Militant's influence among the unions. Hatton had other things in common with the old bosses. His lifestyle, his penchant for flashy suits and expensive restaurants, suggested sources of income other than his attendance allowances and his £10,000 a year 17-hour-week job as community officer with the neighbouring Knowsley council. Hatton's image was not at all the Militant image of austere proletarianism but he was too famous for anything to be done about it. For better or for worse, Liverpool had become the vanguard of Militant's struggle.

In 1985 it had joined with the sixteen rate-capped authorities (although not rate-capped itself) in their campaign of illegal defiance, refusing to set rates until the government had climbed down in the way Jenkin was alleged to have done in face of Liverpool's defiance the previous year. A motion in favour of disobedience of the rate-capping law had been passed at the 1984 Labour conference and it was this which served as the basis for the campaign launched in 1985. The campaign was a flop. The solidarity of the sixteen authorities collapsed, as the Militants had always predicted it would, but Liverpool pressed on towards confrontation. In June 1985 it adopted an illegal deficit budget. Bankruptcy loomed. At the end of August the council issued precautionary redundancy notes to its 31,000 employees. The purpose of this tactic was to advertise Liverpool's plight, increase the pressure on the government to bail the city out, and – as always – to deepen the struggle by raising the consciousness of the working class. The working class, however, saw it differently; the redundancy notices were taken seriously and received with alarm and anger: the tactic was a-too-clever-by-half blunder.

That was the beginning of the end. In his famous speech at the Labour Party conference in Bournemouth Kinnock made contemptuous mock of the Militant regime in Liverpool. 'You start with far-fetched resolutions,' he said – addressing Hatton towards the rear of the hall. 'They are then pickled into rigid dogma, a code, and you go through the years sticking to that, outdated, misplaced, irrelevant to the real needs and you end in the grotesque chaos, the grotesque chaos of a Labour council – a *Labour* council – hiring taxis to scuttle around the city handing out redundancy notices to its own workers. A socialist council delivering redundancy notices to its employees in taxis. (*Uproar.*) You can't play politics with people's jobs!' The use of taxis for this purpose was thought to be particularly shocking, particularly unsocialist.

The speech was a success. For once Kinnock received rave press notices. He had shown himself a fighter, had stood up to the bullies of the Militant Tendency. The next day he stood up to Arthur Scargill as well. When a heckler from the gallery yelled, 'What were you doing in the strike Neil?' he replied, 'Well I wasn't telling them lies. That's what I was not doing.' Before the Bournemouth conference opinion polls had shown the Alliance in the lead with 35 per cent, Labour and the Tories level pegging on 29 per cent. Kinnock's speech shot Labour into a seven point lead – for a while. The speech had drawn attention to his fighting qualities but it had also drawn attention to the presence of his enemies within the Labour Party.

Another inquiry into the Militants now ensued and after much creaking of the constitutional machinery and prolonged legal wrangles another token purge resulted in the expulsion of Hatton and seven other leading Liverpool Militants. But why only the eight Liverpudlians? What about the other 7,000 or so Militants believed to be at large within the Labour Party? And other brands of extremists besides? Kinnock sheltered from his critics behind constitutionality. The Labour Party could act only within its rules, he insisted; not only would it be dragged through the courts if it did not but it was not that sort of party, it was foreign to its nature to offend against the laws of natural justice.

Here was another example of an argument which derived from the delusion that the Labour Movement was a microcosm of the world. The world outside was expected to accept its terms of reference, its rule books, its rites and customs, to accept the transcendental or over-arching character of its class morality, to take as read its family history and tolerate the eccentricities and pathologies which resulted from it. But the world was no longer as willing to do these things, to make these allowances, to accept the mores of the Labour Movement or have its rule books waved in its face; rather it was inclined to regard it as an alien sub-culture inhabited by too many enemies of liberty. The mores which had once ruled working class life no longer held such sway. Less store was set by solidarity. For example, 'Thou shalt not cross picket lines' no longer had the force of an eleventh commandment. Many now saw Eddy Shah not as the wicked boss figure but as the plucky underdog,[34] the Nottinghamshire miners not as 'scabs' but as local heroes.

For most of Kinnock's leadership his party had pinned him down. The miners' strike had rudely interrupted his honeymoon as leader and for a whole year cramped his style. Then he was plagued by the Militants in Liverpool and the loony-Left in London. He said to the *Sunday Times* in September 1985, 'You see it's always the same question . . . Why is your party in bloody chaos? . . . Why aren't you arranging the assassination of Arthur Scargill? . . . They don't want to know what you say or do about South Africa or unemployment.'[35]

So great were his internal preoccupations that he could be forgiven for believing that it was chiefly the 'bloody chaos' of his party which stood between it and power. The popular success of his conference speech at Bournemouth, in which he had roughed up the Militants, and put Scargill in his place for good measure, had reinforced this view within his entourage. After Bournemouth his standing, momentarily, rose in the polls. All he had to do, it was easy to conclude, was to be seen to be standing up to the Militants and Scargill.

This delusion accompanied him down to the General Election and helped him to lose it. His re-education of his party could only move at the pace of his own re-education. He mistakenly supposed that Labour could be made acceptable to the electorate once more without fundamental policy changes. 'I don't believe that the policies on which we fought the election ought to be ejected like some sort of spent cartridge,' he wrote in *Tribune*, shortly before he came to the leadership.[36]

'Change of image is what there is and all there is going to be,' explained one of his aides in 1985, as Labour began to extricate itself from the ruins of the miners' strike. However, the relationship between form and substance is a subtle one and without engaging in bloody battles to reverse past policies Kinnock succeeded in junking a good deal of ideological baggage and making his party at least look a little more electable.

Labour's 'Freedom and Fairness' campaign, launched in April 1986, was the most explicit signal that Labour under Kinnock was coming gradually to terms with the 'Thatcher revolution' and recognising the popular success of certain of its features, notably the sale of council houses and the widening of share ownership. It was also a sign of Labour's coming to terms with the SDP–Liberal Alliance, for it showed that Kinnock now saw the need to compete with it in the centre ground of party politics.

Was he saying, in effect, 'We are the true Social Democrats?' His left-wing critics thought so. 'Is [the Labour Party] to remain basically socialist,' asked Eric Heffer, 'or is it to become a sort of Social

Democratic Party Mark 2? The signs are that it is moving in the latter direction.'[37] Not quite perhaps, or not yet. Kinnock, in a Fabian Lecture towards the end of 1985, had scathingly repudiated the politics of the SDP which, he argued, were 'not concerned with the structure of property ownership, or the transfer of economic power'.[38] For all that, we might do better to judge him by appearances than to analyse the labyrinthine constructions of his prose.

The party political broadcast which launched the 'Freedom and Fairness' campaign out-Saatchied Saatchi and Saatchi. It was slick, glossy and American in style and had been closely market researched. The focus of the broadcast was a pretty little girl, Hannah Roberts, aged 9. We see her running along a dark street and colliding with the reassuring figure of – what the commentary calls – 'a Bobby on the beat'. The message was very different from the message that had been emerging from, for example, the GLC police committee: crime on the streets was recognised for what it was, a popular, predominantly working-class, concern.

The programme played on many of the chords of people's real concerns, about standards of health care and teaching in the schools, the difficulties of first-time house buyers, even the health hazards to children of leaded petrol, and was carefully targeted at the upwardly-mobile 'new' working class to which Kinnock had many times insisted socialism must be made to appeal.

The campaign was the first fruit of the appointment to Labour headquarters of Peter Mandelson to be director of campaigns and communications. Formerly a young television producer, Mandelson was entirely media-minded. The 'Freedom and Fairness' campaign led to jokes about 'designer socialism' and it was true that Kinnock seemed to be increasingly surrounded by young men in business suits, ties, and neatly cut hair, reminiscent of the young functionaries who had accompanied Mitterrand and Fabius to power in France.

Labour pollsters had been telling the party what ought in any case to have been pretty obvious, namely that while its policies on education, health and housing – the social issues – remained widely supported, its image remained outdated and generally negative. In his conference speech at Bournemouth Kinnock had signalled the abandonment of old-style statist socialism for what he then called the 'enabling State'. In February, in a rambling television interview with Brian Walden, he had put the emphasis on production first and distribution second, and had accepted an invitation to liken his approach to that of Franklin Roosevelt and the New Deal. Yet the whole main thrust of Labour's policy since the war had been statist and, in the 1960s and 1970s, corporatist. Images stick and are not changed in a hurry.

In its economic policy, for example, Labour had abandoned the massive reflation it had promised the country in 1983 for a more realistic and pragmatic approach. A more modest expansion in demand would be combined with supply-side measures – billed as 'socialist supply-side measures' – somewhat on the model of Japanese industrial policy. Yet the panoply of boards and acronyms involved in all this – a re-created National Enterprise Board (NEB) and a new National Investment Bank (NIB) – or would that be called the British Industrial Bank (BIB)? – smacked of the 1960s, and 1970s. The talk of obtaining the co-operation of the trade unions – in Hattersley's phrase an 'unspoken bargain' between unions and a Labour government – was still more redolent of the corporatist past. Labour government, it still seemed, would mean more intervention, a more powerful role for trade unions, more spending, more taxes, and almost certainly more inflation. In such broad brush-stroke terms the picture of the future did not look so very different from people's fading photo of the past. To proclaim that Labour was the 'party of production' was not a sufficient answer to the image problem involved here. Labour was not perceived to be the party of production, rather it was seen as the party of producers – a very different matter.

Nevertheless, the launch of the new look Labour Party was a success. It came shortly after the Fulham victory – a Yuppyville London seat – where a nice, moderate, house-trained candidate had trounced the SDP man into humiliating third place. The Prime Minister was floundering still in the pits of Westland. The *Financial Times* went so far as to comment, 'The British Labour Party is again beginning to look like a credible party of government – at least in the sense that it wants office and may achieve it.' This was what was most frequently said about Kinnock – 'he wants to win'. It was a considerable step forward if it meant that – unlike Foot – he was capable of seeing what was required to win and of bringing it about. But what if all it meant was that he believed that Labour could win by packaging and presentation, by putting a smiling face on its policies and wearing a rose in its lapel? 'We are trying to show the Labour Party in its true colours,' said Mandelson. The rose which was adopted as Labour's ubiquitous emblem was symbol of this approach, this way of thinking. It was enough, perhaps, to stave off terminal decline but not enough to win the General Election of 1987.

II

After the Oil

The Conservative Party manifesto of 1987 was to claim that 'decline *has* been reversed'. As the election approached the government's claims to economic success became ever more triumphalist – Britain was the fastest growing economy in Western Europe, the growth in manufacturing productivity was the fastest in the world, investment was scaling new heights, exports achieving new records. Yet if decline had been halted or reversed this was due not to Britain's economy growing at a faster rate than in the past but to the slower growth rates of other countries. It also depended on how you did the sums. The claim that Britain's had become the fastest growing economy in Europe depended on leaving out of account the economic consequences of the first two years of Mrs Thatcher. By starting to reckon from the final quarter of 1981 it could be shown that at an average 2·6 per cent annual growth Britain had done better than everybody other than Japan and Denmark. But if the reckoning begins with Mrs Thatcher's arrival in 1979 Britain, with an annual growth rate of 1·4 per cent, falls to eighth in the league, below the OECD average but in line with the European Community average. This is because output had declined by 3·5 per cent during the government's first two years. Moreover, the average annual growth of 2·6 per cent since 1982, although comparing favourably with the performance of others, was nothing spectacular when compared with Britain's own past performance. In the 1960s the growth rate had averaged 3·1 per cent and in the 1970s 2·4 per cent, performances which had left Britain at the bottom of the league table. Now she was near the top chiefly because the others were doing less well.

Thus to talk about the 'reversal of decline' was somewhat premature. It was calculated that in order to bring British living standards up to those of West Germany, which had moved ahead from around

1970, it would be necessary to grow by 1 per cent faster than the European economies for some thirty years. Nevertheless, it could not be denied that the process of *relative* decline had for the time being at least been arrested. For how long that might prove the case would depend on more fundamental factors to do with the competitiveness of British industry.

An encouraging sign by 1987 was the trend in productivity. Manufacturing productivity really was growing the fastest in the world, at an annual average of 3·5 per cent, even faster than in Japan. That was good news, whichever way you looked at it. It meant that Britain could remain competitive in export markets even though her wage costs did tend to push up a bit faster than other people's. What it meant for the longer term was not so clear. Most commentators were inclined to see it as a cyclical phenomenon. 'The reason why the UK ranks higher on productivity than growth has been that unemployment has risen faster than elsewhere.'[1] It was relatively easy to increase productivity by closing down inefficient factories and reducing over-manned workforces, the difficult part would be to increase efficiency when industry was working at full capacity. In 1987 manufacturing output had still not quite recovered to its 1979 level. Moreover, the productivity record of the economy as a whole was nowhere near so encouraging, and by now manufacture only accounted for about a quarter of total output. Nor had the growth in manufacturing productivity – which, in any case, was no faster than in the late 1960s and early 1970s – made any dent at all in the large gap between Britain's absolute level of productivity and that of most other industrial countries.[2] Britain was a cheap labour country with high unit costs, a most unpromising condition.

Lurking behind the question of Britain's competitiveness, which had deteriorated so markedly in the first two Thatcher years, was the question of what would be done when the oil ran out? It would not run out literally, at least not for a very long while, but run out it would in the sense of ceasing to make up the payments' gap between what Britain could sell and what she needed to buy. The oil from the North Sea had been providential in one sense, the US cavalry coming over the hill just at the very moment the IMF was moving in, but in another sense it had been a qualified blessing – even a curse, some argued – in that it had provided an excuse for not making painful adjustment to the world as it had come to be after the oil shock of 1973. Not only that but as a petro-currency, in some degree, the value of the pound against the D-mark or US dollar bore little relation to the relative efficiency of the British, German and American economies. By forcing Britain to maintain an uncompetitive exchange rate, though aided and abetted in this by the government's dogmatic monetarism, North Sea oil thus helped to bring about the ferocious de-industrialisation which occurred in 1980 and 1981. Manufacturing output fell by some 17 per cent at a cost of two million jobs. For those two years relative decline became absolute with a vengeance.

The question now, as the contribution to output and to the balance of payments made by the oil diminished, as slowly it would, was whether the manufacturing base would prove up to the task of filling the gap. Or, alternatively, the question was whether the service industries could make up both for the falling away of the oil revenues and the decline of manufacture.

These were the fundamental questions asked by the House of Lords Select Committee on Overseas Trade which through 1984 and 1985 accumulated evidence on the course of British decline and the prospects for reversing it. At that moment the proceeds from the North Sea were reaching their very peak. Manufacturing trade had swung into deficit for the first time since the Industrial Revolution.

Britain as the service centre of the world did not seem to offer a very promising alternative future. It was not that providing services was an inferior form of economic activity to the manufacture of goods, although some plainly thought so; it was simply that most services were not for export. In 1985 manufacture may have accounted for no more than 21 per cent of Britain's GDP but it was responsible for half of her exports. Services accounted for half of GDP but only 23 per cent of exports. This meant that for every percentage point by which exports of manufactures declined the export of services would need to increase by 3 per cent. That seemed an unlikely prospect in view of the fact that Britain's share of world trade in services had been declining even faster than her share of world trade in manufactures. Nor was there much reason to suppose that the true vocation of the British lay in providing the world with services. The financial services offered by the City of London were a major export industry but in general the British were not exactly famed for the standard of service in hotels, restaurants, banks, and railway ticket offices.

In any case, as the industrialist Lord Weinstock wondered in his evidence to the Lords Committee, 'what will the service industries be servicing when there is no hardware, when no wealth is actually being produced? We will be servicing presumably the production of wealth by others. We will supply the Changing of the Guard, Beefeaters around the Tower of London. We will become a curiosity. I do not think that is what Britain is about. I think that is rubbish.'[3]

Nor was the rentier income from the investments made abroad during the oil-rich years likely to prove sufficient to keep Britain in the style to which she was accustomed. They would come in handy enough at £3 or £4 billion a year, equivalent to about half the oil revenues at their peak, but even with that help there was no way the books were going to balance without a substantial contribution from manufacturing. By the early 1990s the surplus on oil account would have dwindled away and, unless Britain's industrial performance had improved, the deficit on visible trade could come to twice the surplus on invisibles. On that reckoning Britain could find herself running a deficit of some £12 billion in contrast to the £2·5 billion surplus at the heyday of the oil years.[4] The Select Committee arrived at a similar conclusion while Wynne Godley and his Cambridge colleagues projected apocalypse in the form of a payments' deficit of £20 billion by 1995.[5]

Whichever figures were chosen they indicated the need for a substantial improvement in manufacturing efficiency. For even if exports of manufactures were to grow at double their rate of growth over the period 1979–85, and imports no faster, the result would be a manufacturing deficit of some £10 billion by 1990. That would be three times what it was in 1985. No wonder the Select Committee warned in stark terms: 'It is neither exaggeration, nor irresponsible, to say that the present situation undoubtedly contains the seeds of a major political and economic crisis in the foreseeable future.'

How was this declining trend in manufacture to be reversed? The Select Committee amassed two weighty volumes of written and oral evidence on the subject of Britain's industrial decline. Its inquiries led it into the boardrooms and on to the shop floors, into the classrooms of the schools and the laboratories of the universities, and into the recesses of the national psyche. For at the heart of the problem there seemed to lie some aspect of the British character, or some experience rooted deep in history, which explained why as a people we ticked more slowly than others. How could there be, for example, such a huge difference in efficiency between the Ford assembly plant at Sarlouis in Germany and the Ford assembly plant at Halewood, near Liverpool? The conditions of production were virtually identical at the two factories and yet in Germany they could turn out an Escort in half the time. Overmanning, it seemed, was only a part of the problem. Here is the vice-president of Ford of Europe, Bill Hayden, testifying to the Select Committee:

It takes us an hour to get started in the morning; they then tend to walk off the job before lunch and tend not to come back to time after lunch. You get all the demarcation problems as well. Seventeen years ago, before Ford Europe was formed, in Britain we paid higher wages than in Germany; they had two-and-a-half times the wage increase over that time that the Germans had, but the fact that the German productivity as a whole is greater has meant that the exchange rate has gone from 12DM to 3·6DM and the Germans have ended up earning 40 per cent more than the British.[6]

The Committee was driven to the conclusion – inescapable from the evidence it received – that what had happened to British industry after 1981 had happened not simply, or chiefly, because of North Sea oil but was due to chronic uncompetitiveness going back over many years. The Treasury in its evidence had insisted that the manufacturing deficit – nearly £4 billion in 1984 – was the natural concomitant of the surplus on the oil account. The Treasury witnesses, who included the Chancellor in testy form, did not quite say that manufacturing did not matter but they did argue that it was not the most relevant aspect of Britain's economic problems. As the oil very slowly and gradually declined, the economy would adjust itself – they insisted – and the forces of the market would determine whether it was manufacture or services which took up the slack.

'The government's job,' said Lawson, 'is to create an economic framework and environment best calculated to improve the performance of *all* industries, manufacturing and services alike.' In fact, he did expect to see some revival of manufacture but it would come gradually and 'it is very likely that the manufacturing exports of the future that fill the gap will not be the same manufactures and in many cases not the same industries as the industries which were traditionally relied upon in the past.'[7]

Nor, he insisted, was the challenge facing the country at all a new one or to be measured by the imbalance of trade in manufactures:

Our economy is, or has been in the past, arthritic in various ways . . . not sufficiently dynamic or sufficiently competitive . . . the trade unions and the labour market generally have been highly inflexible, and management in many cases has not been up to the mark.

Hence economists have taken to looking at what they called the 'supply side':

the nitty-gritty, how we can get the economy to perform better, how companies can become more efficient, how we can get better trade union behaviour . . . these are the fundamental problems we should be concerned about and they are not new; they have been with us for a very long time.[8]

This lecture was delivered to a group of men whom Lawson regarded as in part responsible for the condition he was describing. They were drawn from the great and good of the *ancien régime*. The chairman of the Select Committee was Lord Aldington, formerly Sir Toby Low, the chairman of GEC, and an old crony of Edward Heath. Aldington was not one to suffer lectures gladly; 'You are talking to me rather like my tutor spoke to me at Oxford . . .' he complained to one official witness. Among the Committee's members were Lord Kearton, the Courtaulds magnate who had served as head of the Wilson government's Industrial Reorganisation Corporation, Lord Ezra, former chairman of the National Coal Board, and Lord Greenhill, former head of the Foreign Office. Interventionists by instinct and background, they were not likely to be persuaded by Lawson's complacent view that – as Aldington put it – it would 'all be all right on the night'.

Their view was that something very serious had happened between 1979 and 1984. The deficit on manufacturing trade which had appeared in 1984 was the consequence of a long deterioration of exports as a proportion of faster-rising imports. To Lawson's observation that all industrialised countries had seen a decline in the relative importance of manufacture the Committee pointed out that only Britain had experienced a sustained *absolute* decline in manufacturing. It was inclined to attribute this primarily to the differences in attitudes it had discovered to exist between Britain and Japan, Germany and France. There, it seemed, governments, employers, trade unions and banks all united in determination to achieve national success. Their governments and their financial institutions were prepared to look beyond quick profits; their trade unions and workers were more ready to change jobs or working methods, retraining on the way as necessary; their educational systems were geared to producing a technically competent workforce and a highly-qualified élite.

Indeed, the Select Committee once more rediscovered most of the foreign virtues and native deficiencies which, as we saw in Chapter 2, had been perennially observed since late Victorian times. Its conclusion, therefore, was in no way novel, although immensely gloomy. Attitudes must change for Britain's decline to be arrested and reversed. The national character must reform itself. Re-industrialisation, it seemed, was the equivalent of moral rearmament. Otherwise the balance of payments deficit on the scale envisaged would necessitate severely deflationary measures, the Welfare State would no longer be sustainable, unemployment would rise to new and intolerable heights, and the standard of living of the British people would deteriorate.

How was such a cultural transformation to be brought about? For as Lord Weinstock had told the Committee:

> It takes generations to build national attitudes with regard to industry or any general matter in national life, and it will take generations to make fundamental change. I think things are by and large as they are in our country because that is how people want them to be. If we have not responded to the stimuli for change, it is because the British like things as they are and do not want to be like the Japanese.[9]

And as Norman Tebbit, at that time Secretary of State for Trade and Industry, had said in his evidence:

> There are moments when one rather doubts whether we as a society want to achieve [a change in culture] and if we do not want to achieve it, and do not sufficiently value those who help us in that achievement, I doubt if we will make it . . . I think it very regrettable that all too often industry is portrayed as the mucky, dirty lot who ruin the environment and make vulgar things called profits and fight and squabble in their horrid and squalid ways, whereas administration is beautiful and nice and redistribution is even better.[10]

Here was a classic restatement of the old view of the British as a nation of gentlemen in a world of players. And if this was the root of the problem how on earth was it to be eradicated by 1990 or 1995 when, if the gloomsters were correct, the balance of payments deficit would be reaching crisis proportions? If things were anywhere near as bad as the Select Committee alleged there could be little prospect of arresting a decline that had gone so far. The weight of cumulative causation was by now too great. For, however encouraging might seem the cyclical indicators, these long-term non-price or cultural factors would seem to doom the British to perpetual uncompetitiveness.

Gloom of this order was common among the Establishment, indeed self-fulfilling despondency was part of the problem. Sir Edwin Nixon, the chairman of IBM in Britain, had said, 'We had better get used to continuing decline – and in its wake political and social decay and perhaps even democracy itself struggling for survival.' John Harvey-Jones, then chairman of ICI, had told the Select Committee, 'I am bearish about the future for industrial manufacturing in the United Kingdom. I suppose that means I am somewhat bearish about the economy.'[11] Sir John Hoskyns, Mrs Thatcher's policy adviser at Number 10, complained that, 'few, if any, civil servants believe the country can be saved.' John Cassels, director of the National Economic Development Office, said, 'If we have a slightly pessimistic-sounding note in our approach it might be because we know that manufacturing industry has been on retreat in this country for the whole of this century and to suddenly become optimistic and say, "We are just about to get it right," I think is very difficult to say.'[12]

Lawson would have none of this gloom. He took Lord Aldington to task for speaking of a 'crisis'. There was no crisis, rather a healthy revival of manufacture led by exports with productivity, profitability and investment all improving. The cultural change everybody was talking about was happening, under their eyes if only they could see. Far from having squandered the windfall proceeds of the North Sea these had been used to oil the process of adjustment. Now Britain's share of the world markets was growing once more. The decline of manufacture had been halted.

How could such bullish hope and such catastrophic bodings co-exist? Part of the explanation was that in this post-Keynesian era some of the economic problems which for so long had beset Britain were in the process of being redefined as social problems. That meant, for example, embracing the proposition that three million unemployed – some 11 per cent of the work-force – could be consistent with a fast-growing, wealth-creating economy. Another reason was that there was no longer a commonly agreed model against which to measure economic performance. Economies, it seemed, could work in mysterious ways their wonders to perform. 'There is a very wide range of views on how an economy works,' one of Lawson's Treasury officials had told the Select Committee. Were the unemployment figures, as the Keynesians continued to insist, telling us something about the level of demand or were they, as Lawson would have it, telling us something about the quality of supply? The productivity figures, as we have mentioned, could be accounted for in cyclical terms but who was to say whether they might also be recounting some real change in behaviour? At this time the unit costs of production were rising faster in Britain than elsewhere. Earnings were rising at nearly twice the rate of prices and, had it not been for devaluation – or so the Bank of England calculated – unit costs would actually have increased in the period up to 1984. But who was to say for sure whether this was the old English sickness continuing beneath the skin or a symptom of the emergence of a two-tier labour market with its core of highly-paid, highly-productive workers? Moreover, it was perfectly possible for the optimists to be correct in the short or medium term while the pessimists would be vindicated in the longer term. For the problems of the British economy were strategic rather than tactical. As the oil which had cushioned Britain against the world began to dwindle that world was becoming ever more fiercely competitive, as new technology could be transferred with increasing rapidity from the industrialised to the industrialising countries of the world. The important indicators of future performance, therefore, related to education and training, research and development, and Britain's performance in the technology-intensive, design-intensive markets of the world.

Those familiar with the past found it hard to be sanguine about the future. However, against the engrained gloom and doom of much of the Establishment, habituated to shortcoming and failure, itself the product of the long decline as well as a part of its cause, was pitted the faith of those who worshipped at the altar of the market and who had lifted up their eyes to the dawning of the 'enterprise culture' which would falsify all the projections of the past into the future.

There are two aspects of decline. The one, more obvious, manifests itself in actual present performance, measurable falling behind in growth of output, share of markets, wealth per capita, and so on. The other, more insidious, consists in falling behind in the factors which affect future performance – investment, research and development, applications of technology, education and training, management science, and so on. For it to be true that decline had been arrested or halted it would have to be true that the necessary steps had been taken to rectify the more fundamental deficiencies which for many years had been among the chief causes of Britain's relatively inferior performance.

Lawson's bullish confidence in the future was belied by the view which the government took of the future of the Welfare State. We have seen in Chapter 9 how the Cabinet during the first term had flinched from attempting major surgical economies in the health and welfare system. Instead it had engaged in the usual across-the-board economies with the result that there had been a piecemeal deterioration in services, the political consequences of which were soon now to be reaped. On return to office the government had instituted a review of the entire social security system which had been billed as the most thoroughgoing since Beveridge. The social security system was by then costing an annual £39 billion, equivalent to £650 per head of the population. This was one-third of total public expenditure and 11 per cent of GDP. It consisted of 30 different forms of benefit which were administered by a staff of 81,000 at the Department of Health and Social Security plus the 26,000 officers of the Department of Employment who paid out unemployment benefit and 7,800 employees of local authorities who dealt with housing benefits. The administration of supplementary benefit alone involved 40,000 people armed with a handbook 16,000 paragraphs long. The interface between this benevolent apparatus of the State and the indigent public had become the bullet-proof glass which it had been necessary to install in many benefit offices.

Since the war the cost of this system had increased at a rate five times faster than prices. The proportion of national income required to finance it had doubled. Beveridge had envisaged a system based firmly on the principle of social insurance, but something very different had soon emerged. Past contributions became increasingly inadequate for the financing of present claims. Means testing became more and more prevalent, undermining the noble universality of the original concept. In spite of that, half of its cost now had to be financed from general taxation. Beneath the social insurance scheme Beveridge had envisaged a safety net in the form of national assistance, now called supplementary benefit. But at most he had expected it to have to cope with a million people. Today there were eight million. In Beveridge's day unemployment had been the chief source of poverty. Nowadays low pay and the one-parent family blurred the distinction between families in or out of work. There were 1·3 million families in work but with incomes below supplementary benefit level (the 'poverty line') and another 1·8 million less than 20 per cent above it. Working families in poverty were helped by family income supplement and could claim extra for children or to help with the rent. Families out of work received unemployment benefit plus supplementary benefit plus their housing expenses. All families with children were entitled to the child benefit. The system was riddled with anomalies and injustices, and open to abuse. Beveridge had assumed that claimants would not pay tax but the recipients of benefit had been increasingly dragged into paying for them by the net of PAYE. The consequence was the so-called poverty trap: the marginal tax bite which could make people better off on welfare than in work.

It was this mess which the Prime Minister and her Secretary of State for Health and Social Security, Norman Fowler, had set out to reform. For, in spite of the economies which had been made, the cost of the social security system had increased by 27 per cent since 1979. This was due in part to demographic trends but in part to the huge cost of ministering to 3 million unemployed. Nothing had changed since 1982 when the 'Think Tank' had confronted the Cabinet with the economic implications of continuing with universal provision. The cuts which had been made were marginal compared with the scale of the problem as then set out.[13] Some 60 per cent of benefits were covered by election pledges made at some time or another, so the room for manoeuvre was not great. In any case, at the same time as he was seeking to reform the system Fowler was seeking to protect it from the Treasury, which was looking for cuts in the range of £2–4 billion. His review did not live up to its billing as the most important since Beveridge.

The one radical and controversial proposal it contained was for the abolition of the State Earnings-Related Pension Scheme (SERPS). This had been introduced in 1975 with all-party support and was not due to become fully operational until 1998. It was designed to provide the average earner with a supplementary pension, over and above the basic state pension, equivalent to 25 per cent of his earnings. The population was still getting older. In 1985 there were some 9 million pensioners, 3 million more than in 1965. By the end of the century there would be another million, and another million by the year 2035. The government's election promise to keep basic pensions in line with prices would by then cost an additional £22 billion a year. But with SERPS fully in operation the cost to the State would be a further £23 billion. Meanwhile, the falling birthrate would have reduced the number of people contributing to the pension fund.

Before the 1983 election Fowler had said he saw no reason why this should place 'an intolerable burden on future generations'. Now he was saying, 'It would be an abdication of responsibility to hand down obligations to our children which we believe they cannot fulfil.' The scheme to abolish SERPS owed a good deal to the need to make a centrepiece for a review of the social security system that turned out to be less than radical. It was also ideologically inspired. It would constitute a huge measure of privatisation. The Prime Minister herself was much attracted by this. The abolition of SERPS would open the way to a pension-buying democracy to set beside the home-owning democracy. For there were 'two nations' of pensioners: 11 million people in occupational schemes, 10 millions wholly reliant on the State pension.

The Treasury was less enthusiastic about the abolition of SERPS. It would result in a huge saving, but not until the end of the century; the year 2033 was a long while away in political terms, and, in the meantime, abolition would cost more than continuing it would. However, in the present context the chief significance of the plan was what it said of the government's confidence in the future of the economy. It was some measure of decline that what had been deemed affordable on an all-party basis in 1975 was by 1985 judged to be beyond the national means.

Eventually the Cabinet was obliged to abandon the abolition of SERPS although it reduced the level of entitlement and the future cost of the scheme. Once again the government bowed to predominantly middle class protest. As Lawson observed, any change in the welfare system was bound, at least in the short term, to bring benefits to some and disadvantages to others. 'And the disapproval of the latter group tends to be rather more audible than the murmurings of satisfaction from the former.' In the end the Fowler Review yielded minimal savings.

The Welfare State once more proved itself to be beyond the reach of radical Thatcherism. But, if the 'Think Tank' had been at all correct in 1982, the capacity of the economy to sustain it in its present almost open-ended form remained in doubt. It was a vast consumer of resources which might otherwise be directed to other ends relevant to the reversal of Britain's industrial and economic decline. Education was the prime example. While spending on health and social security had risen, spending on education had declined in relation to the total of government spending.

Education rose towards the top of the political agenda in 1986. Partly this was because the teachers had been in dispute over pay and working conditions for the past eighteen months. Their spasmodic disruption of the classrooms had exacerbated public concern about the quality of education, especially as new examinations were pending for the following year. At the same time Sir Keith Joseph had announced his retirement at the end of the current parliamentary session and this at once excited speculation about an early successor to him. Underlying these topical concerns was the deeper one that education was failing the nation and contributing to the process of decline.

Joseph had set out to be a radical reformer. He had proposed steps towards a national curriculum, something which had been recommended in 1938 and considered by Butler in 1943 but, like so many English educational reforms, had been left undone.[14] The curriculum, which was at the discretion of the schools (i.e. the teachers), tended to be too academic, too geared to the entrance requirements of the universities, themselves too much influenced by the traditional standards of Oxford and Cambridge. The schools were failing to equip the majority of school leavers for the society they would enter. It was an appalling fact that some 40 per cent of school leavers left without any kind of qualification at all. It was to rectify this that Joseph had introduced a new and more appropriate school-leaving examination but, above all, he had sought to improve the quality of teaching in the schools. To this end he had proposed a system for assessing the performance of teachers and a scale of salary differentials which would take better account of skill and experience, especially for those subjects in short supply, of which the chief was physics.

No one could doubt Joseph's dedication to learning. He was a scholar himself, indeed a Fellow of All Souls. But his passion for education was matched by his passion for controlling public expenditure. To the Medium-Term Financial Strategy he was as Moses to the Ark of the Covenant, for it was he who in the wilderness of the 1970s had preached the new gospel of monetarism. Twice his party had fought and won on – as he saw it – a mandate to reduce public expenditure; it became a matter of principle for him, therefore, to put doctrine above department, and what he called 'my beloved education service', and never to ask the Treasury for a penny more. Thus, laying out his reform programme in a speech at Sheffield in January 1984, he had re-stated the government's aim to reduce public expenditure overall and insisted therefore that any further funds for education would have to be contingent on 'a sound strategy' for achieving the goals set. In other words, if the government was going to pay, the government should have some control over how the money was spent. For it was an anomaly of the English educational system that government was the paymaster in large degree but had very little control or influence over how the local education authorities and the teachers between them ran the schools. Local control was the price Butler, and educational reformers before him, had had to pay in order to bring the church schools within the State system.

As with social security, and as with the National Health Service, the government had spent more on education for less in service. By 1986 there were a million fewer children in the schools than when Mrs Thatcher had come to power in 1979. Yet as more money was spent on fewer children, standards were falling. Meanwhile, the level of teachers' pay had fallen some 30 per cent below the level set at the time of the Houghton pay review in 1973. The teachers' unions were suspicious of assessment and opposed to salary differentials between different kinds of teachers. To enable the quality of teaching in the schools to be improved they would have to be persuaded, in effect, to sell out their restrictive practices. But the sum of money that Joseph had thought it proper to request from the Treasury was nowhere near sufficient for this task.

Without the teachers' co-operation little or no progress could be made in reforming the secondary school system. Yet the need, which James Callaghan had drawn attention to in his Ruskin College speech in 1976, had become increasingly urgent. In 1985 a comparative study of British and German secondary education reported:

> The German schooling system provides a broader curriculum, combined with significantly higher levels of mathematical attainment for a greater proportion of pupils than does the English system . . . Attainments in mathematics by those in the lower half of the ability range in England appear to lag by the equivalent of about two years schooling behind the corresponding section of pupils in Germany . . . [15]

Halévy, writing of Britain at the turn of the century, had said almost exactly the same:

> It was no longer possible to pass over the fact that a young Englishman on leaving school was intellectually two years behind a German of the same age with the consoling reflection that he made up in character what he lacked in information.

The move to comprehensive education in the 1960s and 1970s had been primarily concerned with making the system more equal. The unpopular 11-plus examination which had segregated British children like sheep and goats into grammar schools and secondary modern schools had been abolished in favour of large mixed-ability schools on American lines. These new schools had mostly done reasonably well, compared with the grammar schools, in turning out

A-levels but considerably worse than the old secondary moderns in educating the bottom 40 per cent of children who were passing no exams at all. The German educational system, on the other hand, was three-tier; yet no more than 10 to 15 per cent of German children left school without diplomas. The technical schools (*Realschule*) were turning out 600,000 qualified apprentices each year; Britain no more than 40,000.

By the time Kenneth Baker took over from Sir Keith Joseph education was high on the political agenda. The dispute with the teachers (which Baker was in the end to settle by imposing a settlement, dismantling the pay-negotiating procedure in the process) had stalled the Josephite programme of reform. Moreover, the Prime Minister had indicated her renewed interest in radical measures of reform. She favoured the idea of education vouchers and she would have liked to have seen some restoration of the direct-grant grammar school of the kind she had attended. Their abolition had been 'one of the biggest mistakes ever made' she was later to say.[16] Joseph had been reluctantly persuaded to abandon the voucher idea in 1984. His officials had convinced him that enabling parents to shop around at will would not be compatible with the State's obligation to make free secondary education available to all. The Prime Minister, however, was undeterred. Baker was again to reject the voucher but, although in general on the left of the Conservative Party, he was willing to go some of the way with the 'New Right' towards breaking the state monopoly in secondary education. He knew, however, that, for better or worse, 93 per cent of the nation's children attended the State comprehensive schools, and he realised that if national standards were to be raised it was here that it had to be done.

As he saw it, education was too 'producer-driven' – by teachers and their unions, by local authorities and professional educationalists; he wanted to see it more consumer-led, more responsive to the wishes of parents and the needs of pupils, more market-orientated. Baker was at the same time a centraliser and a decentraliser; he told the Commons: 'I think all of our society, not just our educational system, can be happier and more stable if more is done at the rim of the wheel and less is done at the hub.' Baker's policy was essentially Joseph's plus money – or *some* more money – plus the political flair that Joseph so singularly and uncompromisingly lacked. In accordance with his rim-hub metaphor he now proposed to act on his belief that education was too serious a business to leave to the professional educationalists, or at least to the local education authorities. The curriculum would be established at the centre, but the schools would be managed by their own heads and boards of governors. This approach was consonant with the government's wish to restrict the intervention of local authority between State and individual, but in the case of the schools this was not Baker's prime motive. His prime motive was to arrest the national decline in the area of British life most crucial to it – education. The best way, as he saw it, to raise the standards in the comprehensive schools was, first, to go ahead with the national curriculum and, second, to inject some competition into the State sector. This he proposed to do by, first, establishing a number of City Technology Colleges which would be funded directly by the central government, in partnership with private enterprise, and, second, by allowing schools whose parents and governors wished to, to opt out of local authority control and manage themselves. In effect, this was a plan to establish a third sector between the private and State – a State-funded independent sector. It would probably be quite small but, or so Baker hoped, it would act as a spur to excellence within the system as a whole. In addition, he proposed to devolve managerial control from local authorities to head teachers, as had been tried with success in some parts of the country, and to permit schools successful in attracting pupils at the expense of the less successful to enrol up to their prescribed physical limits.[17]

He also had some good old-fashioned ideas of his own about what should be taught in the schools. A bibliophile and a bit of a poet (he had published a slim volume) he had made his way in the government as a technology whizz-kid. As Heath's former Parliamentary Private Secretary, and the man who organised (unsuccessfully) Heath's campaign to ward off the Thatcher challenge in 1975, Baker's career had not prospered under the new régime. But as a man of enterprise – some would say he was a bit pushy – he had written her a letter which took her fancy on the importance of information technology and she had rehabilitated him within the government in 1981. He was a man who had thus straddled C. P. Snow's 'two cultures' and was in a strong position to say, as he frequently did, that specialisation was 'the curse of the English education system'. Whether he could himself recite the second law of thermodynamics we do not know, but he could certainly recite A. E. Housman's 'On Wenlock Edge' and thought that every school child should be able to do so.[18] On his visits to schools he liked to get hold of the poetry book and read one with them. He had prospered in the government as something of a trouble-shooter, skilled in the arts of presentation. He had been put in charge of the suppression of Ken Livingstone and the GLC and was then handed the task of devising a means of abolishing the rates. He was a tougher operator than his smooth appearance and gentle manner might suggest; there was some iron beneath the brilliantine. At education his task was to clear up after Sir Keith, to defuse the issue politically. In that he succeeded. Whether the reforms he now proposed were adequate to the task of remedying more than a hundred years of educational deficiency future generations would tell.

For Britain possessed an ill-educated workforce and an inadequate and inappropriate élite. In no other modern country in the world did school-leavers pour from the classroom at the age of 16 each year, without qualification and without vocational training, to take their chances in the labour market. In America the average age of entry into the workforce was 18, in Japan 20; in Germany some 90 per cent of school-leavers went on to receive vocational training. Butler had recognised the problem – as others before him – but still nothing had been done. As Correlli Barnett records, 'It is fair to say that with regard to the whole field of education for competitive efficiency as an industrial nation the vaunted 1944 Education Act offered not so much an executive operational framework as an opened gate to an empty construction site on which local authorities might or might not . . . build the technical and further education system that Britain so desperately needed.'[19] In 1982 the Manpower Services Commission could still report that 'Britain has one of the least-trained workforces in the industrial world . . .'[20]

The MSC had been established by Edward Heath in 1973 as part of his modernising drive to prepare Britain for membership of the European Economic Community. It was the only quango[21] of its kind to flourish under the Thatcher administration. Under the chairmanship of David Young, self-made millionaire and friend of the Prime Minister (of whom she famously claimed, 'he brings me solutions while other people bring me problems'), the MSC set about tackling the excessive rigidity of the labour market by improving the supply of appropriately qualified workers. Out of what had been an emergency response to soaring youth unemployment, due in part to the collapse of apprenticeship and training schemes during the recession, there emerged at last the coherent training policy the country had for so long desperately lacked. By 1986–7 the MSC was spending some £1·5 billion a year on youth training and had become a successful 'assertion of central power' in an area where change was notoriously difficult to achieve.[22] The Youth Training Scheme (YTS) was initiated in 1982 and widely regarded as a palliative for the alarming rate of unemployment among young people. Few credited the claim that it would 'ensure that unemployment among young people under 18 will become a thing of the past.'[23] Yet by 1986 a million young people had been covered by the scheme, now extended to two years and available as of right to all 16-year-olds, two-thirds of whom had progressed into jobs or further education. Young's second major innovation was the Technical and Vocational Education Initiative (TVEI) which was designed to break down the artificial barrier between education and training which had for so long distorted British education. Baker's later scheme to establish twenty City Technology Colleges was a further development along this line of policy. Young was not willing to accept that vocational training should not begin until the age of 16: it should begin in the classroom. The TVEI was in effect a backdoor move towards a national curriculum. Significantly it came from the MSC and not the Department of Education and Science; the MSC, by using the considerable power of its purse strings, was able to side-step local education authorities and exercise effective control over the content and form of this mixture of vocational education and work-training. By 1986 65,000 children aged 14–16 in 600 schools were covered by TVEI schemes, which were now to be extended nationally.

Young's policy was, in effect, to mop up adult unemployment as far as possible with short-run, low-cost programmes while investing in longer-run job creation.[24] The result was that by 1987 the government which had spurned an industrial policy, or a regional policy, or a science policy, had given Britain for the first time in her history a manpower strategy. What had been done fitted broadly into the market-orientated supply-side philosophy of the government; nevertheless, it had involved the dispensation of public funds on a large scale and a considerable degree of centralised intervention. What could and should have been done decades earlier had now been done. Too late? Too late certainly to provide a labour force of the quality required to meet the immediate competitive challenges which faced British industry but in the longer term the economy could hope to benefit from successive generations of better educated, better qualified and better motivated young people.

Whereas the government had been happy to 'throw' money at the MSC – as much as it could spend – the universities had been the one major British institution to suffer real cuts. Their grants had been cut by 10 per cent in real terms since 1979, during which time they had admitted 65,000 more students. They had been obliged, however, to turn away some 30,000 qualified young people. What is more, Sir Keith Joseph had planned to reduce the university population, running at 250,000, as the number of 18-year-olds declined. This seemed to many exceedingly shortsighted in view of the fact that a significantly lower proportion of the eligible population attended university than in most of the developed countries with which Britain was competing in the world.

The proportion of 18- and 19-year-olds attending recognised universities was in Japan 47 per cent, America 42 per cent, Germany 26 per cent, Britain 14 per cent. Percentages of the labour force with a first degree were in America 18, Japan 13, Germany 10, and Britain 6. And, as had been the case since the turn of the century, Britain's output of engineering graduates was miles behind its competitors': Japan was turning out four times as many, Tokyo University more in a single year than in the whole of Britain.

The government, not surprisingly, preferred to cite a different set of figures relating to higher education as a whole. For more than half of Britain's student population was in attendance not at universities but at polytechnics and colleges of further education. On this basis the participation rate of above 30 per cent was higher than Germany's, not far below Japan's but still a long way behind America's. Some two-fifths of these students were part-time, and getting on for a third of them were enrolling for below-degree-level courses. In France, Germany and Japan a much higher proportion of the total were university students – some 80 per cent compared with Britain's 48 per cent.[25]

Joseph's 1986 Green Paper on Higher Education[26] emphasised the importance of the universities in 'generating the qualified manpower the country needs'. It had been prepared in the light of yet another alarming report of British technological backwardness. The emphasis which the Green Paper placed on studies of practical application offended liberal educationalists and was widely regarded as proof of the philistinism of the Thatcher government; Enoch Powell described its approach as 'barbarism'. However, the Green Paper argued that: 'Unless the country's economic performance improves, we shall be even less able than now to afford many of the things that we value most – including education for pleasure and general culture and the financing of scholarship and research as an end in itself.' But how was the country's economic performance to improve if the universities were to be starved of money and obliged to turn away young people qualified to benefit from degree courses? The decline in the relevant age group, far from being an opportunity to reduce the numbers attending university, was an opportunity to broaden the scope of higher education and close the gap with other countries.

The present shortcomings of higher education could not be blamed on the government, only the failure to act to rectify them. Essentially what had happened was that the enormous expansion of university and higher education from the late 1950s through the 1960s had been undertaken without structural reform. Everybody had wanted to be a little Oxford or Cambridge, building quadrangles, offering classics. A vastly expensive and highly élitist form of education was suddenly to be made available to the masses. It had been a last folly of post-imperial grandeur. As Lord Annan, a former vice-chancellor but a critic of the universities, put it in a Lords debate: 'We rightly expanded higher education. We wrongly made it all Rolls-Royce education, from student grants to research facilities.'

Undoubtedly the universities and the polytechnics needed now to re-examine their priorities, make economies, manage themselves better, and look to their relevance to the society they served. But reform cost money and, once again, the government was trying to bring about radical change within a financial straitjacket. Money was needed to make salaries competitive and stem the 'brain drain' and for new laboratories and research facilities if the universities were to shift their emphasis from the arts to the sciences. It was no use blaming Oxford and Cambridge for the ills and distortions of the higher education system. It was true that Oxbridge had a lot to answer for, but there they were, world-class universities by any standard, and it would be the greatest folly surely to dissipate their excellence. But that was what was happening, as chairs went unfilled, as professors and their pupils fled across the Atlantic, as whole areas of scholarship were transferred to American universities only too eager to take over international leadership from Britain. By 1986 Oxford and Cambridge could no longer realistically hope to attract an eminent American academic with more than one child approaching college age. An American turned down one of Cambridge's most desirable chairs because his salary was five times that on offer. Academic eminence was easy to lose in this fashion and would be incredibly hard to regain once lost. One visiting American academic, Robert Collins, spending a year at Balliol from the University of California, was moved to write a letter to the *Guardian*, in which he said: 'To my amazement the policies of the government seemed to be concerned with the emasculation – nay the dismantling – of some of the finest aggregations of talent in the world. Eminent positions unfilled, academic posts of distinction eliminated, funds for research, basic as well as allied, stripped to the bone where, as a non-scientist, I understand that the little money left over is not worth having.'

The renewed brain drain, however, was also in contradiction to the government's declared priority of gearing higher education and research more directly to the needs of the economy. For it was the scientists and technologists who were the most in demand and the most aggressively recruited by predatory American universities. In 1984 more than a thousand scientists and engineers emigrated to the United States. No taker could be found for the chair of design engineering at Salford University which was a model of 'Thatcherism' in that, its grant withdrawn, it had successfully privatised itself as a technical university, closely linked with industry. Its vice-chancellor, John Ashworth, was quoted as saying, 'We know the ideal person for the job but he's in America and can't be tempted back.'

The morale of scientists was by this time, according to Sir George Porter, a Nobel Prize winner and the president of the Royal Society, at its lowest point this century. Traditionally Britain's weakness had lain in failure to develop and exploit commercially the discoveries of her scientists but now there was a crisis in basic research. Pure science had been what Britain was best at but now research was declining at a 'horrifying rate', said Sir Hans Kornberg in his 1985 presidential address to the British Association for the Advancement of Science. Sir Hans challenged the government's belief that only applied research and experimental development yielded commercial result. Pure research preceded technological application. The laser, for example, had been invented before anyone had thought of an application for it. To neglect basic research was 'a recipe for abdicating our future as an advanced nation. I am convinced that we cannot hope to prosper in the long term as exploiters of imported ideas any more than we can hope to prosper as an assembler of imported parts.'

The research budget had declined in real terms each year since 1979. It had borne the chief brunt of the university cuts. Since 1981 some 30 per cent of alpha-rated projects had had to be rejected for want of funds. In 1984 the scientists pleaded desperately with Sir Keith Joseph for more money but that was the year in which he dutifully offered cuts to the Treasury in its drive to contain public expenditure. The government's parsimony was not the only problem, however. Industry in Britain contributed far less to the promotion of science than in other countries. Science had for too long lacked prestige in Britain. The problem, like so many others, began in the classroom. When Joseph in his Green Paper, by implication, blamed the universities for their part in Britain's industrial and economic failure, they riposted that they could only take what the schools provided them with. The undifferentiated salary structure of the teachers had resulted in an acute shortage of, for example, physics teachers, who could earn a great deal more in industry. The schools, for their part, blamed the universities and the examination boards for a bias towards the arts and for requiring children to specialise at so early an age. Whoever was to blame, many children abandoned all science at the age of 13 and there were vacant places for scientists and engineers in British universities.

Britain's overall spending on research and development compared reasonably favourably with others – she ranked fourth in the OECD league – but this was due only to the large amount spent on defence. Britain's civil research budget was way down the table. She spent 50 per cent less than Germany, 20 per cent less than France. Moreover, spending had fallen by some 4 per cent during the first Thatcher term while most other countries had increased their research budgets. To do so was necessary as the fast-developing countries moved into the markets of the developed world, obliging it all the time to move 'up market' into new and more advanced products. For this reason Germany and Japan offered governmental incentives to research and development but Britain did not. Nearly every developed country in the world had a national science policy in some form but Britain did not. Most countries had industrial strategies of some kind in which government co-operated with industry in identifying and giving priority to the sectors which it was in the national interest to support and develop. Britain had no such policy. It ran against the market philosophy of the Thatcher government.

The 1985 annual report on science and technology by the Department of Trade and Industry commented:

> The UK now devotes the smallest share of its gross domestic product to civil research and development. This disadvantage in quantity is not offset by any generally greater effectiveness of R and D in Britain. A combination of different indicators all points to the declining industrial impact of the UK's civil R and D effort.

A country endeavouring, as Britain was, to arrest a long and deep-seated decline needed, above all, to move into the fastest growing markets of the world. Britain was failing to do this. It could have been expected that the effect of the uncompetitive exchange rate between 1980 and 1986 would have been most marked on low value-added products but it was in goods in which technology and design were more important factors than price that Britain had done worse at this time.[27] Highly research-intense industries accounted for half of Britain's exports and 45 per cent of her imports. She was trading at a surplus in two sectors only – chemicals and aerospace equipment. Import penetration in these high-tech sectors had doubled over the decade 1975–85. Moreover, this trend had the character of a vicious spiral; for costly research and development could only be recouped through large-scale production, while large-scale production requires the capture of highly competitive markets and that involved high levels of research and development.[28]

Britain's trade deficit in information technology was deteriorating and by 1985 stood at around £2·5 billion. According to the US National Science Foundation Britain's share of world markets in technology-intensive goods had fallen from 12 per cent in 1965 to 8·5 per cent in 1984. Her share of new US patents was also declining while those of Germany and France had increased. John Ashworth of Salford said: 'It is difficult to exaggerate the extent of the defeat British manufacturing industry has suffered in a highly competitive world.'

The failure sufficiently to apply technology continued. Many of the inventions of British science had been developed and exploited elsewhere. By 1986 only one in forty British factories was using robots and the total number in use was fewer than the increase in Germany in the previous year. In offices the picture was no better. 'No UK company is spending as much on office automation as they are on office cars,' reported one consultant. The chief reason for this was the lack of technical know-how among managers. And how many times over the decades had we heard such complaints about the quality of British management, its lack of drive, weak professional skills, disdain for special training? Now here was the British Institute of Management reporting that in this age of information technology no more than 7 per cent of British managers possessed university qualifications and only 2 per cent a business degree or professional management qualification. Only a tiny proportion were accustomed to use keyboards and micros. 'The lesson seems to be that successful exploitation of high technology is as much about developing people as developing things,' wrote the technology correspondent of the *Financial Times*.[29] He was echoing Lyon Playfair a hundred years before.

These renewed debates about Britain's industrial and economic future took place against an uncertain political background. Having fared badly in the local government elections of May 1985 the government proceeded to lose a by-election in the Welsh seat of Brecon and Radnor to an Alliance candidate. More significantly, Labour did well and finished a close second. That week a senior Whitehall official said privately: 'I think we've seen the start of the next General Election campaign.' The thought had suddenly dawned that the Conservatives could lose.

'Thatcherism' was now entering its seventh year but unemployment was still rising. The Brecon by-election had unleashed a litany of complaint about 'the cuts'. The social issue was beginning to move up the political agenda as complaints mounted about the long waiting-lists for hospital treatment and conditions in some of the schools. The spectre of social violence, raised by the scenes on the picket lines of the miners' dispute, was revived in the autumn of that year when rioting erupted in the Handsworth district of Birmingham and spread to other inner-city areas. Petrol bombing again became a familiar spectacle on the nation's television screens. A few days later in the course of a riot in Tottenham, North London, a police officer was hacked to death in savage fashion.

Meanwhile, the terms of the economic policy debate between the government and its critics had changed somewhat. It was no longer primarily between reflationary 'wets' and deflationary monetarists, although some continued to insist that the high unemployment figure and the reduction in industrial capacity since 1979 indicated a deficiency of demand. But this was a hard position to sustain, politically if not intellectually, when the Chancellor could claim to be presiding over the fastest-growing economy in Western Europe. So the argument shifted gradually on to strategies for job-creation and social improvement. What was called, infelicitously, the 'infrastructure' became an issue of the day. 'Britain is falling to pieces,' complained the CBI (which, in Lawson's view, would always find something to complain about rather than get on with the job). Investment in roads or sewers would provide more employment, it was argued, than the tax cuts favoured by the Prime Minister and the Chancellor; moreover, investment in repairing the housing stock or improving the schools would address the condition of the inner cities which – as the riots had signalled – was potentially explosive; furthermore, investment of this kind – especially in education or scientific research – was essential to the industrial future of the economy, the best insurance against the day the oil 'ran out'.

The 1985–6 annual review of public expenditure which followed the Brecon by-election produced a modest reflation of the economy, financed chiefly by asset sales. The government did not call it such, or admit to any change of policy, but a reflation was what it was. Even the Prime Minister began to make speeches drawing attention to how much money her government was spending rather than how much it was not spending. For example, at the annual Lord Mayor's banquet at Guildhall she said:

> You have only to travel to see it: 180 miles of new trunk roads being built; railways being electrified; tube stations vastly improved; new power stations; £900 million next year to improve the water supply; 51 major hospital projects under construction. This is a colossal programme. And that is just the public sector.[30]

That autumn the price of world oil had started to fall sharply. During the following year the surplus on oil account was halved – from £8 billion to £4 billion. But with the oil price fell the pound, making British exports more competitive. In the early part of 1986 there was a 15 per cent net devaluation of the pound. This was virtually a simulation of the fearsome scenario contemplated by the Select Committee. Therefore it was with a certain smugness that Lawson in his 1986 Budget speech was able to say:

> I am aware, of course, that a report recently published in another place [the House of Lords], and it attracted a certain amount of publicity at the time, predicted, 'As the oil revenues diminish the country will experience adverse effects which will worsen with time' – effects, it was said, of a most alarming nature. Had the authors of that report dreamed at the time they wrote that half the oil revenues were about to disappear within a matter of months, their conclusions would no doubt have been even more apocalyptic.

It was against the background of an extremely buoyant economy, of export-led growth stimulated by devaluation and falling material and fuel costs, that Ministers late that summer went into the annual review which would determine the levels of government spending in the run up to the General Election. Ostensibly it was the most difficult yet to face the government. To remain within the spending targets required by the Medium Term Financial Strategy would be to commit political suicide. Something had to be done, be seen to be done, about the hospitals, the schools and the state of the housing stock. Yet the bids submitted by ministers for additional monies for these purposes exceeded the 'fiscal adjustment', that is the amount of money Lawson had up his sleeve for pre-election tax cuts. The answer, however, proved simple. When Winnie the Pooh was asked if he preferred jam or honey he replied 'both'. So did Nigel Lawson.

Lawson had about him something of the air of an overweight school-boy in possession of an oversize tuck box filled with jam *and* honey. He had gone through life with the intellectual's belief that mind would triumph over matter which, in his case, it had. He was not much concerned with appearances. A brainy boy at Westminster School and Oxford he had joined the *Financial Times* under Gordon Newton, who had believed in recruiting straight from Oxford and Cambridge on the grounds that journalism could be quickly learned while brains were harder to come by. Lawson was not the first Chancellor to have been an economist (in the sense of having read PPE at Oxford) but he was the first to have been a professional financial expert. At the *Financial Times* he had written the influential Lex column and gone on to become the City Editor of the *Sunday Telegraph*. Apart from a brief spell as editor of the *Spectator* he had never been far from money, and had made (and lost) a good deal himself.

When he arrived at the Treasury in 1979 as Financial Secretary he was as well-equipped as any official to wrap his brains around the business of the department. He was less well-equipped as a politician. Patience, tact, and charm were not among his more obvious attributes; his style was not to persuade but to win arguments, which he was used to doing. He had had some difficulty in finding a seat in Parliament and did not manage to do so until 1974, when he was 41, although his political ambitions had become evident when he had worked as a speech writer for Sir Alec Douglas Home in the period before the 1964 General Election.

During his first year as an MP Margaret Thatcher became leader of the Conservative Party. Lawson put his brilliance of mind and grasp of financial affairs at her disposal. She liked facts and figures in a man. He primed her with clever questions to put to Wilson and Callaghan. He was, on economic matters at least, 'one of us'. So the Treasury was his natural berth in 1979. In the number three slot there his role was as a sort of monetarist commissar, one of Mrs Thatcher's blue guards, and it was he chiefly who persuaded the then Chancellor, Geoffrey Howe, against the contrary advice of more pragmatic instincts, to enshrine his money targets in a Medium Term Financial Strategy. In spite of this service the Prime Minister had preferred the younger Leon Brittan when a vacancy occurred for the Cabinet-ranking number two Treasury job. But she did soon after put Nigel in the Cabinet at the Department of Energy where he waited in the wings for the Chancellorship which was to be his in 1983. Thus his progress to the one job for which he was most eminently qualified and most desired was swift and almost direct.

He was not all of one piece, however, not at all. He was more of an eccentric than his reputation for Treasury reductionism allowed. He must be the only Chancellor in modern times to have been told by the Prime Minister to 'get a haircut'. He dared to tease her, occasionally; 'Oh Nigel . . .' she would say. Although 'one of us' on economic matters he was not a Thatcherite through-and-through, too Whiggish in some respects; it is to be doubted if he set much store by 'Victorian values'. He was not a hanger or a book-banner. Although he could be pompous his saving grace was a winning self-deprecation; for all the arrogance of manner he never quite, perhaps, managed to take himself entirely seriously. This may have been because he knew he was a chancer, a gambler by nature. As Chancellor of the Exchequer he was now at the biggest table: he kept his nerve, played high, and won!

Now, in 1986, politics took over from economics. In his autumn statement to the Commons, Lawson, to jeers and cheers on both sides of the House, announced more than £10 billion of additional spending. There were to be £5 billion for education, £3·4 billion for health, £1·3 billion for housing. You can't throw money at problems, money isn't the answer. How many times had Ministers said it? But there was one exception to the rule. You could throw money at a General Election; money was the answer when it came to staying in power. The 'normal pattern of Conservative government' has been resumed, said the *Financial Times*.

Expenditure had never been cut during the Thatcher years. In 1979 the policy had been to reduce it in real terms. It was never achieved. After 1984 the policy was to contain it in real terms. That didn't happen either. If expenditure had not been cut at all – indeed under the Tories it had risen more rapidly than it had during the Labour years 1974–9 – what was all the fuss about, why was everybody screaming about 'the cuts'? Because, apart from the huge cost of unemployment benefit, most of the increase in public expenditure had gone on public sector pay and not on improving services. Thus both statements were true: the government *had* spent more on health, education, and maintaining the housing stock; the health service, the schools and the housing stock *had* deteriorated.

Now the policy was to allow public expenditure to grow in real terms provided that it continued to decline as a percentage of faster-growing GDP. This new target also looked unlikely of achievement, for Lawson had allowed himself only the slightest margin of error. The U-turn at last? The headline writers thought so, dusting off the old cliché. So did the Commons Treasury and Civil Service Select Committee. 'It is now clear,' it reported, 'that in the key factors of public expenditure control, reduction in the money supply and in the use of interest and exchange rates there had been a substantial change in policy.'

The abandonment of the spending targets in the autumn of 1986 was at the same time a last nail in the coffin of monetarism. Who better to bury it than Lawson, for it was he who, as a junior minister at the Treasury under Geoffrey Howe, had given birth to the Medium Term Financial Strategy in March 1980. Those were the days of true belief. 'Control over the money supply', declared the Treasury, 'will over a period of years reduce the rate of inflation.' The theory was that by declaring firm money growth targets, and sticking to them, inflationary expectations could be lowered and, before long, inflation itself brought down. The chosen instrument for this task was Sterling M3, a broad measure of the money supply. But already by 1981 M3 had been found wanting. It had 'not been a good indicator of monetary conditions in the past year.' In the Budget of 1981 M3 was replaced by M1 (a narrow measure of money supply) which was to be assisted by PSL2 (the broadest measure of all).[31] But these new girls were no more faithful than M3. No sooner was PSL made a target than it was overshot by a hilarious amount. It didn't last long. Neither did M1. The government remained as dedicated as ever to controlling the money supply but increasingly incapable of saying what the money supply was or how it was to be controlled. The ritual continued (targets were set) but behind the altar the Treasury increasingly relied upon the exchange rate both as a measure of monetary conditions and as an instrument of policy. In the Budget of 1985 Lawson hopefully announced a new M3 target. Within six months it had been exceeded by twice the amount. So yet another measure took a bow. This one was called M0 and was the narrowest of them all. According to M0 the money supply consisted of the notes and coins in the pockets of the public, no more and no less. This was a particularly useless measure for there was no effective way of controlling its behaviour. All the while the banks were lending money and the liberalisation, and internationalisation, of the City made it increasingly difficult either to monitor or to control the behaviour of money. So in 1985 Lawson waved goodbye to M3. To bring broad money back within the target range would have meant repeating the errors of 1980–1, interest rates that would plunge the economy back into recession.

In his annual Mansion House speech that autumn Lawson announced that in future money targets would be set only for the purpose of indicating trends. 'If the performance of one indicator were to deteriorate we would need convincing evidence from other indicators before concluding that this was acceptable.' In other words, the 'targets' would no longer be targets. Henceforth the Treasury would make up the policy as it went along. In practice, in the absence of all other reliable indicators, the authorities turned increasingly to the exchange rate. For this the instrument of control was short-term interest rates. But according to the savants of Chicago the exchange rate and the money supply could not be controlled at the same time. The implication of Lawson's new policy was that interest rates would be determined chiefly by the needs of sterling and not by money supply considerations.

Whatever this was it was not monetarism. For one reason the new policy implied that prices could be determined by factors other than the quantity of money. That was heresy. For example, if changes in the exchange rate increased import prices why could not prices be determined by changes in wage rates or material costs, as the Keynesians had always supposed? Even if it were true in theory that the growth of the money supply was what determined, in time, the rate of inflation, this had been proved a useless insight because there was no way, it seemed, whereby the rate of money growth could be measured in a modern economy, and no effective means of controlling it.

The political attraction of monetarism had derived from the notion that the automatic enforcement of targets could replace the fallibility and prodigality of governments. Now human judgment was restored. For, as the governor of the Bank of England was to point out, the trouble with money targets was that, 'If the marksman does not have the wit to adjust his aim he may inflict severe injury on the economy.' Exactly.

The intellectual collapse of monetarism was gratifying to those who had held it to be a nonsense in the first place. Nevertheless, to pronounce monetarism dead – as the monetarists had been pleased to say of Keynesianism – was in some ways misleading and unfair. It could be argued that dogmatic monetarism had resulted in unconscionable unemployment and unnecessary loss of industrial capacity but it could not be denied that inflation had been brought down and that, for the time being at least, the economy was expanding healthily with reasonable price stability. Economists might attribute the fall in the rate of inflation chiefly to the fall in world commodity prices and, certainly, the observance – or, rather, non-observance – of Lawson's succession of moving targets had had little to do with it. Yet we may still wonder whether the entrenchment in some form of the government's will to conquer inflation was not a necessary step towards the arrest and reversal of decline. The Medium Term Financial Strategy had instituted a new regime, a dramatic break from the pay and prices diplomacy of the corporatist years. Monetarism may have been a mumbo-jumbo (at least in the crude version practised by the Thatcher government) but the usefulness of a religion for the purpose of exercising social control is not to be measured by the truth of its faith. Now it was time for the early Puritan zeal to give way to a milder Anglicanism. For nearly everyone now was agreed that 'money matters' and, although himself a monetarist of little faith, Lawson remained a sound-money man. Keeping inflation down remained his priority. He also remained a convinced and aggressive supply-sider. As for the Prime Minister, monetarism had become synonymous with Thatcherism (or Thatcherism with monetarism) and she remained wedded to her simple beliefs that governments had no business printing money and that markets must be allowed their play. Monetarism may have been dead but Thatcherism was far from it.

12

Defence of the Realm

The object of British diplomacy since the end of the Second World War had been to make a little power go a long way. It had been a story not of adjustment to reduced circumstances but of failure to adjust. Even if she was more aware than her predecessors had been of Britain's straitened circumstances and lowered standing in the world – if only because by 1979 both had worsened so much more – Margaret Thatcher was no readier than they had been to cut the suit to fit the cloth. Strategic reappraisal was not on her agenda. Indeed part of her purpose in seeking to reverse the decline of the economy was to restore Britain to what she believed to be its proper role in the world. She was a British nationalist.

Immediately after the war Churchill had deluded himself – or deluded the British people – into supposing that Britain remained at the centre of three 'concentric circles': the Atlantic, Europe, and the Commonwealth. Later the British Establishment foolishly supposed that Britain could stand by and watch the progress of the European unification movement. The signing of the Treaty of Rome in 1957 was not considered of major importance. A more realistic assessment of Britain's position in the world actually began when Macmillan – from weakness – sued for late entry to the European Communities but De Gaulle then said, 'No'. Britain joined on unfavourable terms in 1973 but it was not for ten years more, until the General Election of 1983, that the British became effectively reconciled to membership.

Missing the European bus in 1957 had been the most disastrous misjudgment, the legacy of which was so to preoccupy the Thatcher government more than twenty years later. But throughout the whole of the post-war period strategic over-extension, the error of the Roman Empire, continued. Even in 1986 it was a matter of pride to the Thatcher government, not of concern, that although Britain was by now substantially poorer than Germany and France, it spent substantially more than they did on defence. The figures were Britain 5·2 per cent of GDP, France 4 per cent, Germany 3·3 per cent.

Post-imperial delusions persisted throughout the long reluctant transition to a European role. Harold Wilson had insisted that Britain's frontier was at the Himalayas, although economic circumstance later forced him to order withdrawal from East of Suez. Edward Heath, although the most European of recent British Prime Ministers, tried to cling on to the East of Suez role. Callaghan spoke wistfully of the great wide oceans and had no taste for Europe. Thatcher liked the Europe of Brussels even less. She persuaded herself that Britain owed it to the world to show that aggression against the Falklands Islands did not pay. They were romantics all. Yet each of them in succession must have become more realistically aware of the true power position which lay behind the words they used – words such as 'special relationship', 'historic Commonwealth ties', 'world-wide obligations'. What had been lacking was not so much realism as the will to make the adjustments indicated by Britain's changed circumstances. Diplomatic skill came to consist of playing a weak hand.

Of all post-war Prime Ministers Mrs Thatcher was the least experienced in foreign affairs. All the others, except Wilson and Attlee, were at least as experienced in international affairs as in domestic. Thatcher, on the other hand, had held no Cabinet post other than as Education Secretary and no 'Shadow' brief remotely connected with the world beyond Britain's shores. Her instincts were simple and for the most part small town and 'little England'. She shared Norman Tebbit's view that, 'The Ministry of Agriculture looks after farmers, the Foreign Office looks after foreigners.' Diplomacy for her was to become the extension of her prejudices by other means. She was a gut anti-Communist with views very similar to those of Ronald Reagan and the American Right. Her attitude towards the European Community was scarcely more positive. Britain's 'Community partners' were, in her vocabulary, 'they', and 'them' – in other words – foreigners.

To compare Mrs Thatcher with Charles de Gaulle is at once instructive and misleading. De Gaulle might have said, as she did, 'our duty to freedom is to defend our own'. She, like him, saw herself engaged in a mission to restore her country's fallen standing in the world. Moreover, because her nationalist credentials were not in doubt, she succeeded in liquidating problems which had defied others, as he had done with Algeria. She came to terms with African nationalism and faced down the white settlers in Rhodesia, signed away the British colony of Hong Kong, and brought Britain at last to terms with her membership of the European Community. The Irish problem, which in some respects resembled that of French Algeria, eluded her, although even there she did what only a Unionist above suspicion could have done and moved towards an accommodation with Dublin at the expense of the Protestant ascendancy in the North. But whereas De Gaulle identified France with Europe, or rather Europe with France, she was a British and not a European national-ist; and whereas he had spoken of independence, meaning freedom from American hegemony, she was content with Europe's depend-ence upon the United States and saw it as the only guarantee of freedom. Like him she would have nothing of supra-nationalism on the Brussels model, and became the scourge of the European Com-mission, but unlike him she did not aspire to the leadership of Europe or, if she did, she failed to devise a basis for its exercise. De Gaulle had been an anti-Community European; she was scarcely a European at all.

This, perhaps, was the most signal failure of her foreign policy. For the task which remained after Britain's belated entry into the Euro-pean Community in 1973 was to achieve a role of political leadership within it. That the terms of membership were unequal, having been negotiated from weakness, made this task more difficult. Mem-bership of the Community remained a contentious issue in domestic politics. It had been unfortunate, moreover, that the enlargement of the Community had occurred just as the 'long boom', which had brought such prosperity to its original members, ended. It had been hoped that Britain would at last now benefit from the advantages of a large single market but instead Britain became a partner in recession. By 1983, however, the British economy was in the vanguard of the European recovery and by then Mrs Thatcher had outlived politically all the European leaders who had greeted her, with considerable misgiving, on her accession to their club in 1979. Giscard d'Estaing had given way to Mitterrand, Schmidt to Kohl, and the Franco–German relationship had become less intimate. Here would have been a chance to establish at the heart of the Community the political direction which could only flow from a triple alliance of Britain, France and Germany. But by then much ill-will had been accumu-lated around the issue of the British contribution to the Community budget, which had totally preoccupied the Prime Minister's Euro-pean diplomacy in her first term and was not to be settled until the meeting of the European Council at Fontainebleau in May 1984.

She had pursued this matter with a total disregard for both the spirit and the letter of the Community. For the letter of the law, as laid down in the Treaty of Rome and the subsequent decisions of the Council of Ministers, said that the Community should have its 'own resources' in the form of the proceeds of the common external tariff, the levies on agricultural trade, and a share of the value-added tax (VAT) yield in member countries. The effect of this system on Britain was inequitable. She paid in a great deal more than she got out. This was due, on the one hand, to the extent of her trade with non-member countries, on which the tariffs accrued to Brussels, and, on the other hand, to the huge preponderance of agriculture in the expenditures of the Community, from which she received little. The result was a net contribution considerably in excess of what would have been her fair share on a GNP basis. But in prosecuting this grievance, which was legitimate enough, Mrs Thatcher seemed to take positive delight in offending against the European canon. She struck a position entirely nationalistic, demanding 'my' money back.

She admired the manner in which the French ruthlessly pursued their national interests and was determined that Britain should do the same. What she did not grasp was that the French were able to get away with it because no one dared challenge their pretensions or credentials as a European power. She made no concessions to so-called 'Community spirit', the convention by which pork-barrel quarrels among member States are conducted with genuflections to the common and over-arching purpose of 'constructing' Europe. She would have none of this hypocritical nonsense; she did not believe in European unification in any supra-national sense and, she suspected, neither did they. It was against her nature to indulge in theological double-talk and if she understood the contrast between the continental tradition, rooted in the Enlightenment, of proceeding by high-sounding declaration, and the British tradition of pragmatism, she was unwilling to arrange a meeting of minds. And while others were willing to sign their names to academic scraps of paper in the safe knowledge that they would have no practical outcome, she would ostentatiously and irritatingly refuse.

If 'Euro-nonsense' – as she called it – offended against the neatness of her housewifely, tax-lawyer's mind, so even more did the Common Agricultural Policy. She was right that here was an intolerable and insupportable monster, a gross distortion of the original purpose – far from achievement – of establishing a common market for all goods and services, as well as the source in part of Britain's special difficulties. But she found it difficult to accept that German politicians appeased their farmers in much the same way that she herself continued to champion mortgage tax relief. Supporting farm prices, rather than supporting farmers, was Europe's way of dealing with what had become the social problem of its peasantry. This was inconvenient for Britain who, in the days of 'Victorian values', had ruthlessly liquidated her own peasantry, but was insufficient reason for allowing the CAP to stand in the way of all other European progress. It was not within Britain's power to reform European agriculture; it was within Britain's power to contribute political leadership to Europe.

Mrs Thatcher did not rise to this challenge for another reason. She had no real wish to do so. For her foreign policy goals were nationalistic only within the scope of Britain's 'special relationship' with the United States. She wished to preserve the status quo and not to change it. She did not like it when, from time to time, her Foreign Secretary, always under subtle pressure from the Foreign Office, tilted cautiously towards Europe. She was against irritating the Americans with talk of greater European unity within NATO, especially as nothing would come of it in any case. Her instinctive anti-Europeanism had mellowed somewhat over the years of office, although not with regard to the institutions of the Community, especially the Commission; if there was anything she hated more than bureaucracy it was international bureaucracy. However, she came to see Europe as a useful, even necessary, political forum for the exercise of British national influence.

Her attitude towards East–West diplomacy also changed. During her first term she had been content with the 'Iron Lady' soubriquet which the Russians had flatteringly bestowed upon her. She had seen no reason to talk with the Russians and preferred to abuse them from afar. As late as 1983 she had described the Soviet Union as 'a modern version of the early tyrannies of history – its creed barren of conscience, immune to promptings of good and evil'. But after the election that year she changed her mind and made her opening to the East. Why? Sir Geoffrey Howe believed that she had done so as a result of her proximity to nuclear weapons; the awesome responsibility of a finger on the trigger.[1] My own guess is that it was because she became interested. The Foreign Office had been tactfully tutoring her in occasional little seminars with their Soviet experts. Carrington, who had complained about 'megaphone diplomacy', had been working on her from the sidelines; he had continued to have influence even after his Falklands resignation in 1982, not least because he lived near Chequers and was easily available for Sunday morning drinks. To have an Eastern policy was logical in terms of her Western policy, which was founded in the 'special relationship' with the United States and hers with Reagan. The only interest the Soviets could conceivably have in Britain was as America's most intimate ally. They did not suppose that we could act as go-between – the Super Powers had no need of go-betweens – but Britain's knowledge of and judgment about what was going on in Washington was of value.

Once she had made this leap her style of diplomacy was more suited to dealing with the Communists than with her partners in capitalist Europe. For the Russians respected her for not pretending to believe what she did not believe and for speaking her mind; they had thick ideological skins reinforced by decades of official hypocrisy. As with Robert Mugabe, the guerrilla leader who became the first president of independent Zimbabwe, so with the Russians; once she had been persuaded to face the realities of power she enthusiastically engaged with them, relishing the challenge. Her visit to Hungary in early 1985 was her first official venture behind the Iron Curtain, apart from a working funeral in Moscow. Signalling a willingness to engage in dialogue helped to open the way to Gorbachev's visit to Britain in December 1985. That was something of a coup, for he was shortly to succeed the ailing Chernenko and she had backed the right horse. 'He and I can do business,' she said of Gorbachev.

The business they could do, she supposed, was to help to keep the armed nuclear peace. Maintaining Britain as a nuclear power became the chief goal of her foreign policy. For it was the possession of nuclear weapons which above all else gave Britain her residual Great Power status and set her and France apart from the rest in a world dominated by the Super Powers. But it was not simply a question of status or power symbols; for Mrs Thatcher believed passionately that nuclear weapons had kept the peace for forty years and that Britain's own security required the capacity to deter the Soviet Union, alone if necessary.

To this end she had had no hesitation in deciding that the American Trident system was the appropriate replacement for the ageing Polaris. By the mid 1990s the submarines would be thirty years old, their hull-life nearing its end. The Callaghan government had rehearsed all the arguments concerning a replacement but reserved the decision to whoever formed the government after the 1979 election. Callaghan later denied that he had in any way pre-empted the choice in favour of a Trident replacement but his then colleagues were of the opinion that his own mind was virtually made up. In any event, the incoming Thatcher government had no difficulty in accepting the

'Moscow criterion' adopted by successive Cabinet secretaries and senior officials at the Defence Department. This required the British deterrent force to possess the capacity to penetrate known and likely future Soviet defences in order to inflict damage upon what were politely called 'key aspects of Soviet state power'. Hitting the Kremlin was what it meant. Once that standard was set the Trident was the only available choice. The cost in 1982 was estimated at £7.5 billion over 16 years, but by 1986 had risen to almost £10 billion. Over the whole period that would amount to 3 per cent of the total defence budget, at its peak 11 per cent.

Submarine-launched Cruise missiles would not have met the Moscow criterion. They were slow and vulnerable to air defences. Their range would have limited their submarine carriers to a portion of the Norwegian Sea. In order to ensure penetration, and because they were armed with only a single warhead, they would have had to have been deployed in substantial numbers, which would have cancelled any cost advantage. According to official estimates as many as 10,000 Cruise missiles would have had to be deployed in a total of 11 submarines. For all that, the Trident replacement would give Britain a capability far in excess of her true requirements. The four submarines would be armed with 16 Trident D5 missiles, each capable of carrying 14 independently-targeted warheads, a potential total of 224 per vessel. Each Polaris submarine was armed with 48 warheads. Although the government has said that each missile would be armed with no more than 8 warheads (and each vessel, therefore, with a maximum of 128) this nevertheless represented a substantial increase in Britain's nuclear capability.

The second early decision of the Thatcher government concerning nuclear weapons had been to endorse plans, already far advanced, for the modernisation of NATO's intermediate-range nuclear forces (INF). NATO defence ministers meeting in Brussels in December 1979 agreed on the deployment of new American intermediate-range nuclear missiles on European soil. These consisted of 462 ground-launched Cruise missiles and 108 Pershing II ballistic missiles. The Pershings were to be based in Germany but Britain, together with Italy, Belgium and (it was hoped) The Netherlands, was to be one of the hosts of the Cruise missiles. A total of 160 of these were to be stationed at Greenham Common in Berkshire and at Molesworth in Cambridgeshire.

The INF decision was taken for a number of somewhat contradictory reasons. There was a military case for modernisation in order to give NATO a capability at each level of nuclear response ranging from the battlefield to the strategic. A so-called 'grey area' had been identified between the battlefield nuclear weapons which, according to the strategy of Flexible Response, would be used at an early stage of a full-scale conflict with the forces of the Warsaw Pact, and the American strategic weapons which were the last-resort guarantor of European security. This led into another problem which concerned the credibility of the American nuclear guarantee. Would an American president, when it came to it, be prepared to risk Chicago for Hamburg? The question had been asked – by Charles de Gaulle and Henry Kissinger among others – and their answer had been 'no'. In which case, some argued, a lower-level response was required to restore credibility to the concept of extended deterrence, or – as it was put – to 'recouple' Europe to the United States.

These arguments would have had their force whether or not the Soviet Union had been deploying SS-20 missiles – new weapons of high accuracy and with the range to strike anywhere in Europe but not to reach the United States. The Soviets, because of their geographical position, had developed intermediate-range missiles at an early stage and had deployed large numbers in the 1950s. Therefore there was nothing new in principle about the SS-20s, and some evidence that the Soviets had misjudged western reaction to what had been intended only as modernisation of obsolete systems. Nevertheless, the deployment of some 400 SS-20s, each with three warheads, amounted to a capability to destroy all useful NATO targets without inflicting harm on American soil. In this way they intensified fears that the Alliance had become 'decoupled'. But, in any case, the SS-20s gave NATO an excuse to modernise its own nuclear forces in the intermediate-range category. Moreover, a psychological need was felt after the fiasco of the neutron bomb – which after persuading the Europeans reluctantly to accept, President Carter had suddenly cancelled – for NATO as a whole to demonstrate its ability to show that it could carry through a decision to deploy new nuclear weapons.

Yet at the same time, because there was political opposition to importing new American nuclear weapons into Europe, and a mounting general anxiety concerning the breaking down of détente following the 1979 invasion of Afghanistan, it was thought prudent by the European members of NATO to wrap the deployment of the new missiles in arms control proposals. This was the so-called 'two track' policy and was consistent with NATO's long-standing policy of defining its security in complementary terms of deterrence and détente. However, it had the effect of linking a deployment at the same time justified on military and political grounds with a particular category of Soviet missile, the SS-20. And implicit from the beginning in this position was the notion that if the Soviets were to remove all of their SS-20s, NATO would be only too happy not to deploy the Cruise and Pershing missiles. Indeed, this became the West's explicit position when President Reagan proposed the so-called 'zero option' in 1981. However, nobody worried too much about that at the time because it was seen as a cynical propaganda move which there was no possibility of the Soviets accepting.

Once the decision to deploy the new missiles had been taken, carrying it out became a test of NATO solidarity. The Carter administration had been reluctant originally to station the missiles in Europe. It had agreed to do so at the Europeans' request. For them to have reneged on the deal now would have confirmed the worst American suspicions that the virus of neutralism was infecting her European allies. As America swung to the right, sweeping Ronald Reagan to the White House, such suspicions grew, especially as the peace movements grew stronger. By 1981 demonstrators were taking to the streets in their hundreds of thousands. At the weekend of 24–25 October some 250,000 were out in London and four other Western capitals. The Communist Party *Morning Star* called it 'a people's earthquake for peace'. That year also saw the establishment of the women's peace camp at Greenham Common where the first Cruise missiles were due to arrive in December 1983. The Greenham Women were to become the feminist spearhead of the peace movement and part of the left-wing mythology of the times.

In the late 1950s and early 1960s the Campaign for Nuclear Disarmament had grown from nothing into a mass movement, although predominantly of the concerned middle classes. The annual Easter marches from the atomic energy establishment at Aldermaston to Trafalgar Square at their peak had involved hundreds of thousands. Then the CND fell apart in factional dispute and evaporated from the scene almost as rapidly as it had appeared. Now it revived. Its chairman (or chair*person*) Joan Ruddock had an attractive, telegenic personality and she could expound the CND case with cogency and charm. She was a friend of Glenys Kinnock and the two were to be photographed at Molesworth base. The general-secretary who helped to bring the CND to life again was the Roman Catholic priest, Monsignor Bruce Kent. A public schoolboy and a tank officer, he had become a mature student in the 'class of '68', for he had been politicised by his students while chaplain to London University in the ferment-years of 1967–74. By 1983, the 'year of the Cruise', the CND could claim 84,000 members and in the next year it peaked at 110,000.

At the annual conference late in 1983, in the heady atmosphere of the coming of the missiles and the coming of a General Election, Ruddock claimed: 'We have moved to the forefront of the political arena.' 'We are a major political force,' said Kent.

The burgeoning of the peace movements across the whole of northern Europe was a manifestation of the nuclear angst which, as we noted briefly in Chapter 9, had all of a sudden once more gripped people's minds. One cause of it may have been the sheer proliferation of warheads in Europe which had become sufficient to fight a war of total annihilation many times over. Another was the breaking down of détente with the Soviet invasion of Afghanistan in late 1979. The subsequent rejection of SALT II by the US Senate and the repression of the Solidarity movement in Poland contributed to the sense that a new 'cold war' had developed. Dialogue between the Super Powers had virtually broken down and been replaced by 'megaphone diplomacy'. But the chief recruiting sergeant for the CND and the other European peace movements was Ronald Reagan. His 'evil empire' rhetoric, his patent disdain for arms control negotiations, and his celluloid image as a man from the wild west, caused him to be seen by many as a president capable of engulfing the world in nuclear war. These anxieties came to focus on the Cruise and Pershing missiles. Their original and actual purpose had been to provide what had been supposed to be a missing link in the chain of deterrence and, by rendering the American guarantee more credible, make less likely the conflict which would cause NATO to resort to battlefield nuclear weapons. They were seen by their opponents, however, in precisely the opposite light, as evidence of an American willingness to fight a limited nuclear war on European soil. In this respect much was made of Presidential Directive 59, which had been leaked during the American presidential election campaign of 1980 and was taken to be evidence of plans for such limited war-waging. 'No Euroshima!' became one of the slogans of the day.

At the same time the Soviets had mounted an offensive to prevent the deployment of the new missiles. This was a clumsily conducted medley of cajolements and threats but it contributed to the general anxiety and made it even more imperative that Europe should not succumb to a development akin to Finlandisation. The Soviet campaign was to culminate in their walk-out from the Geneva disarmament talks on the eve of the arrival of the first Cruise missiles at Greenham Common and the first battalion of Pershing IIs in Germany in December 1983. That year saw elections in Germany as well as in Britain. Shortly before the two countries went to the polls the

Americans had tabled new disarmament proposals in Geneva. While insisting that they continued to prefer the zero option, they now offered to talk about an interim agreement which would impose a ceiling on the INF deployments of both sides. This move, it was hoped, would help to persuade European opinion that the disarmament negotiations, the second of the 'two tracks', were being trodden as vigorously as the deployment track, and in a constructive and realistic fashion. Meanwhile, in January, Mrs Thatcher had taken the opportunity of the retirement of her Defence Secretary, John Nott, to appoint Michael Heseltine as his successor, with the special assignment to wage propaganda war against the CND. This Heseltine went about in characteristic style, arriving at Greenham Common in a flak jacket and making an appearance on the Berlin Wall.

In spite of the rapid ascent of the CND and the numbers participating in demonstrations – there were to be 70,000 at Greenham Common that Easter – public opinion had shifted very little. Opinion polls on the subject of nuclear weapons are tricky, for public opinion is highly suggestible and questions which mention the Americans and weapons tend to tilt opinion one way while questions which refer to the Russians or stress unilateralism tilt it the other way. But relying upon Gallup's standard unloaded question: 'It has been suggested that Britain should give up relying on nuclear weapons for defence whatever other countries decide. Do you agree/disagree?' in May 1983 – on the eve of the General Election – 23 per cent agreed and 57 per cent disagreed. Unilateral nuclear disarmament, then as now, commanded the support of between a quarter and at very most a third of the electorate. However, within this overall view of the matter, around 50 per cent were opposed to the coming of the Cruise missiles, more when it was stressed that they would be under sole American command; at the same time more people were ready to cancel the Trident than to decommission the Polaris fleet. The shape of public opinion in this regard was politically significant, for support was at its lowest for the idea that Britain should dispense with her own nuclear weapons – the main plank of both the CND and Labour's policies. A similar phenomenon could be observed in Europe; the peace movement flourished in countries such as Germany and The Netherlands where American nuclear weapons were the issue, but it scarcely existed in France where the *force de frappe* was regarded as the means to an armed neutrality. In other words, national nuclear weapons were on the whole popular; hosting American systems was not.

The elections in both Germany and Britain turned out to be major defeats for the peace movements. In Britain Labour was severely handicapped by its policy of unilateral nuclear disarmament and by its association with the CND. The first 16 Cruise missiles duly arrived at Greenham Common. The Russians walked out of Geneva – a tactical error, which strengthened the American claim to be the more willing negotiators – but returned shortly after the re-election of President Reagan in 1984. The following autumn the president met the new Soviet leader, Mikhail Gorbachev, at a summit meeting in Geneva. The fact that at last they were meeting, chatting by the fireside, while Nancy Reagan and Raisa Gorbachev took tea, went a long way towards calming European nerves. The nuclear anxiety had begun to lift from Europe and the peace movements to wane, as the CND had done in the early 1960s. By 1986 its membership had declined from the peak of 110,000 to 84,000, the same as in 1983. The Greenham women soon alienated the public by their tactics of civil disobedience, just as Bertrand Russell and his Committee of 100 had speeded the disintegration of the CND in the early 1960s. Although a broad church of middle class conscience, ranging from Quakers to Communists, the CND had come to be politically dominated by the broad Left, of which Kent himself appeared to be a member. It was his opinion that, 'the churches are handicapped by profound anti-Communist feeling . . . at variance with Christian teaching.' Thatcher's nuclear nationalism was closer to the instincts of the mass of the people than the CND's neutralism, which went further than the Labour Party and was opposed to Britain's participation in NATO with its strategy of nuclear deterrence. For 1987 the CND was to decide upon a tactically low profile in the election campaign with the aim of not embarrassing Labour as it had done in 1983. The conference at which this was decided went almost unnoticed, only five reporters were present and no television cameras. The wheel of protest had turned almost full circle. NATO, however, and Mrs Thatcher, were left saddled with their zero option, the legacy of the brief flowering of the peace movements. In January 1986 Mikhail Gorbachev was to take it up and, to her great consternation, play it back into the American court.

Meanwhile, however, the Prime Minister's goal of preserving the nuclear status quo, and within that her overriding priority of maintaining Britain as a nuclear power, had been threatened from another direction. This was her friend the president's Strategic Defence Initiative, the so-called 'Star Wars' plan. On 23 March 1983, in a speech that was to prove momentous, Reagan had asked:

What if free people could live secure in the knowledge that their security did not rest upon the threat of instant US retaliation to deter a Soviet attack, that we would intercept and destroy strategic ballistic missiles before they reached our own soil or that of our allies? I know this is a formidable technical task, one that may not be accomplished before the end of the century. Yet, current technology has attained a level of sophistication where it is reasonable for us to begin this effort.

This had also been in part a response to the peace movement for, as Henry Kissinger put it, gloomy as ever, to continue to rely on mutual annihilation, 'involves the near certainty of the growth of pacifism or the risk of holocaust as a result of miscalculation or the gradual escalation of peripheral crisis.'

There was general European dismay at Reagan's sensational promise to render nuclear weapons 'impotent and obsolete'. It had obvious 'Fortress America' implications, for if America could make herself invulnerable to nuclear attack why should she defend Europe? Missile defences would undermine the nuclear deterrence on which Europe depended for her security, given the imbalance between NATO and the Warsaw Pact's conventional capabilities. Europe would be made safe for a conventional war. Even if the programme proved unfeasible, which was the general view, it would impose a huge burden on the American defence budget and that would mean that Europe would be asked to pay more towards her own defence. Meanwhile, the pursuit of the chimera of salvation from the nuclear age would jeopardise arms control negotiations and delay the return to détente which, in Europe, was the necessary concomitant of public support for nuclear deterrence. Moreover, if the Super Powers were going to start deploying anti-missile defences – for the Soviets would surely follow suit – Britain and France might find themselves effectively disarmed of their deterrents. But even if that were not the case, here was the president of the United States promising to liberate the world from nuclear weapons at the very moment when Britain and France were engaged in modernising their nuclear forces at great expense and European leaders were endeavouring to persuade their publics to hold to the notion of nuclear deterrence.

The Prime Minister's first instinct was to support the president wholeheartedly. But she was advised that 'Star Wars' was unlikely to work, except on a limited scale, and would destabilise the balance of deterrence. She was also apprised of the implications for Trident. She concluded, however, that it would be pointless to try to persuade the president to abandon the research programme, for his heart plainly was set upon the pursuit of his dream. The best strategy therefore was to support the research programme while subjecting deployment to the 1972 ABM Treaty. Heseltine took a different view. He was much more alarmed by the potential consequences for Trident and saw the SDI as the starting gun for an arms race spiralling into space. He would have preferred to take a position closer to that of the French, which was openly critical of the United States. This was the first of several tensions between the Defence Secretary and the Prime Minister which was to culminate in his resignation from the Cabinet in 1986.

She brilliantly achieved her goal when she met President Reagan at Camp David in the December of 1984. There she succeeded in pinning him down to four points which were to serve as the basis for future British and European 'Star Wars' diplomacy. Neither Caspar Weinberger nor Richard Perle was at Camp David. 'We bounced them,' said a British official, delighted at the coup. In the more sober judgment of the Institute for Strategic Studies, Camp David was 'Europe's most important political accomplishment since the president raised the SDI issue in 1983.'[2] The four points were:

1 The United States and western aim is not to achieve superiority but to maintain balance, taking account of Soviet developments.
2 SDI-related deployment would, in view of treaty obligations, have to be a matter of negotiations.
3 The overall aim is to enhance and not to undermine deterrence.
4 East–West negotiation should aim to achieve security with reduced levels of offensive systems on both sides.

The first point was an undertaking not to upset the nuclear balance, the second implied compliance with the 1972 ABM Treaty (which the British hoped could at some stage be renegotiated to accommodate the SDI programme in some limited form), the third implied the possibility of a mix of offensive and defensive systems, and the fourth implied an eventual deal with the Soviets, a trade-off between SDI and the Soviet armoury of offensive missiles. The Americans, of course, put different glosses on these points and, in any case, attached far less importance to the Camp David four points than did Mrs Thatcher and the Europeans. In Washington they were seldom mentioned and were remembered only with difficulty as the game moved on. Nevertheless, they provided the Europeans with ground to stand on which proved valuable when it came to the Reykjavik summit meeting two years later.

At the preceding Geneva summit in November 1985 – the first such Super Power meeting in six years – Reagan and Gorbachev had agreed to pursue a 50 per cent reduction in strategic arms and an 'interim' INF agreement. But on 15 January 1986 Gorbachev departed dramatically from this with his proposal to eliminate all offensive nuclear weapons by the year 2000. In the course of this Britain and France would have to freeze their nuclear forces at current levels and on those grounds alone the proposal was unattractive to London and Paris. But even less attractive to Mrs Thatcher was any talk of a world without nuclear weapons for, as she saw it, it was the deterrent threat of nuclear weapons which had kept the peace for forty years and its removal would make Europe safe once more for a conventional war which the Russians would win. Nevertheless, Reagan responded positively to Gorbachev's new move. Moreover, he seized upon the one aspect of the Soviet proposals which was most unwelcome to Europe, namely his revival of NATO's 'zero option'.

The Prime Minister by now most strongly preferred the so-called 'interim option' which would leave a balance of intermediate-range missiles on either side. Europe had gone to all the trouble of deploying Cruise missiles, had faced down the peace movements and suffered Greenham Common women. Moreover, 'Star Wars' had given rise to new fears about de-coupling which it had been one of the original purposes of the INF deployment to allay. Anything which could be construed as a step towards the elimination of nuclear missiles undermined the British nuclear deterrent which it was Mrs Thatcher's absolute determination to keep. She wrote to Reagan in strong terms. She warned him that Gorbachev would play it long and be most unlikely to do a deal before the next presidential election. She urged him either to make it plain that SDI was not negotiable or, preferably, to offer the Soviets reassurance against an American breakout from the laboratory and the ABM Treaty. She regretted his part in raising the spectre of a nuclear-free world. She reminded him that nuclear weapons had kept the peace for forty years and that without them Europe would be at the mercy of the Soviet preponderance in conventional might.

In June that year the Soviets tabled important new proposals in Geneva. These marked a turning point in the negotiations and became the framework for the diplomacy which culminated in the Reykjavik meetings. In essence the Soviets were now talking about a strengthened ABM Treaty to contain 'Star Wars' in exchange for deep cuts in strategic weapons. The Americans countered with detailed proposals in a letter from Reagan to Gorbachev on 25 July. The chief defect of these from the Russian point of view was that their effect would not be to constrain SDI. Rather, as a White House official said, 'The president's intention is to get the Soviets to agree to deployment [of strategic defences] at the end of seven years in return for an American commitment not to withdraw [from the ABM Treaty] before then.'[3] From Mrs Thatcher's point of view Reagan's letter to Gorbachev was unsatisfactory, for once again it envisaged the ultimate elimination of offensive ballistic missiles.

Gorbachev had promised at the Geneva summit to attend a second one in 1986. Reagan was perfectly content for this to be another highly-televised getting-to-know-you-session. Gorbachev wanted to do real business. Reagan subsequently arrived in Reykjavik expecting to take part in a preliminary canter round the familiar tracks of START and SDI while agreeing to the outlines of an interim INF agreement as had already, to all intents and purposes, been agreed. The Russians, for their part, arrived with a huge team ready to engage in serious negotiations. At the very first meeting Gorbachev produced a fat manila folder. 'You seem to have a lot of papers,' said Reagan apprehensively.

Gorbachev went further than the proposals tabled previously in Geneva. He proposed a ten-year embargo on withdrawal from the ABM treaty and the elimination of all intermediate-range nuclear weapons from Europe. Reagan rejected this last offer and counter-proposed the world-wide elimination of intermediate missiles. However, a working group was constituted to attempt to refine the positions taken and it worked all through the night. The next morning Gorbachev made further concessions, the result of which was that, without any consultation with the allies, Reagan bought the elimination of all intermediate-range missiles from Europe. London was told this news by telephone call.

During the night progress had also been made on important details concerning the 50 per cent reduction in strategic missiles. 'Suddenly we thought we were making history,' said one of the American officials afterwards. The Soviets shared in the sense of excitement. But the fundamental questions remained: would Reagan be prepared to make the grand compromise between his 'Star Wars' dream and his ambition to achieve deep cuts? Would Gorbachev consummate the progress made on INF without an SDI concession from Reagan? The two leaders met once more to explore the answers to these questions. It was agreed on the American side that Reagan would now accept

Gorbachev's suggestion of a ten-year guarantee of compliance with the ABM Treaty. However, the proposed 50 per cent cut in offensive weapons was scheduled to be made over five years. For reasons of symmetry he was now advised that he should at the same time propose the elimination of all ballistic missiles over the same ten-year period. This suggestion was subsequently attributed to Richard Perle and it was seen by his enemies in Washington as a deliberate wrecking amendment. From the Soviet point of view this proposal remained deeply unattractive. The US would proceed with the SDI programme unconstrained – it had not even confirmed that it would abide by the narrow interpretation of the Treaty – while the Soviets would be obliged to dismantle half of their strategic missiles in five years and the rest of them within ten. Moreover, the Soviets were opposed to the elimination of ballistic missiles for precisely the reason that Perle had put the suggestion forward, namely that it would confer a superiority upon the United States in the form of Cruise missiles and bombers and the new stealth technology that was under development. This was why Gorbachev counter-proposed that all strategic systems should be covered by the ban. But by then the summit was doomed. For Reagan had insisted on his vision of a world in which nuclear offence had given way to nuclear defence, while this was totally unacceptable to Gorbachev. As Reagan, eyes gleaming, tried one last time to sell his vision to the Soviet leader, Gorbachev went even further and called for the elimination of all nuclear weapons. It was at this point that Reagan said, 'Gee, why the heck not?' – or some such – and for one heady moment the vision – for Mrs Thatcher the nightmare – of a world without nuclear weapons loomed before their eyes.

The summit had failed in a manner which was deeply alarming to the European allies and none was more alarmed than Mrs Thatcher. European opinion divided between those who took Reykjavik seriously and those who did not and who saw it as an exercise in posturing for the benefit of public opinion. Mrs Thatcher belonged to the former school. Critics of the president were divided between those who blamed him and his 'Star Wars' delusions for the failure of the summit and those whose complaint was that it had very nearly succeeded. 'Thank God for Gorbachev,' was the view at Number 10, 'for if he'd signed up there and then we could have all bought our tickets to New Zealand.' In public the Prime Minister was, as always, loyal and supportive. There would be no 'wedge-driving' by the Soviets, as she had said many times. In private she was aghast and angry. She did not at all like the zero-option for intermediate-range missiles, which Washington had now effectively conceded, but still less did she like the American proposal for a world without ballistic missiles which officially remained on the table. She gave the American ambassador, Charles Price, an exceedingly hard time demanding to know what difference, if any, there was between Ronald Reagan's position and Neil Kinnock's.

The president may have not meant what he said, or said what he meant, when he acceded to Gorbachev's ploy about banning all strategic systems and, in any case, that was preposterous and unrealistic. But there on the table was an American proposal (Perle's) to ban all ballistic missiles in ten years' time. That would mean no Trident; it would mean her nightmare come true. In the meanwhile, the zero option had been conceded, virtually signed-and-sealed, and was now probably unavoidable. The zero option had been a ploy, not taken seriously at the time, in the propaganda war against the Soviets and against the European peace movements, although it had always been implicit in NATO's original dual-track policy. NATO had at the same time sought to assert the military necessity of the new missiles and the political desirability of getting rid of them. And, as the peace movement had gained in strength, the public had been led increasingly to suppose that the chief purpose of the Cruise and Pershing missiles was as a bargaining counter for getting rid of the Soviet SS-20s. Thatcher herself had declared to the Commons in 1983: 'The best balance between the Soviet Union and NATO is zero.' That was not her view at all. But to the European public the zero–zero deal which had been almost done in Reykjavik seemed eminently to be desired. Thus were the European NATO leaders hoist with their own petard.

The Prime Minister set off once more to Camp David in a bid to retrieve the desperate position brought about by the president at Reykjavik. She obtained from him confirmation of his 'full support for the arrangements made to modernise Britain's independent nuclear deterrent.' They agreed once more on arms control priorities: 50 per cent cuts in strategic missiles, the 'zero option' for INF subject to collateral constraints on shorter-range weapons (although her preference remained for a less-than-zero deal), a ban on chemical weapons, and more urgent efforts to redress the conventional military imbalance. The statement issued afterwards also contained the words, heavily underlined in British briefings:

We confirmed that NATO's strategy of forward defence and flexible response would continue to require effective nuclear deterrence, based on a mix of systems. At the same time, reductions in nuclear weapons would increase the importance of eliminating conventional disparities. Nuclear weapons cannot be dealt with in isolation, given the need for stable overall balance.

Ostensibly she could not have asked for more. She had gone to Washington to speak for Europe. She had demonstrated her power of influence. The president had eaten the words he had spoken at Reykjavik. Yet the scrap of paper she brought home did not entirely dispose of the president's alarming vision of a nuclear-free or, at least, ballistic-missile-free world. That genie would not easily be rebottled. There had been no joint communiqué from Camp David, merely a prime ministerial statement, 'agreed by the White House'. The 'mix of systems' referred to did not preclude a mix excluding ballistic missiles. Even the confirmation of the 'arrangements for replacing Polaris with Trident' fell short of endorsing the principle that Britain should remain an independent nuclear power. And shortly after their meeting Reagan was to say that everything that had been on the table at Reykjavik remained upon the table. For all that, as an exercise in damage limitation Mrs Thatcher's mission was a success.

In this it was in striking contrast with Neil Kinnock's endeavours to sell to the Americans Labour's so-called 'non-nuclear defence policy'. Kinnock visited Washington and some other American cities in December 1986, hard on Mrs Thatcher's heels. His forlorn purpose was to persuade Congressional and public opinion that Britain under a Labour government would remain a loyal member of the alliance, intent upon strengthening NATO, not weakening it.

Labour had fought the 1983 General Election on the policy of unilateral nuclear disarmament which the party conference had adopted in 1980 for the first time since 1961. This had been one of the symptoms of the CND's meteoric revival at that time as East–West relations deteriorated after the Soviet invasion of Afghanistan and nuclear anxiety spread across Europe. But it was also an aspect of Labour's ideological lurch to the Left and the march of the activists through the institutions; 'banning the bomb' was another way of running up the Red Flag. The following year the pro-nuclear, Atlanticist wing of the party had been gravely weakened by the defections to the SDP. The 1983 Manifesto had declared: 'We will propose that Britain's Polaris force be included in the nuclear disarmament negotiations in which Britain must take part.' But it added that a Labour government would 'carry through in the lifetime of the next parliament our non-nuclear defence policy.' The campaign had fallen apart at this illogical seam. Foot, a supporter of the CND since its inception, construed the policy to mean that Polaris would go come what may; Healey that it would only be dispensed with if it could be negotiated away.

The statement of party policy, *Defence and Security for Britain*, issued in 1984, contained no such ambiguity. Decommissioning the Polaris was made in no way contingent upon reciprocal action by the Soviets. At the same time it pledged a Labour government to cancel the Trident replacement programme. It also repudiated the NATO INF modernisation decision of December 1979 and promised that a Labour government would send back the American Cruise missiles now in Britain. More than that, it would de-nuclearise the F-111 bombers at Lakenheath and Upper Heyford and withdraw the facilities for Poseidon submarines on Holy Loch. For good measure a Labour government would remove nuclear battlefield weapons from the Central Front and call upon its NATO allies to do the same. (How non-nuclear British forces would participate in the defence of the Central Front while NATO's strategy remained nuclear was never explained.)

The 1984 policy statement put an end to serious internal party disagreement on defence, on Kinnock's terms. They were all unilateralists now. The myth had grown up that what had lost the election in 1983 was not the policy of unilateral nuclear disarmament itself but the disunity which had developed around it. Moreover, it came to be believed that the public had mistakenly supposed that Labour's 1983 policy had been a policy for leaving Britain defenceless; the new policy would make clear that Labour's purpose was to strengthen Britain's real defences by improving her and NATO's conventional capabilities. Even Denis Healey now fell into line, more or less. He made a number of increasingly evasive statements on the subject. In an interview with *Marxism Today* in 1986 he said bluntly that in 1983, 'It wasn't the confusion, it was the unilateralism that was the damaging thing,' but he went on to contend that the 1983 policy had been 'very negative for the Labour Party because people thought we wanted to see Britain undefended, not unilateral nuclear disarmament.'[4] However, he did concede that, 'So long as the Soviet Union has nuclear weapons there have to be nuclear weapons somewhere in NATO to deter them from using them.'[5] He had on many occasions tried to persuade Kinnock to accept the paradox of deterrence but without success. Healey had always taken the view that politically the most damaging aspect of Labour's policy was its intention unilaterally to dispense with the Polaris force. This, as he had been vigorously reminded at a factory gate meeting in his Leeds constituency on the first day of the 1983 campaign, flew in the face of the patriotic instincts of the British working class. To counter this was the purpose of his claim that he and Kinnock had obtained from Konstantin Chernenko an undertaking that the Soviets would match the decommissioning of Polaris with some equivalent degree of Soviet disarmament, for he knew perfectly well that this would be trivial in terms of the totality of Soviet strategic weapons and of the overall nuclear balance; its only purpose was and could be to counter the allegation of 'onesided disarmament'. He purported to believe that the removal of the American bases would matter less than the decommissioning of Polaris. Like many other military experts he had always been dubious about the military value of the Cruise and Pershing deployments; it was out of loyalty to Helmut Schmidt, and because of the sensitive position of Germany within NATO, that he had kept publicly silent. He offered rationalisations of the removal of the other bases in terms of the advancing obsolescence of the Poseidon submarines and the F-111's in their nuclear role. Probably what he really thought was that it would all be all right on the night, that a Labour government would never actually carry out this part of its policy or that, if it tried to, the negotiations with the Americans could be spun out over years not months, thus avoiding a crisis in NATO.

Towards the end of 1986 Labour produced a glossier version of the 1984 policy, this time bearing the symbol of the rose and entitled *Modern Britain in a Modern World: A Power for Good*, which emphasised the conventional reinforcement that would flow from Labour's non-nuclear defence policy. Peter Mandelson, Labour's director of communications, said, 'There will not be a repeat of 1983. It will not be a choice between defence and no defence, between defence and pacifism. Now the choice is between an incredible defence policy and real defence, a choice between two versions of patriotism.'

The new document claimed that 'strengthening NATO's conventional defence and relieving the United States of the obligation to commit nuclear suicide in response to Soviet attack on Western Europe is fully supported by many Americans.' This was a true statement as far as it went; but it was also true that Labour's means of supposedly working to that end enjoyed no support whatever among influential Americans. The general attitude was summed up by Democratic Congressman Stephen Solarz, who wrote: 'The implementation of Labour's anti-nuclear policy would probably lead to the disintegration of the Alliance Labour says it wants to preserve.'

Kinnock set off to America in the hope of correcting this view. He appears to have believed firmly at that time that the new policy document had done the trick, that his defence policy was now viable and need no longer be an electoral liability. His mood, said a colleague, seemed 'almost euphoric'. It was his second visit to Washington as Labour leader. On his first he had made a singularly poor impression, seeming badly briefed and seriously misinformed, and had been rude to Secretary of State George Shultz. This second visit was no more successful than the first. He received a bad press on both sides of the Atlantic. The headlines he made back home were chiefly about his difficulties in making appointments with anyone of importance. Fairly reported or not, his trip was a public relations disaster at the moment the countdown to the General Election was beginning. He delivered a keynote speech setting out his case at the Kennedy School of Government at Harvard. The essence of this was that since NATO's nuclear strategy was 'incredible' security and stability would be enhanced by moves towards a greater reliance on conventional forces. A Labour Britain would give a lead in this matter, both contributing to the enhancement of NATO's conventional strength and pressing for a general move from nuclear to conventional dependence.

His audience was underwhelmed by the logic of his case. In the United States there exists a substantial community of people expert – or at least literate – in strategic questions. In Britain there are fewer. In recent years representatives of the Labour Party had been conspicuously absent from the seminars and events organised by the International Institute of Strategic Studies or the Anglo-American week-end conferences at Ditchley Park in Oxfordshire. Kinnock's defence policy had been hatched in a world of his own, remote from the world to which he now had to present it or in which he might, just conceivably, have to implement it. Few who heard him at Harvard were prepared to believe that a Labour Britain would in fact expend the Trident savings on conventional rearmament or that this was the real purpose of the policy. Nor was it. The policy was a product of the internal politics of the British Labour Party, not of any serious consideration of the requirements of British or Western security.

It was pointed out that there were non-nuclear members of NATO, Canada, Norway and Denmark among them. It was true. But Britain was not Denmark. It was true that NATO had survived De Gaulle in 1966 but circumstances were much changed since then. American

Congressional and public opinion had grown much more sensitive on the subject of European resolve. The whole Alliance relationship on both sides had grown more fragile as the Atlantic had appeared to grow wider. Some Congressmen saw neutralists under every European bed. At any time, and in any circumstances, the defection of Britain, America's oldest and truest ally, was going to be a psychological shock far more profound than the defection of France; in present circumstances it might well prove terminal.

The American ambassador, Charles Price, took the unusual step of making a public warning on this point even while the Labour Party conference was in progress in Blackpool. He said: 'We would have to think carefully about whether or not it was advantageous to continue to maintain bases in Great Britain.' Kinnock replied: 'It would make absolutely no sense for them to cut off a nose to spite a face when we say we are going to become another non-nuclear power in NATO. It wouldn't make sense in strategic terms.' But this was a misreading of American opinion. It was the other way round: Washington tended to shrug off European neuroses with the thought that the US didn't need NATO but NATO needed the Americans.

If the purpose of Labour's policy was to hasten the conversion of NATO to a conventional strategy then it was hard to see how this would be assisted by dealing it what might well prove a mortal blow. It was true that there was a growing body of informed opinion in favour of moving towards a 'no first use' or, at least, a 'no early first use' posture in place of Flexible Response. But not one influential proponent of this view was prepared to endorse Labour's means of allegedly going about it. Hardly anyone was prepared to support it – among European leaders only Papandreou!

Moreover, even if – as few believed – a Labour government would increase conventional military spending, or do so for very long, the impact this would have on the conventional force imbalance between NATO and the Warsaw Pact would be very small. The cost of moving to a non-nuclear strategy was immense. ('As soon as you say the word conventional you say the word expensive,' George Shultz had said.) There were no signs of any general willingness in Europe to undertake it. Even so, as Healey had pointed out, NATO would need some nuclear weapons for as long as the Soviets possessed them. The only time nuclear weapons had ever been used was by America against Japan, who had none with which to deter.

Kinnock floundered in still deeper trouble when it came to deterrence. He could not bring himself to grasp the paradox that, although unusable, nuclear weapons do deter or that, because their effects are so horrendous, a low degree of credibility can achieve a sufficient degree of deterrence. At Blackpool he had said: 'If we're not prepared to use the weapon system ourselves, we certainly would not be asking anyone else to jeopardise themselves by the use of that nuclear weapon. It would be immoral to do so.' This line of thought led down the road to neutralism, for he seemed to be rejecting the American umbrella altogether. Yet if his position was essentially a moral or an emotional one, as we must suspect it was at heart, why was he spending so much time trying to argue it in practical terms of credibility and cost? Without carrying practical conviction Kinnock's policy of unilateral nuclear disarmament lost much of its moral force.

Labour leaders hoped, and some sympathetic commentators suggested, that Reykjavik would politically disarm Labour's unilateral nuclear disarmament policy. Was not Ronald Reagan himself proposing, in effect, that Europe become a nuclear free zone, like Sheffield or Lambeth? Was not Gorbachev now widely regarded as a man of peace? But they misjudged. The tide of nuclear anxiety, of which Labour's deeper and deeper commitment to unilateral nuclear disarmament had been a part, had turned and was fast receding; hopes were running high of a new nuclear accord between the Super Powers. There would be survival in our time. Labour's proposals, in the meanwhile, seemed irrelevant, unconvincing, and potentially dangerous.

The background to the Labour and Tory conferences of 1986, to the Prime Minister's dash to Camp David and Kinnock's ill-starred visit to the United States was a strong revival in the government's poll standing brought about in part by a sharp decline in the fortunes of the SDP–Liberal Alliance as a result of its own confusions on defence. Indeed, it had been the unilateralist vote at the Liberal Assembly in Bournemouth which – to the great good fortune of the Tories and the great misfortune of the Labour Party – had brought the defence issue to the top of the agenda once more.

The salience of the defence issue, as measured by opinion pollsters, is a poor guide to its electoral importance, especially over the long haul between elections when images are made or amended, to be reinforced but seldom changed in the brief intensity of the campaign itself. Defence policy is the badge of a party's patriotism. In Labour's case it was a CND button. People may not spend a great deal of time thinking about it but, perhaps because it is something which they expect to leave to governments, it is one of the litmus tests of a party's competence and fitness to govern. For the leaders of parties it provides a crude macho test, the one so spectacularly failed by

Michael Foot when he appeared at the Cenotaph on Remembrance Day in his CND kit.

In so far as Kinnock's and Labour's commitment to unilateral nuclear disarmament helped to lose them the 1987 General Election the battle lines were already drawn by the end of 1986. In so far as the Alliance's disarray harmed its chances of breaking the barrier of the two-party electoral system the same was true. There were not, as Mandelson had said, 'two versions of patriotism'. There was only one and Margaret Thatcher had it cornered.

Nevertheless, the game was played out to the end. Undeterred by his December trip to the United States Kinnock undertook a further journey to Washington, this time for a date at the White House itself, on the eve of a long-planned pre-election trip by the Iron Lady to the Kremlin. All that the electorate needed to know, or was likely to want to know, was contained within the symbolism of these back-to-back visits.

Some of his advisers urged Kinnock not to go. He was walking into a right-hook. To show up at the White House on the eve of her arrival at the Kremlin was to invite unfavourable comparison, probably ridicule. The president owed her a favour or two. He would be set up for the British press which had poured scorn on his previous visit. But Kinnock had explained his lack of invitation to the White House in December by saying that his meeting with Reagan had been arranged for a second and later trip. To back out now would look chicken. He was by now trailing in the opinion polls, with an election imminent. He desperately needed, if he could, to repair the damage done by his earlier visit and show that he could sit down with the president man to man. His colleagues regarded his decision to go ahead as the stupidest he had ever taken.

If go he must, he should take the opportunity – they had urged – to make his disarmament commitments more flexible of implementation, preferably negotiable. This would be his last chance to do so, for any trimming on his return from the White House would be made to look as if he was bending to Reagan. He would not or could not bring himself to modify his basic position on deterrence. However, in the light of the latest developments in the European missile saga (Gorbachev had removed the post-Reykjavik linkage between a zero–zero INF deal and START), he was willing to declare a stay of unilateral execution on the Cruise missiles pending the final outcome of the Geneva negotiations. He did not want to 'jog any elbows' he said rather grandly. Yet the extent to which he was obliged still to watch his left wing became apparent when, the very next day, he felt it necessary to make clear to reporters that his reprieve did not apply to the F-111s or the Poseidon bases. The opportunity to make his entire policy contingent on the Geneva talks – the only escape from the hook on which he was caught – was at this point finally lost.

Protocol requires that visiting political leaders of opposition parties receive thirty minutes of the president's time. Kinnock emerged to engage in a demeaning dispute as to whether he had received his full ration or, as the White House put it out, a few significant minutes less. Reagan had surrounded himself with Cabinet officers and aides – Shultz and Weinberger among them – and (accidently on purpose?) mistaken Dennis Healey for the late British ambassador to Washington, Oliver Wright. It was at this level that the encounter was reported, assessed, and contrasted with Mrs Thatcher's triumphant sweep through the gate of the Kremlin to a three-star VIP welcome. 'A total, total disaster,' said one of the 'Shadow' Cabinet colleagues who had most strongly advised Kinnock not to go.

Meanwhile, in Moscow . . . She had set out prepared to face a big bust up and the bold tactics were to pay off. Gorbachev, it turned out, appreciated the Thatcher style in a way that European Community leaders or Commonwealth prime ministers had not. He apparently had decided in advance to make her visit a success. He gave her star treatment, allowed her thirteen hours of his time and permitted her 50 minutes of uncensored television time, unprecedented condescensions to the visiting leader of a middling European power.

She treated him, it seems, pretty much as she was accustomed to treat anyone else. She gave him a hard time. 'At moments I thought he was going to throw us out,' said an aide, 'but, then, one or other would laugh and break the tension. "Oh aren't I awful?" she would say.' Of course both were actors, both putting it on – and both knew that the other knew it. Hers, however, was a stunning virtuoso performance, and she knew it. She came home positively glowing, radiant with self-achievement, adrenalin at full blast, hyped by her encounter with power.

On foreign affairs a good deal of what he had said to her she had regarded as 'utter propaganda drivel, the sort of rubbish you read in *Pravda*.' She had not given him an inch. 'Why don't we trust you, Mr Gorbachev? Hungary, Czechoslovakia, Afghanistan . . .' so she went on. He gave as good as he got at this level – Northern Ireland, racism in British cities, three million unemployed, the thousands of homeless. On nuclear weapons it was more businesslike but the real business could be done only in Geneva, as both of them knew. Her purpose was to make plain that Europe would not accept his vision of a nuclear-free continent. That was her message in public and in private. 'We won't let all nuclear weapons be removed from Europe,' she declared. 'I want peace not abolition . . . Nuclear weapons are a deterrent . . .' He said, 'It is beyond our understanding how one can heap praise on nuclear arms. For political and moral reasons, we cannot accept that notion.'

But it was on domestic matters, his plans and dreams for the Soviet Union, his *glasnost* (openness), his programme for reconstruction, that they really engaged. She was fascinated. More than that, she was convinced. She spotted him as a fellow 'conviction politician'. She liked the way he talked. When he spoke he made it sound as if it was going to happen. He persuaded her that life could be made better for the Soviet people. A few weeks earlier her staff had arranged for her a high-powered seminar of Soviet experts down at Chequers. The general drift of their analysis had been that Gorbachev was genuine, meant business, but would probably fail in his Herculean mission to modernise the Soviet Union. Many had failed before him. That conclusion had been congenial to her. For him to succeed would be bad news for the West, she believed. The best she was prepared to say on setting out for Moscow was: 'We will judge you by results, not by what you say but by what you do.' Now, here she was, flying home and saying, 'A more open society – more open discussion and wider freedoms and an economy based more on incentives – is in the long-term interest not only of the Soviet Union but of the West as well.' 'We wish you well,' she had said on Soviet TV. She said it again in her statement to the House of Commons. It was a remarkable opening of her mind. The Iron Lady had been for turning.

Why had Gorbachev subscribed so handsomely to her re-election campaign? Perhaps to show that *glasnost* was for real? He allowed her to lunch with Andrei Sakharov, breakfast with Iosif Begun, a Jewish refusnik only recently out of a labour camp. In the television interview which she did with three senior Soviet commentators she was able to tell the Soviet people things they had never been told before. 'I wonder why *you* have so many nuclear weapons?' she threw back to a questioner and went on to enumerate: they had more ICBM's, more warheads, more intermediate missiles, more short-range missiles than the west . . . 'You have more than anyone else . . .' And didn't nuclear weapons deter? 'Doesn't the bully go for the weak person rather than the strong?'

They asked her personal questions. Yes, it was true she could manage on five hours sleep. Yes, all she usually had for breakfast was black coffee and vitamin C pills. And a 'very, very light lunch before

Questions.' Questions? What did the Russians know of Prime Minister's Questions? 'When answering questions,' she explained, 'you don't want too much in your tummy.' Was she a workaholic? She confessed to it. 'Frankly work is more interesting than anything else.' Or, as Noël Coward had said, 'work is more fun than fun.' She was having fun.

All the media-managers in the world could not have bought her such an election broadcast. Viewers and voters back home saw her lighting candles in the monastery at Zagorsk, moving among the friendly people in a Moscow suburb, thrilling to the sound of Cossack music in Tbilisi. But above all they saw her, Margaret Thatcher, Prime Minister of Great Britain, being royally received by the Gorbachevs.

She had gone to Moscow as the champion of the status quo in Europe. Her task there had been to make a declaration of Europe's interest in the outcome of post-Reykjavik diplomacy. Europe had seen the spectre of the Super Powers dealing over its head. Before leaving for Moscow she had made a day trip to Paris and Bonn to consult with Mitterrand and Kohl. She had become the staunchest pillar of the Western Alliance. An American diplomat in London told an American correspondent, 'She is leader of the Conservative Party, Prime Minister of Great Britain, and Defender of the Faith.' Kinnock in his Harvard speech had defined Britain's role as that of a 'well developed, well connected, medium-sized power that makes its responsibilities match its capacities to fulfil them.' She aspired to more than that. Yet it was he who suffered from the greater post-imperial delusion of power, for he insisted on believing that by unilateral nuclear disarmament Britain could give a lead to the world, that by a non-nuclear *démarche* Britain could convert the whole of NATO – the Americans too – to a strategy of conventional defence.

At the same time Kinnock underestimated Britain's influence and importance. He underestimated the psychological blow that her defection would administer to the Alliance and to the United States. He also underestimated the influence that the possession of nuclear weapons conferred upon a country. For it was the 'nuclear question' which was preoccupying Europe, preoccupying Washington, and preoccupying Gorbachev as he explored the reaction of America's European allies to the vision of the new order which had been conjured at Reykjavik. 'At this critical moment for Europe,' he said at the Kremlin banquet in Mrs Thatcher's honour, 'it is the nuclear powers – Britain and France – that we are addressing in the first place.'

Following Reykjavik France had proposed nuclear co-operation between France and Britain. The symbolism of this gesture was more important than anything likely to result from it. It was a sign of the times. Europe was in a state of some ferment. Not for the first time public opinion was moving in one direction, governments in another. For the public Reykjavik had been a moment of hope, the dawning perhaps of a new age of peace. Their hope was in Gorbachev. People liked the look and the sound of him. Astonishing changes seemed to be taking place. Switch on the television and the radio and there were Russians talking in English and sounding like Americans, using perplexing baseball metaphors – 'I guess that is not outside the ballpark.' Governments, on the other hand, were still reeling from the shock of Reykjavik, wondering what had hit them. One fear had given way to the other in the cycle of perpetual neurosis which governs transatlantic relations: the fear that trigger-happy America might disturb the peace of the European oasis was giving way to the older fear that isolationist America might leave Europe to her own devices and defences; the complaint that the United States had abandoned arms control was giving way to the complaint that the United States would make arms deals at Europe's expense; fear of renewed cold war was being replaced once more by fear of condominium. Could this be the ending of the Atlantic era as we knew it?

Not if Margaret Thatcher had anything to do with it! She was displeased when Geoffrey Howe thought aloud on these matters in a speech he made in Brussels on 16 March, only a few days before her departure for Moscow. In it he said that, 'We need to be alert to trends in American thinking which might diminish our security – perhaps not today or tomorrow but in the longer term.' 'Europe no longer dominates American thinking as much as it did once in the past,' he observed. Therefore, he suggested, Europeans needed to consult a little more closely, although – of course – always within the Atlantic context. Concerning SDI he noted, 'A distaste for nuclear weapons is not a new phenomenon in America. But I believe it right and prudent to prepare for the possibility in the longer term, of a less-nuclear world.' Nuclear deterrence would continue to apply, he avowed, but relying on smaller quantities of fewer systems. Nor was NATO's strategy fixed for all time. Its concept of deterrence was not based on a pre-determined progress through specific layers of nuclear escalation.

In other words, the United States was no longer wholly or for ever to be relied upon and Europe needed to adjust to the idea, not of a world without nuclear weapons, but a world – and a Europe – with fewer nuclear weapons. She did not like this sort of talk and had toned his speech down a bit. To talk about the unthinkable was only to father the thought, she believed. But not talking about the possibility of some degree of American disengagement, psychological and physical, was not to talk about what everybody was already thinking about, and talking about. Zwigniew Brzezinski, who had been President Carter's national security adviser, was arguing that the threat of war in Europe was no longer sufficient to justify the presence of 350,000 troops, 100,000 of whom could be better deployed elsewhere. An influential consensus had long since formed around the proposition that NATO's Flexible Response strategy was no longer credible or viable. Its inventor, Kennedy's Defence Secretary, Robert MacNamara, had argued so. Henry Kissinger had spoken many times of the incredibility of NATO's doctrine. Ronald Reagan's Strategic Defence Initiative had itself undermined the idea of deterrence. It was the logic of 'Star Wars' which had triumphed at Reykjavik. It would do so again.

4
THE NEW ORDER ESTABLISHED

13

Why Thatcher Won

The 1987 General Election was over before it began. When on 11 May the Prime Minister named 11 June as the day, the poll-of-polls put the state of the parties as Conservative 43 per cent, Labour 30, Liberal–SDP Alliance 25. On polling day the result was Conservative 43 per cent, Labour 32, Alliance 23. Labour had made marginal progress at the expense of the Alliance. That was all that happened. The government was re-elected because of a prosperous economy and a divided opposition. To that extent 1987 was a re-run of 1983.

In spite of the verve of Labour's campaign and the boost it gave to Neil Kinnock's personal popularity Labour managed to improve its position only fractionally. To have won a majority in the House of Commons would have required a swing of 11 per cent, more than twice the change which brought Mrs Thatcher to power in 1979. There was never the slightest sign of such a shift of opinion in the country. At the launch of the campaign in Perth Nigel Lawson had said: 'No British government has ever been defeated unless and until the tide of ideas has turned against it. And so far from turning, the tide of ideas that swept us into office in 1979 is flowing even more strongly today.' Nationally the swing turned out to be 2·5 per cent. Under Kinnock's leadership Labour thus retrieved a third of the losses suffered between 1979 and 1983.

The 1987 General Election confirmed the new socio-political map of Britain which had been unrolled in 1979 and 1983. It gave Mrs Thatcher a more secure base than she had had before. The skilled workers (C2s), who had defected from Labour in 1979 but returned hastily to the fold when hit by 'the Thatcher recession' of 1980–1, and had rallied to her again at the time of the Falklands, now looked as if they were registering a permanent shift in allegiance. Now she possessed a real majority in the land, or at least a real plurality, a sufficient base for a parliamentary majority under the British electoral system for as long as the opposition parties remained a divided force.

Although statistically an improvement on its 1983 showing, Labour's performance was in some ominous regards worse. For it had piled up yet more votes in its diminishing strongholds, won a few back from the Alliance in seats it would never win in the south but made no advance on the battlegrounds of the future. Labour's natural constituency appeared to be reduced to around 35 per cent. It had become more than ever the party of declining Britain. That is the party of the trade unions, the council estates, and the manufacturing centres of South Wales, Scotland and the north. The elements of that core constituency continued to decline. Trade unionists had comprised 30 per cent of the electorate in 1979, now only 22 per cent. Council house dwellers had amounted to 35 per cent of all households in 1979, now to only 27 per cent.

Mrs Thatcher's natural constituency was meanwhile growing. The proportion of owner-occupiers had risen from 52 per cent in 1979 to 66 per cent and of the million who had bought their council houses since 1979 44 per cent belonged to the skilled manual working class which was once more to swing to Mrs Thatcher.[1] Only 7 per cent of the electorate had been shareowners in 1979, now 19 per cent were. Of those who had bought shares in British Gas and British Telecom or the other industries which had been privatised 56 per cent voted Tory, 16 per cent Labour.[2]

As Ivor Crewe summed up his analysis of the BBC–Gallup material:

> The Conservatives are the first party of manual workers in the South (+18 per cent) among owner-occupiers (+12 per cent), and non-unionists (+2 per cent) and only 1 per cent behind in the private sector; Labour retains massive leads among the working class of Scotland (+43 per cent), the North (+16 per cent), council tenants (+32 per cent), trade unionists (+18 per cent) and the public sector (+17 per cent).[3]

Among the middle classes the Tories' support fell for the third successive election – to 55 per cent. These losses occurred chiefly among the university-educated 'intelligentsia' (the Alliance's only true constituency) and public sector employees. The small but hard-core petty bourgeoisie remained solid in the government's support. Nevertheless, the government's attempts to apply Thatcherism to the middle classes had taken their electoral toll. Meanwhile, its populist appeals to the working classes had again paid off. The Conservatives won 36 per cent of the working class vote, their highest proportion ever. They did best among the affluent working classes across the whole of the south. Among working class homeowners they led Labour 44 per cent to 31 per cent, which was better than the result of the election nationally.

The campaign changed nothing. Kinnock's standing as leader improved but from the exceedingly low 25 per cent achieved by his Washington visit to 45 per cent on polling day. Crewe comments, 'His electoral advantage to Labour has been over-estimated. It largely consisted in not being Michael Foot.'[4] Labour made little ground on policies. It narrowly won the education battle, was always well ahead on health, comfortably ahead on jobs and miles behind on defence. Education apart there was no significant movement on these issues although defence moved up the salience scale as Labour's policies came under attack. The number who thought Labour's defence policy was 'dangerous' increased sharply. The Conservatives held on to unassailable leads on inflation and law and order as well as on defence. They won hands down on taxation. But as the campaign went on they came increasingly to be seen as 'the party of the rich' and those who told Gallup, 'I don't like Mrs Thatcher' increased from 9 per cent to 23 per cent. The result of the election could not be construed as an endorsement of the Prime Minister's style of government.

Nearly everybody went on saying that unemployment was the most important issue facing the country, as they had been saying since 1979. Nigel Lawson, for one, had not believed them. He had stuck to his belief that it was inflation that most people cared most about and controlling it had remained his first and overriding priority. Boredom might lose the Tories the election but unemployment, he was certain, would not. He was right. Three million unemployed had not prevented Mrs Thatcher's re-election in 1983 and it did not do so in 1987, although by then the trend was at last encouragingly downward. One reason why unemployment was not the overriding issue it seemed to be was the distinction in people's minds between public issues and issues which affected them personally. Asked to say which issue was most important 'to you personally' health ran unemployment a much closer second. Asked which 'threatens you and your family most' 49 per cent said rising prices to the 43 per cent who said unemployment. When Labour was market-researching its poster campaign people much preferred the hospital poster to the dole queue poster. In spite of three million unemployed consumer confidence in the economy was high. Unemployment had been redefined in people's minds as a social problem rather than as an economic indicator.

Seldom, however, can an election have been fought around two such discrepant accounts of economic and social reality. One was of a country in the grip of a pestilence, writhing under the scourge of 'Thatcherism', its industry laid waste, its social fabric torn asunder, its people suffering. 'For us the only things that are going up are the dole queues and the cost of living,' Labour's industry spokesman, John Smith, had told the Blackpool conference. Another Thatcher victory, said Kinnock, would plunge Britain into a Dickensian nightmare with beggars in the streets and young thugs marauding through the cities. 'Britain is crying out for Labour' was Labour's slogan. The other vision was of a country saved from socialism, pulled back from the abyss of its decline, resurgent, confident and prosperous. 'A bulldog economy,' Thatcher called it, referring to a party poster which depicted a British bulldog dwarfing a German shepherd dog and a French poodle, an economy transformed, 'with better growth, better productivity, more exports, higher earnings.' 'It's great to be great again' was the Tory slogan.

'If things are so good, why are they so bad?' asked Labour's campaign co-ordinator, Bryan Gould, at the end of the campaign. Whether this was a remark made in exasperation or genuine sarcasm, I cannot say. But if things were so bad, why were they so good? Why were the high streets booming, property values rising, the stock markets breaking all records? On the one hand were three million unemployed, some 10 million people living on or below the poverty line, 800,000 families in sub-standard housing. Yet on the other hand, average real living standards had improved by some 23 per cent since 1979, at a rate of about 3 per cent a year since the ending of the recession in 1982. In the two years running up to the election they had increased by 11 per cent. Since 1979 2·5 million families had become homeowners and five million more people had become shareholders.

Perceptions differed sharply along party lines: only 3 per cent of Conservatives thought the economy had deteriorated, only 15 per cent of Labour believed it had improved. Only one in five Labour voters thought their living standards had improved. Perhaps it depended on where you lived. The world could look very different as seen from, say, Swindon and Scunthorpe. North–south was to become during the campaign a metaphor for the 'two nations', a shorthand for 'them' and 'us'. But it was an unequal contest, for one nation had done well out of the six years of economic recovery and greatly outnumbered the nation that had done less well. In 1987 the 'north' fought back, but all the time the 'south' had been moving north.

No doubt the rich had become richer and the poor, relatively speaking, poorer. Between 1979 and 1986 gross earnings of the lowest paid 10 per cent increased by 80 per cent, a real increase of only 3·5 per cent, while the earnings of the top 10 per cent increased by 180 per cent, a real increase of 23 per cent. This growing gap had been exacerbated by the bite of taxation: a family with two children living on £5,800 (half the national average wage in 1987) was paying a larger proportion of its income in taxation than in 1979 while a family on twice the national average (£23,200) was paying less.[5] At five times the average earnings, that is £58,000 a year, the real increase since 1979 was 38 per cent.

These two contrasting visions of Britain in 1987 were, at bottom, a confrontation of moralities. For many, reared in the political culture of post-war Britain, Thatcherism was an evil. There was no other word for it. It was evil because of the callous consequences of the market economics it espoused and practised on behalf of the rich, the strong, and the powerful, whereas it was the proper duty of governments, people had been brought up to assume, to provide for the welfare of the nation and especially to attend to the needs of the weak and the helpless.

Do not let us paint too rosy a picture of a caring nation, eager to volunteer its taxes for the purpose of helping others. We have seen how the crisis of the system which brought Mrs Thatcher to power in 1979 was in part a crisis of the Welfare State brought about by a simultaneous burgeoning of demands upon it and growing unwillingness, during a period of rapid inflation, to pay for it. And still in 1987 one of Labour's chief difficulties lay in its commitment to old-style Croslandite egalitarianism and its implausible claim that this could be financed entirely by taxing only those earning more than £25,000 a year. Labour's taxation policy – if that is the word for the muddle – went a long way towards losing it the election.

Yet, at the same time, many were still not ready – if ever they would be – to accept the ethos of Thatcherism, or not when applied to the Welfare State. From time to time the pollsters had consulted the public on this point and asked which it would prefer, more spending on the hospitals or schools or its taxes cut. The majority remained in favour of the Welfare State. Consistently more people opted for more social spending than for cuts in their taxes, not – we may suspect – on strictly instrumental grounds or because they did not want their taxes cut, but because it seemed the decent thing to say, a way of casting a vote of confidence in an aspect of their society in which they felt pride, or had done and wanted to.

This was what made Thatcherism so offensive to its opponents. For it seemed to make a virtue out of base human nature rather than to desire its improvement, to seek not to bring out the best in people but the worst. It appealed to their selfish instincts rather than to their generosity, was hard-nosed and hard-hearted. Margaret Thatcher simply 'didn't care' – that was the complaint above all. Why did she take such pleasure in making remarks like the one about the good Samaritan? No one would have remembered him, she had said, if he had had only good intentions – he had money as well. Yes, but all the same it was for his good intentions that he was remembered. He crossed the road.

She, for her part, regarded socialism as unmitigated evil, a perversion of human nature and a blight upon the land. This applied to all of its appurtenances, trade unions, nationalised industries, huge council house estates, much of local government. Socialism had reduced the country to the condition in which she had found it and, had she and Providence not intervened, would surely have taken it the rest of the way down the road to being like Eastern Europe. And when it came to caring, let the socialists not throw the first stones. Who was it who ran the schools in which the roofs leaked and there were no proper books? For the most part it was socialist authorities who refused to close under-pupilled schools, who put teachers before children. And why were children leaving the schools without the barest qualifications? In large part, she believed, because of left-wing teachers who wouldn't teach and who filled their pupils' heads with pernicious nonsense about racism and sexism. It was the same with housing. Why were the repairs not done, why did people live with water running down their walls, the lifts all out of order, no lights on the stairs? Because the socialists had imprisoned people in these appalling concrete ghettoes and wished to keep them there, opposing the idea that people should buy and own their own homes, because bureaucrats and trade unions conspired to see that the repairs were not done or, if done, were done at three or four times the cost at which they could have been done. The hospital queues existed in spite of all the money lavished upon the National Health Service. And why was that? Because look how it was managed and look how it was union-ridden – remember COHSE in the 'Winter of Discontent'?

At least the country faced a clear choice. The election was to be a contest between Thatcherism and socialism, the final showdown perhaps. 'Today it is socialism which is in retreat and Conservativism which is advancing . . .' she proclaimed at the launch of her campaign in Perth. 'It is our policies which are in tune with the deepest instincts of the British people.'

The election had another significance for the divided forces of the opposition. On the race for second place might depend the future of the realignment of party politics. Labour was fighting this time for its life. Another result like 1983 would finally destroy its credibility as an alternative party of government. To finish third in terms of the popular votes cast, even while remaining by far the largest party of opposition in terms of seats, would be a profound psychological blow. It would cast doubt on Labour's legitimacy as the leading party of opposition. For these same reasons the election was make-or-break for the Liberal–SDP Alliance. Unless it could trounce Labour into third place, or establish a respectable parliamentary bridgehead, perhaps holding the balance of power in a 'hung' Parliament, the historic fate of the Liberal Party beckoned – to become a party of perpetual protest on the fringes of British politics.

In 1983 the Alliance had run a feeble campaign for the first two weeks and made no headway in the opinion polls. But when Labour's campaign had self-destructed in the final week the Alliance had surged to fill the vacuum. If history were to repeat itself in 1987 the Alliance would be much better placed to break through. For in 1983 it had gone into the campaign with 18 per cent in the opinion polls and finished with 26 per cent of the votes. This time it was starting roughly where it had left off in 1983, for the local government elections on 7 May had suggested that the Alliance would have scored around 27 per cent in a parliamentary election. Moreover, in no election since the war had the third party – until 1981 the Liberals – done worse at the end of an election campaign than at the beginning. What is more, this was the first election at which the third party was to receive equal broadcasting time.

The Alliance's error was to fight the last war. It began by writing Labour off. 'Why should we waste time arguing with people who aren't going to win?' asked Steel. John Pardoe, who had returned from political retirement to be Liberal campaign manager, said, 'In the first week of this campaign we have to convince the British people that Labour are no-hopers, they are losers.' Yet by the end of week-one the Liberal president, Des Wilson, was writing in his campaign diary: 'Any dreams we had then that we would be neck and neck, or even have overtaken Labour, have been shattered. Instead Labour has made the running. The public writing off of Labour at the beginning of the week has made our position worse, for we have publicly failed to achieve a publicly stated objective.'[6]

There was no clear strategy: should the Alliance seek to bury Labour or go for a share of power in a hung Parliament? David Owen was wedded to the latter goal. 'I don't think the main target is to overtake the Labour Party,' he said. 'The main target is, it must and always has been in my book, to be in a position of power and influence for Alliance views and Alliance programmes.' But the implication of this line was that the Alliance, if it were to hold the balance, would use it to keep the Thatcher government in power. Owen was suspected of, in his heart, preferring the Conservatives to Labour. Whether he did or not it was certainly his judgment that Kinnock would be unwilling or unable to deal on any basis that could be acceptable. David Steel for his part defined the task of the Alliance as offering the country 'a clear anti-Thatcher non-Socialist alternative'. He was reluctant to speak of coalition in any terms that implied a willingness to deal with Mrs Thatcher. He said, 'I find it unimaginable – that's the best word I can use – that there would be any circumstances in which a minority government led by Mrs Thatcher could be sustained in office by us.'

The difference between the 'Two Davids' became more and more evident as the campaign developed. They were saying different things, publicly correcting one another. This double-headed leadership – two heads speaking with different voices – became the main scapegoat of the campaign. But the chief reason for not voting Alliance given by the 23 per cent of Gallup respondents who said they had considered doing so was not the dual leadership but their belief that a vote for the Alliance would be a wasted vote. A majority of the electorate (68 per cent) thought either the Alliance could not win or that it would let one of the other parties in. Among the actual defectors, fear of letting the Tories in was twice as potent as fear of putting Labour in.[7] Labour was not as unacceptable as in 1983. It was not going to win the election but this time it was not going to self-destruct. The Alliance, meanwhile, suffered the traditional fate of the third party in a two-party system.

The revival of the Liberals in the 1970s and the birth of the SDP in 1981 had been aspects of the crisis of governability or the politics of decline. Now times had changed. The Alliance was left behind. Its policies were redolent of the 1960s and 1970s, for example its adherence to an incomes policy and its schemes for constitutional reform. Owen rang few bells with statements such as, 'The system of government has failed us. We are out to bust the system.' Most people did not want 'hung' Parliaments or coalitions. As the social issue moved up the agenda the more pig-in-the-middle-like the Alliance seemed. The Two Davids found themselves conducting a running commentary from the sidelines. At best the Alliance's image was a warm blur.

The premise of Labour's campaign was the belief that style could triumph over substance. That had been the story of Kinnock's leadership. 'There's nothing wrong with our policies, it's us they don't like – the Labour Party,' was the belief of Labour's campaign manager, Bryan Gould. Labour had hoped to enter the lists at around 37 per cent in the polls, at the threshold of a parliamentary majority. Then it hoped that its new professionalism would prevail, enabling it to hold, perhaps increase its support, although it had never succeeded in doing so during a post-war election campaign. But Labour found itself entering the campaign with a humiliating 30 per cent, scarcely above the 'catastrophe' mark of 1983. This was due to Kinnock's disastrous outings to Washington and to the so-called 'London effect' which had lost it the Greenwich by-election in February and done it much damage in the local elections on 7 May.

In accordance with its new marketing philosophy Gould had declared that Labour had a 'product to deliver'. The product turned out to be not the Labour Party but Kinnock. The tactic was to interpose the image of the leader between the party and the voters. The master stroke to this end was the election film made by Hugh Hudson, the director of *Chariots of Fire*. It contrived not to mention the Labour Party at all but was entirely about the charm, the courage, the intelligence and the caringness of the Kinnocks. It was hugely successful, not least in that it won the Labour campaign a reputation for professionalism and modernity of style that was to last it through to polling day.

The Tory high command had gone into battle fearing the Alliance more than it feared Labour. It judged, correctly, that Labour could not win. But if in the early stages of the campaign that were to become staringly apparent to the voters there would be the danger that dissident Conservative voters and despairing Labour voters would start leaping on to the Alliance bandwagon. The Tories had a huge respect for Owen. They feared him more than they feared Kinnock. An argument had gone on for months and years about how best to handle the doctor. One view was that the Conservative Party ought to look forward to the day when Labour would be replaced by a moderate non-socialist party; the other view was that the Alliance was as much the enemy as Labour. The debate was largely academic for it did not lead to tactical conclusions. There was no way the Conservative Party was going to assist the Alliance to power. The more threatening it seemed, the more vigorously it must be opposed. However, Norman Tebbit's way of going about this had been much criticised. It consisted in keeping up a Red Scare which would frighten Tory fainthearts into line.

Out of favour though he was, who more appropriate to preside over the apotheosis of Thatcherism than Tebbit? He was the archetypal Thatcherite, lower-middle class, unburdened by class guilt or social conscience, acquisitive in tooth and claw, scathingly anti-Socialist. He prefigured Thatcherism when elected to the Commons in 1970. There he had soon made his reputation as a nasty piece of work. By 1973 he was protesting against the Heath government's too-soft policy towards the unions. When Thatcher became leader of the party he became one of her bother boys. 'A semi-house-trained polecat,' Michael Foot had called him, 'the Chingford skinhead,' someone else. More affectionately he was known as Dracula or, having bought a cottage in Devon, the 'hound of the Baskervilles'.

As chairman of the Conservative Party he had delighted the Thatcherite faithful but sent shudders down the spines of the old guard. He might scare the enemy but, by God, he scared the Whitelaws and the Biffens. As for the public, perhaps they loved to hate him, like a pantomime villain. Tebbit was King Rat, the evil genie, the wicked ogre. 'Fee, Fi, Fo, Fum, I smell the blood of Ken Livingstone.' He was there to be hissed. 'Oh, no you won't', 'Oh, yes I will.' And, oh yes he would, peering over the rims of his granny reading glasses, delivering yet another Tebbitism.

His 'get on your bike' speech at Blackpool in the aftermath of the Brixton and Toxteth riots of 1981 propelled him to national notoriety and made him the darling of the new, slowly emerging, Thatcherite Conservative Party. What he had said was, 'My father didn't riot but got on his bike to look for work.' That had been made to sound as if he had bicycled from the Hartlepools to Harlesdon. What he had done was to ride round the building sites of Edmonton after he had lost his job as a shop manager. 'Get on your bike' became the moral imperative of Thatcherism.

In the Disraeli Lecture of 1985 (for which he was a perverse choice) he said, 'The trigger of today's outburst of crime and violence . . . lies in the era and attitudes of post-war funk which gave birth to the "Permissive Society" which in turn generated today's violent society.' The word permissive from his lips sounded like a sexually transmitted disease. But if people could enter the National Gallery and look at the Rokeby Venus he saw nothing wrong with Page Three of the *Sun*. He was no prude. Indeed he enjoyed a dirty joke. He was an out-and-out populist.

Margaret Thatcher used him – very much 'one of us' – in place of James Prior to get tougher with the unions. He took over the Department of Employment in 1981. In 1983 the 'Parkinson affair' had delayed Tebbit's transfer to Trade and Industry, his next ambition, but once there he began to fall from favour. She suspected him of turning out to be a sheep in wolf's clothing. He was becoming another of the big spenders, lavishing taxpayers' money on British Leyland. He was not sound on free trade: Jap-bashing was more up his street. Although an ideologue by reputation, Tebbit was more concerned with power. But then so was she. His chief offence, perhaps, was to have become her heir apparent. A would-be heir to Margaret Thatcher should make himself extremely unapparent.

It had been understood that he would become in due course party chairman in good time for the next election. Then at Brighton in 1984 he and his wife Margaret had become victims of the IRA bombing of the Grand Hotel. In the coldness of dawn and under the glare of television cameras Tebbit had been unburied from the rubble and lowered on a stretcher, badly injured. He had managed a joke. His wife had fared less well and was to be paralysed for life. The courage he had shown on that occasion was of the redeeming kind. It was impossible ever again to feel or think quite the same about him as before.

He was a man with a public and a private face. In private he was fun and could be very funny but behind the courteous charm and sardonic sense of humour was a prickly character. After the Brighton tragedy colleagues found him more difficult, embittered by what the gods had done to him, as he had reason to be, poor man. He was also in physical pain which he bore in public without complaint.

Mrs Thatcher duly made him chairman in the September 1985 reshuffle. There had been some movement in the party to prevent this. The Brecon by-election that summer had revealed the 'that woman' factor at work. Tebbit seemed hardly the best choice to repair the government's image for uncaringness. More likely he would dance on the nation's social conscience in ammunition boots. But she was committed to him, could not gainsay him after Brighton.

He was soon to fall further out of favour. A nationalist by populist instinct, he took up the cause of the Land Rover on behalf of the party. He was against the decision to permit the bombing of Libya from British bases, although on this there was also a row concerning his position in the inner circle. He had not been one of the Ministers privy to the American president's request, nor had he been summoned to the meeting which drafted the statement to be made late at night to the Commons as the raid became imminent. Cecil Parkinson, as party chairman, had been a member of the inner Cabinet which fought the Falklands War.

Mrs Thatcher by now regretted appointing Tebbit as party chairman. They had 'married' after the affair was over but she was stuck with him, for better or for worse, although in the spring of 1986 she toyed for a moment with the idea of replacing him, for it was then or never. She did not put him in charge of the long-range planning for the election which was set in hand at that time. The all-purpose Sir Geoffrey Howe was made chairman of the 'A-team' and on it Tebbit was outnumbered. The A-team had been John Wakeham's idea. Wakeham did not approve of Tebbit. Increasingly her way of dealing with him was to appoint minders; first there had been Jeffrey Archer, to whom she had taken a shine, then Peter Morrison, who had been with Tebbit at Employment, and finally Lord Young, whom he could not regard as a rival.

Tebbit had been rehabilitated with a well-publicised telephone call just before the summer holidays and at Christmas had been one of the party at Chequers, the nearest equivalent of a place on the podium in Red Square for the celebrations of the October Revolution. But by early 1987 he was out of favour again. She felt that he was bouncing her into an early election, narrowing her freedom of choice with his public statements. She contemplated bringing back Parkinson to run her personal campaign from Number 10, a move that would have placed Tebbit in an impossible position. Nevertheless, Parkinson was around. Moreover, he favoured an autumn election.

Tebbit's campaign was much criticised. Labour had out-Saatchied Saatchi's. It had been a bumpy ride at Central Office. But towards the end of it Tebbit said, 'I'd rather have a lack-lustre campaign and win than a glossy campaign and lose.' He had made up his mind by then that he would go when the election was over. He would care for his wife. The ambition which had burnt so high in him had been the casualty of Brighton in the end. Now there was no heir, presumptive or apparent, no heir at all.

The theme of the Conservative campaign had grown out of the government's difficulties a year earlier as it had staggered from Westland pillar to Leyland post. At that low moment it seemed scarcely probable that it was going to win a third term on its record. What it needed therefore, decided party strategists, was a fresh radical programme. By the time of the party conference in Bournemouth a theme had emerged or, at least, a slogan – 'The Next Move Forward'. Ministers trooped to the rostrum to unveil shiny new plans for improving the schools, reforming the housing estates, and rebuilding the inner cities. The conferences proved a brilliantly successful operation which sent the government into the election with a new sense of *élan*.

The greatest failure of the Thatcher Revolution had been in the application of market economics to the Welfare State. In most cases, as we have seen, this had proved politically impossible. Nor had the suppression of Ken Livingstone and the GLC, the disqualification of Ted Knight in Lambeth or of Derek Hatton and the Militants in Liverpool done anything to change the character of local government in the cities. One lot of lefties had been replaced by another, the second more 'loony' than the first. The policies which the government would put forward in its Election Manifesto were designed to meet both these shortcomings: they would at once simulate the working of market forces within the State sector of education and housing and circumvent the negative or destructive power of local authorities. Thus there was to be a new wave of Thatcherite populism, a third chapter in her Revolution, and in time the Conservative Party would be politically reinstated in the cities from which it had been driven. Mrs Thatcher's ambition to extirpate socialism from the land would be fulfilled at last.

This was a bold project. Yet from the high ground on which they began Ministers were soon forced on to the defensive. In the first phase of the campaign Labour had promoted the social issues by advertising Neil Kinnock's social conscience, in the second by advertising Margaret Thatcher's lack of it. Fuelled by the persistent findings of the pollsters, Labour hung her 'uncaring' image round her neck. An election broadcast showed a slum school without enough books to go round. 'This is how Mrs Thatcher cares for your children's education.' The Tories had 'no children in local schools, know no one on YTS, have no loved ones waiting in pain on a hospital waiting list,' Kinnock told a Birmingham rally. She had said somewhere that there was 'no morality without choice', and that, said Kinnock, was the sum total of her beliefs. 'She locks out of morality all those people who, no matter how much moral obligation they feel, haven't got the money to buy her kind of private provision in health and housing and schooling.'

Before they knew where they were Cabinet Ministers were having to explain their visits to the doctor, apologise for their resort to private medicine, account for where their children went to school. Thatcher floundered in clumsy self-defence. 'I exercise my right as a free citizen to spend my own money in my own way, so that I can go on the day, at the time, to the doctor I choose and get out fast.' They had begun the campaign as populists, but were ending it as plutocrats.

'Why does the Tory Party hate the north?' the Chief Whip, John Wakeham, was asked in an election phone-in. He was stuck for an answer. 'You're living in another world, you've no idea what it's like,' his questioner told him. North–south was more than a metaphor, it was a real divide, although not a simple geographical one. Scotland, for example, where the government was to fare badly and Labour register its greatest gains, was the third most prosperous region of the United Kingdom after the south-east and East Anglia. The really big divide existed between London and the rest of the country. Its GDP per head was 26 per cent above national average, the south as a whole 15 per cent above the average. Not surprisingly the main burden of unemployment had been felt in the old manufacturing regions, chiefly the north, the Midlands and South Wales. What was called the north–south divide was really the map of declining and growing Britain, an old–new divide.

In the south employment was provided by predominantly small firms; it was the large-scale industries – mostly in the north – which were in decline. Over the Thatcher years employment in shipbuilding was down from 31,000 to 5,750, in coal-mining from 36,000 to 16,500, in steel from 22,000 to 9,900. During the same period employment had risen in East Anglia and fallen only by some 2 per cent in the south-east, but it had fallen by 14–15 per cent in the north and north-west and by 10 per cent in the West Midlands. Altogether 94 per cent of the 1979–86 job losses had been in the Midlands and the north. Because hardest-hit by the decline in manufacture, the West Midlands – once synonymous with brash prosperity – had experienced the slowest growth in real disposable income.

Immobility of labour was a part of the problem. Migrations between regions were small. Moving was expensive, particularly for the unemployed. For those in work, although wages were higher in the south than in the north, national wage-bargaining meant that the differentials tended not to be worth the upheavals of moving. A family with a council house in one part of the country had no guarantee of obtaining one in another part of the country. Over the years controls had severely reduced the availability of rented accommodation. While regional wage disparities were not great, housing was a great deal more costly in the south. In the south-east in 1985 people spent 50 per cent more of their income on housing than in the north. A family selling a house in the north might not be able to enter even the bottom of the housing market in the south. In these ways the inhabitants of the other Britain were virtually prisoners within it.

Because it was generally poorer, the north tended to lag behind the south in all kinds of ways. Yet it was easy to caricature the north–south divide. Leaving aside Scotland, where the pattern of tenure is different, it was not true that the working classes of the north were a nation of council-house dwellers while the south was a nation of property-owners. The incidence of owner-occupation ranged from 70 per cent in the south-east, outside London, to 55 per cent in Greater London and in Yorkshire and Humberside. It was true that the north had more cities and the problems that went with them. The new shopping centres (the largest in Europe was in Gateshead) and the new cars on the roads testified to the prosperity which co-existed with the poverty of the north, so did its entries in the *Good Food Guide.*

When hospital waiting lists became an election issue it was easy to assume, as many instinctively did, that the north had been deprived of resources while the south had gobbled up more than its share. Not so; the hospital building programme was heavily centred on the north. In the northern region the waiting list for operations was the shortest in the country (12 per thousand), while the longest was to be found in the north-east Thames area (18·5 per thousand). A report on the nation's health, leaked shortly before the election, was seized upon and forced into the 'two nations' context.[8] What it showed was that the health of upper-income families had improved more rapidly than that of lower-income families, which was not surprising, for poverty and ill-health have always gone hand in hand. But the report also showed that smoking was becoming increasingly a working class epidemic. Among male unskilled manual workers 49 per cent smoked, only 17 per cent of professional men. This was not a simple function of poverty, for although in general poorer families in the north spent more of their incomes on tobacco and drink than in the south, Scotland, the third most prosperous region, had the highest incidence of cancer and heart attacks – the smoking, drinking, and eating diseases.

The junior Health Minister, the ambitious young Edwina Currie, took the north to task for its unhealthy eating habits. But her accusations were not quite true either. For example, the people of Yorkshire and Humberside were eating more fish, less meat and less butter than anywhere else. The unhealthiest eaters were in the Midlands, where habits had been formed in prosperity not poverty. In all countries of the world there are health disparities between socio-economic classes and between regions. There was no evidence that they were greater in Britain, although Britain's health as a nation was in general failing to keep up with that of richer nations.

However, northern patriotism had been excited during the Thatcher years. There was a real sense that the north had borne the brunt of Thatcherism while the south had enjoyed its fruits. The north was a distant country of which the Tories knew little and cared less, Roy Hattersley accused. Labour's Health and Social Security spokesman, Michael Meacher, may not have been far wrong when he described the Prime Minister as 'idolised by millions in the south, detested by millions in the north'.

The battlefield of north against south was the industrial Midlands, where north meets south. No area in the country had been hit harder by manufacturing decline and the unemployment which accompanied it than the metal-bashing industries of the West Midlands. An unusual number of marginal seats were clustered here and in the East Midlands, indicating the changing political character of the region. For example, Birmingham, Northfield, had fallen sensationally to the Tories in 1979. A working class constituency, with half of its population housed in council houses, it was the home of the Austin Rover car plant at Longbridge. It had fallen briefly to a right-wing Labour candidate in a by-election in October 1982, after the suicide of the Tory member, but only by a majority of 289. It had swung again to the Tories in June 1983, but only by a majority of 2,760. If Labour could not win Birmingham, Northfield, it was farewell to Labour Britain. Its housing estates were the kind of places where Labour used to weigh the votes not count them. But three-quarters of the way through the 1987 campaign few Labour posters were in evidence. Canvassing the rows of shabby 1950s housing it was easy to spot those which had been bought by their tenants; they were the houses with painted front doors, built-on porticoes, conservatories at the back. On their doorsteps people said things like, 'We've always been Labour but . . .'; 'We might vote Labour for jobs . . .'; 'Anything to put her out.' They were no longer saying what they had been saying in 1983: 'Labour isn't what it used to be . . .'; 'I'll not vote for them on defence,' although they may have been thinking those things still. The impression was that what was left of the Labour vote was solid enough this time but that there simply wasn't enough left of it. Old allegiances, once broken, fade away; on the first occasion it is hard to vote Tory or Liberal but easier on the second, easier still on the third.

The tradition in this part of the country was of working class patriotism and aggressive local individualism. This, after all, had been Joe Chamberlain country. Now it was responding to another, and similar, brand of populism. The West Midlands had become a multi-racial conurbation and racism was never far beneath the skin of its politics. The 'London effect' had not helped Labour at all, nor the 'black caucus' rally which had been held in Birmingham a few weeks before the election. There was 17 per cent unemployment in Northfield in 1987 and Mrs Thatcher was not loved. But, for all that, the Tory vote across the Midlands had held remarkably solid, and it was holding solid now. A large-scale opinion poll by Marplan for the Press Association in the autumn of 1986 had suggested the region was still sliding ineluctably towards Tory Britain in the south, away from Labour Britain in the north. The Tories held Birmingham, Northfield, on 11 June. Not a single Midlands marginal fell to Labour.

As the end of the campaign neared, stung by the repeated allegations of her uncaringness and by the venom of class hatred which – as she saw it – her opponents had whipped up against her, furious with the party advertising agents, Saatchi and Saatchi, for allowing such an image of her to take hold, there was a brief moment of panic at the Tory headquarters. A maverick Gallup poll had shown a narrowing of the gap. The Tory managers had been taken aback by the evangelical fervour of Kinnock's campaign. One said, as it was all over bar the counting, 'We'd have lost this election without defence.' We shall never know. Certainly, Labour had paid a price for Neil Kinnock's commitment to unilateral nuclear disarmament. He had worn his social conscience on his sleeve but his CND badge on his lapel. Having seized the initiative in the early stages of the election he had lost it when, on the David Frost programme early that Sunday morning (24 May), he described the choice for defending Britain as one between nuclear extermination and 'using all the resources you have got to make any occupation totally untenable'. What did he mean? Guerrilla warfare, said the Tories, 'Dad's army' – an image of the Home Guard armed with pitchforks fending off the Russians. A poster was rushed out, 'Labour's defence policy': a man in a tin hat with his hands up – surrender! It was a ludicrously unreal scenario that Kinnock had been drawn into, yet what he had foolishly said was the logical consequence of his refusal to believe that nuclear weapons could deter. MORI, who were Labour's private pollsters, recorded between the first and second weeks of the campaign an extra 10 per cent of respondents who gave defence as an important issue, against an increase of only 2 per cent who mentioned the National Health Service, which was the issue Labour was pushing to the fore. Nevertheless, it is improbable that the excursions and alarms of the campaign made much difference in the end. The country already knew what it thought of Labour's defence policy, had only recently seen Kinnock and Thatcher back-to-back in Washington and Moscow. Kinnock's gaffe merely reinforced the doubts about Labour's competence to govern, doubts which were centred on its economic and taxation policies.

When the campaign was over some said that Kinnock had won the argument but, if he had, he had won the wrong argument. The election was about more than Margaret Thatcher's conscience. It was she who had won the argument over the eight years which had preceded the three weeks of the campaign. At her final press conference, as Kinnock across the road at Transport House was announcing 'the last days of Thatcherism', she – quietly but passionately, her eyes piercing her questioner – said:

> I shall put it this way: Communism is a system which gives privileges to the few at the top, and none to the many. Capitalism and enterprise is a system that only works by spreading ever more widely to more and more of the population what used to be the privileges of the few. Capitalism could not exist otherwise. It gets its profits and its investment for the future by spreading to the enormous number of people the benefits, whether in terms of consumer goods or capital. It has to be with the people because it is a partnership of enterprise and other kinds of effort. It *is* working. There were times during the past eight years when – believing passionately as I do in the things we were doing – I began to wonder whether there was still the enterprise in Britain that made her the country she was, or whether having got the ball to people's feet they would somehow still have that vivacity, verve, the energy, the vigour, the dynamism the Merchant Venturers used to have. I know now that they have. It *has* worked. It *is* still there. It *is* going on. And it *will* continue.

14
Why Labour Lost

The Socialist Age was coming to an end. What was happening in Britain was part of a world-wide phenomenon: everywhere in the industrialised democratic world the old manual working class was in decline, trade union membership was falling, old class loyalties were crumbling. It was as André Gorz had put it in a vogue book a case of 'Farewell to the Working Class'. In southern Europe socialist parties might still have a role to play as agents of belated democratisation; democratic socialism survived in the small neutralist countries of Scandinavia; but across the whole swathe of northern Europe the mode of politics which had dominated the post-war period, and much of the twentieth century, was in decline.

In part democratic socialism was the victim of its own success. The welfare societies it had helped to build had opened other and less-collectivist avenues of advance. Affluence had eaten into old class loyalties. Education had provided ladders of escape from the working class. But democratic socialism – or, in the continental usage, social democracy – was inflationary. The principle of social advance through the agency of the State when combined with the acquisitiveness of mass consumer societies made them everywhere harder to govern. All across Europe there had been a reaction against the power of trade unions, seen as the engines of inflation, and, as inflation went on the rampage, against the State itself.

The 'fiscal crisis of the Welfare State' became part of the crisis of socialism. The all-providing State was blamed at the same time for the soaring cost of welfare and for its failure to provide enough of it. Socialism became associated also with the warring groups of trade unionists and claimants who did public battle in the corporatist arena. Or, as Mancur Olson had put it, 'The familiar image of the social pie [we would say national cake] does not really capture the essence of the situation; it is perhaps better to think of wrestlers struggling over the contents of a china shop.'[1]

Internationalisation of the economy had made socialism increasingly problematical as a form of national politics. It was doubtful by the end of the 1970s whether even Keynesianism could be practised in one country. When socialism came to power in France in 1981 for the first time since the pre-war Popular Front, nationalising 39 banks and 5 major industries, the world soon foreclosed. In the 1970s the logic of socialism had led the Left in Britain towards a siege economy (the so-called Alternative Economic Strategy) which as well as being patently unfeasible was calculated to forfeit public support.

Meanwhile, the capitalist model offered new attractions or, if not attractions, sobering examples. Europe had felt the blast of competition from the aggressively free-enterprise take-off economies of the Pacific Basin. In the decade after the 1973 'oil shock' the United States, by-passed by the Socialist Age, had generated 16 million new jobs while Europe – statist and highly unionised – had seen unemployment rise to dizzy heights.

The economic difficulties of the 1970s accelerated the disintegration of the old working class. The European social democracies were obliged to adjust their economies to the new world price of oil and to face the competitive challenge from the less-developed countries. It did not matter whether it was called monetarism or, as in Mitterrand's France, socialist modernisation, the effects were the same: steel plants and coal mines closed. Trade unions, the pillars of the social democratic order, had found their strength primarily in the large-scale manufacturing industries and public utilities. It was these sectors which were in most rapid decline while the growth in employment was chiefly in small and high-tech enterprises or private services, sectors traditionally un-unionised and notoriously hard to organise.

The socialist parties of Europe had looked around for new cadres with which to replenish the ranks of the depleted working class. They had found in 1968 the students, the blacks, women, groups struggling to be liberated who might cut across the old lines of the class war. But student behaviour and racial and sexual politics gave offence to the old class constituency and what had been gained on the roundabouts of the new politics had been lost, or more than lost, on the swings of working class conservatism. In Germany, where the Green Party emerged as a rival on the Left, the SPD had felt obliged to espouse the politics of ecology and disarmament in order to attract the support of the new high-tech post working class but these too, they found, alienated their traditional supporters, who were at the same time more susceptible to the politics of the New Right. The fact of the matter was that socialism could no longer command a viable constituency of interest.

At the same time its crisis was ideological. The idea of socialism had lost its appeal, perhaps because it had served its purpose. The idea which had gripped the European mind for more than a century had run its course. A product of the confluence of industrialisation and democratisation, the idea of socialism took hold at the moment when God was pronounced dead and when politics was aspiring to be a universal science. By the end of the 1970s socialists could not be at all sure that they were articulating the aspirations of ordinary people. With the withering class base had come a decline in the moral imperative. Nor could they be sure that history was on their side. The working class struggle was becoming a minority cause.

At about the same time socialism ceased to be fashionable. This was not unimportant, for fashion helps to shape the minds of generations. In France, where the tradition was Marxist and where intellectuals had espoused the Communist Party rather than reformist social democracy, there had been a sharp reaction against the very notion of socialism. Towards the end of the 1970s the Parisian intelligentsia had become possessed of the idea that the Gulag was endemic not merely to Stalinism but to socialism itself. Nobody could seriously suppose that of the SPD or the British Labour Party. Yet even in Britain, thanks to the antics of Arthur Scargill, the London Left and the Liverpool Militants, the illibertarianism of the Left had become more apparent than its libertarianism. And, as Burkhardt somewhere said, 'that religion should again become an affair of the individual and his own personal feeling was inevitable when the church became corrupt in doctrine and tyrannical in practice.' The cults of Yuppidom, the new secular individualism of the age, were not primarily political, they were primarily materialistic – certainly they were not socialist. The 1980s were not at all like the 1970s or 1960s. A *fin de siècle* spirit was taking over. 'Designer Socialism' might flourish still between the covers of *Marxism Today*, the CND had blossomed for a while, and the miners' strike had provided the opportunity for a last indulgence in the nostalgia of class struggle, one last shove so to speak, but now those parties were over. Socialism had come to reek too much of the past. It would live on as a dying creed, perhaps, the priesthood remaining as the congregation departed.

Yet it remains to be explained why the Labour Party had done quite so badly, so much worse than other democratic socialist parties, for no party in Europe had contrived to reduce its support from 48 per cent in 1966 to 32 per cent in 1987. Ivor Crewe attributes Labour's decline chiefly to its failure to appeal to the new upwardly-mobile working class:

> In October 1974, the last election it won (just), Labour took half the skilled worker vote (49 per cent), and the Conservatives less than a third (31 per cent). In 1979 – an election it *lost* – it took 45 per cent of their vote, level pegging with the Conservatives. [In June 1987] it secured barely over a third (34 per cent) of their vote, trailing the Conservatives by 9 per cent. There could be no starker electoral testament to Thatcherism.[2]

Or no starker obituary of 'Labourism'. For the Labour Party's greater failure than continental social democratic parties' may be explained in part by its relationship with the trade union movement. The British Labour Party was umbilically linked to the trade union movement in a way that no continental party was; no other party permitted trade unions to impose their will, and their policies, upon it through the power of the block vote. But that might not have mattered had not the unions been more unpopular in Britain than in any other country. They were more unpopular because they were more powerful and outside the law. The Labour Party, through its institutional ties and financial dependence upon them, had been obliged to conspire with them to keep them beyond the reach of the law.

The power of the unions had been one reason for the lack of success of social democratic government in Britain by comparison with the Continent and that may have contributed to Labour's more spectacular decline. The Labour Party also had remained burdened by an antediluvian ideology, in the form of Clause Four of its constitution, which, although little heeded in government, had been a perennial source of embarrassment in Opposition. Not only that but Britain's brand of social democracy was more statist than any continental version where, by and large, the social market economy had become the model. For all these reasons British socialism went more against the grain than others.

Another difference was the electoral system. Britain was the only west European country forced into a Manichaean mould. Other socialist parties were obliged, for the most part, to adopt more pluralistic strategies and succumb to the compromises involved in the sharing of power. Coalition had been their exit from the wilderness. This had made them generally more responsive to their electorates and freed them somewhat from domination by their activitists.

No continental socialist party had undergone a cultural revolution as disturbing as Labour's in the early 1980s. This had done much to accelerate the electoral decline made manifest in 1983 and 1987. With the dethroning of the Parliamentary Labour Party in 1981 power had been transferred, in Bagehot's phrase, from 'moderate persons close to the scene of action to immoderate persons far removed from it.'[3] By this means the Labour Party was shifted to the left at a time when the country was moving to the right. How important Parliament itself is in a modern televised democracy is hard to say. Probably not as important as parliamentarians and parliamentary commentators imagine. Yet by a mysterious process parliamentary reputations permeate into the consciousness of the electorate. For most of the 1983–7 Parliament the Labour Party was not there. The Labour benches were frequently empty as MPs were preoccupied not with representing their constituents but with appeasing their constituency activists. That was the consequence of mandatory reselection. As Chris Mullins, an ardent Bennite had put it, 'The purpose of reselection is to change the attitude of MPs, not necessarily to change MPs.' The chief significance of the creation of the Electoral College in 1981 was that it increased still further the power of the unions as the arbiters of the Labour Party. This was done at a time when the unions were in decline as an interest in the land. The sovereignty removed from MPs as the elected representatives of the people was redistributed to an unholy and unrepresentative alliance of party activists and trade union bosses.

This had made it even more difficult than before to abandon policies to which the party was committed but which were unattractive or repugnant to the electorate. Unilateral nuclear disarmament was one. This too was a peculiar liability to British socialism in another sense. Social democracy in neutralist Sweden or Austria had not been required to address the dilemmas of nuclear power, although German Social Democracy had had to adjust to a radically altered status in the world, namely a divided Germany. However, the power structure of the British Labour Movement was more germane to such issues as the role of the trade unions and the sale of council houses, both vote losers for Labour. The trade unions had seen to it that the Party could not adopt a policy acceptable to the country while Labour councillors and local activists had seen to it that the desires of council tenants were ignored in the name of socialism.

The decline of socialism in Britain had been further hastened by the earlier onset of the counter-revolution. Margaret Thatcher was the first anti-socialist to come to power in social democratic Europe. That is to say she was the first seriously to challenge the prevailing order with a view to reversing the course of post-war politics. Her success drove new nails into the socialist coffin. The power of the unions was diminished. State industries were privatised, an example that was to be followed in Germany and France. Ownership was extended – of homes, of shares, of pensions. But equally important, perhaps, she exploded the socialist assumption. For since the war the governing classes of Europe, certainly of Britain, had seen themselves as living in the Socialist Age. Indeed that idea had haunted the European mind since the coming of the universal franchise at the turn of the century, for the implication of mass democracy had been the eventual coming of a socialist society. The ruling classes had endeavoured therefore to temporise, appease, postpone or, alternatively, to re-press the forces of socialism. The first technique had proved surprisingly successful, more so than the second. But it had not occurred to them that the advance of socialism could be prevented altogether and that what had seemed the march of history could be halted or reversed. That powerful idea now took hold.

Labour's defeat in 1987 was the occasion for yet another inquest. The Labour Party was accustomed by now to such inquests. They had become something of a ritual. Inquest, however, is the wrong word, for the object of the exercise on these occasions is not to ascertain the cause of death but rather to establish the certainty of resurrection. 'Socialism is dead,' goes up the cry, 'Long live socialism!' One wonders at this triumphalism in defeat, the invincibility of the belief that whatever else changes the validity of socialism remains – 'more relevant than ever today'.

After the defeat of 1959 a famous little book had asked the question, 'Must Labour Lose?'[4] Yes, very probably, was its answer. It pointed to the decline of the working class, to the effects of affluence (embourgeoisement), to Labour's unfavourable 'cloth cap image' as the party of the underdog, and to the unpopularity of many of Labour's policies, especially nationalisation. When Labour narrowly won the election of 1964, and went on to confirm it in the landslide of 1966, the premature obituarists of 1960 were duly mocked. But the pessimists had been correct. Crosland, for example, had predicted after 1959 that, 'the Labour vote will probably decline . . . by about 2 per cent at each successive general election.'[5] Between 1959 and 1987 and over six General Elections (counting the two elections of 1974 as one) its share of the vote had fallen from 44 per cent to 32 per cent.

The terminal decline thesis was revived after the 1979 defeat in much the same terms as after 1959. For not much had changed. In a deliberate echo of the 1960 post mortem Austin Mitchell, Crosland's successor in Grimsby, published a pamphlet which asked 'Can Labour Win Again?' and in which he warned, 'We are a party under threat. The mass party is atrophying. Our policies have never been adjusted to a new situation. The prolonged failure to produce the growth without which many of our aims are impossible and the feeling that a Labour Government cannot "deliver" undermines our efforts. The changing electoral situation threatens to relegate us to third division north status.'[6] Before the 1979 defeat (and before Eric Hobsbawm took to the field) Ivor Crewe and his Essex colleagues had put forward their 'partisan de-alignment' thesis as an explanation of Labour's secular decline, and had attached particular importance to its loss of support in February 1974.[7] The 'catastrophe' of 1983 seemed amply to confirm the thesis that Labour was in long-term and, possibly, irreversible decline.

In 1987 Labour improved its share of the vote from 28 per cent to 32 per cent. That marked a decline of 5 per cent on 1979, which had been a decline of 2 per cent on October 1974. The 1983 result had been Labour's worst since 1918; 1987 was its worst only since 1931. Yet the first reaction to the 1987 result was to scorn once more the premature obituarists. Indeed, before even the first result had been declared Kinnock was trumpeting the achievement of his leadership. 'Take yourself back to 7 p.m. on October 2, 1983,' he told an interviewer. 'I had just been elected leader of the Party. My standing in the polls was 24·5 per cent.' – That may have been his personal rating. In fact Labour (on MORI's figures) stood at 30 per cent in August 1983, 27 per cent in September, and 37 per cent in October – 'We were suffering from self-inflicted damage,' he continued. 'The obituaries for the Labour Party had already been typed. Where are they now? I'll tell you where they are – they're in the shredder. As a party, we're back.'

It was true that Labour had avoided finishing in third place in terms of popular votes. For a moment after the Greenwich by-election that possibility had seemed real. Tebbit had certainly not ruled it out at Conservative Central Office. It would have been a massive psychological blow which would have undermined Labour's legitimacy as the chief party of opposition although, in any likely event, it would have remained by far the largest oppositional force in Parliament. As it turned out Labour finished a clear nine points ahead of the Alliance (in 1983 it had been a bare two) and dancing on David Owen's political grave seemed to some almost as gratifying as victory itself.

So there was talk of the two-party system restored, the mould unbroken. But was it? The disintegration of the SDP–Liberal Alliance which swiftly followed the election certainly gave Labour its opportunity to re-establish itself in the left-centre of British politics at the expense of the new merged party, or old augmented Liberal Party, whichever it turned out to be. But for all that 7 million people had voted for the Alliance on 11 June as against 10 million for Labour. Labour had overtaken the Alliance and moved into second place in 21 Conservative-held seats but the Alliance remained second in 227 to Labour's 146. The third party was still the second party in the whole of the south.

With the detested Owen out of the way there was now talk of some kind of deal or understanding with the Liberals in time for a General Election in 1991 or 1992. Much was made of the anti-Thatcher majority in the land if only it could be mobilised, for she had once again been returned with only 43 per cent of the vote. But if there could be said to be an anti-Thatcher majority consisting of 57 per cent of the electorate there could equally be said to be an anti-Labour majority consisting of 68 per cent of the electorate. Until Labour addressed that stark fact it seemed improbable that any fancy coalition of forces could return it to power.

Encouragement was taken from the idea that Labour, although losing the election, had in some sense 'won the campaign'. But had it? It had won the commentators' plaudits for the slickness of its media management. It was 'a hit with the critics but a disaster at the box office.'[8] Kinnock himself had put up a good fighting show. Gallup's respondents had voted him 'man of the match', especially for his televised performances. Labour had managed to get Thatcher on the run, forcing her to explain her visits to the doctor. But in the end it had not been the shots that Labour had called which governed the outcome: the social issue had not decided the election, it had been decided on her terms, on economic competence.

It was claimed that the result showed Labour's decline to have been halted and reversed but that, as we have seen, was not so. In aggregate Labour's showing was marginally better than in 1983 but its support was more than ever concentrated in the declining classes of the declining areas of the country. As Austin Mitchell this time put it, 'Labour is being relegated to the peripheries of British life because

our structures, ethos and attitudes tie us to a world that is dying.'[9]
While Thatcher had won almost as well as in 1983 without the
'Falklands Factor' Labour had lost almost as badly without the 'Foot
Factor'. Even by Kinnock's own yardstick Labour had not done well.
He and his strategists had drawn the line between 'losing well' and
'losing badly' at 250 seats. Labour had won only 229, twenty more
than in 1983.

Although the campaign was claimed as a success its result discredited the thesis on which it had been fought. This was the same thesis
which had underlain Kinnock's leadership throughout, namely that
the Labour Party could be sold to the electorate rewrapped but
without fundamental change of content. Labour's Manifesto in 1983
had been described as the 'longest suicide note in history'. Kinnock
had seen to it that the 1987 Manifesto was a short list of generalities; it
was 17 pages long. On public ownership it said no more than that 'we
shall extend social ownership by a variety of means.' 'Social ownership' was what used to be called nationalisation. The Labour Party
was committed to renationalise British Gas and British Telecom in
which now millions of working class voters owned shares.

The post mortem took a familiar form. On the Left it was said that
socialism had not been rejected because it had not been on offer. The
party had failed to make a sufficiently radical and socialistic appeal to
enthuse the working classes. 'The general election results proved',
according to Tony Benn, 'that Labour candidates did best where a
strong socialist challenge has been mounted, as in Liverpool.' The
Right blamed the Left. Especially they blamed it for the 'London
Effect'. Kinnock himself saw the Greenwich by-election as an ill-
timed blow of ill-fortune which reinforced public prejudices and fears
about left-wing domination of the Labour Party. Indeed he saw his
whole leadership as having been plagued in this fashion. Scargill and
the miners' strike had lost him one precious year, then he had been
obliged to waste time and energy on the Militant Tendency. The
implication of this view was that without such embarrassing diver-
sions and distractions Labour could have been electable.

But could it? Or will it be? From its own point of view the 'loony
Left' was not as loony as made out. It knew how to put together local
coalitions – Livingstone's place in Parliament was the proof of it; the
trouble was that its style of politics was inimical to winning power
nationally. Yet it came nearer to articulating the plight of the
wretched of the inner cities than did anyone else, with the possible
exception of the Prime Minister. The left-wing municipal socialists
had spotted, as she was now belatedly to do, that 'Labourism' bore

much of the responsibility for the deplorable condition of the inner cities, the rotting housing estates, the de-educating schools, and the acres of dispiriting blight. But her ambition next to show that 'Thatcherism' could be the redemption of the cities meant that in her third term, as in her second, left-wing Labour-controlled authorities would be in the firing line and the public eye.

Constitutional reform was the leadership's chief hope for in time reducing the power of the Left in the party. Kinnock had always favoured one-person, one-vote as the way of carrying out mandatory reselection. The purpose of this was to reduce the power of small numbers of activists who could easily stack the general management committees of local parties. The price of this and of all such attempts to curb the power of party activists would be to enhance the power of the trade union bureaucracies. One-person, one-vote was the only reform Kinnock had attempted on becoming leader but he had been beaten by the block votes. This time he would buy off the unions by allowing them to send delegates as usual to selection conferences while the rest of the individual membership voted individually. As he saw it, there was nothing he could do about this. Ending the block vote, or breaking the umbilical link with the unions, was not on his agenda, not within the realm of practical Labour Movement politics. Hattersley conceded this publicly on television, accepting with a shrug that Labour looked like the 'party of the trade union bureaucracy'.

Some in the party spoke in terms of making more of a virtue of the trade union connection. One of the up-and-coming Kinnockites, Gordon Brown, MP for Dunfermline East, pointed out that the Labour Party had the smallest membership of any socialist party in Europe yet there were six million trade union members affiliated to it by virtue of paying (or failing to contract out from) the political levy. 'For this army of supporters now waiting in the wings individual membership should be inexpensive to buy and attractive to hold.' But of this great army only 42 per cent had even managed to vote Labour. Among the growing body of middle class trade unionists (professionals, executives, technicians, and so on) 37 per cent had voted Conservative and half of the remainder for the Alliance.

Nobody could see how the defence policy was to be reversed. In the same post-mortem TV interview Hattersley had said: 'The present defence policy is held with such passion amongst members of the party that the damage it would do to change it would be almost irrevocable.[10] It was not clear whether Kinnock now thought the policy should be reversed. Recognition that Labour had lost the election chiefly because of its feeble claims to economic competence encouraged the complacent view that the defence policy had not been as damaging as its critics made out. Encouragement was found in the prospect of British nuclear weapons becoming caught up in a Super Power deal. To this extent the future of socialism lay in the hands of Mikhail Gorbachev and President Reagan's successor. But more likely they would make Labour's dilemma in 1992 even more acute than in 1987. For by then Trident would no longer be cancellable on economic grounds. The complicating issue of the American Cruise missiles would have been resolved. Except in the improbable event of the abolition of ballistic missiles from the world the issue of the British deterrent would then present itself in the fashion most harmful to Labour, as a straight issue of nuclear nationalism. And the more uncertain the American commitment to the defence of Western Europe, the more problematical the future of the Atlantic Alliance, the more hesitant the progress of West European unity, the more developed the process of East–West détente, the stronger would be the case for the ultimate re-insurance provided by national nuclear deterrence.

With the nuclear and the union questions almost insoluble within the terms of Labour Movement politics the post mortem took the form chiefly of thrashing around for new visions of socialism. 'Talking of socialism we talk to ourselves, and in a language which is counter-productive in the wider community,' said Austin Mitchell, but nobody was listening to him. The task was easy to define: how to weld together a new winning coalition which could combine the underclass, the traditional working class, and sufficient elements of the new middle classes. But that had always been the problem and solving it had always been easier said than done. For example, for Michael Meacher, who from a left-wing position was valiantly, if somewhat belatedly, attempting to come to terms with the Thatcher Revolution, it was necessary now for Labour to broaden its class appeal. 'It is the technocratic class – the semi-conductor chip designers, the computer-operators, the industrial research scientists, the high-tech engineers – who hold the key to Britain's future. That is the class that Labour must champion and bring to power if it is to break out into the Midlands and the south.' But what was the evidence that these people at all wanted what Labour had to offer?

In a perverse way Labour in its defeat could take heart in Mrs Thatcher. Had she not shown that radical convictions could bring electoral success? Did not her example indicate sticking to principles? Benn had frequently made this point, setting socialist convictions against her 'conviction politics'. Joan Ruddock, the CND campaigner, now in the new Parliament, had made a similar point before the election concerning Labour's policy of unilateral nuclear disarmament. 'If we have got something hard to sell,' she had said, 'we must sell it hard. Look how Mrs Thatcher has successfully pushed ahead with policies which should have been hard for the public to accept.' Labour found it difficult to grasp that Mrs Thatcher's 'conviction politics' went with the grain, Labour's against the grain. To embrace the idea that Thatcherism was actually popular was asking too much, although Meacher came near to it when recognising her 'ideological dominance'. The election had suggested that Thatcherism was a good deal more popular than Mrs Thatcher. She had delivered the goods that people wanted.

What could Labour offer? Individualism became the buzz word. This was another familiar feature of what passed for re-thinking in the Labour Party. The latest notions could be incorporated through hyphenation. By the use of the word 'socialism' as a prefix, or the word 'democratic' as a reassuring prefix to the word 'socialism', most problems could be solved. Thus, during the election we had Hattersley talking about 'our socialist supply side policies' and now, preposterously, Kinnock was talking about 'socialist individualism'. There was nothing socialist about individualism. Socialism had been invented as the antithesis of individualism. That was the point of it, the assertion of social or collective values over the values of an atomised, individualistic society. But here was Kinnock: 'With the dispersal of the population, the experience of being part of a collective is not as strong as it used to be. Our initial approach has got to be from the party to the individual. They have got to be *told* [sic] that socialism is *the answer for them* because socialism looks after the individual.'

Perhaps the germ of this new ideological line was to be found in the famous 'Kinnock and the rose' election broadcast. Hugh Hudson's film had laid the basis for a new myth of potential political significance, a myth to set against the Thatcher myth of grocer's girl made good. For here were Neil and Glenys, the children of the Labour revolution, reared on the free milk of the Welfare State, nourished by educational opportunity, the first in their families 'in a thousand generations' to get to university. And why was this? Because their forebears had no 'platform upon which they could stand,' had been denied their fair and proper chance. Not a word here about the collective advance of the working class, instead a tale of individual achievement as a result of a greater equality of opportunity. Here was planted the subliminal notion of Labour yuppiedom – or Yukkies, Young Upwardly-Mobile Kinnocks. But the difference between the miner's son and the grocer's daughter was that he hadn't left his conscience behind him, wasn't the sort to pull up the drawbridge.

Kinnock emerged from the election firmly in charge. He was credited within the party for a successful campaign. He had heartened the faithful. He was still only forty-five. No one could lay a finger on him as leader. The Electoral College was a wonderfully immobilising device which made it virtually impossible to remove a leader. The hard Left in the party was isolated. It had never recovered from the schism of 1981 when Kinnock and others of the Tribune Group had refused to support Tony Benn. The parliamentary party had undoubtedly shifted to the left as the result of re-selection, or retirement under pain of re-selection. For the first time in post-war history the Left had a majority over the Right but it was predominantly a soft Left majority, loyal to Kinnock. The Tribune Group had become the party establishment. Kinnock's writ ran. The broad future direction of the party was agreed. The trend would be towards more of the same or, rather, a little less of the same – labourist socialism watered down by individualism, more responsive to market forces.

During the campaign he had been surrounded by young men intent on power. None more so than Bryan Gould. Kinnock's absence from London during most of the campaign had rocketed Gould to prominence. It had been only the previous autumn that he had been elected to the 'Shadow' Cabinet for the first time. He was eminently reasonable, always courteous, and the acme of competence. He was exactly the sort of chap you would appoint to run the national whelk stall. He was the kind of boy any mother could be proud of. A New Zealander, a Rhodes Scholar of Oxford, he was suitably deracinated, and unscarred by the English class system. He was no ideologue. A market socialist? More of a market-research socialist perhaps. Or perhaps there was no great difference. 'Market socialism' was the new intellectual fashion. It had originated in the East European experience and reflected the full-turning of the wheel: for whereas socialism had originally been a reaction to the tyranny of the market, 'market socialism' was a reaction to the tyranny of the State. What exactly it consisted of mattered less than that it offered a convenient code for signalling new concern for the consumer and the individual. Gould spoke of a politics of 'self interest'. It was a way of coming to terms with Thatcherism.

Would there be socialism after market socialism, somebody had asked? But who cared? Not, we may suspect, these New Revisionists.

Gould, remember, had fought the campaign on the premise that Labour's policies were not its problem, the Labour Party was the problem – the noise and the people. What passed for rethinking was not so much rethinking as the continuing process of repackaging. In 1987 Labour's image had been strong as a caring party. By 1992 it must acquire the image of a competent party. For there were not enough carers in the country to constitute a political majority. If Labour was to extend its appeal beyond its declining class base, from the council estates into the Waites estates, from the rust belt of the north into the silicon belts of the south, it would have to build a new coalition of interest around a claim to competence in the matters of managing the economy, training and educating the cadres of a modern society, promoting competition and combining popular ownership with social control.

It was with such hopes and ambitions that the New Revisionists attended the final days of Margaret Thatcher. For surely her third term would be her last? Surely one day the pendulum would have to swing? They were young enough to wait. But what if the pendulum did not swing? In Europe, where the parties of the Right had split, as in Scandinavia, the Left had been in almost perpetual power. But where it was the forces of the Left which were divided, on sectarian or religious grounds, the hegemony was of the Right. Had Britain now joined that second club?

15

Third Party Disarray

The election brought swiftly the end of the Alliance, the disintegration of the SDP and the destruction, or self-destruction, of David
Owen. Within hours of the declarations Roy Jenkins and David Steel
pulled the trigger for merger between the two parties. Steel may have
done so partly to signal that Liberal colleagues who were already
throwing their hats into the leadership ring were wasting their time.
As far as Steel was concerned there would be no vacancy. But he must
have known also that the move would be regarded by Owen as a
challenge, an invitation to a showdown. For Steel could have been in
no doubt whatsoever that, as far as the other David was concerned,
the two parties would merge over his politically dead body. That is
exactly what was to happen.

Owen had pitted himself against merger from the very moment he
became leader of the SDP in June 1983. He had from the very
beginning of the SDP been unenthusiastic about the Liberals. After
the break with Labour in 1981 he had seen the first priority as
establishing the identity of the new party as an independent force.
Roy Jenkins, he believed, had seen the SDP only 'as a transit camp on
the way to a merger with the Liberal Party'. Owen recognised that at
some stage there would have to be a tactical understanding with the
Liberals for fighting an election but saw no hurry for this. He
regarded the Alliance formed at the Liberal Assembly in Llandudno
in September 1981 as premature. He had not himself attended that
conference. He believed the Alliance to have been plotted behind his
back. Jenkins had shanghaied the SDP at birth.

On replacing Jenkins as leader in 1983 Owen set out to re-establish
the identity of the SDP in contradistinction to the Liberals. It may by
then have been too late. The two parties were drawing together
willy-nilly on the ground where there was a good deal of natural

fraternisation. At the top the view was widely held in both parties that the dual leadership with which the 1983 General Election had been fought had been a liability, bewildering to the voters. Owen therefore might have sought to make a virtue of necessity and tried to establish the SDP, although the smaller party, as the dominant force within an increasingly integrated alliance of the two parties. David Steel at that time was in deep depression so the moment would have been favourable for Owen to establish himself as the dominant leader. Instead he pitted himself against all forms of closer collaboration, regarding them as the thin end of the wedge of merger.

As he saw it the continued existence of the SDP was in doubt. It was defying the laws of political gravity. The 1983 election had been a severe blow to earlier hopes. In 1981 it had seemed as if the old party system was in rapid disintegration. For a dizzy moment at the end of that year Gallup had put the Alliance in the lead with 50 per cent. On the eve of the Falklands War the three parties had been level pegging at around 33 per cent. By June, with the Falklands gloriously retaken, the Alliance was trailing a poor third, the Tories with 44 per cent and it with 24 per cent. It had gone into the election with around 17 per cent and made no headway in the first two weeks of the campaign. Then Labour under Foot's leadership had collapsed. The Alliance had filled the vacuum. It had finished with 26 per cent of the votes cast, barely two points behind Labour.

Was this realignment? Yes, in the sense that, at least for the time being, there had been a major shift in party allegiances. The Labour vote had all but collapsed. Mrs Thatcher had recruited to her camp an unprecedented number of working class voters. Many others had deserted to the Alliance. In Kinnock's own constituency, as solidly Labour as they come, 22 per cent had voted for an SDP candidate. But there had been no realignment at Westminster. There the iron law of the British electoral system had been enforced. The Alliance's 26 per cent of the vote had yielded it 3 per cent of the seats, 23 in all. Of these the SDP had won six. That was the party Owen now led.

He was in no position to deal with the Liberals from strength. Mere survival would be a considerable feat. But there was another reason why he set himself so adamantly against merger or anything that smacked of it. This was his belief that merger was the device by which his enemies would seek to destroy him. For his former comrades of the Gang of Four, co-founders of the SDP, had become in his eyes the enemy within, eager to throw open the gates to the Liberal foe. Increasingly Owen saw Jenkinsites under every bed, or restaurant table. He firmly expected that Jenkins, Rodgers and Williams, and their acolytes, would before the next election gang up with Steel to demand a single Alliance leader and by that means dump him.

In this there was a good deal of paranoia but also a good deal of truth. The remaining Gang of Three found Owen hard to take as leader, although for somewhat different reasons. Jenkins's own leadership had failed and he had been supplanted by a younger man. Owen when Foreign Secretary had treated him in most shabby fashion as President of the European Community. Owen had never been quite one of 'Roy's boys' but it had been a betrayal of friendship nonetheless the way he had slighted the older man, pandering to the Labour Party view that Jenkins was some kind of renegade or Euro-traitor. Moreover, the paternity of the SDP was in dispute between them. As Jenkins saw it, the Dimbleby Lecture made him indisputably the founding father. Owen saw the SDP as the offspring of the Labour Party and himself as prime mover in that breakaway. He had resented Jenkins's triumphal return from Brussels and blamed him for betraying the true cause of social democracy. Jenkins for his part found it hard to accept the idea of Owen as leader of *his* party.

Shirley Williams and William Rodgers had been Owen's comrades at arms within the Labour Party. They had not at first differed with him seriously either about the direction the new party should take or its relationship with the Liberals. But they had put their careers on the line with his. They had set out as a collective leadership in what was to be a daring and noble enterprise. Now he was leader and they were not. He was in Parliament and they were not. He was a famous and glamorous figure while they faced the prospect of fading from the public eye. They had to earn their livings. He did not. In so far as they may have suffered the pangs of regret, secretly wishing themselves back in the Labour Party, Owen was the embodiment of their apostasy.

As leader they now found him arrogant and monstrously macho. The repeated observation that the SDP was a one-man band was an insult to them. But one-man band it was. To make a mark as the leader of a fraction of six and give it credibility as a political party was a remarkable feat. Impossible though they might find him, Owen was the SDP's one huge asset. He looked the part of an alternative Prime Minister in a way that Steel never could or would. The relationship between the Two Davids was an unequal one all round. As leader of the Liberal Party Steel saw himself as the senior partner. He had more troops than Owen: three times as many MPs (although only 17) and a vast if motley army of irregulars who could be mustered to fight parliamentary by-elections. The Liberals had been in the by-election game since Orpington in 1962. They had been up and down that roller coaster a good few times since then. They regarded the SDP as amateurs when it came to street politics, *real politics*. Yet plainly in another sense Owen was the senior partner. Steel recognised Owen's credentials as someone who had held senior Cabinet office. He was prepared to defer to him on policy matters. He was not prepared, however, to be regarded as Owen's creature. He resented deeply his caricature on the *Spitting Image* programme as a diminutive figure cooing sycophantically from Owen's pocket.

Owen for his part regarded the education of the Liberal Party as a kind of White Man's Burden that had fallen upon him. He behaved towards it somewhat like a colonial governor. He did not regard it as a serious political party. 'I see certain anarchical tendencies in the Liberal Party which make it difficult for it to stand firm on key policy issues.' In other words, they were a shower. 'The Alliance must be more consistent,' he told them sternly. 'Far too many Liberal candidates espoused different and conflicting policies at the last election.' He could not understand why Steel had not sorted his party out long ago instead of appeasing it as he did. He was particularly mistrustful of the Liberals on defence and made this his litmus test of whether they were to be regarded at all as a potentially serious partner in power.

However, while Owen had no high regard for Steel as a leader, and considered him to lack seriousness on policy matters, he saw in him a ruthless and treacherous operator, very different from his public image as Mr Nice. For he had witnessed the son of the Manse playing Macbeth at Ettrick Bridge during the 1983 election. There, at a crisis summit called at his lowland Scottish home, Steel had put Roy Jenkins ferociously to the dagger. He had demanded his resignation as 'Prime Minister Designate' of the Alliance in the most cruelly wounding fashion and, when this was not forthcoming, had pushed Jenkins brutally aside for the remainder of the campaign. Why Jenkins had forgiven Steel but never Owen we do not know.

Steel would have preferred the two parties to have merged after 1983 but knew, given Owen's attitude, that it was not on. He tried saying to Owen, 'I don't want a merger any more than you do but let's come together naturally on the ground.' But Owen wasn't having that either; he was opposed to fraternisation by the troops and did what he could to stop it. He saw it as the thin end of eventual merger, which it was. He succeeded in blocking joint policy formulation until 1986. He resisted the appointment of joint spokesmen for the two parties although this was eventually done in the months before the election, and with some success. He would not even sit next to Steel in the House of Commons.

Nevertheless, the Two Davids achieved a *modus vivendi* of a kind. They were obliged to, for they were like two mountaineers roped together. The differences between them were less ideological than of style and temperament. Steel saw himself as a man of the Left and was at ease in that role. The mission of the modern Liberal Party, as he saw it, was to provide a non-socialist alternative to Labour on the Left of British politics. 'We are not just a party of the Left but *the* party of the Left,' he had once said.[1] He felt a greater affinity for the Labour Party than he could ever conceivably feel for the Tories. He liked Kinnock and most cordially disliked Thatcher. He could not bring himself to admire her or anything much that she had done. 'Thatcherism must be stopped,' he said, 'and how to stop it should be at the top of the agenda of every politician in every party who wants a new way ahead of partnership and progress.'[2] Owen's position was more complicated. He too was of the Left by instinct and conviction but his feelings towards Labour were coloured by his apostasy. Defence had become for him an issue of overriding principle. The credibility of the Alliance as a party aspiring to break the system, he judged, would depend upon the country seeing it as a force capable of governing with authority and no nonsense. People must be able to trust it to face down a Scargill or see off a Galtieri. 'The country will not vote for our Alliance if they sense at that time any weakness of purpose, indecisiveness or lack of resolve,' he declared. 'What this party needs is balls,' he had told one of the SDP's leading feminists.

For a third party struggling to be taken seriously in a two-party electoral system, tactical assessments of this kind do not easily convert into battle plans. Hours might be spent arguing about whether to go for Tory or for Labour votes but what was actually said or done in the end was probably not very different. Owen's view, for what it was worth, was that Labour could not and would not win. Therefore he was in the market for Tory votes. Steel was of the same opinion about Labour's chances but was reluctant for the Alliance to be seen as tilting in any way towards the Tories. This was for reasons of personal preference but also because it was the only manner in which the Liberal Party could be led. For Liberals were accustomed to point their guns against whoever was the local enemy, Tory in some seats and Labour in others; this way of fighting battles made it difficult to take sides in the war. Grimond had once said of the parliamentary

Liberal Party that it was a body of men united only in fear of losing their seats.

Steel was not opposed to the idea of coalition. Far from it, the thrust of his leadership had been entirely in the direction of sharing power; he had tried throughout to educate the amateur millennialists of his party in the disciplines involved in such a project. But Steel could not forbear from saying that he would find it exceedingly uncongenial to share power with Mrs Thatcher. Owen did not exactly wish to get into bed with Mrs Thatcher (although a newspaper advertising poster on display during the 1987 election showed him in that compromising position) but it was his judgment that Kinnock, even if willing, would be unable to come to terms with the Alliance in a hung or, as he preferred to call it, 'balanced' Parliament. The Labour Party would not allow it. Moreover, he was determined to make it clear that the Alliance could have no truck with Labour's unilateralist disarmament policies in any form. But for these reasons, whenever Owen spoke of coalition he was liable to be interpreted as leaning towards a coalition with Thatcher and not with Labour. And Steel, for that reason, preferred him not to speak of coalition at all.

Much had been made also of Owen's espousal of the social market economy at the first SDP conference he had addressed as leader. The speech he had made at Salford in 1983 had contained nothing new or original but was intended to signal the return to the true notion of social democracy which had inspired him and the others who had left the Labour Party. He took this to be the partnership between the market, for the purpose of creating wealth, and the State, for the purpose of distributing it more equally. The social market, as he understood it, was the compromise between socialism and capitalism which the German SPD had accepted at its 1959 Bad Godesberg conference. In other words, what Owen thought he was saying was that the SDP belonged in the tradition of the SPD of Helmut Schmidt. What he was taken to have said was that the SDP should be more like the Conservative Party of Mrs Thatcher. The Liberals (or at least some of them) regarded themselves as the champions of Keynesian economic management. Keynes had been a Liberal. Williams, Rodgers and most of the ex-Labour people were anxious to remain true to what they took to be their basic principles. It was their position that the Labour Party had betrayed these, not themselves. So everybody was pleased to fall upon Owen for moving too far to the Right. For example, when Owen supported privatisation Williams and Rodgers did not. The Liberal Council passed a motion condemning his social market theories. Under party pressure Steel criticised him publicly at Oxford. Roy Jenkins warned, 'Post-Thatcher the country will not want a sub-Thatcherite alternative.'[3]

Williams and Rodgers shared with the Liberals the project of creating an alternative to Labour on the Left. They took that to have been the original Social Democratic project. But the Owenites preferred to talk about the 'New Politics'. The 'New Politics' was a phrase that could be used to suit everybody's convenience. But what Owen usually meant was a politics in which co-operation between parties, and coalition governments, became positive virtues rather than the freakish outcome of a mathematically 'hung' Parliament. Realignment was not a transitional process but consisted in a permanent shifting pluralism made possible by proportional representation. This was a somewhat Utopian vision: it was proving difficult enough to achieve three-party politics within the British electoral system without insisting on a multi-party model. Moreover, the public did not share Owen's enthusiasm for hung Parliaments. MORI polls commissioned by *The Economist* consistently said so. They saw it as a recipe for weak government. Disraeli was right, the English did not love coalitions. Electorally Owen was on to a loser, but he went on plugging his line. However, the 'New Politics' had one great advantage for the Owenites. In a pluralistic world there would be no need for merger between the SDP and the Liberals: they could happily compete and co-operate for ever, drawing strength from diversity.

Defence had always been Owen's test of Liberal seriousness and at the bottom of his line when contemplating any deal with the Labour Party. Unilateral nuclear disarmament had been one of the reasons for his despairing of the Labour Party and leaving it. The Liberals had long been ambivalent on the subject of nuclear weapons. They had always been opposed to the idea of Britain as an independent (or 'so-called independent') nuclear power. They had soon become opposed to the stationing of Cruise missiles in Britain. But they had refrained from adopting an out-and-out CND position. Short of ban-the-bomb decisions Steel had been able to live with his party on nuclear weapons although it had on occasions defeated him. One such occasion, as Owen had been quick to note, had been on the very morning after the consummation of the marriage with the SDP at Llandudno in 1981 when the Assembly had voted to support a nuclear 'freeze'. In 1984 Steel, under pressure from Owen, had taken on his party and lost. In that year the Assembly reaffirmed its 'opposition to the maintenance of an independent British nuclear deterrent.' Steel managed to persuade it to refrain from unilaterally dispensing with Polaris (which was to be included in arms control negotiations) but it had defied him by voting for the unilateral removal of the Cruise missiles. The SDP was committed to maintaining Britain's existing nuclear capability and replacing it if necessary, although not with Trident which was regarded as too powerful and too expensive.

As a means of containing these differences and in the hope of resolving them Owen and Steel had in 1984 appointed a joint commission of senior party members under the chairmanship of a former ambassador. For an agreed policy to be possible one fundamental question had to be answered. What was to happen when the obsolescent Polaris force became finally obsolete? The two parties were agreed in their opposition to Trident but the clear implication of Liberal policy was that there should be no replacement at all, while the SDP wished Britain to retain a deterrent capability. Owen was adamant that it must. The commission, not surprisingly, was unable to resolve this difference substantively but attempted to do so procedurally: it recommended that no decision need be taken for the moment, or should be taken until all the facts and circumstances were known, concerning 'whether or, if so, how' the Polaris should be replaced. This was a kind of compromise, for it involved the Liberals in recognising that the question of replacement remained open while falling well short of the commitment to maintaining a nuclear deterrent upon which Owen insisted.

The commission was ready to report in June 1986. Before it was able to publish its findings officially they were leaked. The way in which this happened revealed the true state of relations between Owen and Steel and within the leadership of the Alliance. Steel lunched with journalists from the *Scotsman*, the result of which produced headlines which declared, 'Alliance Report Rejects UK Deterrent – Owen's Nuclear Hopes Dashed.' Owen, in fury, took the opportunity of the Council for Social Democracy's quarterly meeting in Southport two days later to reject the commission's findings in advance of publication. He said:

> I must tell you bluntly that I believe we should remain a nuclear weapons State. If we are to carry conviction in our decision to cancel Trident after an election, we ought to be prepared to say that we will find a replacement for Polaris . . . Certainly you should know quite clearly that I definitely do not believe that I would carry any conviction whatever in the next election were I to answer – on your behalf – on the question of the replacement of the Polaris, that that would have to depend on the circumstances of the time. That would get and would deserve a belly laugh from the British

electorate. That sort of fudging and mudging was what I left behind in the Labour Party.

This statement was lethal in a number of ways. Not only did it explode the attempt at compromise between the two parties but publicly accused his own colleagues on the commission, one of whom was Rodgers, of the kind of unprincipled fudging which had driven them from the Labour Party. At the same time he was saying to Steel, 'OK, if you want to play rough . . .' Steel wrote to the *Scotsman* dissociating himself from their report, claiming not even to have seen the commission's findings, but nothing was going to persuade Owen that Steel had not knifed him in the back once more. Things were never to be the same again after this incident. The two parties of the Alliance were placed on a collision course which would remain until Polling Day and lead afterwards to the rupture between the Owenites and the mergerites. Trust would never again exist between the Two Davids. The SDP was now irrevocably split. The bitter factionalism within the leadership was brought into the open in all its pent-up vehemence. Rodgers wrote to *The Times* that a replacement for Polaris was 'not a question of principle and ought not to be a test of political virility'. Williams wrote in the *Daily Mail*, 'It would be excellent if he's prepared to listen to other points of view and possibly even consider whether there is room for some movement on his part as well as on the part of the rest of us.' While the Owenites closed ranks around their man others began to see in him a party-wrecker who would not be content until he had destroyed the Alliance and with it the SDP. Told that Owen had said what he had said because of a report in the *Scotsman*, Jenkins – puce with fury – spluttered, 'In that case the man's totally unfit to hold public office.'

Owen and Steel that summer attempted to patch up a compromise which would at least get them through their conferences. In September the Alliance stood at around 25 per cent in the polls. That summer it had been clocking up scores of 30 per cent or more in local government by-elections. If the defence row could be contained its prospects looked none too bad. The idea was to wrap up a Polaris replacement in what Owen called 'Euro-cladding'. The commission provided a foundation for this in the stress it had placed upon the European pillar of NATO. The Two Davids set off on a European tour, the result of which was the notion of a 'European Minimum Deterrent'. Like many such compromises its strength was that nobody could be seriously expected to believe in it. But even if a French or Anglo–French alternative to the Trident could be devised it seemed improbable that the British public would warm to the idea of exchanging their dependence on the United States for a dependence on their traditional enemy within the European Community.

The resolution put before the Liberal Assembly at Eastbourne asked it to welcome 'closer co-operation in defence policy and procurement between Britain and its West European partners to develop a more effective British contribution to the collective defence capability of the European pillar of NATO.' That was the wrapping in which the Assembly was to be sold the open option of a Polaris successor. But an amendment had been tabled to the effect that this British contribution to NATO should be 'non nuclear'. This, as Steel at once saw, would be construed as tantamount to a decision in favour of unilateral nuclear disarmament. He was happy enough himself with the prospect of a non-nuclear Britain – that had been his own position since the early 1960s; but he was not a unilateral nuclear disarmer (although his wife was) and, always the politician, did not wished to be tarred with that brush. The Labour Party had demonstrated beyond peradventure that unilateral nuclear disarmament was a vote loser. Steel was in the vote-winning business. At the same time Steel knew that whatever he did or said a good many Liberal candidates would fight their elections exactly as they pleased, many of them on CND tickets of one kind or another. The Liberal Party being the Liberal Party, there was nothing much he could do about this. Quarrelling with his party in public, and probably losing as in 1984, did not seem the best idea therefore. Owen might be right concerning the credibility of the Alliance's posture on the British deterrent but the credibility of the Alliance as an electoral force also depended upon its unity. Owen had struck that a mortal blow. For these reasons Steel resolved not to speak in the debate himself and to hope for the best.

Ostensibly the debate at Eastbourne was about whether Britain's contribution to NATO could (not necessarily *would*) continue to be nuclear or whether that would be specifically excluded. But it was a more momentous occasion than that for the fragile future of the Liberal–SDP Alliance. For the Liberal Assembly was meeting under unprecedented public gaze. Britain's nuclear future was the question but the credibility of the Alliance as an electoral force was at stake. Would the Assembly pass the test – Owen's test – of a serious party aspiring to a share in government or would the old anarchist Adam out?

Steel's distaste for his own party – especially when it gathered before his eyes once a year at some polite resort or spa – was second only to Owen's. He positively dreaded the annual Liberal Assembly. He would cut his sojourn as short as possible and spend as much time as he could in the more congenial company of the press. His only control as leader over the Assembly's proceedings was his veto over its decisions, to which he clung as to a lifeline. Who came to the Assembly and who voted there depended on geography and the weather as much as anything else. The previous year's Assembly in Dundee had gone off quietly because the rail fare had acted as a deterrent. Eastbourne was but a day trip from London, uncomfortably close to the southern bastions of the CND. In theory there were rules governing who could come and who could vote but in practice they could not be enforced because there was no central register of members. It was a part of the Liberal ethos that there should not be. More or less anybody who showed up and paid up was likely to be counted as a Liberal, for the day at least. Some most unsatisfactory people were likely to appear, many of them creeping from under the stones of Hebden Bridge. Hebden Bridge in Yorkshire, not far from Leeds, was the headquarters of the Association of Liberal Councillors which Steel had described, accurately, as a 'party within a party'. The ALC, like so much else in British politics, had grown out of the 1960s scene. Its balding, hairy convener was Tony Greaves, the sight or mention of whom was enough to plunge Steel into depression. Greaves, however, could point out that whereas Steel spoke for 17 MPs at Westminster he could speak for some 2,000 or more elected councillors around the country. The vast majority of constituency activists did not have Liberal MPs to support, did not expect to have Liberal MPs to support, and in some cases did not want Liberal MPs to support. MPs tended to be regarded as a small and unrepresentative élite corrupted by the London life. This was the endemic defect of a party fifty years out of power: it had become an extra-parliamentary party aspiring to parliamentary power.

Whereas Steel's party was for the most part straddled between Westminster and the Celtic fringes, Greaves's party was based chiefly in the cities of the north. It was the party of 'community politics', derived from the 1960s participation movement. The idea was to build the 'Liberal Society' from the bottom up. What exactly the 'Liberal Society' was had never been satisfactorily explained but it would be some kind of unstructured New Jerusalem in which individualism would reign and no central writ would run. 'Liberalism', suggested *Liberator*, the theoretical organ of the ALC, 'is a rich cocktail of anarchism, socialism and a very strong green strand.' Community politics, however, was more organisational than ideological in its thrust. Community politics was a cult of activism and a form of local populism; at its best it was a radical politics of involvement, at its worse a Tammany-style pork-barrel politics of promises.

The Liberal Party had long since ceased to represent any great interest in the land. Rather, in its modern form, it was a great conglomeration of individuals, special interests, single issues, and lost causes. Tom McNally, one of the Labour Party defectors to the SDP, described the culture shock of his first Liberal Assembly in terms of people 'chewing celery and wearing open-toed sandals'.[4] A Liberal Assembly is more fringe than conference; the actual proceedings take place in the midst of a vast bazaar of lobbyists, charities, publicity stands, information desks, commercial stands and tables of home-made produce. De Gaulle, in one of his moments of exasperation with the French, had asked how was a nation which made 1,756 – or whatever it was – different kinds of cheese to be governed? Steel must have wondered how power was to be achieved by a party which could at the same time support quite so many causes as well as manufacturing goodness knows how many different kinds of fudge and organic honey.

As the election drew nearer Steel had increasingly seen policy-making in Alliance terms: not so the members of Greaves's party or the left wing of his own party at Westminster. It suited Steel to be able to plead the greater good of the Alliance against what Grimond used to call the 'wee free' Liberals, his party activists or the more left-wing Liberal MPs. In the eyes of the grassroots activists the SDP represented everything that was wrong with Steel's Liberal Party writ large: it was centrist, élitist, growth-orientated, corporatist, managerial, metropolitan, media-conscious, and Atlanticist. The Liberal Assembly was the annual forum for asserting the superior virtues of community politics over parliamentary politics. This year at Eastbourne this impulse was the stronger as a result of the belief that Steel was increasingly in Owen's pocket. It was not Alliance policy that was being thrust upon the party, it was Owen's policy. By sabotaging the commission's report Owen had placed Steel in an intolerable and impossible position. For any subsequent compromise could only fan suspicions that Steel was Owen's dummy. Moreover, any plea from Steel to put Alliance above party would carry little weight with his own people when Owen had so often made plain his contempt for the Liberals as Alliance partners and had seldom himself been prepared to defer to the common cause. The defence row was itself a spectacular example of his refusal to do so.

The debate at Eastbourne was mismanaged. Indeed it was not

managed at all. Steel did not speak. The supporters of the 'no nuclear' amendment had the better of the debate. Their emotional appeal was the stronger. The Euro-fudge was not up to the weight now placed upon it. But that was not really the problem. Not for the first time the Liberal Assembly went ape. One speaker denounced the 'misguided, misconceived so-called realism which has more to do with power politics than the values we share and know will succeed.' Another appealed to delegates to ignore the advice to 'keep your heads down, the electorate might see you'. Was this a party 'preparing for power' as Steel had enjoined it ten years earlier in his very first speech as leader? 'We are on the verge of responsibility,' declared Bermondsey MP Simon Hughes as he set out to explore the wilder shores of irresponsibility in a speech of such emotional incoherence that it brought the Assembly roaring to its feet while Steel sat hunched in miserable silence. The argument about nuclear weapons (if argument it was) had soon been lost in declarations about Liberalism. 'We are Liberals . . .', Liberal this, Liberal that. 'At Liberal Assemblies we make Liberal policy,' said MP Michael Meadowcroft, a member of the CND national council. Otherwise, 'we might as well all go and join the SDP,' said Greaves, as if that would be a fate worse than nuclear holocaust.

The debate took place as if the world did not exist. The electoral implications for the Alliance of what was at issue were scarcely mentioned or considered. It ended in a spirit of jubilation and self-satisfaction. The amendment was carried – by 652 votes to 625, but carried all the same. The Liberal Assembly had asserted itself, shown who made Liberal policy – and it was not David Owen. But they knew not what they did. The following morning's headlines were along the lines of 'Ban the Bomb Vote Shatters the Alliance', 'A policy in pieces', 'Bad day for the Alliance'. They were read with bemused surprise by many of the Liberals at Eastbourne. One said, 'OK, it may not have been too good for the Alliance but it was good for Liberals, it's made us feel better.' Paddy Ashdown (who had spoken against the amendment) called it 'a vindication for democracy'. Hughes, whose speech had done such damage to the Alliance cause, proclaimed 'a new style of politics'. Meadowcroft complained that the press, 'didn't understand the process'. Apparently we had seen 'democracy in action'.

Steel took a different view. We had seen, he told the Assembly, the Liberal Party reverting to its old habit of preferring purity of principle to practical politics; he compared the resolution passed to the proclamation of a nuclear-free zone on a lamppost in Lambeth; he described as a 'breathtaking misjudgment' the notion that the Assembly was somehow strengthening his hand in negotiations with David Owen; and he went on:

> We are either in Alliance or we are not. We must live and breathe the Alliance . . . I am reported as being angry with this Assembly. My emotion is not that of anger but of profound frustration that what you hope for and what I hope for, namely electoral victory for Liberalism and the Alliance, may have been temporarily and unnecessarily put at risk.

Never before had he spoken to his party in such terms. But it was too late. The damage had been done and it was to be lasting and severe. Eastbourne triggered a fission which was to be immensely damaging to the Alliance. It gave the government its chance to make a pre-election issue of the defence of the realm, turning on the Labour Party which had been trying to keep quiet on the subject. This contributed to the Conservative revival that autumn. By Christmas the Alliance was looking a much less plausible contender for power. Its credibility as a vote-winning force – the only credibility that really mattered – had been damaged in the crucial run up to the election. Steel and Owen subsequently put together a more or less agreed position but they were never able to carry conviction on the matter of the Polaris replacement. As Owen had predicted this proved damaging to the Alliance during the election campaign. But, as Steel had tried to tell him, far more damaging was the spectacle of disarray which he had helped to bring about by his imperious behaviour.

The Alliance went into the election campaign with brokered policy positions, two leaders, and no agreed tactical or strategic objective. It was never settled whether the objective was to maximise their vote in the hope of relegating Labour into third place or to win the balance of power. They had no agreed answer to the question of whom they might coalesce with in a hung Parliament. They had no answer at all to the question of what the Polaris would be replaced with, for on this it was agreed only that nothing could be said. Perhaps this made no difference to the result on Polling Day. The Alliance's problems were more fundamental than these. However, the campaign fertilised the seeds of the sectarian disarray that was to follow swiftly upon its ending.

The first move, agreed by the Two Davids, was to go for the Tories in the hope of sidelining Labour. Its next move, after a tactical reappraisal, was to go for Labour in the hope of establishing itself as the plausible alternative force of opposition. Its third move was to proceed in contrary directions, Owen increasing his investment in coalition, Steel endeavouring to appeal to what he took to be the 'anti-Thatcher majority in the land'. Steel was not against coalition as such – he had spent most of his political life advocating it in one form or another – but he feared that every time Owen mentioned the word it signalled his readiness to do a deal with Thatcher and drove the anti-Thatcher majority into Kinnock's arms. But Steel, as always, was under pressure from his party and may have had in mind the difficulties he might encounter after the election. As the campaign entered the last week he was convinced that, in any case, Mrs Thatcher was on her way to victory.[5] For Owen this was no time for playing party politics or for prissy Liberal inhibitions: the only credible tactic that remained was to persuade voters that the Alliance could yet hold the balance of power and for that reason would not be a waste of a vote.

The campaign ended with the two of them defiantly plugging their respective lines to their travelling press corps, openly contradicting each other in radio and television interviews. The Two Davids Act had fallen apart, on stage and in the dressing room. It had been devised as the surrogate for a single party or a single leadership: the Two Davids would become inseparable, be seen to go together like eggs and bacon, become a national institution like Morecambe and Wise. Now they were scarcely on speaking terms. They had taken to avoiding each other at the morning press conference. On 3 June, after another public disagreement about who would coalesce with whom, they met in Nottingham but refused to get into the same car together. For Owen, Steel had become 'that moralising little Scottish creep'. Steel, perhaps, consoled himself with the thought that the aftermath of the election would soon show who was in whose pocket.

For Steel had had a bad campaign. He blamed that to a large extent on Owen, if not on Owen personally then on his insistence on the dual leadership. In a report to the officers of his own party he said, 'I do believe that if either David Owen or I had been running the campaign as single leaders it would have had a sharper image and strategy.' But it was not only that; the requirement to work together had brought out something of the worst in both of them: Steel had appeared before his own people at the joint campaign headquarters as a man lacking in decision and resolve, devious and slippery, who would say one thing and do another, for whom ten minutes was apparently a long time in politics. Owen's manner did not endear him to the campaign staff but few could remain in doubt as to which was the bigger man of the two. *Spitting Image* was too near the knuckle.

The minute the election was over Liberal MP Paddy Ashdown made remarks which were taken – by Steel at least – to mark the opening of a succession race in the Liberal Party. Steel moved swiftly to pre-empt and, having informed Owen that he intended to lay before his party officers on Tuesday a memorandum which would set out the options as he saw them, ten minutes later leaked it to the BBC. Steel's options amounted to 'merger – or else!' Roy Jenkins had already written in that day's *Sunday Times*: 'there is no alternative to a merger if the Alliance is to have a serious future.' On the Monday it became known that Steel would be a candidate to lead the new party which he had even given a name – 'Liberal Democratic Alliance'.

The SDP became engulfed in civil war. All the bitterness and hatred and jealousy which its failure had created now burst forth in violent recrimination. Owen stood out to the last, as he had said he would. He would not lead a merged party, he would not join a merged party. He and his followers would remain the true Social Democrats, let those who wanted to desert to the Liberals do so. He endeavoured to put an ideological gloss on his stand – a merged party would not uphold Britain's nuclear defences, would not remain true to the social market philosophy – but the struggle was not about policy but power. It was also about David Owen. The assassins were closing upon him as he had long known they would. Merger had been sharpened by his rivals as the dagger that would finish him. It was almost as if he could not wait to assist them, Brutus to his own Caesar. A small band of devoted disciples huddled around him, some egging him on, others seeking to restrain him. By a series of petulant and uncompromising moves he ensured a fatal splitting of his party and condemned himself to the wilderness. For although he spoke of 'multi-party politics' as the 'New Politics' the old British electoral system remained in force. It was hostile to a third party. The prospects for a fourth were negligible. But it was Owen who precipitated a ballot of the membership on merger. It went against him – by a comfortable 57·4 per cent to 42·6 per cent. On 6 August 1987 David Owen resigned as leader of the SDP. A month later it was he who forced the issue: 'amicable' split or breakaway. His conference turned him down. There had been an air of inevitability about these proceedings. Owen was destined, it seemed, to become a leader without a party.

He had been the second most dominant figure of the Thatcher era. To have achieved that reputation was remarkable for the leader of a party of half a dozen struggling for survival in the hostile conditions of the British two-party system. Yet by some triumph of the will, and with an energy of conviction comparable only to hers, he had played in her league as no one else had done or begun to do.

The macho bit was in part the product of his character and temperament but was also in part the rôle he was required to play as the leader of a party that was scarcely a party. He did believe, it would seem, in the virility principle, for he was constantly talking about 'guts' and 'balls' and, searching for words, had invented the concept of 'fudge and mudge'. Some by temperament prefer to regard politics as the 'art of the possible', some are more interested in the impossible. But there was nothing inhuman about Owen, not at all; it was in the way of an actor of genius that he actually became the part he had been cast to play, that of Man of Destiny. Unfortunately the same urges, or demiurges, which can lead a man to the pinnacles of power and fame lead also to the wilderness.

Impatience was one of his energies. Cambridge had not interested him at all; he had been too impatient to get on with it. He had done his medicine and been a houseman at St Thomas's (across the river from Westminster) and was in Parliament by the time he was twenty-eight. Callaghan had jumped him up to Foreign Secretary at the age of thirty-eight. But by then he had already done a junior stint at the Ministry of Defence (Navy Minister) under Denis Healey and at the DHSS (Health Minister) under Barbara Castle. Either he had been lucky and had the jobs he had cared about or he had cared about the jobs he had had. One way or the other, experience stuck hard to him as he went.

To be made Foreign Secretary at the age of thirty-eight, quite suddenly, when not even in the Cabinet, had been a shattering experience, exhilarating and wonderful but at the same time frightening. Almost his first task had been to accompany Callaghan to Washington on a visit to the Jimmy Carter White House. Nothing could have been more glamorising. He was glamorised; he was also fawned upon and importuned like a pop star. Youth, good looks, the allure of his life, and the women's magazine romance of it all brought him fame far greater than usually attached to the office of the Foreign Secretary – take Sir Geoffrey Howe for example. There had been nothing like Owen since Curzon or the young Eden. Yet he was not at all at home in the job and not a success. The Foreign Office is the Rolls-Royce of departments. Some feel at home in it, some do not. It knows how to make a passable Foreign Secretary out of a mule and could have made an Eden out of Owen; but he would not let it or did not know how to. Instead, he was chippy; a monoglot in the presence of clever multilinguists, he took pleasure in writing 'balls' on their elegant despatches and in describing his senior officials as 'second class minds'. Unsureness of himself was an aspect of the arrogant manner.

Youth, fame and glamour were to be among his chief allies as the Man of Destiny. 'The whole key to success for any initiative', he wrote in a pre-launch memo to the SDP, 'is that it is new, different, young and fresh looking. For every 60-year-old establishment figure there must be a late thirties/early forties radical thinker . . .' He was writing a job description for himself. The new party was being set up by disappointed renegades, has-beens; the high-flying doctor was its tomorrow's man.

It was lucky for him that when the new party was launched neither Roy Jenkins nor Shirley Williams was in Parliament. He was *de facto* the parliamentary leader from the outset and the Falklands debates had given him the chance to impose himself upon the House as a patriotic statesman. Although a poor speaker, he made himself into a formidable parliamentary performer at Question Time. After 1983 he was more effective as a one-man Opposition than Kinnock with the whole of the Labour Party behind him. The Tories feared him and respected him. The Prime Minister was alleged to have said that she wished that she was a football manager for then she 'could have sold Heseltine and bought Owen'.

He was ubiquitous on television. One of his chief political talents was the swiftness and sureness of his judgments. He was always up with the game, covering a wide range of issues. All this was done with minimal back-up. He installed a Press Association tape machine in his office and won public attention by his quick reactions to events. For example, when the young policewoman, Yvonne Fletcher, was murdered by a Libyan gunman in St James's Square it was Owen who broke the news to the 'World at One'.

He was the first politician to take the measure of the Thatcher Revolution. He saw that the world would never be the same again and tried to stake out positions for his party that would give it a place in the future. His colleagues in contrast seemed determined to cling to the past, to offer – as Ralf Dahrendorf had put it – 'a better yesterday'. Owen was not interested in putting that Humpty together again. He was trying to shift the political argument on to new ground, reaching out for something more than watered-down Labourism or boned up Liberalism. But what exactly was it? The trouble was that what Owen called 'social democracy' had also failed, also belonged to the past. Thatcher's were the only 'new politics' on offer for the moment. It was she who prefigured the post-socialist society, or half of it – the other half was still a vacant space.

The Alliance's election campaign had exposed not only a lack of strategy but something much more basic. It had exposed to the protagonists their own lack of real purpose and conviction. What were they offering? What exactly was their alternative? What was the nature of their project? Why were they there? It had been a noble enterprise at the beginning. A stand had been taken for something open and democratic which would tackle the problems of the country in a decent and moderate spirit. Yet in some way the enterprise had brought out the worst in them all, turned them against each other, and destroyed four good careers. Here was the stuff of tragedy. Faced with the horror of where they were, of the hollowness of their cause, most could not wait to retreat into the familiar past. Owen set off alone into the unknown future.

The SDP had been a child of the crisis of ungovernability. Reform of the political system had been its distinctive remedy for Britain's economic ills. It had diagnosed them as primarily systemic and incapable of cure under the existing two-party regime. There were plenty of sensible things to be done but no way of doing them for as long as Britain, uniquely in Western Europe, persisted with her winner-take-all adversarial politics.

But the new party had never been rooted in an interest in the land. Nor had the modern Liberal Party. There was no foundation for it comparable to the mercantile middle classes on which Peel attempted to reset a modern Conservative Party and Gladstone succeeded in founding his new Liberal Party. There was nothing comparable to the newly enfranchised and trade unionised working classes on which the Labour Party had based its rise to power. The nearest the SDP had come to representing such an interest was its support among the university-educated salariat. It had achieved a foothold but scarcely a base. Nor was there a great issue capable of forging a realignment of the parties – nothing comparable to the franchise, Ireland or tariff reform. Political reform had been the nearest to it but the SDP had aroused more interest as a critic of the system – 'an anti-party party' as Roy Jenkins was to put it – than it had done with its calls for proportional representation and constitutional reform.

The SDP had set out to be a new left-of-centre party but had never succeeded in attracting significant support in the Labour parts of Britain. It had become, like the Liberals, another southern-based middle class party. The Volvo was no joke. You might meet a better class of person than with the Liberals but fewer of them. The SDP lacked troops. What it did have was an officer corps. What had been attempted was, in effect, a *coup*. The Limehouse Declaration was an invitation to the electorate to overthrow the system. If it was to be done like that it would have to happen quickly, before the novelty of the new party wore off and before the wasted-vote argument took hold again.

It was this attempted coup that failed finally in 1987. In truth it had already failed in 1983. The crisis of governability had passed, at least for the time being. The mood of the country had changed. Thatcherism had come to pass. The Labour Party had refused to leave the stage. Too weak to win power it remained too strong to be removed from the scene. Meanwhile, the argument was conducted on Mrs Thatcher's terms. The centre was no longer as vacant as it had been in 1981. The SDP broke up on the rock of her present invincibility. It was she not they who had shattered the mould. They now lay scattered among the pieces.

So was the two-party system now restored? Not quite; the two-and-a-half party system perhaps. In the two-and-a-half party system the Liberal Party plays an essential role as mid-term safety valve. In exchange for performing this useful function its Right Honourable leader is permitted to stand at the Cenotaph once a year, to attend State banquets at Buckingham Palace and rise in the House to express his condolences on the death of the president of the Seychelles, or whoever. In the leader of the Liberal Party are combined, as Bagehot would have spotted, both 'dignified' and 'efficient' functions. But the Alliance with the SDP for a while had got everybody dancing to the three-party tune. 'Three-party politics are here to stay' became a conventional cliché of the times. In bringing this about the Alliance after 1983 had been helped by opinion polls which consistently suggested the possibility, if not probability, of a hung Parliament. The enterprise had had a certain credibility therefore. The Liberals? Or their new, augmented Alliance Party or whatever it would call itself? The Liberals are the Liberals are the Liberals. Nevertheless, there were still 7 million voters in the country, getting on for a quarter of those who had voted, who had declared for 'neither of the above'. They also were unlikely to go away.

16

Permanent Revolution?

The Thatcher Revolution? What revolution? Is it permanent? Britain's decline, is it halted or merely slowed for a while? The Old Order gone for ever? One consensus smashed, a new consensus formed? Socialism dead? Can it be true that we have lived in such exciting times?

Think back for a moment to where we were on page one. That world of the 1970s seems an age away. The Winter of Discontent, the economy under surveillance by the IMF, Tony Benn, Jack Jones (Jack who?) more powerful than the Prime Minister, today we have to pinch ourselves to be sure that we were not dreaming these things. And who then could have supposed that with three million unemployed – more than two-and-a-half times its level in 1979 – Margaret Thatcher would be re-elected and re-elected again? Who would have predicted that the frontiers of the State would have been rolled back to the tune of £20 billions' worth of assets with some 600,000 employees transferred from the public to the private sector? Who then would have predicted that the government could withstand for more than a year a strike in the coalfields and inflict unconditional surrender upon Arthur Scargill? Who would have believed that the trade unions would be marginalised to the extent that by 1987 only 1 per cent of voters would consider trade union power to be the chief issue facing the country, when in May 1979 73 per cent of people had believed this to be so? And who would have supposed that a million council tenants would have purchased their homes or one in five of the population become shareholders? Or that the Labour Party would split and a new party rise and fall in so brief a time? Who in 1979 would have expected that Margaret Thatcher would be Prime Minister at all in 1987 let alone Prime Minister supreme?

The curbing of trade union power is the most singular of her achievements. It was done not only by the three successive Acts of Parliament but by everything else that comes under the head of 'Thatcherism' – high unemployment, sound money, reduced income taxes, privatisation, the extensions of ownership. The world in which trade unionism had prospered and grown powerful was changed around it. The most important of the Acts was that of 1984 because its provision for secret ballots before a strike and for the election of union executives enabled the other changes which were taking place in society to be reflected in the democratic preferences of union members. In this way the trade unions were made more representative institutions. But at the same time they became less important. Before long we may look back and wonder how it was that so much energy and anger went into the institutionalisation of work-place conflict and so little into the enlargement of the rights of the citizen in his and her other capacities as consumer, tenant, parent, or patient.

Whereas trade union reform had been high on the new government's list of priorities in 1979, privatisation was not. It rated four paragraphs tucked away in the Manifesto. Yet it became the centrepiece of the Thatcher Revolution in its second phase. This not because the selling off of State monopolies to become private monopolies changed anything very much for the consumers of gas or telephone services but because privatisation became synonymous with popular ownership. The first privatisations were motivated primarily by considerations of efficiency. It was an article of Thatcherite faith that private enterprise could run things better than the State. It was not until the Telecom sale that revenue-raising and popular ownership became the chief considerations. Here was a Tory government practically giving money away. Yet the great majority of those who bought shares did not take the quick profits available but remained shareholders. In the case of British Telecom 2·2 million people bought shares originally (half of them for the first time in their lives) but in 1987 the company had 1·7 million shareholders. In the case of British Gas there were 4·5 million original buyers, 4 million shareholders in 1987. Between 1979 and 1987 the proportion of the population owning shares increased from 7 to 20 per cent and, if further privatisations take place as planned, could by 1992 become the highest in the world, exceeding the 26 per cent of Americans.

As with the sale of council houses, privatisation appears to have had a symbolic impact far greater than the aggregate effects of wider ownership. The sales of British Gas and British Telecom were highly publicised events which served as powerful earnests of the idea that Thatcherism stood for owning things while socialism did not. Conservatives had talked about this for long enough but had got on with owning most of the property and wealth themselves, or so it seemed to those who had none. Moreover, ownership is an idea that permeates as assets increase in value. In the West Midlands at the time of the 1987 General Election were families who, having bought at a discount for, say, £8,000 council houses valued at, say, £12,000 in 1982, knew of similar houses which had changed hands for over £20,000 at current prices. It was not just a case of a garden path to call your own, here was financial security among the working classes of a kind known previously only to the middle classes. Here was something to hold on to and hand on to children; and as children who were already buying their own houses on mortgage inherited houses or shares of houses from their parents, so wealth – capital! – would accumulate.

On coming to power Margaret Thatcher was faced with a prospect of continuing decline more alarming than even she had realised. Relative decline – as the Bank of England at that time had warned – could very easily have become an absolute decline. She pleaded for extra time. 'One did not realise the extent to which we had the most colossal overmanning and inefficiency.' She had originally hoped for ten years in which to turn the country round. Towards the end of her first term of office she began to talk about the need for a third. More recently she has mooted a fourth.

The first two years of her first administration can be seen as a salutary, short sharp shock to a nation on the slide, or as the dogmatic vandalisation of the manufacturing base. Which it was will depend upon whether the cultural or attitudinal changes brought about by that treatment will in the longer term outweigh the short-term loss of output and capacity. What can be said is that the government did not for one moment plan to drive unemployment first above two million and, then, above three, nor anticipate that unemployment at that sort of level would become a chronic condition. The assessment of the Thatcher government's economic record, as we have seen in Chapter 11, depends greatly upon whether the reckoning is done from day one or from the end of the 1980–1 recession. The latter calculation chimes better with anecdotal evidence which suggests that some kind of shift in attitudes did occur and that the economy is on a more virtuous path than for many years. This is a crucial judgment because another five years of sustained export-led and investment-led non-inflationary growth could turn an impressive recovery into a remarkable transformation.

We should not forget that oil came gushing to the rescue at the moment of her coming to power. The Thatcher age will have co-incided almost exactly with the providential boon of the North Sea. Indeed, it is impossible exactly to disentangle the positive (or negative) effects of 'Thatcherism' from changes which were already in train. Unemployment was already rising when she came to power, the trend towards a greater inequality of income already well established,[1] and the new underclass of the cities was already growing. The oil crisis of 1973 had accelerated the shift away from the old nineteenth-century centres of manufacturing and of population from inner city to suburbia, and from north to south, and in the process – in A. H. Halsey's words – 'a pattern has emerged of a more unequal society as between a majority in secure attachment to a still prosperous country and a minority in marginal economic and social conditions, the former moving into the suburban locations of the newer economy of a "green and pleasant land", the latter tending to be trapped into the old provincial cities and their displaced fragments of peripheral council housing estates.'[2]

We call this 'Mrs Thatcher's Britain' but it is not a Britain of her making. What is described here is not a dislocation brought about by 'Thatcherism'. However, the process of polarisation between the People and the Underclass (Disraeli's 'Two Nations', remember, were the 'Privileged' and the 'People') was exacerbated by policies designed to speed the adjustment rather than to soften its economic and social pains. It was a tougher regime she ushered in and she presided over some of its consequences, it may be thought, with too great an equanimity.

This polarisation was qualitative as well as quantitative. The Britain of the peripheral council estates, planning disasters on a vast scale, and of the declining inner city areas has become increasingly another country. 'This is not simply inequality of income and living standards between different areas. It is the emergence of two entirely different socio-economic systems. In the rest of the nation there is a market economy. On the outer estates there is a local economy which subsists entirely on State provision and administrative fiat.'[3] Across the country there were in 1987 some 6 million local authority tenants, not all of them of course in these abandoned ghettoes; but 2 million of them were claiming supplementary benefit, 1 million were retired, and some 300,000 were one-parent families. Only 35 per cent of the heads of these households were employed, compared with 70 per cent of owner-occupiers. Half of the long-term unemployed were the inhabitants of council estates where the unemployment rate was on average 25 per cent; among home owners it was 4 per cent.[4] The cost of living rose considerably faster for council house tenants, while their incomes were rising less rapidly. Higher income families with tax-relieved mortgages did considerably better under the Thatcher governments.

If Supplementary Benefit is taken as the poverty line, more than 8 million people, 17 per cent of the population, were living on or below it in 1987, 33 per cent more than in 1979. They included more than 2 million children, 16 per cent of all children, an increase of 72 per cent since 1979. Unemployment and the growth of one-parent families were the chief causes of these steep increases. The government cannot be blamed for the latter trend, which was sharply upwards throughout the 1970s, but the steepest increase in the numbers of the poor took place between 1979 and 1981 – the years of recession and the first experiment in Thatcherism. The number of families with children in poverty rose by 580,000 to 1,171,000.[5]

This poverty, although by no means exclusive to inner city areas, is heavily concentrated in them as they are dragged down by multiple deprivation while those who are able move out to join the rest of Britain. The report of the Archbishop of Canterbury's Commission on the Urban Priority Areas, *Faith in the City*, painted Britain in 1986 as 'an elaborate picture of inequality': 'In the foreground appear the shabby streets, neglected houses and sordid demolition sites of the inner city, in the middle the vandalised public spaces of the peripheral estates, while in the background are the green and wooded suburbs of middle Britain.' As for the city, the report went on, it remained 'part magnet to the disadvantaged newcomer, part prison to the unskilled, the disabled, and the dispirited, part springboard for the ambitious and vigorous who find escape to suburbia, and part protection for enclaves of affluence.'[6] In other words, the inner city is a paradigm of Thatcherite Britain.

All revolutions are permanent revolutions in the sense that when they lose momentum they cease to be revolutions. Plainly the Thatcher Revolution has yet to run its course. To what degree its achievements, or its consequences good and bad, will prove permanent is another question. We may be certain that 'Thatcherism' will not reign for ever and still less will Mrs Thatcher. The question is whether subsequent governments will be obliged to come to terms with her New Order, as the Tories came to terms with the post-war order in 1951, and whether 1979 was a year like 1906 and 1945 in which British politics became set in a new pattern.

For the first time since 1964 one government will have been in power for more than a decade pursuing a broadly consistent strategy. Electoral volatility persists between elections but the rapid succession of weak or failed governments has given way to a continuity of strong government. Moreover, there is today less prospect than at any time in the post-war period of what has been done being quickly undone. The Thatcher Revolution is entrenched in several ways. It is entrenched in a diffusion of private ownership to the point at which nationalisation (except on a casualty basis) has ceased to be practical politics for any party aspiring to election. It is entrenched in the international financial system which makes it virtually impossible for a government to reimpose exchange controls. This effectively excludes the practice of socialism in one country and would make difficult even the practice of Keynesianism in one country. The diminution of trade union power is not yet so permanent in the eyes of the TUC – or, in this matter, its servant the Labour Party – but with the passing of time it will become increasingly difficult, and eventually impossible, to reinstate it as the Fifth Estate. What is more, while the trade union movement looks to a Labour government to restore it to power a Labour government can no longer rely upon trade union members to elect it to power. That is a profound change.

As history books are written we shall become more aware of the continuities which lie behind what we call the Thatcher Revolution. Many of its features are prefigured in the politics of the post-war era which have been the story of Britain's struggle to adapt to lost power and reduced circumstances. The 'property-owning democracy' was a 1950s phrase of Anthony Eden's and it was the Edward Heath government which sold the first council houses to their tenants. Privatisation, or denationalisation, was not a new Tory theme. The steel industry has been denationalised and renationalised. Sound money was what Thorneycroft and Powell had resigned over in 1958. Denis Healey was Britain's first monetarist Chancellor. Successive attempts had been made to bring trade unions within the law, by Wilson and by Heath. It was James Callaghan who initiated the 'Great Debate' on educational standards. Yet it was Margaret Thatcher who had the will to do these things, to succeed where others had failed and to press forward where they had drawn back.

It was her ambition, she had declared, to 'kill' socialism. That had not before been made explicit. However, she from time to time gave somewhat conflicting versions of how this project was to be achieved. On occasions she has appeared to envisage herself as the agent of a realignment at the expense of the Labour Party, on other occasions she has spoken of the Labour Party itself abandoning socialism. In

1985, in her annual interview with the *Financial Times*, she explained how wrong she considered the SDP defectors had been; they should have remained within to fight to restore what she called 'the true old-fashioned Labour Party', the Labour Party of Gaitskell and Attlee. But by 1986 she appeared to regard the Labour Party as incorrigibly socialist and said, somewhat gnomically, to the *Financial Times*, 'I think you could get another realignment in British politics.' After another Tory victory? 'After two more victories.'[7] But whichever way it was to be, 'killing socialism' was her mission.

How far has she succeeded? It is not only in Britain, but across a large swathe of Western Europe, that for the first time in this century the governing classes no longer assume that socialism in some form is what history has in store. The initiative has passed and government is no longer the art of procrastination. At the same time, as I have argued, the socialist idea is on the wane and in Paris today, for the first time since the French Revolution, the intelligentsia has no left-wing project.[8] These are profound intellectual changes.

In more parochial British terms she has presided over a considerable, although far from complete, change in attitudes. Something remarkably close to the 'common ground' which Sir Keith Joseph spoke of in the 1970s has been established. Its assumptions are individualistic rather than collectivist, preferring private to State ownership, putting the rights of the member before the interests of the trade union, and sound money above the priming of the economy. But if this has the makings of a new consensus it does not yet extend to the Welfare State, where the assumption remains that the condition of the people is primarily the responsibility of the State and that health, social security and education are proper areas of public provision. In these regards the Thatcher Revolution is far from complete or total. However, if socialism is taken to be at heart a doctrine concerning production and ownership it would seem to be pretty effectively dead in Mrs Thatcher's Britain.

The Labour Party is another matter, although for the time being she has dished it electorally – or it has dished itself. Between 1979 and 1987 she constructed a new majority (or, strictly, a new plurality) in the land, an anti-socialist coalition involving the prosperous working classes of the south and Midlands. This is what makes 1979 a year to go down with 1906 and 1945. But at the same time she had provided no institutional foundations for her counter-revolution. By reforming the voting system she could, if she wished, cast her anti-socialist counter-revolution in cement. But electoral reform at the same time would bring an end to the Thatcher revolution. She is not the sort of player to leave the tables and cash in her chips. Yet for as long as Britain's electoral system remains Labour *can* win and if Labour is what she means by 'socialism' her revolution cannot be secure. The rise and fall of the SDP, furthermore, suggests that the project of a moderate realignment on the centre-left is forlorn for as long as the Labour Party retains a regional base strong enough to command some 200 seats in the House of Commons.

So what does she have in mind? The application of Thatcherism to the cities in order to destroy these last bastions of socialist Britain. She would show that the divided nation, which in the election had been blamed on callous Thatcherism, was the result not of capitalism but of callous socialism, of the dependency which it engendered in people, of the mismanagement and inefficiency which was endemic in that whole collectivist nexus of town hall bureaucracy and trade unionism. It was they who were responsible for the de-education of people's children in the schools, they who spent money on redundant teachers which could have been spent on more books or repainted walls. It was they who presided over those disgraceful estates, seeping with damp and creeping with mould, where nothing ever worked or was repaired – littered, vandalised and plagued by violence.

She was motivated in this latest enterprise not by a change of heart, although stung by the things which were being said about her, but rather by a new determination to prove that what her enemies – with a hiss – called 'Thatcherism' was the moral and intellectual superior of what she – with a hiss – called 'socialism' and was as relevant to the cities as to the suburbs and the shires. By this means she would reinstate the Conservative Party in the great cities of the north. The south would move north. Tory Britain would invade and conquer Labour Britain. Her revolution would be complete. Her realignment would be accomplished.

This breathtaking project was hit upon, as with privatisation, almost by accident. It had grown out of narrower preoccupations. In education, for example, her chief animus was exasperation with left-wing authorities who permitted, or encouraged, their teachers to fill the heads of children with pernicious propaganda and drivel. This, combined with her hankering after the education voucher, the pet scheme of the Thatcherite 'Think Tanks' for applying market economics to education, resulted in the scheme to establish new independent schools within the State system, especially in the cities. 'In inner cities,' she said on television during the election, 'I think the grammar school was the ladder from the bottom, however far one wished to climb, for many a young person that would never have had it . . .';

and she added, 'I would like to see more because, if you look at the House of Commons, many of us have got there through a grammar school system.'[9] Was this, the memory of her own grammar school and what it had done for her, the limit of her vision of the 'enabling society'? Perhaps the establishment of high quality independent schools as free ladders of opportunity would catch the imagination of the working classes as had done the sale of council houses and shares in British Gas and British Telecom. Perhaps, in the third phase of the Thatcher revolution, it would take on a symbolic significance going far beyond the number of the schools themselves. But the likely scale of the scheme was hardly commensurate with the scale of Britain's educational neglect. Nor was it obvious that what might be appropriate in a few left-wing multi-racial boroughs was relevant to the educational needs of the great majority of authorities. Loony-Left London was scarcely the best perspective from which to address the problem of the Two Nations of Britain.

Resources on a great scale would be necessary to repair the ravages of Britain's cities and make good the deficiencies in education which lie at the heart of Britain's decline. For the social problem and the economic problem are at bottom the same. The social conditions in which people have been required to live have bred the ignorance and apathy with which the challenge of decline has been approached. To attribute these national shortcomings to Thatcherism or to the excesses of local socialism is equally to underestimate the nature and the scale of the challenge which remains. Eight years have been too short a time in which to rewrite the folk memories of industrial Britain or make much mark of any kind upon it. For the old centres of the Industrial Revolution, which had been the 'depressed areas' of the 1930s, in decline since Edwardian times, the shock of 1973 had meant but yet another chapter in a long book of painful adjustment.

The Thatcher years had seen the recovery of one Britain, not at the expense of the other but at the cost of its neglect. Sir Keith Joseph and education was the relevant parable to set against the romantic project for carrying the word of Thatcherism to the heathen of the cities. He had declared that 'monetarism is not enough'. He had seen clearly that education lay somewhere near the heart of Britain's decline. (Callaghan had drawn powerful attention to the crisis in his 'Great Debate' speech of 1976.) Joseph had drawn up radical plans but had refused to back them with resources. Time was lost and nothing was achieved. He had demonstrated that Thatcherism was not enough.

The contradiction here was fundamental. Mrs Thatcher was not averse to bending the spending targets in an election year. She was more a politician than an ideologue. Milton Friedman, no less, had complained that his doctrine was being invoked 'to cover anything that Mrs Thatcher at any time expressed as a desirable object of policy'.[10] Power was her game. She was fascinated by it in others (Reagan and Gorbachev), she accumulated it for herself, and determinedly denied it to her enemies (the unions, left-wing councils and the rest). But the scale of the resources required to regenerate the cities, reform the secondary school system and restore civilisation to the housing estates was at huge variance with the canons of her housekeeping finance. That is why it was an article of Thatcherite faith that 'money wasn't the answer'. It was the spirit of enterprise that was lacking in the cities, it was the drug of dependency that was holding them back. The problem was political, cultural, anything but financial. One Nation she believed, she *had* to believe, could be built on sound money.

That we shall see. But that will be the test. For with the aid of powerful symbols, supported by improvements in economic/performance and real increases in prosperity, the 'Thatcher Revolution' is, perhaps, half a revolution. It is a revolution in half of Britain. Whether it can be more than half a revolution must depend upon its ability to address the needs of the other half of Britain. This is not merely to apply a test of conscience but a standard of legitimacy. For Britain remains not only 'Two Nations' but in two minds, torn between the old welfare ideal and the new enterprise ideal, rejecting socialism but not yet at moral ease with the new order. Thatcherism mitigated by riot would be unlikely to endure.

Perhaps a natural state of equilibrium has been reached between a market-orientated economy and a State-provided welfare system, a new compromise between the spirit of acquisitiveness and the spirit of solidarity. If so the Thatcher Revolution will have run its course. For, in any case, time will strengthen the hand of the consolidators over the revolutionaries. During her second term of office 'Thatcherism' ceased to be an issue within the Conservative Party. Thatcher became the issue, *'that woman'*. For it was feared that by her style and manner, or by simply pressing on regardless, she might place at electoral jeopardy all that had been achieved and thereby betray her own revolution. Now, in her third term, that dilemma becomes doubly acute. For minds will turn to 'after Thatcher' as in France they did to *'après de Gaulle'*. What will she leave behind? A post-socialist Britain in some form, for – as I have tried to show throughout – Margaret Thatcher was as much a consequence as a cause of the collapse of the *ancien régime*, a product of the ending of the socialist era. She was Britain's first post-socialist Prime Minister.

The character of the post-socialist society we may only glimpse. Its policies, perhaps, will be less to do with producers and more to do with consumers. They will be less centred on the place of work and more centred on the neighbourhood, the school, and places of leisure. We shall learn to think more in terms of citizens and speak less often about 'the workers'. The post-socialist society will be characterised by a majority of haves over have-nots. It will be a two-thirds, one-third society. For a society to see itself in this new way, not as a society of 'them' and 'us' but as a society in which most of 'us' are part of 'them' represents a profound change. And when it is realised that not only the poor but the 'working class' are political minorities it may become more feasible to build new coalitions of interest or conscience around issues of justice and liberty. For issues will begin to transcend class in the way that class previously transcended issues.

The counter-revolution of collectivist expectations of the Thatcher years may have excited other, individualistic expectations, for more liberty and greater equality. For, as even the Labour Party has begun to realise, these values are not exclusive to socialism and do not have to be cast in a collectivist mode. Politics is usually about what people want, what they want for themselves and their families, what they want for their society and their country. Mrs Thatcher has excited expectations of a certain kind. She had taught more people to want to own their homes, to want to own a stake in things, to want a better chance for their children. To demean these as 'materialist', or even 'selfish', is to fail to understand the equality and freedom which material prosperity confers. But even with that important proviso 'Thatcherism' has been about something more than material advancement. She, more powerfully than anyone else, has articulated the moral doubts and yearnings of her age. For what people wanted, surely, was an end to decline, release from the corrosive sense of failure, a government which governed, and a country to begin to be proud of once again. The future may not be hers but she has set its agenda.

Notes

1 POST-WAR DISCONTENTS

1 Paul Addison, *The Road to 1945*, 1975, p.14.
2 Trade union legislation of 1906 and 1913 gave immunity to trades unions from civil actions for damages resulting from industrial disputes.
3 Anthony Sampson, *The Changing Anatomy of Britain*, 1982, p.37.
4 Philip Williams, *Hugh Gaitskell*, 1979, pp.313ff.
5 Philip Norton and Arthur Aughey, *Conservatives and Conservatism*, 1981, p.132.
6 C. A. R. Crosland, *The Future of Socialism*, 1956, pp.521–4.
7 Susan Crosland, *Tony Crosland*, 1982, p.13.
8 Ben Pimlott, *Hugh Dalton*, 1985, p.625.
9 C. A. R. Crosland, *Socialism Now*, 1974, p.75.
10 Aubrey Jones, *Britain's Economy*, 1985, p.99.
11 Peter Jenkins, *The Battle of Downing Street*, 1970.
12 Students led protests in the streets which resulted in violent clashes with the police.
13 A. H. Halsey, *Change in British Society*, 1986, p.40.
14 On 6 October 1973 – the Day of Atonement – Israel was attacked by Egypt across the Suez Canal and by Syria from the Golan Heights.
15 Norman St John Stevas, 'The Disappearing Consensus' in Anthony King (ed.), *Why is Britain Becoming Harder to Govern?*, 1976, pp.58–9.
16 Joel Barnett, *Inside the Treasury*, 1982, p.49.
17 Bernard Donoughue in A. King (ed.), *The British Prime Minister*, 1985, p.58.
18 Barnett, op.cit., p.23.
19 Susan Crosland, op.cit., p.376.
20 William Rodgers, 'Government under Stress. Britain's Winter of Discontent, 1979', *Political Quarterly*, vol.55, no.2, April–June 1984, p.173.
21 Ibid.

2 *THE POLITICS OF DECLINE*

1 Kenneth O. Morgan, *Labour in Power*, 1984, p.498.
2 Sidney Pollard, *The Wasting of the British Economy*, 1984, p.6.
3 Keith Smith, *The British Economic Crisis*, 1984, pp.193ff.
4 Peter Burke in *Daedalus*, Summer 1976, pp.142–3.
5 Carlo Cipolla, *The Economic Decline of Empires*, 1970, p.9.
6 J. H. Elliott, *Imperial Spain*, 1963, Penguin edition, p.380.
7 R. B. Haldane, quoted in E. Halévy, *History of the English People*, (Epilogue: 1895–1905), 1926. Pelican edition, 1939, p.13.
8 Michael Fores, 'Britain's Economic Growth and the 1970 Watershed', *Lloyd's Bank Review*, January 1971, p.32.
9 Correlli Barnett, *The Collapse of British Power*, 1972, *passim*.
10 E. J. Hobsbawm, *Industry and Empire*, 1968, p.149.
11 N. F. R. Crafts, *British Economic Growth During The Industrial Revolution*, 1985, pp.155ff.
12 Fores, op.cit., p.39.
13 G. C. Allen, *The British Disease*, 1979, p.43.
14 E. Halévy, op.cit., pp.42–3.
15 Ibid., pp.44–5.
16 Ibid., p.42.
17 Hobsbawm, op.cit., p.161.
18 Norman Stone, *Europe Transformed*, 1983, p.18.
19 Barnett, op.cit., pp.94, 109.
20 W. E. H. Lecky, the Liberal historian, quoted in W. O. Lester Smith, *The Government of Education*, 1985, p.81.
21 Wynne Godley in Wilfred Beckerman (ed.), *Slow Growth in Britain*, 1979, p.228.
22 Roger Bacon and Walter Eltis, *Britain's Economic Problems: Too Few Producers*, 1976, p.5.
23 Ibid. p.19.
24 Cipolla, op.cit., p.1.
25 C. P. Snow, *Two Cultures*, and *A Second Look*, his lecture of 1959.
26 Barbara Castle, *Diaries*, 1980, pp.219–24.
27 'The United Kingdom in 1980', *The Hudson Report*, 1974, p.1.
28 *The Economist*, 2 June 1979.
29 Martin Wiener, *English Culture and the Decline of the Industrial Spirit, 1850–1980*, 1981, pp.157ff.
30 Mancur Olson, *The Rise and Decline of Nations*, 1982, p.90.
31 Elliott, op.cit., p.382.
32 See Ronald Dore, *The Origins of National Diversity in Industrial Relations*, 1973.
33 Richard Caves and Lawrence Krause (eds), *Britain's Economic Performance*, 1980, pp.19, 185.

3 *CONSENSUS OR CONVICTION POLITICS?*

1 Butler lowered tax thresholds and slashed food subsidies. His Budget inaugurated the gradual ending of the austerities imposed during the War and by the 1945–51 Labour government.
2 In 1970 Edward Heath and the Conservative 'Shadow' Cabinet met for a weekend at the Selsdon Park Hotel, Croydon, where they drew up a programme of measures which were generally regarded as a Right-wing departure from the post-war consensus.
3 Eric Hobsbawm, *The Forward March of Labour Halted?*, 1981, p.78.
4 Tony Benn, *Arguments for Socialism*, 1979, p.16.
5 Ibid., pp.163–4.
6 *The New Politics: A Socialist Reconnaissance*, Fabian Tract 402, 1970, pp.16–17.
7 Barbara Castle, *The Castle Diaries, 1974–76*, 1980, p.414.
8 Arthur Marwick, *British Society Since 1945*, 1982, p.182.
9 Douglas Hurd, *An End to Promises*, 1977, p.142.
10 George Gardiner, *Margaret Thatcher*, 1975, pp.159–60.
11 Sir Keith Joseph's speeches at this time are collected in *Stranded on the Middle Ground*, Centre for Policy Studies, 1976.
12 Television interview, 1977, quoted in Trevor Russel, *The Tory Party*, 1978, p.29.
13 Ian Gilmour, *Inside Right*, 1977, p.96.

4 *A MORAL ISSUE*

1 Speaking on 'Christianity in Politics', 30 March 1978.
2 Mrs Thatcher, to the Conservative Party conference in Brighton, 1976.
3 Quoted in Trevor Russel, *The Tory Party*, 1978, p.107.
4 Geoffrey Pearson, *Hooligan*, 1983, pp.207, 212.
5 Robert Hewison, *Art and Society in the Sixties*, 1986, pp.xv–xvii.
6 Quoted, ibid., p.297.
7 Quoted with approval by Stokely Carmichael in David Cooper (ed.), *The Dialectics of Liberation*, 1967, p.134.
8 Marcuse in ibid., pp.187–9.
9 The councillors had refused to raise rents. Councillors who fail to discharge their financial responsibilities can be made to pay any shortfall out of their own pockets.
10 Pearson, op.cit., p.210.
11 A. H. Halsey, *Change in British Society*, 1986, p.113.
12 The Black Papers were occasional pamphlets by 'New Right' educationalists opposed to the trend towards comprehensive secondary education.
13 Arthur Marwick, *British Society Since 1945*, 1982, p.128; Halsey, op.cit., p.60.

5 *UNCONVENTIONAL WISDOM*

1 Lord Harris of High Cross, founder of the Institute of Economic Affairs.
2 *Listener*, 26 October 1978.
3 Allan Mayer, *Madam Prime Minister*, 1979, p.43.
4 Ibid.
5 Ibid., p.29.
6 8 oz. = 227 grammes, 2 oz. = 57 grammes. 1s. 2d. would today be 6p., but of course prices were lower in the 1940s.
7 According to her then Permanent Secretary, Sir William Pile, in Hugo Young and Anne Sloman, *The Thatcher Phenomenon*, 1986, p.26. Macleod became Chancellor of the Exchequer in June 1970, when she became Secretary of State for Education, but he died within months.
8 David Butler and Dennis Kavanagh, *The British General Election of 1979*, 1980, pp.339–40.
9 Reference to 'Selsdon Man' was made by Harold Wilson as a joke after Edward Heath's Selsdon Park conference, see Chapter 3, note 2.
10 Stuart Hall and Martin Jacques (eds), *The Politics of Thatcherism*, 1983, pp.25–6.
11 Butler and Kavanagh, op.cit., p.350.
12 Philip Norton and Arthur Aughey, *Conservatives and Conservatism*, 1981, pp.168–9.
13 Ibid., p.175.
14 Samuel Beer, *Britain Against Itself*, 1982, pp.107ff.
15 Ivor Crewe in Dennis Kavanagh (ed.), *The Politics of the Labour Party*, 1982, p.10.
16 Quoted in Norton and Aughey, op.cit., p.181.
17 Crewe in Kavanagh, op.cit., pp.9–45.
18 Butler and Kavanagh, op.cit., p.350; Crewe in Kavanagh, op.cit., pp.10–12.
19 John Curtice and Michael Steed in Butler and Kavanagh, op.cit., pp.394ff; Norton and Aughey, op.cit., p.186.
20 The SDP (Social Democrats) was formed after a breakaway from the Labour Party in early 1981. Later that year it entered into electoral alliance with the Liberal Party.
21 Anthony Heath, Roger Jowell and John Curtice, *How Britain Votes*, 1985, pp.74–5.
22 Robert Blake, *The Conservative Party from Peel to Thatcher*, 1985, p.338.
23 Ian Gilmour, *Inside Right*, 1977, p.121.
24 Clause 4, part iv, of the Labour Party constitution is regarded by those on the Left of the party as its *raison d'être* and as the true undiluted socialist objective: 'To secure for the workers by hand or by brain the full fruits of their industry and the most equitable distribution thereof that may be possible upon the basis of the common ownership of the means of production, distribution and exchange, and the best obtainable system of popular administration and control of each industry and service.'

25 Ian Gilmour, speech at Amersham, Bucks, 30 January 1975; Gilmour, *Inside Right*, 1977, pp.131, 142–3, 257.
26 Alan Walters, *Challenging Complacency: A First-Hand Look at the Government's Experience*, 1983, p.9.
27 Jock Bruce-Gardyne, *Mrs Thatcher's First Administration*, 1984, p.99.

6 *MOVING LEFT*

1 *Determinism* is the doctrine that human action is not free but necessarily determined by motives which are regarded as external forces acting upon the will. *Sectionalism* confines interests to a narrow sphere with undue accentuation of economic, social and political distinctions. *Economism* was originally used disparagingly to describe the less dogmatic trend of the Russian Social Democratic Party in the 1890s and 1900s. There were two main trends, the first maintaining that the worker's task was to fight for economic gains while politically supporting the constitutional movement of the Liberal bourgeoisie. The other emphasised that policy should be dictated to the party by the workers.
2 Eric Hobsbawm et al., *The Forward March of Labour Halted?*, 1981, p.18.
3 Royden Harrison in Hobsbawm, op.cit., p.54.
4 David and Maurice Kogan, *The Battle for the Labour Party*, 2nd edition, 1983, p.26.
5 Richard Crossman, introduction to Bagehot, *The English Constitution*, Fontana edition, 1963, pp.41–2.
6 Barry Hindness, *The Decline of Working-Class Politics*, 1971, p.161.
7 Quoted in ibid.
8 Hobsbawm, op.cit., p.169.
9 Paul Whitely, *The Labour Party in Crisis*, 1983, p.55.
10 Ibid.
11 Quoted in Hindness, op.cit., p.34.
12 Anthony Heath, Roger Jowell and John Curtice, *How Britain Votes*, 1985, p.36.
13 Ivor Crewe in Dennis Kavanagh (ed.) *The Politics of the Labour Party*, 1982, p.20.
14 *Political Studies*, March 1981, p.80.
15 Austin Mitchell, *Can Labour Win Again?*, 1979, p.10.
16 Set up at the 1979 conference to inquire into the future constitutional reforms, namely the election of the Leader and the drafting of the Manifesto.
17 Robert Harris, *The Making of Neil Kinnock*, 1984, p.139.
18 A popular uprising in 1381 led by Wat Tyler.
19 Susan Crosland, *Tony Crosland*, 1982, p.52.
20 The Department of Energy, where Benn was made Secretary of State, was not quite a power station but the nearest thing. It is situated by the Thames at Millbank.

21 Kogan and Kogan, op.cit., p.114.
22 Benn, *Arguments for Socialism*, introduction to the Penguin edition, p.19.
23 Harris, op.cit., p.156.

7 *THE BIRTH OF THE SOCIAL DEMOCRATS*

1 Orpington was the archetypal commuter suburb. The first in an intermittent series of spectacular by-election victories by the Liberal Party occurred there in 1962.
2 David Butler, *Coalitions in British Politics*, 1978, p.114.
3 *Guardian*, 26 July 1965.
4 The *Manchester Guardian*, 2 February 1929.
5 Jo Grimond, *Memoirs*, 1979, p.216.
6 The Representation of the People Act 1867 extended the borough franchise in England and Wales to householders subject to a one-year residential qualification and to the payment of rates. Lodgers who had lived for a year or more in lodgings worth £10 per year were also enfranchised. In the counties the franchise was extended to those occupying land worth £12 a year and a property franchise was introduced for those with lands worth £5 a year.
7 Ronald Inglehart and Jacques-René Rabier, 'Political Realignment in Advanced Industrial Society', *Government and Opposition*, 21.4, Autumn 1986, p.471.
8 Peter York, 'Recycling the Sixties' in *Style Wars*, 1980.
9 Anthony Heath, Roger Jowell and John Curtice, *How Britain Votes*, 1985, p.59.
10 The Dimbleby Lecture, 'Home Thoughts from Abroad', is republished in Roy Jenkins, *Partnership of Principle*, 1985, p.9ff.
11 S. E. Finer (ed.), *Adversary Politics*, 1975, p.16.
12 Sir William Harcourt was Home Secretary 1880–5, Chancellor of the Exchequer three times, and Leader of the Liberal Party 1895–8.
13 Hugh Stephenson, *Claret and Chips*, 1982, p.30.
14 Sarah Barker Memorial Lecture, 8 September 1979.
15 Since this was written Owen has given his own account of these events in *David Owen, Personally Speaking to Kenneth Harris*, 1987.
16 David Owen, *Face the Future*, 1981, p.6.
17 Robert Skidelski in *Encounter*, April 1979, p.38.
18 Quoted in Ian Bradley, *Breaking the Mould*, 1981, p.132.
19 Giles and Lisanne Radice, *Socialists in the Recession*, 1986, p.16.
20 Owen, op.cit., abridged and revised edition, 1981.

8 *THE THATCHER FACTOR*

1 The figures were: Williams (SDP) 28,118 (49·1 per cent), Butcher (Con.) 22,829 (39·8 per cent), Backhouse (Lab.) 5,450 (9·5 per cent).

2 Alan Walters, *Britain's Economic Renaissance*, 1986, p.15.
3 See Chapter 11 below.
4 John Fforde, quoted in Jim Tomlinson, *Monetarism: Is There an Alternative?*, 1986, pp.24–5.
5 For assessment of the Thatcher record see Peter Riddell, *The Thatcher Government*, 1983, pp.69–79.
6 Quoted in Martin Holmes, *The First Thatcher Government, 1979–83*, 1985, p.209.
7 It is possible that the Alliance victory in the Glasgow, Hillhead by-election, at which Roy Jenkins was returned to Parliament, would have given a new boost to its fortunes. The Hillhead election was on 25 March, the Falklands were invaded on 2 April. In April Gallup showed the Alliance back in the lead: Cons. 31: Lab. 29: All. 37. The Task Force set sail and South Georgia was recaptured on 25 April. In May the Tories were at 41, Labour at 28, the Alliance at 29. The December–March figures are the best guide to the pre-war trend.
8 Alexander Haig, *Caveat*, 1984, p.266.
9 Ibid., p.265.
10 My impressions have been confirmed by David Sanders, Hugh Ward and David Marsh (with Tony Fletcher) in *British Journal of Political Science*, no. 17, 1987, pp.281–313. By a process of correlating the course of the government's popularity/unpopularity with macro-economic factors they conclude that the 'Falklands Factor' as such was fairly negligible – perhaps worth a temporary 3 per cent – and a chief cause of the government's reviving popularity, and the electoral victory in June 1983, was an upsurge in personal expectations resulting principally from reduced taxation.
11 John Curtice and Michael Steed in David Butler and Dennis Kavanagh, *The British General Election of 1979*, 1980, p.363.
12 Anthony Heath, Roger Jowell and John Curtice, *How Britain Votes*, 1985, p.99.
13 Richard Rose and Ian McAllister, *The Nationwide Competition for Votes*, 1984, p.149.
14 Ibid., p.95.
15 Heath, Jowell and Curtice, op.cit., pp.74–85.

9 PRIME MINISTERIAL GOVERNMENT

1 Francis Pym, *The Politics of Consent*, 1985 edition, p.xi.
2 *Sunday Times* interview, 27 February 1983, quoted in Martin Holmes, *The First Thatcher Government 1979–83*, 1985, p.210.
3 Quoted in John Gyford, *The Politics of Local Socialism*, 1985, p.69.
4 Andrew Gamble, *Marxism Today*, November 1980, p.17.
5 George A. Boyne, 'Rate Reform and the Future of Local Democracy', *Political Quarterly*, vol.57, no.4, Oct.–Dec. 1986, p.427.
6 Ibid., p.428.
7 *Observer*, 25 February 1979.

8 Hugo Young and Anne Sloman, *The Thatcher Phenomenon*, 1986, pp.42, 43.

9 Peter Hennessy, *Cabinet*, 1986, p.263.

10 Quoted in ibid., p.94.

11 Young and Sloman, op.cit., 1986, pp.46–7.

12 Ibid., p.49.

13 Dennis Kavanagh, *Thatcherism and British Politics*, 1987, p.277.

14 I reported at that time: 'Mr Heseltine is more urgent in his alarm at the way things are going, especially in the cities, and could even be brewing up towards a spectacular resignation': *Sunday Times*, 13 October 1985.

15 The minutes of the Cabinet are kept by the Cabinet Secretary who is skilled in the art. The Cabinet Secretary is the servant of government not of history. What is actually said in Cabinet and what is recorded as having been said or decided are not necessarily the same thing. The Prime Minister has the last say in that.

16 *Fourth Report from the Select Committee on Defence, Westland plc: The Government's Decision Making.* House of Commons 519, para.144.

17 Ibid., paras 144–7.

18 Of the Democratic Party National headquarters for the purpose of placing bugging devices. The headquarters were housed in the Watergate complex overlooking the Potomac.

19 Select Committee on Defence, op.cit., paras 144–7.

20 Ibid., para.162.

21 Michael Heseltine, *Where There's A Will*, 1987, p.143.

22 In the summer of 1985, however, he beat the Prime Minister in Cabinet – in fact isolated her – when he successfully insisted that an order for a new frigate should go to the Merseyside yard of Cammell Laird although another yard had tendered more competitively. This incident rankled and contributed to their confrontation over Westland.

23 In fact that is exactly how the Official Secrets Act does work. While Ministers and senior officials speak to the press as they see fit, petty bureaucrats and clerks risk discipline for the most trivial disclosures. In theory it could be a prosecutable offence to reveal the number of cups of tea consumed in Whitehall each day, although perhaps that *should* be kept a State secret.

24 Number 10 Downing Street and the Cabinet Office in Whitehall are connected by a corridor.

25 Hennessy, op.cit., 1986, p.23.

26 Quoted in ibid., p.23.

27 Official Report, 27 January 1986, col.657.

28 Select Committee Report, para.184.

29 Official Report, 23 January, col.454.

30 A committee consisting of all backbench members of the Conservative Party, so named after a famous meeting in 1922, the upshot of which was to end the war-time coalition under Lloyd George.

31 Select Committee Report, para.183.

32 Ibid., paras 213, 214.

33 MORI's figures.

34 John Biffen, 'The Conservatism of Labour', in Maurice Cowling (ed.), *Conservative Essays*, 1978, p.155.

10 *COMRADES AT ARMS*

 1 Robert Harris, *The Making of Neil Kinnock*, 1984, p.31. This is the chief source on Kinnock before he became leader of the Labour Party and contains much useful autobiographical interview material.
 2 Ibid., p.108.
 3 Quoted in ibid., p.138.
 4 Quoted in ibid., p.126.
 5 Martin Adeney and John Lloyd, *The Miners' Strike, 1984–5*, 1986, p.27.
 6 Ibid., p.33.
 7 Michael Crick, *Scargill and the Miners*, 1985, p.26f.
 8 Adeney and Lloyd, op.cit., pp.34–5.
 9 Ibid., p.28.
10 Quoted in ibid., p.300.
11 Sartre had said, 'violence like Achilles' lance can heal the wounds that it has inflicted.' Aron was right, although as many in Paris said at that time, 'better wrong with Sartre than right with Aron'.
12 Adeney and Lloyd, op.cit., pp.111–13.
13 Ibid., p.103.
14 André Gorz, *Farewell to the Working Class*, 1980, p.74.
15 Harris, op.cit., p.164.
16 Adeney and Lloyd, op.cit., p.294.
17 Quoted in Michael Leapman, *Kinnock*, 1987, pp.88–9.
18 John Gyford, *The Politics of Local Socialism*, 1985, p.27. A useful book on which this section heavily relies.
19 Ibid., p.67.
20 Ibid., pp.102–3.
21 Ibid., p.105.
22 John Carvel, *Citizen Ken*, 1984, p.39. (This is the indispensable book on Livingstone and I rely heavily upon it in this section.)
23 Ibid., p.40.
24 Later to become the Workers' Revolutionary Party, this was the sectarian rival to the Revolutionary Socialist League, otherwise known as the Militant Tendency.
25 Carvel, op.cit., p.47.
26 Ibid., pp.90–1.
27 Peter Gerard Pearse and Nigel Matheson, *Ken Livingstone or 'The End of Civilisation As We Know It,' A Selection of Quotes, Quips and Quirks*, 1982.
28 Carvel, op.cit., pp.201–9.
29 In 1981 fares on the London Underground system were reduced by 25 per cent with the help of a subsidy. The 'Fares Fair' policy was later outlawed by the House of Lords.

30 Anne Sofer, *The London Left Take Over*, 1987, pp.19, 105.
31 See for example Beatrix Campbell and Martin Jacques in *Marxism Today*, April 1986.
32 Michael Crick, *The March of the Militants*, 1986, p.233.
33 Ibid., pp.229–30.
34 Eddy Shah, new style newspaper proprietor who in 1983 found himself in violent confrontation with the print unions over his denial of a 'closed shop' at his Lancashire and Cheshire plants. Later he became the pioneer of Fleet Street's technological revolution.
35 Quoted in Leapman, op.cit., p.95.
36 *Tribune*, 15 June 1983.
37 Eric Heffer, *Labour's Future, Socialist or SDP Mark 2?*, 1986, p.114.
38 12 November 1985.

11 *AFTER THE OIL*

1 *Lloyds Bank Economic Bulletin*, April 1987.
2 G. F. Ray, 'Labour Costs in Manufacturing', *National Institute Economic Review*, no.120, May 1987, p.73.
3 House of Lords, *Report from the Select Committee on Overseas Trade 1984–5, vol.2*, Oral Evidence, p.474.
4 *Lloyds Bank Economic Bulletin*, January 1986.
5 House of Lords, op.cit., vol.1, p.41; *Cambridge Bulletin*, March 1986.
6 House of Lords, op.cit., vol.2, pp.225, 227.
7 Ibid., p.555.
8 Ibid., p.573.
9 Ibid., p.468.
10 Ibid., p.718.
11 Ibid., vol.2, p.467.
12 Ibid., p.542.
13 An OECD report in 1985 took a different view. Taking account of more favourable demographic trends, it saw the prospect for social spending to grow in line with economic growth for the remainder of the century. (OECD, *Social Expenditure 1960–1990*, March 1985.)
14 Correlli Barnett, *The Audit of War*, 1986, p.298.
15 *National Institute Review*, May 1985.
16 At the Young Conservatives' conference, Scarborough, 7 February 1987.
17 The Prime Minister was more ambitious. In an interview with me she expressed the hope that 'most' schools would opt out. The *Independent*, 14 September 1987.
18 On Wenlock Edge the wood's in trouble;
        His forest fleece the Wrekin heaves;
    The gale, it plies the saplings double,
        And thick on Severn snow the leaves.
19 Barnett, op.cit., p.291.
20 *Youth Task Force Report*, HMSO, 1982.

21 Quango: quasi-non-governmental organisation. Such public boards had proliferated in the Wilson years. For the 'New Right' quango was a term of abuse.
22 Editorial, *Political Quarterly*, vol.57, no.3, July–September 1986, p.229.
23 *Training for Jobs*, HMSO, Cmnd 9135, 1984.
24 Andrew McArthur and Alan McGregor in *Political Quarterly*, p.248.
25 Department of Education and Science, *Statistical Bulletin 9/84*, July 1984.
26 *The Development of Higher Education into the 1990s*, HMSO, Cmnd 9542.
27 *Midland Bank Review*, Autumn 1986, p.8.
28 Ibid., p.13.
29 *Financial Times*, 9 June 1986.
30 11 November 1985.
31 PSL: private sector liquidity. It included everything – building society savings as well as bank deposits – everything bar 'monopoly' money.

12 DEFENCE OF THE REALM

1 In Hugo Young and Anne Sloman, *The Thatcher Phenomenon*, 1986, p.105.
2 ISS, *Strategic Survey 1986–87*, p.14.
3 Ibid., pp.56–7.
4 *Marxism Today*, April 1986.
5 *Tribune*, 28 March 1986.

13 WHY THATCHER WON

1 According to Gallup–BBC figures; MORI records a swing of Alliance to Labour but no change in the level of Conservative support. The two sets of figures are (C2s = 27 per cent of the electorate):

	1983	1987
MORI:		
Con	40	40
Lab	32	36
Lib (SDP)	26	22
Gallup:		
Con	39	43
Lab	35	34
Alliance	27	23

2 Harris ITN Exit Poll.
3 Ivor Crewe, *Guardian*, 15 June 1987.

4 Ibid., 16 June 1987.
5 *The Economist*, 23 May 1987.
6 Des Wilson, *Battle for Power*, 1987, p.231.
7 Ivor Crewe, *Guardian*, 16 June 1987.
8 Health Education Council, *The Health Divide*, 1987.

14 *WHY LABOUR LOST*

1 Mancur Olson, *The Rise and Decline of Nations*, 1982, p.44.
2 *Guardian*, 15 June 1987.
3 Quoted by Peter Pulzer in an article which makes the same point, *Financial Times*, 24 June 1987.
4 Mark Abrams, Richard Rose, Rita Hinden, *Must Labour Lose?*, 1960.
5 Anthony Crosland, *Can Labour Win?*, 1960, reprinted in *The Conservative Enemy*, 1962, p.163.
6 Austin Mitchell, *Can Labour Win Again?*, Fabian Tract 463, September 1979, p.29.
7 Ivor Crewe, Bo Särlvik and James Alt, 'Partisan de-alignment in Britain, 1964–74', *British Journal of Political Science*, vol.7, 1977.
8 Ian Gilmour, *Independent*, 21 July 1987.
9 *Independent*, 24 July 1987.
10 LWT's 'Weekend World', ITV, 14 June 1987.

15 *THIRD PARTY DISARRAY*

1 *New Statesman*, 11 August 1967.
2 *New Statesman*, 30 January 1987.
3 Roy Jenkins, *Partnership of Principle*, 1985, p.6.
4 Quoted in Ian Bradley, *The Strange Rebirth of Liberal Britain*, 1985, p.170.
5 Des Wilson, *Battle for Power*, 1987, p.293.

16 *PERMANENT REVOLUTION?*

1 Central Statistical Office, *Social Trends*, 17, 1987, p.17.
2 Ibid., p.19.
3 Andrew Broadbent in *New Society*, 14 May 1986.
4 *The Economist*, 4 July 1987.
5 Church of England, *Not Just for the Poor*, 1986, p.46.
6 Church of England, *Faith in the City*, 1985, pp.21, 25.
7 *Financial Times*, 14 November 1985, 19 November 1986.
8 Sir Isaiah Berlin, in conversation.
9 ITV, 'This Week', 4 June 1987.
10 Quoted by John Newhouse in a profile of Margaret Thatcher, 'The Gamefish', *New Yorker*, 10 February 1986.

Select Bibliography

Abrams, M., Rose, R. and Hinden, R., *Must Labour Lose?*, Penguin, 1960

Addison, Paul, *The Road to 1945*, Jonathan Cape, 1975

—— *Now The War Is Over*, Jonathan Cape, 1985

Adeney, Martin and Lloyd, John, *The Miners' Strike, 1984–5*, Routledge, 1986

Allen, G. C., *The British Disease*, Institute of Economic Affairs, 1979

Bacon, Roger and Eltis, Walter, *Britain's Economic Problems: Too Few Producers*, Macmillan, 1976

Bagehot, Walter, *The English Constitution*, Fontana, 1963 edition, with an introduction by Richard Crossman

Barnett, Correlli, *The Collapse of British Power*, Alan Sutton, 1984

—— *The Audit of War*, Macmillan, 1986

Barnett, Joel, *Inside the Treasury*, André Deutsch, 1982

Beckerman, Wilfred (ed.), *Slow Growth in Britain*, Oxford University Press, 1979

Beer, Samuel, *Britain Against Itself*, W. W. Norton, 1982

Bell, Daniel, *The Coming of the Post-Industrial Society*, Heinemann, 1974

Benn, Tony, *Arguments for Socialism*, Jonathan Cape, 1979, Penguin, 1980

—— *Arguments for Democracy*, Jonathan Cape, 1981

Blackaby, Frank (ed.), *De-Industrialisation*, Heinemann/National Institute of Economic and Social Research, 1979

Blake, Robert, *The Conservative Party from Peel to Thatcher*, Methuen, 1985

—— *The Decline of Power 1915–1964*, Granada, 1985

Bogdanov, Vernon and Skidelsky, Robert, *The Age of Affluence, 1951–1964*, Macmillan, 1970

Bosanquet, Nick, *After the New Right*, Heinemann, 1983

Bradley, Ian, *Breaking the Mould*, Martin Robertson, 1981

—— *The Strange Rebirth of Liberal Britain*, Chatto, 1985

Bruce-Gardyne, Jock, *Mrs Thatcher's First Administration*, Macmillan, 1984

Burridge, Trevor, *Clement Attlee, A Political Biography*, Jonathan Cape, 1985
Butler, David (ed.), *Coalitions in British Politics*, Macmillan, 1978
—— and Kavanagh, Dennis, *The British General Election of 1979*, Macmillan, 1980
—— and Stokes, Donald, *Political Change in Britain*, Macmillan, 1969
Campbell, Beatrix, *Wigan Pier Revisited*, Virago, 1984
Carvel, John, *Citizen Ken*, Chatto, 1984
Castle, Barbara, *The Castle Diaries, 1974–76*, Weidenfeld & Nicolson, 1980
Caves, Richard and Krause, Lawrence (eds), *Britain's Economic Performance*, Brookings Institution, 1980
Cipolla, Carlo, *The Economic Decline of Empires*, Methuen, 1970
Coates, David and Hillard, John, *The Economic Decline of Modern Britain*, Wheatsheaf, 1986
Cooper, David G. (ed.), *The Dialectics of Liberation*, Penguin, 1968
Cowling, Maurice (ed.), *Conservative Essays*, Cassell, 1978
Crafts, N. F. R., *British Economic Growth During The Industrial Revolution*, Oxford University Press, 1985
Crick, Michael, *Scargill and the Miners*, Penguin, 1985
—— *The March of the Militant*, Faber, 1986
Crosland, C. A. R., *The Future of Socialism*, Jonathan Cape, 1962
—— *The Conservative Enemy*, Jonathan Cape, 1962
—— *Socialism Now*, Jonathan Cape, 1974
Crosland, Susan, *Tony Crosland*, Jonathan Cape, 1982
Crossman, Richard, *The Diaries of a Cabinet Minister*, Hamish Hamilton and Jonathan Cape, 3 vols, 1975, 1976, 1977
Currie, Robert, *Industrial Politics*, Clarendon Press, 1979
Donoughue, Bernard, *Prime Minister, The Conduct of Policy under Harold Wilson and James Callaghan 1974–1979*, Jonathan Cape, 1987
Dore, Ronald, *The Origins of National Diversity in Industrial Relations*, Macmillan, 1973
Elliot, J. H., *Imperial Spain, 1469–1715*, Edward Arnold, 1963; Penguin, 1970
Finer, S. E. (ed.), *Adversary Politics and Electoral Reform*, Anthony Wigram, 1975
Foot, Michael, *Loyalists and Loners*, Collins, 1986
Franklin, Mark, *The Decline of Class Voting in Britain*, Clarendon Press, 1985
Gamble, A., *Britain in Decline*, Macmillan, 1981
Gardiner, George, *Margaret Thatcher*, Kimber, 1975
Geiger, Theodore, *Welfare and Efficiency*, Macmillan, 1979
Gilmour, Ian, *Inside Right*, Quartet Books, 1977
Gorz, André, *Farewell to the Working Class*, Pluto Press, 1982
Grimond, Jo, *Memoirs*, Heinemann, 1979
Gyford, John, *The Politics of Local Socialism*, Allen & Unwin, 1985
Haig, Alexander, *Caveat: Realism, Reagan and Foreign Policy*, Weidenfeld & Nicolson, 1984

Hall, Stuart and Jacques, Martin (eds), *The Politics of Thatcherism*,
  Lawrence & Wishart, 1983
Halsey, A. H., *Change in British Society*, Oxford University Press, 1978
Harris, Kenneth, *David Owen*, Weidenfeld & Nicolson, 1987
Harris, Robert, *The Making of Neil Kinnock*, Faber, 1984
Heath, Anthony, Jowell, Roger, and Curtice, John, *How Britain Votes*,
  Pergamon Press, 1985
Heffer, Eric, *Labour's Future, Socialist or SDP Mark 2?*, Verso Editions,
  1986
Hennessy, Peter, *Cabinet*, Blackwell, 1986
Heseltine, Michael, *Where There's a Will*, Hutchinson, 1987
Hewison, Robert, *Too Much: Art and Society in the Sixties*, Methuen, 1986
Himmelweit, Hilde et al., *How Voters Decide*, Academic Press, 1981
Hindness, Barry, *The Decline of Working-Class Politics*, MacGibbon &
  Kee, 1971
Hobsbawm, E. J., *Industry and Empire*, Weidenfeld & Nicolson, 1968
—— *The Forward March of Labour Halted?*, NLB in association with
  Marxism Today, 1981
Hodgson, G., *Labour at the Crossroads*, Martin Robertson, 1981
Holmes, Martin, *The First Thatcher Government, 1979–83*, Wheatsheaf
  Books, 1985
Howard, Anthony, *RAB. The Life of R. A. Butler*, Jonathan Cape, 1987
Howell, David, *British Social Democracy*, Croom Helm, 1980
Howell, David, *Blind Victory*, Hamish Hamilton, 1986
Hurd, Douglas, *An End to Promises*, Collins, 1977
Ionescu, Ghita, *Politics and the Pursuit of Happiness*, Longman, 1984
Jenkins, Peter, *The Battle of Downing Street*, Charles Knight, 1970
Jenkins, Roy, *Partnership of Principle*, Secker & Warburg, 1985
Johnson, R. W., *The Politics of Recession*, Macmillan, 1985
Jones, Aubrey, *Britain's Economy*, Cambridge University Press, 1985
Joseph, Keith, *Stranded on the Middle Ground*, Centre for Policy Studies,
  1976
—— *Monetarism is not enough*, The Stockton Lecture, 1976
Kavanagh, Dennis (ed.), *The Politics of the Labour Party*, Allen & Unwin,
  1982
—— *Thatcherism and British Politics*, Oxford University Press, 1987
Keegan, William, *Mrs Thatcher's Economic Experiment*, Penguin, 1984
—— *Britain Without Oil*, Penguin, 1985
King, Anthony (ed.), *Why is Britain Becoming Harder to Govern?*, BBC,
  1976
—— *The British Prime Minister*, Macmillan Educational, 1985
Kinnock, Neil, *Making Our Way*, Blackwell, 1986
Kogan, David and Kogan, Maurice, *The Battle for the Labour Party*,
  Kogan Page, 2nd edition, 1983
Leapman, Michael, *Kinnock*, Unwin Hyman, 1987
Lester Smith, W. O., *The Government of Education*, Pelican, 1965
Lipsey, David and Leonard, Dick (eds), *The Socialist Agenda: Crosland's
  Legacy*, Jonathan Cape, 1981

Maddison, Angus, *Phases of Capitalist Development*, Oxford University
    Press, 1982
Marquand, David, *Parliament for Europe*, Jonathan Cape, 1979
Marwick, Arthur, *British Society Since 1945*, Penguin, 1982
Minogue, Kenneth and Biddiss (eds), *Thatcherism, Personality and
    Politics*, Macmillan, 1987
Mitchell, Austin, *Can Labour Win Again?*, Fabian Society, 1979
Morgan, Kenneth O., *Labour in Power, 1945–51*, Oxford University
    Press, 1984
—— *Labour People*, Oxford University Press, 1987
Nevin, Michael, *The Age of Illusion*, Gollancz, 1983
Norton, Philip and Aughey, Arthur, *Conservatives and Conservatism*,
    Temple Smith, 1981
Olson, Mancur, *The Rise and Decline of Nations*, Yale University Press,
    1982
Owen, David, *Face the Future*, Jonathan Cape, 1981, 2nd edition
    (abridged and revised), Oxford University Press, 1981
—— *Personally Speaking to Kenneth Harris,* Weidenfeld & Nicolson,
    1987
Patten, Chris, *The Tory Case*, Longman, 1983
Pearse, Peter Gerard and Matheson, Nigel, *Ken Livingstone or 'The End
    of Civilisation as we know it'*, Proteus Books, 1982
Pearson, Geoffrey, *Hooligan*, Macmillan, 1983
Pimlott, Ben, *Hugh Dalton*, Jonathan Cape, 1985
—— (ed.), *The Political Diary of Hugh Dalton, 1918–40, 1945–60,*
    Jonathan Cape, 1986
—— and Cook, C. (eds), *Trade Unions in British Politics*, Longman,
    1982
Pollard, Sidney, *The Wasting of the British Economy*, Croom Helm, 1982
Pym, Francis, *The Politics of Consent*, Hamish Hamilton, 1984, revised
    2nd edition, Sphere, 1985
Radice, Giles, and Radice, Lisanne, *Socialists in the Recession*, Macmillan,
    1986
Rhodes James, Robert, *Ambitions and Realities, British Politics 1964–70,*
    Weidenfeld & Nicolson, 1972
Riddell, Peter, *The Thatcher Government*, Robertson, 1983
Rose, Richard and McAllister, Ian, *The Nationwide Competition for Votes:
    1983 British Election*, F. Pinter, 1984
—— *Voters begin to Choose*, Sage, 1986
Russel, Trevor, *The Tory Party*, Penguin Special, 1978
Sampson, Anthony, *The Anatomy of Britain*, Hodder, 1962
—— *The Changing Anatomy of Britain*, Hodder, 1982
Selbourne, David, *Left Behind*, Jonathan Cape, 1987
Seldon, Arthur (ed.), *The Emerging Consensus*, Institute of Economic
    Affairs, 1981
Sissons, Michael and French, Philip (eds), *The Age of Austerity*, Hodder,
    1963, Oxford University Press, 1986
Smith, Keith, *The British Economic Crisis*, Penguin, 1984

Snow, C. P., *Two Cultures and A Second Look*, Cambridge University Press, 1964

Sofer, Anne, *The London Left Take Over*, A. Sofer, 1987

Stephenson, Hugh, *Claret and Chips*, Michael Joseph, 1982

Stone, Norman, *Europe Transformed, 1878–1919*, Fontana, 1983

Strachey, John, *The End of Empire*, Gollancz, 1959

Talbott, Strobe, *Deadly Gambits*, Picador, 1985

Thatcher, Margaret, *In Defence of Freedom*, Aurum Press, 1986

Tomlinson, J., *Monetarism: Is There an Alternative?*, Blackwell, 1986

Villiers, Charles, *Start Again Britain*, Quartet, 1984

Walters, Alan, *Britain's Economic Renaissance*, Oxford University Press, 1986

Whitely, Paul, *The Labour Party in Crisis*, Methuen, 1983

Wiener, Martin, *English Culture and the Decline of the Industrial Spirit, 1850–1980*, Cambridge University Press, 1981

Williams, Philip, *Hugh Gaitskell*, Jonathan Cape, 1979

Wilson, Desmond, *Battle for Power*, Sphere, 1987

York, Peter, *Style Wars*, Sidgwick & Jackson, 1980

Young, Hugo and Sloman, Anne, *The Thatcher Phenomenon*, BBC, 1986

Young, Wayland (ed.), *The Rebirth of Britain*, Weidenfeld & Nicolson, 1982

Biographical Index

Adenauer, Konrad (1876–1967)   Federal Chancellor of West Germany, 1949–63, Foreign Minister, 1951–55

Annan, Lord   Former vice-chancellor of London University

Archer, Jeffrey   Novelist and former Conservative MP, deputy-chairman of the Conservative Party, 1985–87

Armstrong, Robert   Secretary to the Cabinet, 1979–87

Ashdown, Paddy   Liberal MP for Yeovil since 1983

Asquith, H. H. (1852–1928)   Home Secretary, 1892–95, Chancellor of the Exchequer, 1905–08, leader of the Liberal Party and Prime Minister, 1908–16

Atkinson, Norman   Labour MP for Tottenham, 1964–83, treasurer of the Labour Party, 1976–81

Attlee, Clement (1883–1967)   Leader of the Labour Party, 1935–55, deputy Prime Minister in Churchill's War Cabinet, 1942–45, Prime Minister, 1945–51

Baker, Kenneth   Conservative MP since 1968, Secretary of State for the Environment, 1985–86, Secretary of State for Education since 1986

Baldwin, Stanley (1867–1947)   Leader of the Conservative Party, 1923–37, Prime Minister, 1923, 1924–29, 1935–37

Barnett, Joel   Labour MP for Heywood and Royton, 1964–83, Chief Secretary to the Treasury, 1976–79, created Lord Barnett, 1983

Basnett, David   General secretary, General Municipal Workers Union, 1973, General Municipal and Boilermakers Trades Union, 1982–85

Beaumont-Dark, Anthony   Conservative MP for Birmingham Selly Oak since 1979

Beckett, Terence   Former chairman of Ford Motor Company, director general of the Confederation of British Industry, 1980–86

Begun, Iosif   Jewish Soviet dissident (eventually allowed to emigrate to Israel in January 1988)

Bellos, Linda   Labour leader of the London Borough of Lambeth Council

Benn, Tony   Labour MP for Bristol South-East, 1950–60, 1963–83, Secretary of State for Industry, 1974–75, Secretary of State for Energy, 1975–79, Labour MP for Chesterfield since 1984

Bevan, Aneurin (1897–1960) Labour MP for Ebbw Vale, 1929–60, Minister for Health and Housing, 1945–51, Minister of Labour, 1951

Beveridge, William (1879–1963) Director, London School of Economics, 1919–37, Liberal MP for Berwick, 1944–45, chairman of the Social Services Inquiry which published reports (1942, 1944) laying plans for the establishment of the welfare state

Bevin, Ernest (1881–1951) Former leader of the Transport and General Workers Union, Labour MP, 1940–51, Minister of Labour, 1940–45, Foreign Secretary, 1945–51

Biffen, John Conservative MP since 1961, Chief Secretary to the Treasury, 1979–81, Secretary of State for Trade, 1981–82, leader of the House of Commons, 1982–87

Birch, Nigel Conservative MP, 1945–70, Secretary of State for Air, 1955, Economic Secretary to the Treasury, 1957–58

Blunkett, David Labour MP for Sheffield Brightside since 1987, formerly Labour leader of Sheffield City Council

Boyson, Rhodes Conservative MP for Brent North since 1974, Under Secretary of State for Education, 1979–83, Minister of State for Social Security, 1983–84, Minister of State in Northern Ireland, 1984–86, Minister for Local Government, 1986–87, knighted in January 1988

Brandt, Willy Federal Chancellor of West Germany, 1969–74, chairman of the United Nations Commission on Development Issues

Brittan, Leon Conservative MP for Cleveland and Whitby, 1974–83, and for Richmond, Yorkshire, since 1983, Home Secretary, 1983–85, Secretary of State for Trade and Industry, 1985–86

Brook, Norman (1902–67) Secretary to the Cabinet, 1947–62

Brown, George Deputy leader of the Labour Party, 1960–70, Secretary of State for Economic Affairs, 1964–66, Foreign Secretary, 1966–68

Brown, Gordon Labour MP for Dunfermline East since 1983, opposition spokesman on trade and industry since 1985

Bruce-Gardyne, Jock Conservative MP, 1964–74, 1979–83, Economic Secretary to the Treasury, 1981–83, life peer, 1983

Butler, R. A. (1902–82) Conservative MP, 1929–65, Minister of Education, 1944, Chancellor of the Exchequer, 1951–55, leader of the House of Commons, 1955–61, Home Secretary, 1957–62, Foreign Secretary, 1963–64

Callaghan, James Labour MP, 1945–87, Chancellor of the Exchequer, 1964–67, Home Secretary, 1967–70, Foreign Secretary, 1974–76, Prime Minister, 1976–79, leader of the Labour Party, 1976–80, life peer, 1987

Campbell-Savours, Dale Labour MP for Workington since 1974

Carrington, Lord Secretary of State for Defence, 1970–74, Secretary of State for Energy, 1974, Foreign Secretary, 1979–82, secretary-general of NATO, 1984–87

Castle, Barbara Labour MP for Blackburn, 1945–79, Secretary of State for Employment, 1968–70, Secretary of State for Social Services, 1974–76, member of the European Parliament since 1979

Chamberlain, Joseph (1836–1914)   President of the Board of Trade, 1880–85, Liberal MP, 1885–1906, Secretary for the Colonies, 1895–1903

Chamberlain, Neville (1869–1940)   Son of Joseph Chamberlain, Conservative MP, 1918–40, Chancellor of the Exchequer, 1923–24, 1937–40, Minister for Health, 1924–29, Prime Minister, 1937–40

Channon, Paul   Conservative MP for Southend East since 1959, Secretary of State for Trade and Industry, 1986–87, Secretary of State for Transport since 1987

Chernenko, Konstantin   General Secretary of the Soviet Communist Party, 1984–86

Churchill, Randolph (1911–68)   Conservative MP, 1940–45, author and son of Sir Winston Churchill

Churchill, Winston (1874–1965)   Conservative MP, 1900–04, 1924–64, Liberal MP, 1904–22, Chancellor of the Exchequer, 1924–29, Prime Minister, 1940–45, 1951–55

Crosland, Anthony (1918–77)   Labour MP for Grimsby, 1959–77, Secretary of State for the Environment, 1974–76, Foreign Secretary, 1976–77, author of 'The Future of Socialism' (1957)

Crossman, Richard (1907–74)   Labour MP, 1945–74, Minister of Housing, 1964–66, leader of the House of Commons, 1966–68, Secretary of State for Social Services, 1968–70, author of famous Cabinet diaries

Currie, Edwina   Conservative MP for Derbyshire South since 1983, undersecretary for Health and Social Security since 1985

Dalton, Hugh (1887–1962)   Labour MP, 1924–59, president of the Board of Trade, 1942–45, Chancellor of the Exchequer, 1945–47

De Gaulle, Charles (1890–1970)   President of France, 1959–69, wartime French Resistance leader

Disraeli, Benjamin (1804–81)   Conservative MP, 1837–81, Chancellor of the Exchequer, 1852, 1858–59, 1866–68, Prime Minister, 1868, 1874–80

Douglas-Home, Alec (Lord Home)   Conservative MP, 1931–51, 1963–74, Foreign Secretary, 1960–63, Prime Minister, 1963–64

Eden, Anthony (1897–1977)   Conservative MP, 1923–57, Foreign Secretary, 1935–38, 1940–45, 1951–55, Prime Minister, 1955–57

Edmonds, John   General secretary of the General Municipal Boilermakers and Allied Trades Unions since 1986

Ezra, Lord   Chairman of the National Coal Board, 1971–82

Foot, Michael   Labour MP, 1945–55, and since 1960, Secretary of State for Employment, 1974–76, leader of the House of Commons, 1976–79, leader of the Labour Party, 1980–83

Fowler, Norman   Conservative MP since 1970, Secretary of State for Transport, 1981, Secretary of State for Social Services, 1981–87, Secretary of State for Employment since 1987

Gaitskell, Hugh (1906–63)   Labour MP, 1945–63, Chancellor of the Exchequer, 1950–51, leader of the Labour Party, 1955–63

Gilmour, Ian   Conservative MP since 1962, Secretary of State for Defence, 1974, principal House of Commons spokesman on foreign affairs, 1979–81

Giscard d'Estaing, Valéry   President of France, 1974–81

Gladstone, William (1809–98)   Liberal Prime Minister, 1868–74, 1880–85, 1886, 1892–94

Gould, Bryan   Labour MP, 1974–79, and since 1983, Labour campaign coordinator, 1986–87, Shadow Secretary of State for Trade and Industry since 1987

Gow, Ian   Conservative MP for Eastbourne since 1974, parliamentary private secretary to Mrs Thatcher, 1979–83, Minister for Housing, 1983–85, Minister of State at the Treasury, 1985

Greaves, Tony   Liberal party activist, former general secretary of the Association of Liberal Councillors

Grimond, Jo   Liberal MP, 1950–83, leader of the Liberal Party, 1956–67, May–July 1976, life peer, 1983

Hailsham, Lord (Quintin Hogg)   Conservative MP, 1938–50, 1963–70, Lord President of the Council, 1957–59, 1960–64, Lord Chancellor, 1974–79, 1979–87

Hammond, Eric   General secretary of the Electrical Engineers and Plumbers Trades Union since 1986

Harris, Ralph   Lord Harris of High Cross, director of the Institute for Economic Affairs

Hattersley, Roy   Labour MP for Birmingham Sparkbrook since 1964, Secretary of State for Prices and Consumer Protection, 1976–79, deputy leader of the Labour Party since 1983, Shadow Home Secretary since 1987

Hatton, Derek   Leading member of the Militant Tendency, former deputy leader of Liverpool City Council

Havers, Michael   Conservative MP, 1970–87, Attorney General, 1979–87, Lord Chancellor, June–December 1987

Healey, Denis   Labour MP since 1952, Secretary of State for Defence, 1964–70, Chancellor of the Exchequer, 1974–79, deputy leader of the Labour Party, 1980–83

Heath, Edward   Conservative MP since 1950, leader of the Conservative Party, 1965–75, Prime Minister, 1970–74

Heffer, Eric   Labour MP for Liverpool Walton since 1964

Henderson, Nicholas   British Ambassador to the United States at the time of the Falklands War, formerly British Ambassador in France and to the United Nations

Heseltine, Michael   Conservative MP since 1966, Secretary of State for the Environment, 1979–83, Secretary of State for Defence, 1983–86

Hobsbawm, Eric   Professor of Economic and Social History, University of London, since 1982

Howe, Geoffrey   Conservative MP since 1964, Chancellor of the Exchequer, 1979–83, Foreign Secretary since 1983

Hughes, Simon   Liberal MP for Bermondsey since the 1983 by-election

Hurd, Douglas   Conservative MP since 1974, Secretary of State for Northern Ireland, 1984–85, Home Secretary since 1985

Ingham, Bernard   Press secretary to Mrs Thatcher since 1979

Jenkin, Patrick   Conservative MP, 1964–87, Secretary of State for Social Services, 1979–81, Secretary of State for Industry, 1981–83, Secretary of State for the Environment, 1983–85, life peer, 1987

Jenkins, Clive   General Secretary of the Association of Scientific, Technical and Managerial Staffs since 1970

Jenkins, Roy   Labour MP, 1959–76, Home Secretary, 1964–67, 1974–76, Chancellor of the Exchequer, 1967–70, SDP MP for Glasgow Hillhead, 1981–87, leader of the SDP, 1981–83, life peer, 1987

Jones, Jack   General secretary of the Transport and General Workers Union, 1968–78

Joseph, Keith   Conservative MP, 1956–87, Secretary of State for Social Services, 1970–74, Secretary of State for Industry, 1979–81, Secretary of State for Education, 1981–86, life peer, 1987

Kent, Monsignor Bruce   General-secretary, 1980–85, and vice-chair since 1985, the Campaign for Nuclear Disarmament

Kinnock, Neil   Labour MP since 1970, leader of the Labour Party since 1983

Kitson, Alex   Deputy general-secretary of the Transport and General Workers Union, 1980–86, Chairman of the Labour Party, 1980–81

Kohl, Helmut   Federal Chancellor of West Germany since 1982

Law, Andrew Bonar (1858–1923)   Conservative and Unionist MP, 1902–10, 1911–23, leader of the House of Commons, 1916–21, Chancellor of the Exchequer, 1916–18, Prime Minister, 1922–23

Lawson, Nigel   Conservative MP for Blaby since 1974, Secretary of State for Energy, 1981–83, Chancellor of the Exchequer since 1983

Litterick, Tom   Labour MP for Birmingham Selly Oak, 1974–79

Livingstone, Ken   Leader of the Greater London Council, 1981–86, Labour MP for Brent East since 1987

MacDonald, Ramsay (1866–1937)   Labour MP, 1906–18, 1922–35, 1936–37, Prime Minister, 1923–24, 1929–35

McGregor, Ian   Chairman of the National Coal Board (British Coal), 1983–86, chairman of British Steel since 1986

McIntosh, Andrew   Leader of the Labour opposition on the Greater London Council, 1980–81, life peer, 1982

Macleod, Iain (1913–70)   Conservative MP, 1950–70, leader of the House of Commons, 1961–63, Chancellor of the Exchequer, 1970

Macmillan, Harold (1894–1987)   Conservative MP, 1945–64, Chancellor of the Exchequer, 1955–57, Prime Minister, 1957–63

McNally, Tom   Special advisor to James Callaghan, 1976–79, Labour MP, 1979–81, SDP MP, 1981–83

Mandelson, Peter   Labour Party director of communications

Marquand, David   Labour MP, 1966–77, chief advisor to the Secretariat General of the European Council, 1977–78, Professor of Contemporary History and Politics, Salford University, since 1978

Mayhew, Patrick   Conservative MP for Tunbridge Wells since 1974, Solicitor General, 1983–87, Attorney General since 1987

Meacher, Michael   Labour MP for Oldham West since 1970, Shadow Secretary of State for Employment since 1987

Meadowcroft, Michael   Liberal MP for Leeds West, 1983–87

Mitchell, Austin   Labour MP for Grimsby since 1977

Mitterrand, François   Socialist President of France since 1981

Morrison, Peter   Conservative MP for Chester since 1974, deputy-chairman of the Conservative Party since 1986, Minister of State for Energy since 1987

Mugabe, Robert   Prime Minister of Zimbabwe since 1981, President since 1987

Mullins, Chris   Editor of *Tribune* newspaper, 1982–84, Labour MP for Sunderland South since 1987

Murray, Len   General secretary of the Trades Union Congress, 1973–84, life peer, 1985

Nott, John   Conservative MP, 1966–83, Minister of State at the Treasury, 1972–74, Secretary of State for Trade, 1979–81, Secretary of State for Defence, 1981–83

Onslow, Cranley   Conservative MP for Woking since 1964, chairman of Conservative backbench '1922' Committee since 1984

Owen, David   Labour MP, 1966–81, Minister of Health, 1974–76, Foreign Secretary, 1976–79, SDP MP since 1981, leader of the SDP, 1983–87, 1988

Pardoe, John   Liberal MP for Cornwall North, 1970–79

Parkinson, Cecil   Conservative MP since 1970, chairman of the Conservative Party, 1981–83, Secretary of State for Trade and Industry, 1983, Secretary of State for Energy, 1987

Peel, Robert (1788–1850)   Prime Minister, 1834, 1841–46, founder of the modern Conservative Party

Phillips, Morgan   General secretary of the Labour Party, 1944–62

Powell, Enoch   Conservative MP, 1950–74, Minister of Health, 1957–60, Ulster Unionist MP for South Down, 1974–87

Prentice, Reg   Labour MP, 1957–77, Secretary of State for Education, 1974–75, Conservative MP, 1977–87, Minister of State for Social Security, 1979–81

Prior, James   Conservative MP, 1959–87, Minister for Agriculture, 1970–72, leader of the House of Commons, 1972–74, Secretary of State for Employment, 1979–81, Secretary of State for Northern Ireland, 1981–84, life peer, 1987

Profumo, John   Conservative MP, 1950–63, Secretary of State for War, 1960–63

Pym, Francis   Conservative MP, 1961–87, Secretary of State for Defence, 1979–81, leader of the House of Commons, 1981–82, Foreign Secretary, 1982–83, life peer, 1987

Rees, Merlyn   Labour MP since 1963, Secretary of State for Northern Ireland, 1974–76, Home Secretary, 1976–79

Ridley, Nicholas   Conservative MP since 1959, Secretary of State for Transport, 1983–86, Secretary of State for the Environment since 1986

Rippon, Geoffrey   Conservative MP, 1966–87, Secretary of State for the Environment, 1972–74

Rodgers, William   Labour MP, 1959–81, Secretary of State for Transport, 1976–79, SDP MP, 1981–83, vice-president of the SDP, 1981–87

Ruddock, Joan   Chair of Campaign for Nuclear Disarmament, 1981–85, Labour MP from Deptford since 1987

Scanlon, Hugh   President of the Amalgamated Union of Engineering Workers, 1968–78, life peer, 1979

Scargill, Arthur   President of the National Union of Mineworkers since 1979

Schmidt, Helmut   Federal Chancellor of West Germany, 1974–82

Shah, Eddy   Founder of *Today,* pioneer of the newspaper technological revolution

Shinwell, Emanuel   Labour MP, 1922–24, 1928–32, 1935–70, Minister for Fuel and Power, 1945–47, Secretary of State for War, 1947–50, Minister of Defence, 1950–51

Shore, Peter   Labour MP since 1964, Secretary of State for Trade, 1974–76, Secretary of State for the Environment, 1976–79

Silkin, John (1923–87)   Labour MP, 1963–87, Government Chief Whip, 1966–69, Minister for Agriculture, 1976–79

Slater, Jim   President of the National Union of Seamen

Smith, John   Labour MP since 1970, Secretary of State for Trade, 1978–79, Shadow Chancellor of the Exchequer since 1987

Sofer, Anne   Labour member, 1977–81, SDP member of the Greater London Council, 1981–86

Steel, David   Liberal MP since 1965, leader of the Liberal Party since 1976

Stevas, Norman St John   Conservative MP, 1964–87, leader of the House of Commons, 1979–81, life peer, 1987

Tatchell, Peter   Labour candidate in the historic Bermondsey by-election of January 1983

Tebbit, Norman   Conservative MP since 1970, Secretary of State for Employment, 1981–83, Secretary of State for Trade and Industry, 1983–85, chairman of the Conservative Party, 1985–87

Thorneycroft, Peter   President of the Board of Trade, 1951–57, Chancellor of the Exchequer, 1957–58, Secretary of State for Defence, 1964, chairman of the Conservative Party, 1975–81

Underhill, Reg   Labour Party national agent, 1972–79, life peer, 1979

Wakeham, John   Conservative MP since 1974, Government Chief Whip, 1983–87, leader of the House of Commons since 1987

Walden, Brian   Labour MP, 1964–77, journalist

Walker, Peter   Conservative MP for Worcester since 1961, Minister for Agriculture, 1979–83, Secretary of State for Energy, 1983–87, Secretary of State for Wales since 1987

Wall, Pat   Labour MP for Bradford North since 1987

Walters, Alan   Professor of Political Economy, Johns Hopkins University, since 1976, personal economic advisor to the Prime Minister since 1979

Weinstock, Lord   Managing director of General Electric Co. Ltd. since 1963

Whitehouse, Mary   President of the National Viewers and Listeners Association

Whitelaw, William   Leader of the House of Commons, 1970–72, Secretary of State for Northern Ireland, 1972–73, Secretary of State for Employment, 1973–74, Home Secretary, 1979–83, deputy Prime Minister, 1979–88, Lord President of the Council, 1983–88

Williams, Shirley   Labour MP, 1964–79, Secretary of State for Prices and Consumer Protection, 1974–76, Secretary of State for Education, 1976–79, SDP MP, 1981–83, president of the SDP, 1982–88

Wilson, Des   Chairman of the Campaign for Freedom of Information since 1984, campaign director, Friends of the Earth, since 1985, president of the Liberal Party, 1986–87

Wilson, Harold   Labour MP, 1945–83, president of the Board of Trade, 1947–51, leader of the Labour Party, 1963–76, Prime Minister, 1964–70, 1974–76, life peer, 1983

Woodcock, George (1904–79)   Assistant general secretary, 1947–60, and general secretary, 1960–69, of the Trades Union Congress

Wyatt, Woodrow   Labour MP, 1945–70, chairman of the Horserace Totaliser Board since 1976, journalist and author

Young, David (Lord)   Chairman of the Manpower Services Commission, 1982–84, Secretary of State for Employment, 1985–87, Secretary of State for Trade and Industry since 1987, life peer, 1984

Younger, George   Conservative MP for Ayr, Secretary of State for Scotland, 1979–86, Secretary of State for Defence since 1986

General Index